792.
092

Loie Fuller

"Do call me Loïe. It is so much my name."
—Loie Fuller to Mme Jules Clarétie, ca. 1907

Loie Fuller

GODDESS OF LIGHT

Richard Nelson Current
& Marcia Ewing Current

NORTHEASTERN UNIVERSITY PRESS
BOSTON

Northeastern University Press

Copyright 1997 by Northeastern University Press

All rights reserved. Except for the quotation of short passages for the purposes of criticism and review, no part of this book may be reproduced in any form or by any means, electronic or mechanical, including photocopying, recording, or any information storage and retrieval system now known or to be invented, without written permission of the publisher.

Frontispiece: Loie Fuller, about 1898.
(Photograph by Langfier; courtesy of Roger-Viollet.)

Library of Congress Cataloging-in-Publication Data
Current, Richard Nelson.
Loie Fuller, goddess of light / Richard Nelson Current & Marcia Ewing Current.
p. cm.
Includes bibliographical references and index.
ISBN 1-55553-309-4 (cloth : alk. paper)
1. Fuller, Loie, 1862–1928. 2. Dancers—United States—Biography. 3. Modern dance. I. Current, Marcia Ewing. II. Title.
GV1785.F8C87 1997
792.8′028′092—dc21
[B]   96-52659

Designed by Virginia Evans

Composed in Fairfield Medium by
G & S Typesetters, Inc., Austin, Texas.
Printed and bound by Thomson-Shore, Inc., Dexter, Michigan.
The paper is Glatfelter Supple Opaque Recycled, an acid-free stock.

MANUFACTURED IN THE UNITED STATES OF AMERICA
01 00 99 98 97   5 4 3 2

*In loving memory of our parents,
Mildred and Bob, Anna and Park,
each of whom, like Loie,
used creativity to enhance the lives of others*

CONTENTS

Illustrations / *xi*
Preface / *xv*

1. From "Louie" to "Loie" / 3
2. The Serpent and the Serpentine / 23
3. Extraordinary Success, Extraordinary Failure / 45
4. Why Can't I Be Salome? / 71
5. The Mistress of Fire / 93
6. A Theater of Her Own / 119
7. Sada, Isadora, Marie, the Curies, Rodin / 145
8. Wanderers in Glory / 167
9. La Loïe and Her Muses / 193
10. Little Loïe and Big Alma / 221
11. More Missions to America / 245
12. The Lily of Life / 267
13. Light and Shadow / 291
14. The Dying of the Light / 309

Epilogue / 335
Appendix / 343
Notes / 353
Bibliography / 381
Index / 391

ILLUSTRATIONS

Loie Fuller, ca. 1898 / frontispiece

Loie with her father, ca. 1867 / 9

Loie as Little Jack Sheppard, 1886 / 18

Loie in costume, 1889 / 28

Serpentine dance, 1892 / 34

A "nude-appearing" photograph / 37

Loie in "Dance of the Serpents" / 49

Posters in Paris streets / 52

Loie and her furs / 56

Loie in "Dance of the Flowers" / 73

Loie in Silvestre's *Salomé* / 82

Loie, her mother, and the Flammarions / 87

Dumas fils with Loie, 1894 / 89

Loie dancing "The Butterfly," 1896 / 107

"La danse du Lys," 1900 / 113

Portrait of Loie given to Gab Bloch / 121

Photo of Loie given to Rodin / 123

Photographic study for a sculpture by Rodin / 126

Loie's creation of a "flower" / 127

Time-release photo of Loie dancing / 133

Pierre Roche artworks for Loie's 1900 theater / 136

Entrance to Loie's theater / 138

Color plates (following page 144)

Loïe Fuller Gavotte *sheet music*
La Loïe Fuller/Vivante Fleur
Oil painting by Pierre Roche
Gypsograph by Pierre Roche
Fire Dance poster by Jules Chéret
Fire Dance poster by Georges Meunier
Fire Dance poster by PAL
Four gilt bronze lamps by François-Raoul Larche
Two posters by PAL
Two lithographs by Toulouse-Lautrec
Bronze figure by Clara Pfeffer
Bronze vase by Hans Stoltenberg-Lerche
Porcelain lamp by Paul Teresziuk
Stoneware charger by Massier and Lévy-Dhurmer
Two posters by Manuel Orazi
Poster by Paul Colin
Necklace inspired by Loie

Loie among her trunks / 161
Loie driving an automobile / 169
Rodin and Loie in rickshaws / 173
Poses from d'Humière's Salome / 181
A letter from Loie to Rodin / 183
Loie with her mother / 188
Loie with her Muses / 197
The dance troupe in front of the Sphinx / 219
Alma Spreckels / 223

Illustrations

{ xii }

Loie with the Rodins in Rome / 233
Loie and The Thinker / 251
Christmas 1916 at the Rodins' / 260
Sam Hill and Gab Bloch / 263
Queen Marie of Romania / 285
Loie after surgery / 299
Loie on her deathbed / 332

Illustrations

PREFACE

This, the first full-length biography of Loie Fuller in the English language, is based almost entirely on primary sources. For making our research possible, we are indebted to librarians, curators, and archivists at the following institutions: New York Public Library for the Performing Arts, Lincoln Center, New York City; Bibliothèque Nationale, Bibliothèque de l'Arsenal, Bibliothèque de l'Opéra, and Musée d'Orsay, Paris; Newspaper Library, London, and Theatre Museum, London; San Francisco Performing Arts Library and Museum, San Francisco; Chicago Historical Society and Newberry Library, Chicago; Hinsdale Historical Society, Hinsdale, Illinois; and Wellesley College Library, Wellesley, Massachusetts.

For special assistance in our research, we are obligated to Colleen Schafroth of the Maryhill Museum of Art, Goldendale, Washington; Virginia Krumholz of the Cleveland Museum of Art, Cleveland, Ohio; Hélène Pinet of the Musée Rodin, Paris; Denis Gallion and Daniel Morris of Historical Design Inc., New York City; Jo-Anne Birnie Danzker and Michael Buhrs of the Museum Villa Stuck, Munich; and Larry Matlick of Macklowe Gallery, Ltd., New York City.

We owe thanks to Pat Woodstrup of Sycamore, Illinois, for providing us with copies of documents pertaining to the Fuller family, of which she is a member.

Finally, we are grateful to William A. Frohlich, director of Northeastern University Press, without whose encouragement we would never have written the book.

R.N.C./M.E.C.

Loie Fuller

1

From "Louie" to "Loie"

S he once was the most famous dancer in the world, though some who saw her perform wondered whether what she did was really dancing, and she herself had her doubts. What brought her fame was her way of manipulating voluminous folds of silk while having beams of colored light play upon them. She may or may not have been a true mistress of terpsichore, but she certainly taught the light to dance.

In fact, this woman did much, much more than that. She broke the mold of traditional choreography and prepared the way for the development of modern dance. She helped to launch other pioneers, among them Isadora Duncan. A "magician of light," she made important contributions to stage lighting and lesser ones to cinema techniques. She became the personification of Art Nouveau, the inspiration for artists who, idealizing her, portrayed her more often than any other woman of her time. She, in turn, promoted the work of her artist friends and was responsible for the founding of two art museums. An inspiration for poets as well as artists, she served as a symbol of the symbolist movement.

She was born in America but was made in France, or so she said. Paris was where (in 1892) she became an overnight sensation, where she spent most of the rest of her life, and where (in 1928) she died and her ashes were deposited. Paris was also where she met the woman who was to be her lifelong companion. Her other Parisian friends included such famous people as the novelists Alexandre Dumas *fils* and Anatole France, the sculptor Auguste Rodin, and the scientists Pierre and Marie Curie and their daughter Eve. During World War I she repaid France by urging her fellow Americans to join the conflict on that country's side, and by persuading them to contribute to the relief of its wounded and its war widows and orphans. Still, there was ambivalence in her national loyalties. Francophile though she became, she always kept her U.S. citizenship and her quintessentially American character.

She could boast of friendships not only with French celebrities but also with American tycoons and with Romanian and other royalty. One of the closest of all was her friendship with the ravishing Princess and then Queen Marie of Romania.

This remarkable American was something of a paradox. A tall and lovely sylph in posters and sculptures, she was in reality a rather chubby woman with a fairly plain face. A dance innovator, she possessed no formal training in choreography. Eventually a cofounder of art museums, she had never even seen an art exhibit before going to Paris at the age of thirty. A close and respected associate of some of the most learned men and women in the world, she could claim no institutional education beyond that offered by the common schools of Illinois in the 1860s and 1870s.

What she did have, in addition to her winning ways, was a dauntless will to get ahead, together with enough intelligence, resourcefulness, and ingenuity to give effect to that will. These qualities were not only recognized but often admired by others, including the prominent art critic Arsène Alexandre, who in 1900 lauded her vitality and positive drive and proclaimed her to be *a very pushing woman* in the best sense of the word. The strength of these traits enabled her to keep going in the face of repeated disappointments and disasters.

She was humiliated when her husband of nearly three years turned out to be a bigamist — indeed, a trigamist. As an impresario, she once put on a play that not merely flopped but was one of the worst debacles in the history of the New York stage. She confronted financial ruin when, because of the illness of her mother, she broke a contract to perform in Russia and was sued for damages. Though one of the highest paid performers of the period — and one who benefited from a succession of bountiful angels — she bore heavy expenses, mismanaged her money, and was continually in debt. Her kind of dancing was strenuous; it was especially exhausting when she was weakened by one of her frequent colds or bronchial infections. She sometimes feared she was going blind, and her eyesight suffered terribly from the glaring light to which, year after year, she was exposed. Yet, like the trouper she was, she carried on.

When too old and fat for a performer, she became a teacher, one who instructed girls in "natural dancing" and directed their performances as long as she lived. Through her pupils she continued, time after time, to come up with some new and wonderful spectacle. She won applause with her showmanship even when she was in her sixties and had to compete with Josephine Baker, the young and terrific African American dancer, for the attention of the Paris public.

She rose to extraordinary heights from a quite modest background. Her accomplishments were such that she might well have been satisfied with an unadorned account of her beginnings. She was not. Once she had achieved celebrity, she knocked several years off her age and made up fantastic tales about what was left of her early years. She created her own myth.

A century after her sudden rise to fame, she was no longer remembered except among people interested in modern dance or in Art Nouveau. Even they could have only a sketchy and inaccurate conception of her personal life. The full and true story remained to be told.

Her earliest universe, so far as her own memory went, was a Chicago boardinghouse as it existed soon after the Civil War. Her father, Reuben Fuller, owned and ran the boardinghouse with the assistance of her mother, Delilah. Living there also were her brother Frank, several years older than she, and varying numbers of servants and boarders. She was then a plump little girl with a round face, turned-up nose, big blue eyes, and light reddish brown hair. Her name was Marie Louise and she was called Louie for short.[1]

As she grew up, her memory was stretched farther back through the recollections of her parents. Fullers on her father's side and Eatons and Paddocks on her mother's, she learned, had served with bravery and sacrifice in the Revolutionary War, so that she was entitled to join the Daughters of the American Revolution, but never did.

Reuben Fuller, when a small boy, had come west from New York State with his father, Jacob, and other members of the family, traveling in covered wagons. According to family tradition, the wagons got stuck in the mud when they reached the marshy site of Chicago, which at that time was only a cluster of huts near a frontier outpost, Fort Dearborn. About sixteen or seventeen miles farther on, the Fullers arrived at land they liked, high and dry, around Brush Hill. Here Jacob bought a large tract from the federal government and began to farm.

Reuben Fuller and Delilah Eaton were married when he was nearly twenty-three and she nineteen. That was in 1850, when the lure of gold was attracting tens of thousands of young men to California. Reuben resisted as long as he could, then left his bride to join the gold rush. He took the roundabout sea route, going by way of New York City and the Isthmus of Panama. After two long years he suddenly reappeared, to the surprise of Delilah, who had heard nothing from him about his coming home. He now told her of his experiences while away — how, for instance, he had barely managed to save himself when his ship caught fire on the return voyage in the Gulf of Mexico. Years later there was still a tinge of bitterness in her voice when she gave her account of that trying time to her daughter.

Whether or not Reuben had struck gold in California, he now had enough money to buy a large farm, which was located about two miles east of Fullersburg, the hamlet that had grown out of the original Jacob Fuller settlement and was inhabited mainly by Jacob's relatives and descendants. As a farmer, Reuben was more interested in raising horses than in raising anything else. He bred and trained trotters and ran them in the harness races at the county fair each fall. A first-rate fiddler and graceful dancer, he provided music for both barn and ballroom dances when not doing a few steps himself. In the winter, when farming was slow, he sometimes took over the management of the Fullersburg tavern that belonged to his father. Abraham Lincoln supposedly stopped there when traveling between Springfield and Chicago.[2]

In January 1862, when Delilah was expecting, the day-to-day temperatures ranged far below zero and the farmhouse was impossible to keep warm. At the tavern the general room was heated by a tremendous stove. There a bed was set up for Delilah and there Marie Louise was born, as Delilah afterward related in impressive detail. "On that day the frost was thick on the window panes and the water froze in dishes two yards from the famous stove," the daughter remembered hearing, and at the "very moment" of her birth she caught a cold that she "never got rid of."[3]

Fullersburg and the Reuben Fuller farm still seemed to have a bright economic future. The plank road from Chicago — with boards laid across wooden beams sunk in the earth — ran past the farm and through the village. For a toll, farmers and other haulers could take goods to market much more expeditiously than on an ordinary dirt road. By 1862 there was talk of something much better yet, a railroad. Surveyors for the Chicago, Burlington, and Quincy soon began to investigate possible routes. The Fullers expected the tracks to follow the plank road, but the surveyors finally chose a line one mile to the south, where the new village of Hinsdale consequently grew up.

Reuben did not soon forget the shattering of his hopes: he was still talking about it when Louie was old enough to understand what it was all about. "I remember the time that the railroad put the station a mile away from us," she wrote decades later. "Father was terribly hurt about it and disappointed. He had worked hard to put that little place [Fullersburg] on the map."[4]

Chicago — which not so long ago the Fullers had bypassed for Brush Hill — now was an incomparably more up-and-coming place. Indeed, it was the biggest of boomtowns, the fastest growing city in the United States. To Reuben, the city began to appeal more than the country, and innkeeping more than farming. When Louie was about two years old, he disposed of his farm, moved to Chicago with his family, and opened his boardinghouse.[5]

In Chicago the Fullers did not go to church on Sunday; they went, instead, to the Progressive Lyceum along with other freethinkers. At the Lyceum's Sunday school there was a recitation period for children. Not long after the Fullers' arrival, little Louie, uninvited and unannounced, climbed up onto the platform, bowed like the orators she had seen up there, and then knelt and recited the prayer she had been taught to say at bedtime: "Now I lay me down to sleep; / I pray the Lord my soul to keep . . ." This was more amusing than shocking to the audience of freethinking parents, who laughed when she finished. They laughed again when, too small to walk down the steps, she slid down, bumpety-bump.

The next Sunday, properly introduced, she curtsied and then spoke another piece, "Mary Had a Little Lamb," which brought enthusiastic applause. Again she bumped down the steps, but this time no one made fun of her. Throughout her life she treasured her mother's report of these two performances. They amounted to her stage debut, she liked to think in retrospect, and they illustrated her precocious showmanship as well as her inborn quickness at learning her lines. She must have memorized "Mary Had a Little Lamb" on hearing her brother read it only once, or so she afterward assumed.[6]

When Louie was five years old, her parents sent her to the nearest public school. Attendance was not compulsory in Illinois in those days, but the

Loie with her father, Reuben, in Illinois, about 1867. (Courtesy of the Dance Collection, the New York Public Library for the Performing Arts.)

Fullers wanted their children to have the benefit of an education. Louie never forgot her first school day. "I returned home full of indignation," she recalled long afterward. "How could they send me there — one only needed five minutes to learn 'that' and I had lost a whole morning." She nevertheless had to keep on going, and she continued to resent it. Never willingly idle, she hated "sitting in the same place for hours doing nothing and waiting for the lesson to be learned" by the other pupils.

When Louie was seven, her mother gave birth to a second boy, Delbert. The next year, 1870, the federal census taker found eight persons living at the boardinghouse in addition to the five Fullers. Her parents and brothers provided good company for Louie, but she could have obtained little companionship or inspiration from the other residents. These included two domestic servants: Kate Duffy, fifteen, and Susan Black, eighteen. The boarders were John Miller, thirty, a machinist; Robert Sewell, twenty-nine, a day laborer; Richard Lichfield, twenty-three, a bookkeeper; William Ames, forty-seven, a carpenter; W. T. Judson, twenty-five, a harness maker; and M. C. Davis, twenty, unemployed. A local census the following year indicated that the number of boarders had increased from eight to thirteen.[7]

That was the year of the great Chicago fire. The summer and fall of 1871 were unusually hot and dry, with continual strong winds from the southwest. On Sunday night, October 8, the conflagration started in a poor Irish neighborhood of wooden shacks and sheds. If the fire had moved straight north, it would eventually have engulfed the Fuller House, which was located at 164 West Lake Street, about five blocks west of the Chicago River's south branch. Luckily for the Fullers, the wind drove the flames to the northeast. Flying embers carried them across the river and through the business district, where brick and stone as well as wooden structures were destroyed. By Monday night, most of the city's core lay in blackened ruins, and more than three hundred of its inhabitants were dead. The spectacle — the orange glow at night, the billowing smoke by day — had been clearly visible from 164 West Lake Street. Crowds of refugees moved through the street and brought the sights and sounds of the catastrophe close to home.[8]

For the time being, though not rich, Reuben remained reasonably well off. The 1870 census credited him with $1,000 in real and $2,000 in personal property — quite respectable sums for the period. The personal property consisted largely of horses, which he was buying and selling to supplement his income. An 1872 city directory listed him as a "horsetrader" (a term that carried the connotation of "sharp bargainer" or, in more modern discourse, "used-car salesman"). Chicago recovered rapidly from the fire until September 1873, when a financial panic set off a nationwide depression. The following year, no longer satisfied with his prospects where he was, Reuben decided to move again.

One of her first trips of any length, the new move was exciting enough at the time, though nothing as compared with the countless journeys by land and by sea that she was eventually to make. It was a two-hundred-mile train ride on the Chicago, Burlington, and Quincy, which ran through Hinsdale and on southwest across the state of Illinois. At Monmouth, a growing and promising town of a few thousand, Louie and the rest of the family got off the train. Here, in a prime location near the center of the business district, stood the National Hotel, an almost new three-story brick building with elegant stone trim on the windows and a stylish cornice at the eaves. This hotel, with her father as proprietor and manager, was now Louie's home.

"We move to Monmouth & I go 'puddling' in the mud," she remembered, "and am surprised by fashionable callers." This suggests that Louie, at twelve, was something of a tomboy, and also that, as newcomers, the Fullers received a warm welcome from the socially elect among the townspeople. Reuben had something to show and impress the visitors. It was a "rare curiosity in the shape of an old English Bible," containing quaint language such as this title: "The whole Booke of Psalmes, collected in English meeter . . . and . . . conferred with the Hebrew with apt notes to sing them with."[9]

As a big-city girl in a small town, Louie had plenty of confidence in herself, and she quickly made her way into community activities. During her first winter in Monmouth she joined with prominent women to help raise money for the local unemployed, whose numbers had increased with the deepening of the business depression. "The entertainment given by the ladies of Monmouth last Friday, for the benefit of the poor, was a very decided success," the *Monmouth Weekly Review* reported on March 5, 1875. "After paying all expenses, they had something over one hundred dollars left. The music, recitation by Miss Fuller, and the 'Original Tom Thumb Family' gave life and enjoyment to the occasion."

Meanwhile Louie was busily rehearsing for a play, *Ten Nights in a Bar Room*. The Monmouth Dramatic Club and Literary Association planned to present it at Union Hall and donate the net proceeds to the Monmouth Temperance Reform Club.

Temperance agitation in Illinois had reached a peak. A recent state law made liquor dealers liable for injury or damage caused by an intoxicated person to whom they had sold drinks. German brewers and Irish saloonkeepers demanded repeal of the measure while the antidrink people, mainly native Protestants, agitated for an even stricter law, one that would bring about statewide prohibition. Many of the evangelical clergy, though they looked askance at ordinary playacting, were more than willing to endorse a temperance drama such as *Ten Nights in a Bar Room*.

For more than twenty years this play had been a favorite for amateur theatricals throughout the North. It was a tearjerker with a lurid plot, in which the local saloon dooms a whole town to sorrow and despair. Night after night the angelic Mary Morgan bravely appears among the drunkards in the barroom to make her touching appeal: "Father, dear father, come home with me now!" This choice role of Mary Morgan was Louie's. Unfortunately, when the day came for the one and only performance, she was indisposed and an understudy had to take her place.[10]

Disappointed though she was, Louie managed to salvage something from her part in the play. It inspired her to speak out against the evils of drink. Regarding her presentation in the nearby village of Kirkwood, the *Monmouth Weekly Review* reported on May 21, 1875: "Miss Louie Fuller, of Monmouth (aged 13), delivered a lecture on temperance, in Columbian Hall, on Saturday evening, to a slim house. It was pronounced good by all who heard it."

Louie gained further recognition when the Prince Imperial Club held its second annual masquerade ball on Christmas Eve. About fifty masked couples had gathered in Union Hall when, at nine o'clock, the band struck up the grand march. Before the judging of the costumes, the crowd heard and applauded a "fine concert" by "the famed 'Tennesseans,' a band of colored jubilee singers," who were on their way to the Centennial Exposition in Philadelphia. The Tennesseans may or may not have been pleased to see some of the masqueraders in blackface, representing a "Plantation Darkee with Pickaninny," "Two African Ladies," and "Two Orphans (colored)." None of these contestants won the prize, and neither did Louie, who was dressed as a "Fairy." "The $10 gold coin prize, for the best impersonation of characters, was awarded to Miss Lottie Schultz, who appeared as Mother Goose."

Louie's moment came after the unmasking, when the waltz contest was held. She and her dancing partner, Perceval Brewer, had to compete with the grownups but nevertheless came away with the grand prize, "youth proving too much for the 'old folks.'" In retrospect she wrote: "I gain the prize for waltzing & fall in love at the same time."[11]

It was no wonder that Louie could dance so well. Not only was she blessed with natural grace and a sense of rhythm, but she also had the benefit of instruction from a terpsichorean expert, her father. "Mr. R. Fuller has opened the 'Monmouth Dancing Academy' in Wallace's Hall," the *Monmouth Daily Review* announced on January 14, 1876. "Mr. Fuller himself is an accomplished dancer, thoroughly acquainted with the principles of the art, and skilled in imparting to his pupils that graceful habit of body and ease of movement so essential to the complete enjoyment of this delightful accomplished art." The Academy started with a class of twenty of "the finest young men of the city," who were to meet twice a week, on Tuesday and Friday nights.

The National Hotel and the Dancing Academy did not hold Reuben Fuller in Monmouth very long. After a two-year stay he sold the hotel and took his family back across the state to Westville, a smaller town located near the Indiana line about 150 miles south of Chicago. His daughter wrote down few recollections of this phase of her life, but she seems to have had pleasant memories of it, as indicated by the summary she once made: "We move

From "Louie" to "Loie"

to Westville. The pretty lady. The church and the paper says she is 14 or 16 — a question anxiously asked by the young men!"

After living a year in Westville, the Fullers returned to Chicago. Reuben now had no occupation (none, at any rate, that was listed with his name in the city directory). Delilah provided for the family by operating a notions store, where Frank was employed as a clerk. Bert was still going to school. And Louie, in the turmoil of adolescence, was trying to find herself and her career.[12]

Stagestruck, the teenager started out by accepting whatever bit parts she could find in one theater or another in Chicago. Opportunities for performers, high and low, were multiplying throughout the country as both the legitimate theater and the variety show expanded in response to an increasing demand for commercial entertainment. The opportunities for Loie Fuller, as she began to call herself, were limited mostly to melodrama, farce, and burlesque (not girlie shows but parodies of serious drama), in which her role was usually that of an ingénue, a soubrette, or a boy. Still, in the course of a decade, she managed to reach Broadway and attain at least a certain degree of stardom on the American stage.

When only fifteen, Loie reportedly joined the Felix A. Vincent Comedy Company in Chicago and went on a nine-month tour with it. Other roles followed. "I play a part with three words & it leads to an engagement when I learn that I must be prepared for theatrical intrigue & I get my chance when critics pronounce me a coming star." Then "I join Frank Mayo's Company at a moment's notice and make a hit without knowing it." That, at any rate, was the way she liked to remember her early years on the professional stage.[13]

Actually, she was nineteen when she got her first chance at something more than a very minor role. William F. Cody — the frontier scout and war veteran popularly known as Buffalo Bill — had arrived in Chicago to present a "soul-stirring, blood-curdling drama," *The Prairie Waif,* for one week at the Olympic Theatre. There was more to the program than merely this gripping play. There was also "an exhibition of Fancy Rifle Shooting" by

Buffalo Bill himself, and there were "wild and weird Songs and Dances" by four Winnebago chiefs, a Pawnee chief, and an Indian maiden whose tribal affiliation was not disclosed.

"The lady who played the part of the Waif, in Chicago, was not particularly friendly to [Jule] Keen, who, at that time, was the stage manager," a friend of Keen's related. At one matinee the actress did not arrive until the end of the first act, in which she was supposed to appear. "She came in with a sweep and a flashy eye and exclaimed, 'What is going on here? How dared you raise that curtain without my being here?'" The stage manager was not well impressed, and apparently he fired the haughty thespian, or she quit.

In either case, here was an opening for Loie. She had to strum the banjo but learned to do so easily enough and, just as easily, memorized the lines of the waif. Then she went on tour with the Buffalo Bill troupe, which traveled as far east as Brooklyn. There, at the Grand Opera House, they appeared in January 1882. By this time the play had been changed to *Twenty Days, or Buffalo Bill's Pledge*, but Loie's role was pretty much the same as before: she was now Miss Pepper, "a conventional crusher and deserted waif." Before she had quite finished the season with Buffalo Bill, she came down with a light case of the smallpox and had to leave the show.

It was a few years before she got another part as good as that of the waif. According to her recollections, she meanwhile toured Illinois in a farce that she had written and had titled *Larks*. For a couple of years she took voice lessons from the music editor of the *Chicago Tribune*, making her first public appearance as a singer in the chorus at a Chicago summer music festival. She apparently traveled for a time with her own musical group. Almost a half century later she reminded Julius Witmark: "when you were a very young boy, with a beautiful head of black, curly hair, and a voice like an angel, you sang in my concert company and went with me throughout America." Witmark, born in 1870, a popular boy soprano, became a partner in the firm of M. Witmark & Sons, the nation's largest publisher of sheet music.[14]

The young Loie dreamed of becoming an opera star.

> At 18 years of age she could sing all right, but was living in dire poverty, managing to indulge in one meal a day, and that

From "Louie" to "Loie"

one sometimes not more than a crust of bread. She was anxious to go into opera, but managers laughed when the half-starved, ill-clad girl walked into their offices and asked for an engagement.

At last . . . she read in the Chicago papers that Murray and Murphy were playing in a farce, called "Our Irish Visitors," at Hooley's Opera House, under the management of J. M. Hill.

Miss Fuller, with a roll of music under her arm, haunted Hooley's Theatre for several days before she managed to corral "Jim" Hill. The day she did a rehearsal was going on and Hill was mad. The play was going all wrong, the lack of singing material being the main cause. Hill . . . looked up crossly as the young girl entered.

"What do you want?" he said gruffly.

"I want an appointment," was the prompt reply.

Hill looked curiously at the diminutive figure in front of him. He saw a girl with a shock of blonde hair, hollow cheeked and with dark circles around the eyes and miserably clad. His sympathies were aroused in a moment.

"What can you do?" he asked gently.

"Anything and everything," was the prompt reply. "I can sing, dance and act. Know Shakespeare by heart, but can't get an engagement at that. I want to do something that will enable me to eat two or three times a day."

In a few minutes Hill was leading the girl back to the stage where the rehearsal was going on. She walked quietly to the piano, unrolled her music, and after a short prelude a glorious soprano voice vibrated through the walls of the theatre in an aria from "Trovatore." She was signed at a salary of $50 a week [a good salary at the time].

That is what a newspaper reporter gathered from Loie a quarter of a century later, when she was fantasizing, as she often did, about her past. It is true, at least, that she was hired by Murray and Murphy for *Our Irish Visitors*, but she was then twenty-four or twenty-five, not eighteen, though she looked even younger than that. In this play she was the leading lady, and she danced as well as sang. Afterward a Bostonian recalled her appearance at the Boston Theatre in August 1885. At that time, "in her skirt and her jersey-like waist, she created excitement, and people flocked in to see what the newspapers called a 'sensational dance,' which some even called 'daring,' just because the dancer wore no corset, and the muscular sway of her young figure was visible."[15]

The next year she made her New York debut, at the Bijou Opera House, in *Humbug*. In this farce, a bit of humbuggery indeed, a German cobbler's son takes the name of a distinguished Southern family to win a woman he thinks is a rich widow; she has no money and marries him for his presumed status. Dominating the proceedings was a comedian named Roland Reed, who was noted for his "picturesque grimaces" and his "vocal squeals." From time to time he interrupted the play to introduce songs. "In a medley of airs from 'The Mikado' Mr. Reed was assisted by a Miss Fuller, who is better as a songstress than as an actress," the *New York Times* commented. "She has yet to learn the value of repose and the meaning of gesture and facial expression. But she has been taught to sing, and she has a fairly good voice." *Humbug* ran for six weeks, closing on August 14, 1886.[16]

No matter what the critics thought of her performance in that play, Loie had done well enough to gain the attention and approval of Nat C. Goodwin, one of the greatest comic actors of the period, a master of burlesque. "That is burlesque," the *Times* explained, " — to imitate a serious work, and in imitating it to make it ridiculous, and it is in the accomplishment of that not very lofty purpose that Mr. Goodwin is pre-eminent upon our stage today." After going to London and buying the rights to four plays that had succeeded there, Goodwin sold the rights to three of them to help finance the production of the fourth, *Little Jack Sheppard*, at the Bijou, where it opened on September 13, 1886. This "grotesque caricature of melodrama" contained very little narrative but an abundance of rollicking music, rhyming dialogue, and far-fetched puns. Goodwin had chosen Loie for the title role, the central character of Jack.

From "Louie" to "Loie"

Loie in the title role of Little Jack Sheppard, *Bijou Theatre, New York, 1886. (Photograph by Sarony; courtesy of the Dance Collection, the New York Public Library for the Performing Arts.)*

Loie, as Jack, got contradictory reviews in the New York press. The *Daily Mirror* sourly reported:

> We regret we cannot commend the management's choice of Loie Fuller for the title role. Miss Fuller evinced improvement, it is true, but she has not the vivacity or the peculiar

accomplishments that go to make up a successful performer in this line of work. Her Cockney accent was such only in the dropping of h's; in all other respects it savored of interior New England. Miss Fuller sings prettily, but she cannot dance, and therein does she vastly fall short of such a role.

The *Times,* while noting that it was Goodwin who attracted people to the theater, gave Loie a very complimentary report:

The scene in which young Jack is supposed to cut the letters of his name upon the wall of his prison while he mournfully sings . . . possesses exactly the spirit that true burlesque should have, because it reflects the meaning of the original and puts it in a comic light. Miss Loie Fuller, as the hero of the piece, does this little bit very neatly, and indeed Miss Fuller's impersonation is very commendable throughout the play. She looks like a boy, as few women do in breeches, and she acts like one, which is still less frequently accomplished.

One evening a newspaper editor and his wife took their six-year-old daughter with them to see *Little Jack Sheppard.* The girl wanted to meet Jack, so her father arranged to introduce her to Loie. "I had succeeded so perfectly in taking a boy's part," Loie remembered, "that the little girl could not believe but that I really was one, and when she had been presented to me, she asked: 'Well, why does Jack wear girl's clothes?'" Loie succeeded in the illusion despite her physique, which was not boyish in the least. Small though she was, she had a fully rounded female figure.[17]

Little Jack Sheppard ran for three months, until attendance drastically declined. To provide something else at the Bijou, Goodwin bought back one of the other burlesques he had imported from England — *Turned Up* — which he recently had sold for five hundred dollars and for which he now was compelled to pay one thousand dollars plus 10 percent of the gross receipts. This play, opening in December 1886, was billed as a "New and Original Melo-dramatic Farcical Comedy," and in it Loie again was given an important role. "We thought we were in for a run of at least one season and

From "Louie" to "Loie"

maybe two," Goodwin recalled. But, much to his and Loie's surprise, the managers of the Bijou very soon decided that the play, if not actually losing money, was making too little profit.

To replace *Turned Up,* Goodwin was offered *Big Pony,* with a libretto by A. C. Wheeler, a New York dramatic critic, and music by Woolson Morse, "a very clever composer." Goodwin wanted to revise and update the second of the three acts. "The dialogue referred to political issues that were long since dead. Wheeler insisted that the play should be performed as he had written it." So, accepting the manuscript as it was, Goodwin went ahead and, at the Bijou in March 1887, lavishly presented "the first production on any stage of the Original American Comic Opera" — *Big Pony* — with "Indians, Cowboys, Mexicans, Monks, Spanish Girls, Squaws, Bucks, Soldiers, etc." Loie was one of the Spanish Girls, Senorita Marie. She and the rest of these people were lively enough, but not Goodwin with his prescribed dialogue. "I was compelled to deliver funny lines which I knew were funereal," he lamented; "the second act was so terrible that the play proved an unmitigated failure." After a few weeks Goodwin revived *Little Jack Sheppard* and took it on tour, with Loie again playing the part of Jack.[18]

Loie next performed in *Aladdin, or The Wonderful Lamp,* at the Standard Theatre in New York in the fall of 1887. According to its promoters, this extravaganza offered the most spectacular lighting effects in the history of the American theater. There had been dazzling spectacles before; in the long-running favorite *The Black Crook,* for example, a fountain took on all the colors of the rainbow when light was projected on the water through a prism. But *Aladdin,* with its magical transformations, was even more impressively staged. In one of the transformations, while scenery was being changed, colored lights played on a curtain of steam. In another the stage appeared to be "filled with elephants and beautiful girls lying among sunrise clouds, with yellow, buff, gold, and silver blending in a rich harmony of color."

Again a male impersonator, Loie, as Aladdin, rubbed the magic lamp to bring about the miraculous changes of scenery. She did not look like a boy this time. While one critic mentioned her among the "clever people" in the cast, another declared that "Loie Fuller's shapely form" was one of the "extra features of the production." No doubt the experience contributed to her future success, since it provided lessons she could use for her subsequent career as an innovator in lighting effects.

Before coming to New York, *Aladdin* had enjoyed the longest run in the history of the Chicago stage. Scenes were added and the cast was enlarged for the New York audience, and at the Standard Theatre the revised play opened to a sizable enthusiastic house. But it lasted there for less than a month, then played in Brooklyn for only a week.[19]

Loie's next engagement, beginning on November 29, 1887, at Niblo's Garden in New York, also proved to be more of a learning experience than a theatrical triumph for her. She had secured a part in *She*, another spectacular, which was based on H. Rider Haggard's grotesque novel about the two-thousand-year-old woman Ayesha. "There is nothing in his books to inspire a dramatist," the *New York Times* remarked, "but there is plenty of material in them to tempt the mere playwright, the painter of scenery, the inventor of 'transformations,' the costumer, and the gasman." (The "gasman" had charge of the gaslights in a theater.) As staged, *She* displayed lighting effects almost as amazing as those in *Aladdin*. There was, for example, a storm with thunder and lightning and "a vast rolling sea, breaking clouds, a lurid sunset." There was also a "cave of the sacred fire of life," where the beauteous Ayesha twice "goes into the flame" and emerges the second time as a "wrinkled hag of hideous aspect."

In these goings-on Loie had a relatively unimportant part. She later joked that "she used to roll, bumpety-bump, down the steps of the property pyramid. She was given the role, not for any special histrionic ability, but because she was willing to fall farther and harder for a $10 stipend than any other member of the company." When she told that story, she was forgetting that one critic had said she played her part "earnestly and with abundant dramatic intelligence." To be sure, another observer complained that Loie and the rest of the cast "lacked, collectively, that glitter which compels a playgoer to hurry to the theatre to be enchanted by actors' efforts."

She remained at Niblo's for four weeks and then went on the road. Loie now had a chance to go bumpety-bump down the steps in Chicago, where she had done much the same thing in her precocious stage debut more than twenty years earlier.[20]

When Loie played in Chicago, her mother and father went along with her

From "Louie" to "Loie"

and visited friends and relatives in Fullersburg. Her parents accompanied her on other trips, too. "Pa & Ma are both here with me," she wrote from Boston, May 31, 1887, to her cousin Eunice L. Rogers in Illinois. "Pa just returned from a trip to Binghamton [in his native New York, where some of his family still lived]. Had a nice time. But doesn't say anything about it." Loie was repaying her cousin, in $10 installments, for a $50 loan. Already she was demonstrating a talent that, along with her theatrical one, was to grow tremendously with the years — a talent for going into debt.[21]

Despite the unsuccessful plays in which she had a part, Loie had attained at least a modest standing in the American theater by 1888, when she was twenty-six. She had been invited to perform in numerous benefits in New York and Boston, and she gave gladly and generously of her time to these charitable events. While doing so, she shared the stage with some of the best-known actors and actresses of the period, among them not only Nat Goodwin but also Lillian Russell and Steele MacKaye. But the career that made her world-famous was yet to begin.[22]

2

The Serpent and the Serpentine

When Loie Fuller was twenty-seven she got married—or thought she did. The arrangement was bizarre and the outcome even more so. Meanwhile, after repeated setbacks in her career, she made an amazing breakthrough, transforming herself into a new kind of dancer with an act that was eventually to bring her worldwide fame.

The man she came to consider her husband, Colonel William B. Hayes, passed as a nephew of former president Rutherford B. Hayes—which he was not. Fat and fiftyish, with a flowing mustache, Colonel Hayes glittered with diamonds on his fingers and on his shirtfront. Generally, he impressed people as a prosperous man of affairs, one who was making money as a railroad lawyer, a New York stockbroker, and a dealer in Florida real estate.[1]

Loie sought an acquaintance with Hayes because she needed money for a theatrical venture she was planning in cooperation with William Morris, a well-known actor. She was to be the leading lady and Morris the leading man in the play *Caprice,* which featured a sort of Pygmalion theme: an uneducated farm girl meets a well-bred artist from the city and, under his tutelage, tries to improve herself enough to be worthy of him. Loie and Morris were going to take the play to Jamaica.

Some time in the fall of 1888 Loie went to Hayes's Broadway office in New York with a lawyer friend, Henry W. Bates, who introduced her to Hayes. She offered him a promissory note signed by her and Morris in return for a loan. Hayes declined at first, but granted the loan when Loie gave him a note that she, Morris, and Bates all cosigned.

Not long after that, Loie again appealed to Hayes, saying she could not put on her play unless she raised enough money to buy new costumes for her troupe, and asking to borrow much more this time. For security, she offered photographs of herself standing on a pedestal and clad only in tights. In one of the pictures she was bent slightly forward with her arms crossed over her breast, her hair falling loosely over her shoulders, and a coy smile on her face. Underneath, the following words were written in a feminine hand: "Pardon, monsieur, I am not dressed." Hayes accepted the photographs and handed Loie a personal check.

By January 1889 Hayes had become infatuated with Loie, and shortly before she was to leave for the West Indies he proposed to her. When she objected that he already had a wife, he told her he was getting a divorce and would have it by the time she came back to New York.

Loie embarked on the first of her countless voyages when, with Morris and other members of the cast, she sailed from New York on one of the city's wintriest days. They had not been under way long when a storm blew up, the ship began to pitch and rock, and Loie found herself miserably seasick. It was a relief to enter the mild air and quiet water of the Caribbean, and a pleasure to land at Kingston, Jamaica, the "island paradise" that was already attracting winter tourists from the United States. Opening in Kingston on January 15, Loie and Morris began to put on three performances a week.[2]

While there, Loie corresponded fairly often with Hayes, who kept expressing his eagerness to be with her. In a telegram she told him not to come to Jamaica until he received an explanatory letter. In the letter, addressing him as "My Own Dear H———," she said she was sorry they could not be together. "But it is impossible. People would talk if you should follow me around, and so I suppose I must wait. Now, of course, if you only had an interest in the company, that would be enough excuse for you to follow me around. You wouldn't be after me, but after your own interests." Taking the hint, Hayes agreed to meet Loie and Morris and talk business with them in New Orleans, where they and their troupe arrived on an English tramp steamer on April 1, 1889. Loie and Morris informed Hayes that they were going to organize a new company, for an extended West Indian tour, and would sell him a one-third interest for twenty-five hundred dollars. He signed a contract, made a down payment by check, and was named treasurer of the Morris-Fuller Company (which never produced a single play).

Then Loie and Hayes took a train to Jacksonville, Florida, where he had some business to attend to. Since he seemed to have easy access to money, she thought he might be able to help her father. Having recently acquired some land near Tampa, Florida, Reuben Fuller was living there with Delilah while he tried to develop the property. By telegram, Loie advised him to come up to Jacksonville. "He came and immediately began to borrow," Hayes later said. "I introduced him to a banker, to whom he tried to mortgage about $500 worth of sand lots for $8,000." The banker, under the influence of Loie's persuasive charm, promised to provide the loan.

From Jacksonville, Loie and Hayes proceeded to New York. Renewing his marriage proposal, he showed her a document that he said was a decree of divorce from his former wife, and Loie then agreed to a wedding. He objected that a regular ceremony would attract public attention, which would be bad for his business. He was planning to start a bank, he explained, and his prospects as a banker would be ruined if it was known that he was married to a burlesque actress.

If Loie were to refuse Hayes, she would risk losing a financial backer, the only one she had. So she accepted his suggestion of a secret common-law marriage. Her mother, now in New York, was present when, on May 11, 1889, Hayes and Loie got together in Loie's Broadway boardinghouse room. The nearest thing to a marriage certificate they were to have was a piece of paper that the couple signed and Delilah witnessed. It read: "I, William B. Hayes, in the presence of God, do take Loie Fuller for my lawful wife. And I, Loie Fuller, do take William B. Hayes for my lawful husband."[3]

Discontinuing her partnership with Morris, Loie soon found a role in *The Chimes of Normandy* at New York's Grand Opera House. She "was sprightly and amusing," a critic wrote in regard to opening night. "She sang passably well, although not endowed with any too much voice. It was noticeable that her antics and dancing smacked of burlesque and the variety show, but vivacity of any kind was gladly welcomed."[4]

She aspired to much greater things. *Caprice*, which had not done very well in Jamaica, ought to do vastly better in England, where theatergoers were so much more numerous. Loie decided to become the impresario and star of her own show and to present it in one of the theatrical capitals of the world—London. A bold decision it was, but she could find reassurance in the expectation that her husband would stand behind her with his financial support. He, for his part, hoped that his investment in her enterprise would pay off with a handsome profit. Both she and he were to be badly disappointed.

Embarking on the steamer *Umbria* on September 3, 1889, Loie made the first of her innumerable Atlantic crossings. Some time after she reached London, her parents arrived there, and so did Hayes. He told the proprietor of the Hotel Victoria, where she was staying, that he was her husband and would be responsible for her debts. Soon he left for the United States, but not before he and Reuben had engaged in a financial transaction that led Reuben to believe Hayes had cheated him out of almost four thousand dollars.

Loie meanwhile leased one of London's leading theaters, the historic Globe, and proceeded to line up a cast. She also engaged an English playwright to revise *Caprice* so as, presumably, to adapt it to local tastes. The Englishman "ruthlessly cut the dances and some of the music-hall business," it was said, but Loie insisted on keeping "two or three 'turns'" in her part. She had got permission to use the play from Clara Beaumont, to whom its American author supposedly had assigned the rights. But Minnie Madden—an actress with whom William Morris had performed in the play before he and Loie took it to Jamaica—contended that the rights belonged solely to her. She accused Loie of "barefaced robbery," and the *New York Dramatic Mirror* repeated the charge. Then Loie, in one of her soon-to-be-frequent litigious moods, threatened to sue the paper for libel.[5]

On opening night, October 22, there was some trouble with the cow that, together with a few live chickens, was supposed to lend realism to a barnyard scene. The cow "licked off enough paint from its property shed and property food to give it a terrible fit of indigestion," according to the *Stage*, a London theater journal. And "several members of the company were compelled during the evening to give it doses of peppermint and other warming mixtures, so overcome was the poor beast with its new surroundings."

Caprice received quite a bit of additional attention in the theatrical press. Reading the reviews, Loie could take what comfort there might be in the fact that, on the whole, her own performance was viewed more favorably than was the play she had chosen to present. "Our fair visitor is a little woman, full of dainty graces, plump and personable, gifted with a power of pleasant pathos and humour, but she threw herself away in this long, spun-out tepidity," said one reviewer. Another declared that seldom had "a

Loie in costume, probably for Caprice, *London, October 1889.*

weaker or more invertebrate play than *Caprice* been brought across the Atlantic," but thanks to "Miss Fuller's individual grace and charm, the piece passed muster," though her singing and piano playing were "of a decidedly mediocre character" and "narrowly missed evoking some unfriendly demonstrations."

Regarding Loie's acting talent, two of the critics were as contradictory as they could possibly be. One said: "She has an artless, impulsive style, and her representation of emotion is natural and apparently spontaneous." The other thought it would be hard to find a "more unnatural and self-conscious actress."[6]

Theatergoers did not like the play any better than the critics did. Loie's lease of the Globe was to have run for three months, until Christmas, but after a few weeks she had to close the play and give up the lease. Now that *Caprice* had proved a money-losing rather than a profit-making venture, she received no more encouragement or aid from Hayes. He had been sending poorly spelled but affectionate letters, which he addressed to "My Darling Girl" or "My Darling Wife" and which he signed "Your Loving Husband." But he was not paying her bills, as he had promised to do, and finally he quit writing, though he realized she was "in straitened circumstances."

Loie was left with her mother to make her way in London as best she could when Reuben returned to New York to confront Hayes. Loie and Delilah were terribly shocked to learn that Reuben had died, on June 5, 1890, and they were still more shocked when they heard about the circumstances of his death. According to what they were told, Reuben and Hayes had been dining together at a hotel in Fort Lee, New Jersey, across the Hudson River from upper Manhattan. After the dinner, Reuben suddenly fell dead, and Hayes had the body embalmed with suspicious haste. The death certificate gave typhoid fever as the cause, but Loie came to believe that her husband had poisoned her father.[7]

For almost a year, Loie could find very few paying jobs in London. In the winter and spring of 1890 she did give a series of "humorous ballad concerts" at Athenaeum Hall, and she appeared briefly in a variety show at the Gaiety Theatre, singing "Marguerite" and reciting "Pyramus and Thisbe" to the "great enjoyment of the audience." But that was about all. Eventually Loie and Delilah found themselves in serious difficulty, though probably not in quite such desperate straits as she long afterward imagined:

> We could no longer afford our comfortable living quarters; a very cheap hotel sheltered us, reminding us persistently of the long list of unpaid bills it was hoarding for us. Many times

The Serpent and the Serpentine

when food became a deep problem, if a great many *real* American friends had not come to our aid, I am sorely afraid we would have starved to death in our garret!

Although these trials were hard on us both, mother and I tried to be cheerful. I made my calls regularly on the agents, and was as regularly told that there were no openings. All this time we were pawning everything we had.[8]

Opportunities improved considerably during the 1890–91 season, and Loie got more frequent, if not quite steady, work. She now appeared in a number of London theaters: Drury Lane, Opera Comique, Avenue, Terry's, Shaftsbury, and Gaiety. She served as an understudy in one production, took part in a couple of curtain raisers, and performed in quite a few special matinees, sometimes as many as three different ones in a single day. In her light and airy roles she gained more nearly unanimous approval than she had done in *Caprice*. In the "farcical comedietta" *Two or One?* there were "some very charming snatches of melody (to which Miss Fuller did perfect justice)," and she "threw a humorous earnestness into her madness that was very amusing." In *Zephyr*, in which she played Zephyrina Winn, she "gave a charmingly natural performance of the warm-hearted little commoner."[9]

Plaudits of this kind were pleasing enough, but they had little to do with Loie's ultimate success. So far as that success was concerned, her most important experience during her London stay was one that neither she nor the critics really noticed at the time: her learning experience as a performer at the Gaiety Theatre.

The Gaiety Theatre was especially noted for its dancers, the Gaiety Girls, and one of their most popular numbers was a skirt dance. The skirt dancers manipulated long and flowing gowns while following some pattern of steps and bodily movements, different performers presenting different routines. Among the early performers the most famous was Kate Vaughan, for whom the Gaiety dancing master had choreographed a special act. Her successor, Letty Lind, was doing a similar skirt dance in *Carmen-up-to-Data* while Loie acted in a curtain raiser for that comic opera. Loie may have substituted briefly for Letty Lind or for another of the Gaiety Girls, Florence St. John. Whether she took part or not, Loie had plenty of opportunity to observe the kind of dancing on which she was to base her own distinctive style.[10]

That, however, lay in the future. At the time Loie left London, in the summer of 1891, she did not yet think of herself as primarily a dancer (though, of course, she had danced in *Caprice* and in many other plays). She took with her the rights to one of the plays she had recently acted in—*Zephyr*—and she expected to put on this comedy and star in it in New York. Her unhappy experience with *Caprice* had not discouraged her from trying again as the impresario and leading lady of her own show.

On the return voyage, aboard the comfortable liner *Teutonic*, Loie participated in a concert on the evening before the ship docked in New York. She demonstrated on this occasion, as on later ones, that she had a way with bigger and better businessmen than William B. Hayes. The shipboard master of ceremonies was Chauncey M. Depew, president of the New York Central Railroad and a well-known raconteur and wit. Loie was much impressed by Depew's management of the ship's concert. "His services in that capacity were rendered in such a manner as to suggest that if he were not the president of a great big railroad corporation he would be eminently qualified to guide the fortunes or misfortunes of a theatrical company," she thought—and no doubt told him so. "I sang at the concert and I shall never forget how my heart was touched when Mr. Depew, in introducing me to the audience, said: 'A song by our own Loie Fuller.' That was American, wasn't it?"

So Loie said after she landed, according to a reporter. "Time has brought no changes in this clever woman," the stagestruck interviewer gushed. "She is the bright, happy, sympathetic little creature that she was when local theatergoers knew her as one of the sparkling ornaments of the burlesque stage, unaffected in her manner, gay, spirited and light-hearted as ever." The newspaperman quoted her as saying further:

> As for my sojourn abroad, well, it was punctuated with all kinds of experiences—some pleasant and delightful, others

The Serpent and the Serpentine

less so. I won't say gloomy, for I never allow an element of gloom or sorrow to enter into my affairs. I believe that life is but short at most, and one's duty is to allow nothing but the bright side to manifest itself. My sojourn in London was really an epoch in my life. I met so many nice people there, and the theatrical folk was so generous and kind to me! I regretted the circumstances which compelled me to leave London, but America is home, and so many ties existed here that I began to feel like a refugee away from it all.

No, I didn't do much in the way of work over there. I only appeared a limited number of times, and, in fact, only went over to study the different methods employed by artists in my particular line of stage work, with a view to perfecting my art.[11]

In the interview Loie mentioned her plan to stay in America and present the comedy *Zephyr,* but said nothing about the real reason she had gone to England—to present the comedy *Caprice.*

Unable to get financial backing for *Zephyr,* Loie gave up the idea of managing her own show again and looked, instead, for a role in someone else's production. She found a job in another play, one that did not amount to much but nevertheless made possible her breakthrough from B-grade actress to nonpareil performer.

In *Quack, M.D.* she was called upon to do a little skirt dance as an entr'acte in addition to taking the lead role as a young widow whom the quack doctor hypnotizes. During a six-week tour with the play, she developed the essentials of her new and distinctive dance routine, which involved the waving of a filmy robe while varicolored lights were projected on it. *Quack, M.D.* finally reached New York, to open at the Columbus Theatre on October 20, 1891, and to close soon after.

Loie was left with her new routine and nowhere to perform it. Though she was acquainted with a number of New York theater managers, they knew her as an actress and a singer, not as a professional dancer. One manager told her that if he wanted a dancer he would get a real one—a star like Letty Lind of the Gaiety in London. Another manager, Rudolph Aronson of the Casino Theatre, was unenthusiastic but willing to try her out.

When Loie arrived at the Casino on the appointed night, the stage was lighted by only a single gas jet, and there was no piano for her accompaniment. She nevertheless went ahead and put on her costume over her street clothes, then "hummed an air and started to dance very gently in the obscurity." Aronson, who had been sitting in the orchestra pit apparently bored, came up on the stage to get a closer look. "I continued to dance, disappearing in the darkness at the rear of the stage, then returning toward the gas jet," Loie remembered. "Finally I lifted a part of my robe over my shoulders, made a kind of cloud which enveloped me completely and then fell, a wavering mass of fluffy silk, at the manager's feet."

Now anything but bored, Aronson soon had a name for Loie's act—the "Serpentine Dance," he called it—and he had the music for it, the soon-to-be-popular French waltz "Au Loin du Bal." He also had a production into which the dance would fit. It was a variety show, the main feature of which was *Uncle Celestin,* the translation of a musical comedy that had been quite popular in France. The show was about to go on the road, and Loie toured with it during the winter of 1891–92.[12]

Not until the company reached the larger cities of the East—Philadelphia, Brooklyn, Boston, and finally New York—were the theaters able to provide suitable lighting for Loie's performance. Along the way she nevertheless got enthusiastic notices, much better notices than did *Uncle Celestin* itself. Critics generally had a kind word only for three of the vaudeville acts: the warblings of a bird imitator, the antics of a comedian with an "automatic piano," and above all the serpentine dance of Loie Fuller.

A reviewer for the *New York Spirit of the Times* attended the performance at the Park Theatre, Brooklyn, to see if *Uncle Celestin* "would do" at the Casino Theatre in New York. "The only artistic feature is the Serpentine Dance, introduced by Loie Fuller, whose name was not on the bills," the *Spirit of the Times* man discovered.

The Serpent and the Serpentine

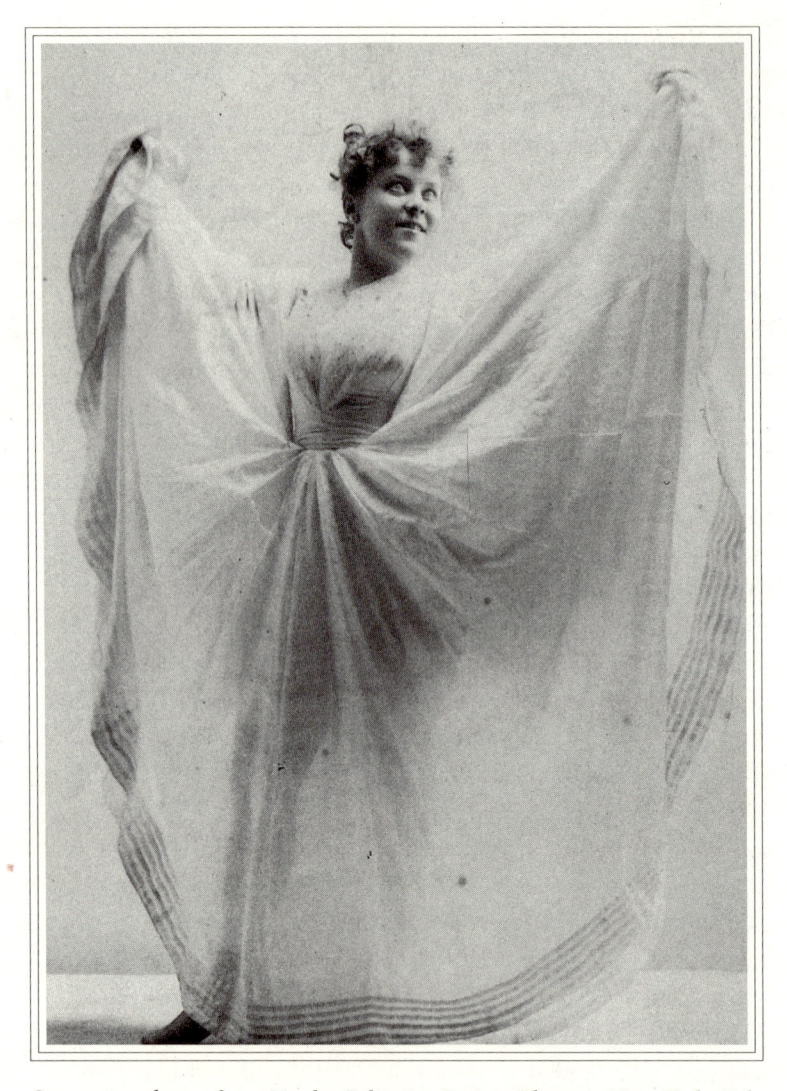

Serpentine dance from Uncle Celestin, *Casino Theatre, New York, February 1892. (Photograph by Sarony; courtesy of the Dance Collection, the New York Public Library for the Performing Arts.)*

Suddenly the stage is darkened, and Loie Fuller appears in a white light which makes her radiant and a white robe which surrounds her like a cloud. She floats around the stage, her figure now revealed, now concealed by the exquisite drapery which takes forms of its own and seems instinct with her life. The surprised and delighted spectators do not know what to call her performance. It is not a skirt dance, although she dances and waves a skirt. It is unique, ethereal, delicious. As she vanishes, leaving only a flutter of her robe upon the stage, the theatre resounds with thunders of applause. Again she emerges from the darkness, her airy evolutions now tinted blue and purple and crimson, and again the audience rise at her and insist upon seeing her pretty, piquant face before they can believe that the lovely apparition is really a woman. Let us have the Serpentine Dance at the Casino and it will be the talk of the town.

It was indeed the talk of the town after Loie appeared at the Casino, to face a crowded house, on the evening of February 15, 1892. The next day the New York papers had nothing but the highest praise for her performance. It "was watched last night in a breathless silence deserved by its novelty and beauty," said the *Times*. It "made a genuine sensation," declared the *Post*, "which alone would cause the Casino to be crowded for some time, and justly so, for the dancing garments of Miss Fuller, thrown into all sorts of lines and graceful rotatory movements, with ever-changing illumination, are infinitely more artistic than the toe-dancing of the greatest *prima ballerina*."

According to the *Sun*, Loie "received three hearty encores for the marvelously and graceful way she manipulated a gauze skirt that alluringly revealed her supple form." Some in the audience thought her dance perhaps a little too daring, but the *World* came to her defense, insisting that the "only one indiscreet thing" occurred when the stage was "illuminated brilliantly" from the back: "Miss Fuller then dances in front of this light, and the transparent effect of the drapery adds something to the sensational effectiveness of the dance." Afterward, the *World* reporter asked Loie: "And what about the moral side of it all?" She replied that a performer had to be guided by her own conscience and by "a sort of inaudible voice from the audience just how far to go."[13]

※

Of more concern to Loie than the moral side of her stage performance was the moral side of her personal life, an issue that came to a head just as her new career was so spectacularly taking off. "Mr. Hayes has repeatedly referred to me as his cast-off mistress," she learned to her dismay. Boasting that he had filthy pictures of her, he insinuated that she was a monster of immorality.

Loie determined to punish Hayes and shut him up. She could have charged him with murder, but convinced though she was of his guilt, she had no real evidence that he had killed her father. She could have sued him for slander. But she thought she had an open-and-shut case against him on the grounds of bigamy. While in England she had received a letter from a woman who claimed to be Hayes's wife and threatened to take legal action against Loie unless she stopped calling herself Mrs. Hayes. By January 1892 she no longer doubted that Hayes was married to another woman.

While in Philadelphia with the touring company of *Uncle Celestin,* Loie took a train to New York on the afternoon of January 18, 1892. Accompanied by her lawyer, she went directly to the Jefferson Market Police Court and obtained a private interview with the judge. Her lawyer applied for a warrant for the arrest of William B. Hayes, and Loie brought out the piece of paper on which, nearly three years before, Hayes and she had declared themselves husband and wife. Giving her age as twenty-nine (it was actually thirty), she now stated, in an affidavit, that "on May 11, 1889, W. B. Hayes did feloniously take unto himself a wife, he at the time having one wife alive"— Amelia E. Hayes. Then she hurried back to Philadelphia for her evening performance at the Chestnut Street Theatre.

On the following day Hayes was arrested and released to await trial. He gave his age as forty, which was at least ten years shy (he would have been only twelve at the time of his marriage to Amelia, which took place in 1864). When interviewed, he swore he had never married Loie but had only

One of the "nude-appearing" photographs that Loie gave William B. Hayes as collateral for a loan in the fall of 1888. (Courtesy of the Dance Collection, the New York Public Library for the Performing Arts.)

helped to finance her and William Morris, much to his own impoverishment. "Mr. Hayes says that Miss Fuller is a playful, innocent thing to all appearances, but that in reality she is extremely wide awake." He also said she was "expensive." He laughed when asked about Loie's story of his dining with her father in Fort Lee and afterward having him embalmed with suspicious haste. "He said that he was not in Fort Lee at the time of Mr. Fuller's death, but went there immediately afterward to attend to the removal of the body, and found it already embalmed."

After Hayes displayed the nude-appearing pictures of herself that Loie had given him, a reporter asked her about them, and she said: "I admit that he has several of my photographs, but they were taken in tights, as I can prove by the photographer." Then, denying Hayes's claim that the marriage paper was a forgery, she insisted that the two had indeed been married, though she maintained with equal conviction that they had never lived together as man and wife.[14]

The case came up on January 29, after repeated postponements to accommodate Loie, engaged as she was in Philadelphia. Several "theatrical people," friends of hers, were in the courtroom, and so was Amelia Hayes, who constantly demonstrated her loyalty to her husband. On the witness stand Amelia was asked if she knew Loie, and she answered that, yes, she had met her in her boardinghouse about May 6, 1889 (five days before the date of the marriage paper), after having heard a rumor that Loie was going to marry Hayes.

> "I called on Miss Fuller and asked her if she knew that Mr. Hayes already had a wife. She said that she did. Then I asked her if the rumor was true. She said that it wasn't; that her relations with Mr. Hayes were purely of a business character."
>
> During this testimony Miss Fuller rolled her eyes as though shocked, and lifted her hands in horror. "Heavens, what a lie," she whispered. "I never saw that woman in my life until I saw her in the court room the other day."

Again for Loie's convenience, the case was put off for a couple of weeks more, when she would be performing in New York. As Hayes left the room with Mrs. Hayes, a detective arrested him on a new charge, that of perjury, which another woman had brought against him.[15]

On February 16, the day after Loie's smashing debut at the Casino Theatre, her lawyer was back in court trying to persuade the judge to reopen her case. The judge had dismissed it on the grounds that the marriage paper was not sufficient proof that Loie and Hayes had been legally married. When the judge refused to reconsider, Loie's lawyer still had the option of suing Hayes for slander. To head off such a move, Hayes issued the following sworn statement:

> I, William B. Hayes, of my own free will and accord, do hereby publish and declare that I firmly believe that Loie Fuller is free from all taint of immorality or misconduct of any kind. Her conduct and relations with me and in my presence, hearing and observation, have always been [of] the most pure, upright and honorable kind and nature, and I regret exceedingly that by any act or word I have cast the slightest reflection on her good name or character, injured her reputation and wounded her feelings. I wish further to emphasize that I have never advanced any moneys to her except in the course of business relations. I never had any indecent or nude pictures of Loie Fuller, nor do I believe that any such picture has ever been taken. I hereby retract any and all remarks I may have uttered reflecting upon her honor and chastity, and apologize to her for having uttered them.

With this "confession and apology," together with her serpentine dance, Loie had "won a double success," or so an admiring newspaperman declared.[16]

Besides that, she was to win a vicarious victory over Hayes in the other case pending against him. He would go to prison not for bigamy but for perjury, though perjury was really the least of his offenses against the poor woman who brought the indictment. The testimony in this case exposed him as even more of a snake than Loie had come to consider him.

Nearly twenty years after marrying Amelia, while the two were living in Detroit, Hayes met a seventeen-year-old girl at a skating rink, a girl named

The Serpent and the Serpentine

Anna Keating, who worked in a department store. He told her he was divorced, but when he learned that she was a Roman Catholic he "was afraid she would have nothing to do with a divorced man," so he changed his story and said he was really a widower. When he asked her to be his wife she consented, and he gave her a ring. There was no wedding but there was a honeymoon, Hayes and Anna occupying the same stateroom on a lake steamer. She was pregnant by the time she discovered that he was already married.

After Hayes and Amelia moved to New York City, Anna came and stayed with them for a while, then went to a "foundling asylum," where her baby was born. Amelia wanted to adopt the "little one." A childless invalid, she thought she might regain her husband's love if she could mother his child, but Anna would not give her baby up.

To make amends, Hayes gave Anna a promissory note for two thousand dollars, payable in two years. He failed to pay the note when it fell due, so Anna sued him and won a judgment against him. He then swore that he had never signed any such note, and he was brought to trial on account of this false affidavit.

Meanwhile Anna had two more children by Hayes, the second of them born in September 1889—four months after Hayes had "married" Loie Fuller. Loie's name was often mentioned in the course of the perjury trial, though she never attended it (she was out of the country by that time). Amelia, the "faithful wife," was constantly present and so was Anna, a "sweet-faced little woman," both of them weeping copious tears. A "bevy of females" came to court to catch a glimpse of Hayes, the ladies' man. "The women cried out that it was a shame that Col. Hayes should be locked up and have to eat just like a common prisoner." That was when he was consigned overnight to the Tombs and before he began to eat just like a common prisoner day after day in Sing Sing.[17]

After taking Hayes to court and failing to get a conviction, Loie became a party to more and more litigation, three lawsuits within a short time, all of which she lost. Finding herself unable to prevent what she considered unfair competition in New York, she decided to take her serpentine dance abroad, preferably to Paris.

Her disillusionment had begun as soon as she made her dazzling debut at the Casino Theatre. As she understood her agreement with the manager, Rudolph Aronson, her name would be featured in posters and other advertisements. Only on this condition had she agreed to perform for the good but not great salary of fifty dollars a week. The *Uncle Celestin* playbill did give her the following mention: "Incidental to Third Act: the Serpentine Dance, by Miss Loie Fuller (specially engaged), as performed by her 100 nights at the Gaiety theatre, London"—which, though not exactly true, was gratifying enough. And huge lithographs, plastered on walls and billboards, displayed her likeness and the words "The Serpentine Dance," but not her name.

Protesting to Aronson, she insisted that she would have to have more money if she were to stay at the Casino. Aronson complied—or she got the impression that he did—and indicated that he was going to raise her weekly salary from $50 to $150. On that assumption, she gave both a matinee and an evening performance on Washington's Birthday, exactly one week after the first appearance at the theater. The next day, however, Aronson made it clear that he would no longer need her services if she could not provide them at the existing rate. So she quit.

That night the Casino playbill included her name and dance as usual. When the curtain fell on the last act of *Uncle Celestin* and the crowd waited expectantly for Loie and the serpentine, a man appeared on the stage and announced that she was ill. Many in the crowd hissed and booed, then stampeded the box office to get their money back, one man enforcing his demand with a drawn pistol. The following night Aronson had a replacement for Loie: one of his chorus girls, Minnie Renwood, who had been studying Loie's technique.

As for Loie, she went to another theater, the Madison Square, and asked for a contract at $150 a week. Charles H. Hoyt of Hoyt & Thomas, who managed the Madison Square, was willing to pay that much but would sign the contract only with the proviso that he could cancel it at will. Hoyt feared that the competition from Minnie Renwood at the Casino might lessen the public interest in Loie at the Madison Square. "I was obliged to accept the conditions which he imposed," she remembered bitterly, "but I experienced all the while an access of rage and grief as I saw in what a barefaced manner they had stolen my invention." On February 29, 1892, she began a long run at the Madison Square Theatre, performing between the acts of the farce *A Trip to Chinatown*.[18]

Her anger at Rudolph Aronson and Minnie Renwood grew when she found that the Casino continued to use the posters displaying *her* picture and advertising *her* dance. She sued, asking for one thousand dollars in damages and an injunction against the New York Concert Company, Ltd., which operated the Casino, and against all the company's employees and officials, among whom Aronson was president. She charged that the corporation, by giving the false impression that she was still at its theater, was defrauding both her and the public.

Months later, on June 14, 1892, the case came to trial before the Court of Common Pleas in the New York City Court House. Loie, with her attorney, was on hand. Aronson testified that, of the 1,000 lithographs that had been made, only 250 had been distributed, and these he "was trying to get back as rapidly as he could." His attorney argued that, after all, Aronson had "originated the title of the dance" and that Loie had "violated her contract in leaving the Casino." Aronson's lawyer seems to have been smarter than Loie's. Hers had brought suit against the New York Concert Company, Ltd., not against Aronson personally. His lawyer stoutly denied that the corporation, as such, had ever had anything to do with Loie! When he moved to dismiss the complaint, the judge promptly dismissed it and ordered Loie to pay the defendant's costs.[19]

Her next defeat came in just a couple of days. While still under contract at the Madison Square Theatre, she was also dancing for another employer, Amberg's Theatre. The Madison Square management, Hoyt & Thomas, had applied for a restraining order against her, and the case was heard in the Superior Court. Loie pointed out, in her defense, that she had "expressly refused to sign a contract with a clause to the effect that she was to appear with Hoyt & Thomas exclusively." The judge decided that, nevertheless, her performance was, "according to her own description, unique, and being so, the spirit of her employment by Hoyt & Thomas must be that they should be entitled to her exclusive services."[20]

LOIE FULLER

Two days after that verdict, another went against Loie, this one in the federal case of *Marie Louise Fuller v. Minnie Renwood Bemis*. Minnie Renwood was no longer performing at the Casino, *Uncle Celestin* having closed shortly after she replaced Loie in the program, but she was dancing the serpentine during the summer on the roof of Madison Square Garden. Loie had taken the precaution of copyrighting a description of the dance she had invented. According to this description, the dance consists of three "tableaux," each of which begins with the dancer invisible on a darkened stage, then suddenly revealed as beams of light strike her. Through the various motions of her dress and changing colors of illumination, she proceeds to create the effect of large flowers, breakers or surf, and a gigantic spiderweb and a huge butterfly. Each tableau concludes with the lights off, then on again, and the dancer out of sight. On the basis of this copyrighted material, Loie now sued Minnie for infringement of copyright, requesting an injunction to keep her from continuing with her imitation.

In the U.S. Circuit Court for the Southern District of New York, Loie's attorney exhibited her "copyrighted composition" and argued that, by virtue of it, she possessed "not only the sole and exclusive right and liberty to print and publish such dramatic composition, but also the sole and exclusive right to act, perform, and represent the said dramatic composition," which she had been able to perform "with great success and pecuniary profit" because of its "originality and extraordinarily novel nature." But the judge, unconvinced, handed down the following decision on June 18, 1892:

> An examination of the description of complainant's dance, as filed for copyright, shows that the end sought for and accomplished was solely the devising of a series of graceful movements, combined with an attractive arrangement of drapery, lights, and shadows, telling no story, portraying no character, depicting no emotion. The merely mechanical movements by which effects are produced on the stage are not subjects of copyright when they convey no ideas whose arrangement makes up a dramatic composition. . . . Motion for preliminary injunction denied.[21]

The Serpent and the Serpentine

Ten days after that, on June 28, 1892, Loie secured an immediate release from her Madison Square Theatre contract, which was to have run until August 1. Hoyt & Thomas promptly replaced her act with one in which "four demure widows, in deep mourning," suddenly "burst into a whirlwind of 'Ta-ra-ra Boom-de-ay,' accompanied with a skirt dance and high kicking."

Loie was giving up her "pecuniary profit" in America to gamble again on the chance of even greater success in Europe. As was her wont, she had been generously contributing to various charities by taking part in recent benefits. For one of her benefit performances, at the German Theatre in New York, a Romanian orchestra provided the accompaniment. After having watched her, the orchestra leader advised her to go to Paris, where an "artistically inclined public" would give her dances "the reception they deserved," as she was to recall. "From that moment on this became a fixed idea with me—to dance in Paris. Then the manager of the German Theatre proposed to me a tour abroad, beginning with Berlin."[22]

3

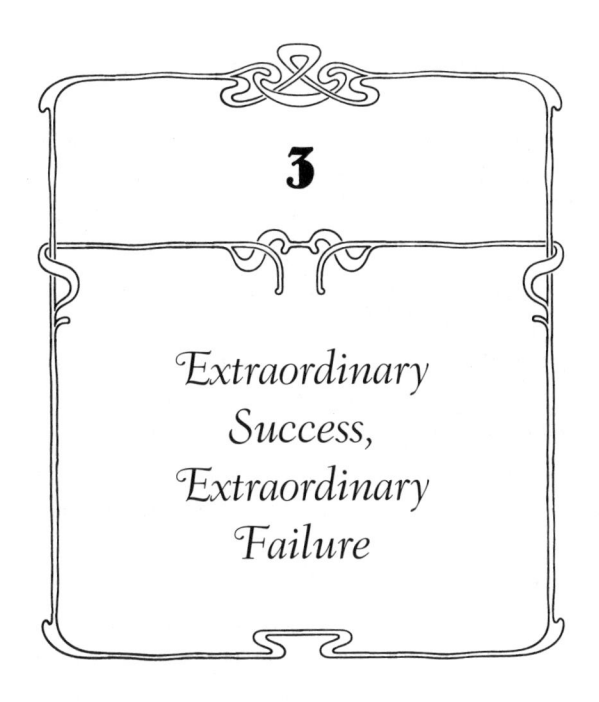

Extraordinary Success, Extraordinary Failure

*A*board a Hamburg-bound ship in the late summer of 1892, the thirty-year-old Loie Fuller thrilled with the anticipation of a glorious future. But her mother, remembering the trip to England and Loie's disappointment there, could not help worrying. As it turned out, this new foreign adventure justified both the hopes of the one and the misgivings of the other.

At first, Loie had reason to be optimistic. She had been a hit in New York and could expect to be one in Berlin, where, with her contract, she could count on an opportunity to perform. She was further reassured by the success of her performance on shipboard, after the captain asked her to take part in a customary entertainment for the benefit of a German seamen's charity. Here was a chance for her to try out some new steps and costumes that she had devised since her last appearance in New York. A stage was improvised on deck, with a German flag as a drop curtain and signal lanterns as spotlights. The night was still, the sea calm, the ship steady. Loie presented six tableaux, each of which brought gratifying applause from passengers and crew. Then she took up a collection—the largest ever, the captain declared. "I felt," she wrote in retrospect, "that I had taken my first step in the conquest of a new world."[1]

There came a letdown when the German theater manager met the Fullers at Hamburg and took them to Berlin. Loie was not going to perform in the opera house, as she had been led to expect, but in a mere music hall, the Wintergarten of the Central Hotel. She made a good first impression there. What amazed the spectators, a Berlin newspaper said, was not so much the dance itself as the staging of it, together with the remarkable quickness and dexterity of the dancer's movements. Spectators were particularly impressed by the lighting effects—the contrast between the inky blackness at the beginning and the diamondlike brilliance that suddenly followed; then the constantly changing colors that came from the electric lamps.[2]

Still, Loie made no such hit in Berlin as she had already made in New York and was soon to make, on a much grander scale, in Paris. After a month her German manager told her he would not longer need her services. She was left with only enough money to pay her hotel bill. As if this were not sufficiently disheartening, her mother fell ill and the weather turned dismal.

When the outlook was darkest, Loie chanced to meet an English-speaking theatrical agent, Marten Stein, who was able to secure some modest engagements for her. She went back to Hamburg, where she gave a dozen performances in a beer garden, and then to Cologne, where she "had to dance in a circus between an educated donkey and an elephant that played the organ." Her "humiliation was complete," as she never forgot.

Paris remained her goal. Desperate though she was, she kept her sights high. She wrote to Pedro Gailhard, director of the Paris Opéra (Académie Nationale de Musique). Without waiting for a reply, she proceeded to Paris with her mother and her agent, Stein, in late October 1892. She signed in at one of the city's finest and most expensive hotels, the Grand, which was strategically located across the street from the Opéra. Immediately, before going to her room, she sent Stein across the street to speak to Gailhard.

Stein came back with a disappointing report. Gailhard had not been much impressed with Loie's act as she had described it in her letter to him. He was not sure that he could afford to engage her at all, but if he could, it would be for no more than four performances a month. And that would hardly pay enough to support Loie and her mother. They and Stein dined in the elegant *salle* of the Grand Hotel, while an orchestra entertained them and their fellow guests with a classical concert. Stein had in mind another place for Loie to try her luck. It was the Folies-Bergère, to the manager of which he had written from Germany in Loie's behalf. After dinner he and the Fullers took a carriage to 32 rue Richer, about a half mile away.[3]

The Folies-Bergère, like the Wintergarten in Berlin, was a music hall, the most important one in Paris. It had started out as one of the city's many cafés-concerts, where customers could listen to singing for the price of a cheap meal or a beer. It developed into a type of circus, in which the performers were mainly animal trainers, acrobats, clowns, and the like. Under the management of Edouard Marchand it was undergoing a further transformation into a grand vaudeville theater that offered a great variety of acts, many of them bawdy. Not quite respectable, it was yet to become an innocuous tourist attraction featuring seminude chorus girls.

The interior of the Folies-Bergère was "ugly and . . . splendid . . . of an outrageous and exquisite taste," with plaster statues here and there and a ceiling of gilded cloth. At the rear was a large open area, the *promenoir*, where some customers found cheap standing room to watch the show, and others negotiated with the high-class whores who frequented the place. "No matter where one sat or stood, one's ears were filled with a medley of waltzes and polkas and finale chords blaring over the cries of program hawkers and shoeshiners, audience chatter and applause. Everywhere the air was laden with perfume scents and the acrid odors of cigar smoke, beer, and dusty rugs."[4]

When Loie, along with her mother and Stein, arrived at the Folies-Bergère, she was shocked to see a poster advertising a "Danse serpentine" already being performed by Miss Mabelle Stuart. Inside, Loie asked to see the manager and was told he would not be available until the end of the evening show, which included a pantomime, "eccentric" singing, and other acts in addition to the serpentine dance. The three visitors were given seats in a far corner of the balcony, where they could watch the show while waiting to talk with the manager. Loie was relieved upon observing Mabelle Stuart's performance; she was sure it could not compare with her own.

But the manager, Marchand, did not find Loie very prepossessing when, shortly before midnight, she appeared at his office door. To him, she looked a little strange in her thick veil, voluminous overcoat, and high button shoes. He had no reason to be dissatisfied with Mabelle Stuart, who, according to the Paris daily *Le Figaro*, was drawing good crowds to the Folies-Bergère and, indeed, was having at least as much success there as she had recently had in London. With Stein serving as interpreter, Loie nevertheless persuaded Marchand to let her demonstrate her act for him then and there. (Actually, Marchand needed no interpreter; he had a good command of English, as she afterward found out.)

On the Folies-Bergère stage that night, Loie had only a violin for accompaniment and the footlights for illumination (circumstances much like those of her earlier tryout at the Casino Theatre in New York). Still, once she was out of her street clothes and in her dancing robe, she succeeded in working her magic on Marchand. He promptly agreed to take her on as a replacement for Mabelle Stuart.

During the next several days Loie was busy rehearsing her dances and overseeing the stagehands and electricians as they made preparations for her special kind of staging and lighting. While she was thus engaged, Mar-

Loie in the "Dance of the Serpents." (Photograph by Reutlinger; courtesy of the Bibliothèque Nationale.)

chand took her one day to the office of *Le Figaro* for her to perform for its editors and obtain some advance publicity. She overwhelmed them. On November 5, 1892, *Le Figaro* announced that Miss Loie Fuller, "la créatrice de la danse serpentine" (the creator, as distinct from the imitator), would debut at the Folies-Bergère that evening. "Voilà—an act that all Paris will rush to see," the paper declared with prophetic accuracy, "for no dance has ever been more alluring or more magical."

That evening Loie presented four of her tableaux: the "Serpentine," the "Violet," the "Butterfly," and the "White Dance." Each aroused deafening applause and calls for repeated encores. Loie had to keep going for forty-five minutes—until she was ready to drop from fatigue. Then members of the audience crowded around her with congratulations and practically carried her to her dressing room.[5]

Paris had never experienced anything quite like the Loie craze that followed. Throughout the 1892–93 season she attracted unheard-of crowds to the Folies-Bergère. She enthralled not only its usual patrons but many others who seldom if ever had been inside such a lowbrow music hall. In doing so, she helped to transform the Folies-Bergère, giving it a new respectability, and she made herself one of the city's top celebrities.

She had performed there only three times when *Le Figaro* reported: "Miss Loïe Fuller, the charming creator of the serpentine dance, is winning every evening at the Folies-Bergère a success without precedent at that theater, which has enjoyed many a brilliant success in the past." After one more performance, those wanting to see her act had to reserve seats several days in advance. "Never has there been seen such enthusiasm on the part of the Paris public." Soon it was impossible to get any seat, or even standing room, without booking at least ten days ahead of time—"a fact without precedent at the Folies-Bergère."

The "incomparable" Loie was doing as well as ever when, on January 26, 1893, she gave her hundredth Folies-Bergère performance. She received an ovation and heaps of flowers, and each member of the audience received, as a souvenir, a fan decorated with a picture of her dancing. Her 150th performance, on March 6, was her "150th triumph." A month later, when she returned after a brief absence, she was greeted with a "triple salvo of applause," and once more the stage was strewn with flowers when she left it.[6]

Loie was such a drawing card that, by herself, she could assure Marchand a sold-out house for a long time. But Marchand was not content with that. While extending Loie's contract, he proceeded to surround his "star of the first magnitude" with new if lesser lights, making the program more varied and elaborate than ever before.

Marchand kept Mlle Duclerc, the original Ta-ra-ra-boom-de-ay girl, whom he had engaged at the same time as Loie, and whom he had expected to be an equally brilliant star. He added successively, over a period of several months, the following acts (among others): Wallenda and his Great Danes. Techow and his educated cats. The tightrope walkers Ara, Zebra, and Vora. Fatima the belly dancer. Sullivan the kangaroo boxer from Australia. Sherman and Morrissey, American blackface comedians. The Girards, musical clowns. *Fantasies parisiennes,* a ballet-revue. *The Lotus Flowers,* a pantomime ballet. Ralph Terry with his animated shadows. (From this last number Loie may have got the germ of an idea for future use. She was, years later, to feature gigantic animated shadows of her own.)[7]

Accompanied by an orchestra of forty musicians, Loie regularly presented four dances—"La Serpentine," "La Violette," "Le Papillon," and "xxxx"—near the end of the second half of the show. ("Serpentine" had become both a specific and a generic term: it referred to a particular dance of Loie's but also to her style of dancing in general.) No matter how many performers were added to the program, she continued to outshine them all.

On the playbill she was the headliner, her name standing out in much the largest and blackest type. She was billed as "La Loïe Fuller." The "La" was significant: it emphasized that this was *the* Loie, the genuine article, not to be confused with any of the imitators that kept springing up. The dieresis in "Loïe" was necessary to preserve the pronunciation, which, without those two dots above the "ï," would be "Lwah" in French and would mean "the goose," or "law." She promptly began to use the French spelling in her signature.[8]

No longer did she suffer from a lack of suitable publicity. Aware as always of the uses of advertising, she commissioned some of the very best lithog-

Extraordinary Success, Extraordinary Failure

Posters advertising Loie's performances at the Folies-Bergère were displayed not only on walls and kiosks but also on handcarts pulled through the streets of Paris. (Courtesy of the Dance Collection, the New York Public Library for the Performing Arts.)

raphers to make her posters. These were not only placed outside the Folies-Bergère and put up on walls elsewhere but also pulled through the streets on carts. "The poster says, 'Serpentine'! ah! what a poor word to describe the impalpable, intangible, ethereal, supernatural essence that arises from the floating of the soft material, from the quick glimpses of pink flesh, from the dazzling magic of the colored lights—a voluptuous poetry!" So rhapsodized one theater critic, giving further advertisement to Loie's act. "The show is the most unusual, the most attractive, the most unforgettable that I have ever seen," declared another. "And there is no pornography, no unwholesome nudity, no coarseness, nothing but the most poetically artistic. This Loïe Fuller is a great, a very great artist." There were only rave reviews. "It is fair to say that such an artist has never been seen before." "Go see Loïe Fuller!"[9]

As an artist, Loie attracted other artists to the Folies-Bergère, among them painters who were fascinated by her use of color. "Since Loïe Fuller has been on the program at the Folies-Bergère," said *Le Figaro* only nine days after her first appearance there, "that pretty theater has become the rendezvous of all lovers of exquisite things, the rendezvous of the most stylish and select Parisians." Aristocrats began to rub elbows with the newly rich, and the reservations list came to resemble a social registry. "There is nothing so curious as the rapid change that has been made in the clientele of the Folies-Bergère," *L'Echo de Paris* commented after Loie had been performing there for only a month. "One now sees black dress coats with a gardenia as a boutonniere; every evening there appears on the rue Richer a long file of carriages decorated with coats of arms; the aristocracy is lining up to applaud Loïe Fuller."[10]

Loie further enlarged and diversified the Folies-Bergère clientele by taking part in family matinees. At first, she refused to "appear in public in the daytime"—her evening performances were fatiguing enough—but after two weeks Marchand persuaded her to try an afternoon show. The first matinee, featuring Loie but also offering some other acts from the evening program, drew a larger crowd than ever. According to *Le Figaro,* more than a thousand people were turned away. The audience consisted mostly of mothers and children—people of a kind that had never been in the music hall before. Loie, "having already won the acclaim of the grown-ups, now received the cheers of the little ones." Thereafter a series of matinees was scheduled for Saturdays and eventually for Saturdays, Thursdays, and holidays. These performances continued to attract large and enthusiastic crowds.[11]

Loie was soon in demand for daytime appearances away from the theater. A number of hostesses followed the Duchess de la Torre in engaging her for their salons. "She is asked to perform at most of the fashionable five-o'clock teas," it was reported in February 1893, "and the most prudish American ladies see no harm in her serpentine dance." She graced official as well as private gatherings, dancing for a reception at the American legation, for another at a French ministry, and for still others elsewhere. She also performed for charity, as when she presented three of her numbers to help raise money for the aid of impoverished literary people. Thus every week, besides doing her act seven nights, she did it as many as three or four afternoons.[12]

It was grueling work, and after each performance Loie was exhausted.

Her arms constantly ached from the strain of manipulating the many yards of cloth. Heated as well as fatigued from the exertion, she had to make her way from the theater to her room at the Grand Hotel until, early in the winter, she caught a bad cold. Not wanting her to miss any of her performances, Marchand and his wife arranged an apartment for Loie and her mother in a building adjoining the Folies-Bergère at the rear. A doorway was cut through the intervening wall so that the Fullers could get to their rooms without going outdoors. There were two flights of stairs to go up, however, and Loie was sometimes too tired to make the climb. Two strong men would carry her up the stairs in a chair.[13]

Loie and her mother decorated their little apartment with mementos of Loie's conquest of Paris. These included works of painters and sculptors who did their best to capture the "airiness and witchery" of the serpentine dance. Poets also paid their respects. Léon Charly honored Loie with several lines of verse, the last of which refers to her as "the one who plays with the rainbow." Stéphane Mallarmé, the leader of the symbolists, praised her as a kindred spirit and devoted to her a serious article entitled "Considerations on Loïe Fuller and the Art of the Dance." She, like Mallarmé and the symbolists, attempted to express the inexpressible, to surmount the limitations of language. Her dances seemed to him like poems without words. They constituted the "theatrical form of poetry par excellence." They had the effect of "witchcraft."[14]

There was at least one dissenting view. The novelist J. K. Huysmans detested the theater but yielded to the persuasions of a friend and accompanied him to the Folies-Bergère. Huysmans sat quietly through Loie's performance. "Loïe Fuller—strange," he thought. "Mediocre dancing. After all, the glory goes to the electrician. It's American." But Huysmans kept his opinion to himself, confiding it only to his journal.

Loie came to be celebrated in music as well as poetry when a "talented young composer," A. Hamburg, wrote the "Loïe Fuller Gavotte." It was available as sheet music in arrangements for either piano or orchestra, and with two flattering pictures of Loie on the cover. *Le Figaro* predicted that the music would "soon become as popular as she who inspired it."[15]

The Loie craze extended even to clothing styles—in Paris, the world capital of fashion. High-toned department stores, such as Bon Marché and

Louvre, were selling Loie Fuller skirts, Loie Fuller hats, Loie Fuller ribbons, Loie Fuller shoes, Loie Fuller petticoats. Modistes, "in making up their fashions for the year," were "selecting the colors worn by Miss Fuller in her stage costume." Men's as well as women's clothes were affected, and boulevardiers were wearing Loie Fuller hats, scarves, and ties. (Loie was no fashion model in her own street clothes but wore some of the most godawful getups.)[16]

Loie had achieved instantaneous fame, helped along by journalists, artists, poets, composers, and merchandisers. But her lasting reputation owed much more to one person than to all of those people put together. That person was Roger Marx, an art critic and art bureaucrat, the inspector general of provincial museums for the French government. "Little did I dream . . . that he would be *the* man of all others to send me down to posterity," Loie remembered with regard to her very first meeting with him.

Roger Marx, enchanted by her performance, had called at her apartment to interview her, but he did not speak English and she did not yet speak any French. "He was too young for a beard," she mused, "but he had one." (Actually, he was three years older than she, and she was turning thirty-one.) Though timid and nervous, he managed to make her understand that he wanted her to meet his wife, who would act as an interpreter. Thus, with the Marxes, began one of Loie's closest and most valuable friendships.

The first thing that Roger Marx did to send Loie "down to posterity"— but by no means the last—was to write an article about her choreography for the intellectual magazine *La Revue encyclopédique*. This essay was the most perceptive of the early analyses of her style of dancing. She presents a new kind of dance, he wrote, one that originated in America but can be truly appreciated only in such a country as France, where the "esthetic instinct" is so pervasive and so refined. "One is tempted to imagine that she found her inspiration and her model in ancient Greece, since she so much reminds one of a Tanagra figurine."

Her success "is due to the contrast between her kind of dancing and that to which we have recently been subjected." Too many *danseuses* have been giving poor imitations of "the Andalusian's impish stomping," or have emphasized a swaying of the hips and a rotation of the pelvis, or have resorted to other bodily contortions. These women wear as little as they can get by

Though a Parisian for more than thirty-five years, Loie never acquired a French sense of style. She is pictured around 1900, at left, and in 1916, at right, her love of furs unabated. (Left photograph courtesy of Roger-Viollet; right photograph by Maude Stinson, courtesy of the Dance Collection, the New York Public Library for the Performing Arts.)

with, and what they wear accentuates the buttocks and the breasts. Loie Fuller is utterly different. She keeps her body straight, and she derives her effects from the very profusion of her garments.

At the beginning of her act the theater is dark, the stage and the scenery draped in funereal black. "From this night the apparition escapes, takes form, comes to life under the caress of the electric beams. She detaches herself from the gloomy background, takes on the dazzling whiteness of a diamond, then is covered with all the colors of a jewel box full of precious gems." Some of the fountains at the Paris exposition of 1889 were illuminated in much the same way, but they were stationary and inanimate. Here is a human being with feminine grace and charm.

In the polychromatic waves of light, the exquisite phantom runs back and forth, skims the floor like a dragonfly, skips along like a bird, flaps her wings like a bat. Now she spins and her long skirt puffs out, to give the appearance of an upside-down calyx of a flower. Then, her arms lengthened by batons, she throws the material high above her head in spirals. Next, she ruffles it so as to give the illusion of rising and falling waves, and the waters become increasingly agitated when stirred by blasts from an electric fan. Finally, the pace quickens and whirlwinds arise. "The material, dizzily swirling, is tinged successively with all the hues of the rainbow; and the vision is never so splendid, so magical, so enrapturing as at the moment when she is about to disappear, to be plunged into nothingness, to be lost in the darkness again."[17]

This kind of praise in Parisian magazines and newspapers might have turned Loie's head—or turned it even more than it did—if she had been able to read French. As it was, she remained, or at least gave the appearance of remaining, quite unspoiled. So it seemed to the Paris representative of the London periodical the *Sketch* who visited her at the "quaint little apartment charmingly fitted up for her." The female journalist was delighted by the "straightforward, unaffected American girl"—"the young lady who came forward with both hands outstretched, pleased to greet the English-speaking visitor." The young lady had tiny hands, the caller noticed, and tiny feet.

This little American "girl" was careful not to belie her seemingly tender years when the interviewer asked her about her past. "I made my debut at the age of two and a half years at a Sunday-school recitation party," Loie replied. "A little later I began acting children's parts, and I played more or less all over the United States." She gave the impression that she had been born about 1871. If she were to be taken as only twenty-two in 1893, she obviously would have to have been a mere child when she started her professional career twelve or fifteen years earlier.[18]

Mabelle Stuart, who preceded Loie at the Folies-Bergère, was by no means the only so-called serpentine dancer with whom Loie had to compete. Numerous rivals, European and American, in Paris and elsewhere, introduced variations of their own but tried to do essentially what she was doing. One of them pretended to be Loie herself. Another took the name Ida Fuller (her real name was Ida Pinckney) and said she was Loie's sister-in-law. Ida, who temporarily was performing somewhere in Russia, would eventually become the most successful and longest-lasting of all the copycats, one who would often be confused with Loie.

In Paris, during that winter of 1892–93, theatergoers could choose among a number of the new kind of dancers. At the Nouveau Theater "twenty or thirty Loïe Fullers" formed a "graceful ensemble," and at the Menus-Plaisirs the beautiful Emilienne d'Alençon "imitated her model with a great deal of dexterity." At the Ba-ta-clan could be seen the "pretty Miss Mathews," and at the Concert-Européen, Amy Feyton, who was said to be "one of the originators of the genre in America." At the Eldorado "the admirers of Loïe Fuller could see how the no less famous Jenny Mills" executed her futuristic and fantastic serpentine dance supposedly of the year 1992, a century later.

But, according to some observers, the best of Loie's rivals was Marie Leyton, "The Electrical Serpentine Dancer," currently at the Tivoli in London. Dressed in a blue jacket and floating blue gauze, she would appear to catch fire as varicolored beams struck her one after another. "The effect is startling, and everyone in the audience sits spellbound."[19]

This Marie Leyton insisted that she had not copied from Loie. She maintained that, instead, she and Loie had obtained their inspiration from the same source, London's Gaiety Theatre. The costumer there had designed a dress for the dancers in *Carmen-up-to-Data* and *The Nautch Girl*. "All the girls' dresses were made like that with very short waists and very full gauzy skirts," Marie Leyton told an interviewer from the *Sketch*. "And you must know Miss Loïe Fuller, the American actress, was over here at the Gaiety. She saw the 'Nautch Girl' and she got Miss Fisher, the costumer here, to make her a dress like it, to take back with her to America for a specialty dance."[20]

Earlier, while Loie was still performing the serpentine in New York, an American periodical had similarly traced the dance's origin to the Gaiety Theatre. Loie "went to London, and for eighteen months was with the Gaiety Company," *Munsey's Magazine* stated (erroneously, since by no means was she "with the Gaiety Company" during her entire stay of approximately eighteen months in London). "There she acted as Florence St. John's understudy, and learned from Letty Lind some of her terpsichorean skill. The so called serpentine dance . . . is an evolution of her own, based upon Miss Lind's 'flower dance.'"

It is hard to know who besides Loie herself could have supplied this information—or misinformation. At any rate, when she had her interview with the *Sketch*, several weeks after Marie Leyton's with the same magazine, she denied the implication that either her costume or her dance was anything but entirely original. She declared:

> A great many accounts have been given of how I first came to start this kind of dancing, and people have said that I took the idea from someone else, or, at least, from some old mythological pictures. This is quite a mistake. The idea came to me quite by accident, and I will tell you how. An Indian officer presented me with a funny little white robe or skirt—in fact, an old Hindoo costume [a sari?]. . . . One day, while on tour [in *Quack, M.D.*], I put on the little gown in order to act a small part for which I thought it appropriate. At the end of the second act . . . there was a kind of little dance. I was in a great hurry, and did not wish to change my skirt, and so danced with the one I already had on. The thin Indian mus-

lin flew and blew round about me. This delighted the public, and I received quite an ovation. Well, that set me to thinking, and I thought to myself that probably something more could be made out of the idea.

In subsequent years Loie repeated this story with elaborations and variations.

Meanwhile, several months after her interview for the *Sketch*, she was interviewed for the *New York Spirit of the Times*. "To a *Spirit* representative," this paper reported, "Loie Fuller explained that she invented the serpentine dance in order to make use of a long robe of the finest India silk which was left over from the Oriental costumes ordered for the Savoy Theatre, London, by D'Oyly Carte, and was presented to her." So now the garment was of silk, not muslin, and it came from the Savoy Theatre, not from a British officer in India.

Less than two weeks later Loie told a *New York Herald* reporter:

> A friend of mine had sent me from Calcutta a Nautch girl's dress and I put it on. I began to pose before a large mirror and to dance about, holding the edge of the voluminous skirt in my hands. The strong sunlight shining through a stained glass window fell upon me and the air caught the silk and floated it about me in graceful and fantastic forms.
> I had discovered a dance.

What had been an "old Hindoo costume" became a "Nautch girl's dress"—that is, an Indian dancer's skirt—which may or may not have been the same thing. But whatever the garment, it had led Loie, according to her recent statement, to make her great discovery while she was posing in her room, not while she was acting on the stage as she previously had said.[21]

Long afterward she gave a quite different account to yet another interviewer. She said she had received her inspiration when she and her mother were nearly starving in a London hotel garret. One day she got an opportunity to replace a dancer who had fallen ill, but she had to be ready to perform that very night. She possessed no costume and no money to buy one. Her mother "suggested that the old trunks that surrounded us might contain something that would be of use."

> At first it appeared almost hopeless—nothing but old-fashioned gowns that would be impossible for a dancer to wear. But finally we came upon a find—yards and yards of cheese-cloth! . . . The yards and yards of material were finally arranged about me in a rather becoming manner, held together by the few pins we were able to collect. . . .
>
> After a great deal of practice I finally discovered that by lifting and waving my arms I was able to twist and sway the cheese-cloth in such a way that it . . . gave a most delightful effect. My first dance had been created![22]

Silk, muslin, or cheesecloth? A gift from India, a leftover from D'Oyly Carte, or a find in a hotel garret? An accidental and utterly original invention, or merely an adaptation of what was already being worn and already being done at the Gaiety Theatre? Probably, like many another invention, Loie's dance owed its development to a combination of influences: to earlier models, chance revelations, and a great deal of thought, experiment, and hard work.

To protect herself from what she considered unfair competition, Loie could not rely on copyrighting a description of her dances, as she had learned from the U.S. District Court in New York. But, as a French legal expert pointed out, she could patent physical objects that she used in her performances.

Accordingly, Loie obtained in France (April 8, 1893) and later in England and the United States a patent on a "garment for dancers" that she had devised. This consisted of triangular pieces of "light fluffy material" sewn together "so as to produce a skirt very broad at the base and narrow at the top." The top was "affixed to a suitable crown" that fit the head. Inside the skirt and attached to it were two "wands" of a light substance such as aluminum or bamboo. This arrangement, with the dancer manipulating the wands, would facilitate "the creating of the waving motion in the folds of the garment" and would assist the dancer "in performing statuesque poses

Extraordinary Success, Extraordinary Failure

and in imitating different styles of wings." By "hanging the skirt from the head"—not "around the waist or close under the arms"—the wearer could produce "more rounded and graceful evolutions of the garment."

While this patent was pending, Loie announced (in January 1893) that she was going to bring action against anyone who, without her personal authorization, gave performances similar to hers. But the French jurisconsult doubted whether she could win a case. He noted that, in France, anyone could patent anything but could secure protection for it only if the thing was entirely new and had never been publicly exhibited. And Loie had already exhibited her inventions through her performances in the United States, Germany, and France.

To keep her skirts from being copied, Loie had them made as secretly as possible. "My serpentine robe was painted by hand on thin silk in sections, so that the artists should not know what they were working at," she explained. "All my dresses are made in America." Fashionable ladies at her private performances tried to get a close look at her costumes and asked: "What kind of material are they made of?" Loie, who knew the value of mystery, replied: "That is my secret." And she would not let anyone touch the cloth.[23]

But what gave Loie her best protection was neither secrecy nor the law. It was the ingenuity and the assiduity that enabled her to make improvements faster than her competitors could copy them. She had started out ahead and she managed to keep ahead. As one of her Parisian admirers commented, "Like every creator of a genre, Loïe Fuller has acquired followers, but there is a vast distance between the original and the copies. And her success increases at a much faster rate. This is why: after having looked at an imitation pearl necklace, one is always pleased to admire a genuine pearl."

"And I attribute Loïe Fuller's great success to the sense of the ideal and the infinite that she evokes," another French admirer wrote.

> Is she pretty, this American? I do not know about that, but I know she has no need to be pretty. She is more than lifelike. She is an apparition, not a woman of flesh and blood.
> As every original has its imitations, so the multicolored

gown now appears everywhere, but it is only a copy and a counterfeit of Loïe Fuller's mysterious gown.

A strange thing—it is the American, less than a tenth as pretty as the beauteous Emilienne d'Alençon or one or another of the Nouveau Theatre serpentine ballerinas—it is the creator of this singular, unreal, fantastic dance who remains the fairy queen of the new kind of entertainment that has made a convert of all Paris.[24]

Suddenly, on April 20, 1893, Loie disappeared from the Folies-Bergère and from its newspaper advertisements. "Already a distant dream!" *Nos Parisiens* commented. "Loïe Fuller comes and goes like a meteor, leaving behind her a luminous trail of purple and gold and emerald. Where *is* the blonde Loïe?" Unannounced, she was off on an unwilling mission that proved disastrous for her financial well-being.

At the Folies-Bergère she had been extremely well paid. She received, in French francs, the equivalent of five hundred dollars a week, which was ten times as much as she had made when she initiated the serpentine dance at the Casino Theatre in New York. She recently was earning more in a week than most American day laborers earned in a year. Among Parisians she was thought to possess good business sense because of her precaution in seeking patents. "Like a good American," one Frenchman said, "she shows a very practical regard for her material interests." But she did not have enough regard for her interests to keep herself from facing the prospect of financial ruin.[25]

The trouble had begun months earlier, shortly after her debut at the Folies-Bergère, when she signed an agreement to perform in Russia in the spring of 1893. Marchand had made the arrangement with the Russian manager and took a personal interest in it. As the time approached for Loie's trip to Saint Petersburg, she became more and more concerned about her mother's health, which would make it hazardous either to take her mother along or to leave her in Paris by herself. But Loie was given to understand that, if she should breach the contract, she would have to pay a forfeit amounting to forty thousand dollars.

Marchand insisted that Loie go to Saint Petersburg. She was committed—and he was committed—to her going. She seemed to have no choice. Then, on the very day she and her mother were planning to depart for Russia, her mother suffered a stroke and had to be put to bed. Loie did not want to leave her in that condition, but Marchand compelled Loie to take the train. She left the train at the first opportunity and returned to Paris. Marchand threatened to have her jailed unless she immediately started for Russia again. This time, at the Russian border, she received a telegram that said her mother was dying. With great difficulty, she managed to make her way back to Paris, arriving just in time to save her mother. "From the moment of my return she began to improve."

The Russian manager sued her to collect the forfeit. He won the case and secured an attachment of her salary. This meant that, until the debt was paid, her weekly income from the Folies-Bergère would be not five hundred dollars but zero.[25]

Soon after her return to Paris, the Folies-Bergère closed for the summer, not to reopen until September. Anxious to pay off the debt, she looked for temporary employment elsewhere. "And London, Miss Fuller: are we never to see you in England?" the *Sketch* reporter had asked. "Why, I hope so, some day," Loie replied. "You know, I have acted over there; but that was before I discovered my dance." Having discovered it, she could now expect better luck in London than during her previous experience.

She did quite well in England this time. "Why," she stated soon afterward, "the last three weeks of my stay in London, when I performed in two theatres on a percentage, brought me $7,500, or $6,000 above expenses, and I pay my Paris manager for a release until October $3,200." Nevertheless, she decided to leave London and spend six weeks in New York—"believing that I can couple with a visit to New York profit enough to outweigh my forfeit." And she imagined that it would be more profitable to stage a grand variety show than to rely on her own performance alone. She was daring to gamble as an impresario once again. In London she found plenty of American entertainers willing to revisit New York on the promise of generous compensation. Having enlisted a manager and a number of performers, she sailed hopefully for her homeland. The consequence was another disaster.[27]

———

Loie's new fame had preceded her to the United States, where it became mixed with her old scandal. The New York press in particular had been giving her glowing publicity. The *Spirit of the Times* proudly claimed to have discovered her and to have "predicted the world-wide celebrity" that she had since attained. Decorating its front cover with a fetching picture, tinted pink and celadon, of Loie in one of her diaphanous costumes, the *Dramatic News* reported: "Americans returning from Paris are in a condition of amazement over the extraordinary success that she has achieved in the French capital."

The Paris correspondent of the *New York Times* viewed Loie's "sensational success" as a sign of growing American influence on the culture of France. He wrote:

> America is coming wonderfully forward now; grave minds are studying the Constitution, religious tolerance, the situation of the Government as regards labor associations, and so on.
>
> While the statesman, the philosopher, and the student look to the shining and humane light across the broad sea, *tout Paris* raves about Loie Fuller and her comparatively graceful and chaste dancing. The knowing people go back to the walls of the Pompeiian bath ruins to seek the origin of the serpentine dance, but they find that the exquisite posing is something more original. It is funny to see the cancan attraction pale before the Yankee dance.

So far as Loie was concerned, however, there was bad news as well as good news in the continuing reports of the William B. Hayes perjury trial. The good news was of Hayes's conviction and his eight-year prison sentence (of which he was to serve only about two years). When Loie heard it she was "almost delirious with joy." The papers reported that, in Sing Sing, Hayes had been "placed in the trouser manufacturing department" and was spending "much of his time sobbing over his work."[28]

The bad news was that Loie's name was continually linked with Hayes's during the trial, and thus the scandal of her unfortunate "marriage" to the bigamist was kept alive. At one point the defense introduced some letters that had figured in her own case against Hayes. The judge said he hoped he was not going to see Miss Fuller in *this* case. "No," Hayes's lawyer responded, "most people prefer to see her on the stage." Especially embarrassing for Loie was the implication that a loan from Hayes had actually come from his wife. "Is it not a fact," the prosecuting attorney demanded of Mrs. Hayes, "that you gave your permission to your husband to advance to the actress, Loie Fuller, $3,000, or $3,500?" The judge would not permit her to reply.

But after the trial Mrs. Hayes, while confined to a hospital, sued Loie for thirty-eight hundred dollars. She said this was the amount she had loaned through her "agent" (her husband). The chief justice of the New York Court of Common Pleas arranged for Loie to give her testimony in Paris. She testified that, at the time of the loan, she did not even know of the existence of a Mrs. Hayes, and that she had reimbursed William B. Hayes for all she had borrowed from him. She said her lawyer held receipts for the repayments. Apparently Hayes had pocketed the money without telling his wife. She did not have a good case against Loie, and eventually she dropped it.

The Fullers also were suing. Loie's mother, Delilah, had inherited from her late husband, Reuben, a claim against Hayes, whom Reuben had accused of "stealing $4,000 in cash while in London." This case had never been settled when, in 1900, Hayes petitioned a court to declare him bankrupt. His second-largest creditor was Delilah, as administrator of Reuben's estate, whose claim had been reduced to $3,750. "Colonel Hayes is best known as the man Loie Fuller, the dancer, had arrested in 1892 on a charge of bigamy," the *New York Times* stated. "That started the wreck of his fortune." So fell the man who, eleven years earlier, had wanted his "marriage" to Loie kept secret because, as he then said, it would ruin his reputation if it was known that she was his wife.[29]

Meanwhile, Loie was still quite newsworthy when she arrived in New

York on the steamer *Spree* on August 10, 1893. Several members of her company already in town were nervous and confused, wondering whether their show would ever go on. "It fell to Miss Fuller as her first duty to put them at ease," the *New York Times* learned from her. "This she proceeded to do as soon as she had fortified herself with a breakfast at the Waldorf." The confusion arose from the fact that no theater had been secured. "Miss Fuller's generalship needed first to be exercised on calming her associates by assuring them that she knew precisely what she was about, and that they might quit worrying and prepare to keep their contracts."

Loie was assuming that she could best make the necessary arrangements after she was on the ground. She sent her manager, Robert Grau, to try the Casino Theatre (which was under new management). Grau learned that at the Casino a deposit of five hundred dollars would be required and the rent of one thousand dollars a week must be paid in advance. Loie wanted a less risky "percentage contract," according to which she would be guaranteed a share of the receipts. Grau succeeded in making such an arrangement with the Garden Theatre, but only for a little more than two weeks, while the Garden had nothing else booked.

"Well content with the day's work, Miss Fuller attended the American Theatre [that] night and told about it. She had arrayed herself in a China silk dress and a big white hat, which she said bore her own name in Paris and was made of what she called crystallized crinoline." She described the entertainment she was preparing for New York. "It will be," she said, "a show at which persons arriving at any time in the evening will see something complete—each act standing by itself, as in vaudeville."[30]

The program for "LOIE FULLER and Robert Grau's Celebrities Organized in Europe" was a curious hodgepodge even for a variety show. It was to begin with two plays, the second of them *The Visit,* a moody and talky piece translated from the Danish of Carl Edvard Brandes. Then would come Alice Shaw, "La Belle Siffleuse," who would whistle "Il Bacio" and other popular tunes. Next, Loie herself was to appear, performing six of her dances. She was to be followed by "A Plantation Idol [sic]," with one woman singing songs of the Old South and another playing the part of a "pickaninny." The program would conclude with "The Gayety Dancer" Florence Levey.

"Miss Fuller asks the kind indulgence of the audience during her changes of costume," the playbill noted. It added: "Under no circumstances shall the ushers demand or accept payment for seats." But what caused the terrible commotion on opening night was neither a delay for a costume change nor an usher's attempt at extortion.[31]

It was a hot summer night, and the theater was packed with people who had come to see the famous Loie. Fanning themselves, they sat patiently through the first play, a boring and inane comedy. Then the curtain went up for *The Visit,* which began with the following "situation" (as described by a New York newsman):

> A man who has led a wild life in Copenhagen (a town which for wild living can give points to Trenton, N.J.) marries a poor girl in a remote neighborhood ... and settles down to a quiet life. He believes his wife to be pure and innocent. A friend of his bachelor days comes to visit him. When the friend and the wife meet, they start, stare at each other, and act so guiltily that the stupidest husband in the world would infer that they had met before.

Sitting before a stage fire—which made those in the audience feel all the hotter—the actors impersonating the husband and his friend droned on in a long conversation. This was mostly inaudible, what with the street noises coming in through the doors, which had been left open for ventilation. The crowd grew more and more restless.

Playing the part of the wife was Olga Brandon, an experienced and talented actress who had been a London hit in the same role. When she came onstage and supposedly recognized her husband's friend as her former lover, she keeled over as if in a dead faint. This struck many in the audience as hilarious, especially the "ill-bred crowd in the back of the house." They "applauded derisively, groaned, and laughed." The play stopped. One of the actors stepped forward to request consideration for Miss Brandon. He was met with hisses and catcalls. Miss Brandon left the stage in tears, and the curtain dropped, never to rise again on that play.

Obviously, it had been a mistake to include a serious, avant-garde drama in a bill designed to appeal mainly to vaudeville fans. Olga Brandon afterward said she had "told Manager Grau, when he proposed to include 'The Visit' in the programme, that it would be entirely out of place in a variety show." But the production was Loie's, and the ultimate responsibility for the fiasco was hers.

As for Loie's own part of the entertainment, it went very well on opening night, once she had finally made her appearance at ten o'clock. "She was rapturously received and, on the whole, deserved to be," the *New York Times* critic wrote. "Her dance has been greatly elaborated and improved, the colored light effects are extremely beautiful, and her management of her voluminous draperies is bewildering." The critic expressed one reservation. In a patriotic touch, Loie had had the magic lantern project upon her gown the image of the first and then of the incumbent president of the United States. These "stereoptic portraits of Gen. Washington and Mr. Cleveland that decorated the person of Miss Fuller" seemed as much "out of place" as the Brandes play had.

In revising the program, Loie discarded that play and arranged her own appearance earlier, putting three of her six dances ahead of the intermission. The show went on, but her troubles were not over.[32]

Her performers became increasingly discontented as Grau fell farther and farther behind with their pay. Especially exasperated were Guy Standing and his wife, Isabelle Urquhart, who constituted the cast of the comedy that remained on the program. Standing threatened to quit. When Grau, at the theater, told him his salary was awaiting him at the hotel, Standing shouted: "You're a liar!" Then "the ladies screamed and everybody expected a physical encounter between the men, but Grau was not equal to the emergency." Poor Grau was indeed in bad shape. He had been drinking, and he was promptly taken to a sanatarium to dry out. "Mr. Grau has behaved himself in a most disgraceful manner for some weeks past," Standing complained. "He has taken all the receipts and has squandered them in rum." Standing and his wife were later to sue Loie for back pay.

Despite the bickering, Loie and her company lasted for their allotted time at the Garden Theatre, from August 15 to September 3, 1893. She then began to perform, by herself, between the acts of the long-running play *Panjandrum* at the Broadway Theatre. Desperate as she was for money, she soon took on an additional entr'acte engagement at the Standard Theatre.

Every weekday evening she had to appear in the one place at 9:30 and in the other an hour later. Every Saturday she had two afternoon as well as two evening performances, with matinees at 3:30 and 4:30. As if such a schedule were not sufficiently killing, she danced on some days at a third theater, either the Columbia in Brooklyn or the Opera House in Harlem.

After surviving almost a month of this, Loie left for Paris without having cleared nearly enough to pay off the tremendous debt that was hanging over her. "I like New York," she said, "but Paris has been kinder to me." She could at least find cheer in her continuing preeminence in her special kind of dancing. She was still "La Loïe"—the original—even though "The Only Marie Collins, The Serpentine Wonder," was billed at the Imperial Music Hall in New York, and Ida Fuller, back from her Russian tour, was scheduled to appear at the Columbia Theatre in Brooklyn.[33]

4

Why Can't I Be Salome?

"This evening the marvelous serpentine dancer Loïe Fuller reappears at the Folies-Bergère, having returned from a veritable triumph in America." So ran the theater's press release for October 20, 1893. "She comes back to us with several new dances and lighting effects, to which the Folies-Bergère has the exclusive rights."

Her reception that evening was all that she could have wished. "La Loïe Fuller, recalled by the enthusiastic bravos of the crowd, had to take several bows," *Le Figaro* reported. "This performance must be counted among the most beautiful of her brilliant artistic career."[1]

Despite this auspicious beginning, Loie's second season at the Folies-Bergère proved less gratifying than her first. She finally decided to try a more elevated kind of presentation, one that would enable her to rise out of the music-hall class. Her bold effort resulted in something less than a complete success.

Meanwhile, at the evening shows, she continued to hold her devoted fans, among them the bohemian poet Jean Lorrain, who lauded "the beautiful girl who, in her floating draperies, swirls endlessly around in an ecstasy induced by divine revelations." She still drew plenty of people to the matinees on Sundays, Thursdays, and holidays—and, for Christmas, on both December 24 and 25. She seemed almost as popular as ever when she gave her three-hundredth Folies-Bergère performance on January 6, 1894.[2]

Though her dances this season were hailed as "new," the novelty was beginning to wear thin, or so Edouard Marchand apparently thought. As manager of the Folies-Bergère, he kept on revising its program, adding performers and acts that presumably would have a greater and more lasting appeal. In doing so, he changed the basic character of the program, making it more and more a girlie show and downgrading Loie and her act.

The first of the new girlies was Emilienne d'Alençon, the same ravishing beauty who, the previous year, had been imitating Loie's serpentine dance at another music hall. A French demimondaine who became a mistress of King Leopold II of Belgium, she was hired to take part in a "pantomime ballet." On the stage she affected a monocle and wore a short skirt and a low-cut, tight-fitting bodice.

Next came the Barrison Sisters, "dancers and singers of remarkable originality," as *Le Figaro* introduced them. There were five of them, Americans

Loie in costume for the "Dance of the Flowers." (Photograph by Paul Boyer; courtesy of the Bibliothèque Nationale.)

all, not really sisters but similar in size and shape and identical in their scanty costumes and strawberry-blond wigs. They sang as one, in uniformly girlish voices, and they danced as one, kicking, bending, turning, gesturing in unison and precisely in time to the music. Thus, though comparatively few, they formed a modern chorus line. There was said to be a special charm in the "sensuous seething of their frilly and beribboned underwear."

And then Caroline Otero, "La Belle Otero," made her Folies-Bergère debut. She already had a reputation as a provocative singer and spectacular dancer—and also as the most aggressive gold digger among Paris courtesans. An Andalusian, she had dark eyes, blood-red lips, coal-black hair, and a way of "rearing up and throwing her head back like a young thoroughbred," according to *Le Figaro*. "The gyrations of her hips and legs drive men crazy."

"Then there is la Loïe Fuller, who could say, like Medea, 'I alone am quite enough!'" *Le Figaro* observed. "La Loïe Fuller, who for more than a year has had her poster outside the Folies-Bergère, and with whom the public signs a new lease every month!" But she no longer enjoyed top billing on the printed programs or in the newspaper ads. La Belle Otero was first, the Barrison Sisters were second, and Loie was tied with Emilienne d'Alençon for third in publicity.[3]

All this belied the words of a reporter from London's *Strand Magazine* who called on Loie about a year after the Paris correspondent of the London *Sketch* had done so. "The dancing of La Loïe," the *Strand* woman wrote, "has so raised the reputation of the Folies-Bergère that now the most particular Parisian has no hesitation about taking his wife or lady friends there." That remained the case with the family matinee but was ceasing to be true of the evening show. Nor was the writer quite accurate or prophetic when she went on to say:

> Miss Fuller has done wonders in improving the public taste and proving that dancing is not an art that degrades, but, with modestly draped figures and graceful movements, an educator, as everything that is beautiful ought to be. Let us hope that the craze for high kicking, unnatural straining of the muscles, and the hideous short skirts and scanty bodice will

become a thing of the past, and that a mere display of skill and agility without the elegance or grace which ought to characterize the Terpsichorean art will die a natural death.

Like the earlier *Sketch* correspondent, the *Strand* writer was impressed by Loie's youthfulness, naturalness, and cheerfulness. "The dancer in private is simply a bonnie, blue-eyed little woman, plain in her dress, and with a sweet frankness of manner and speech which render her eminently attractive."

In reality, Loie was not quite so frank, open, and honest as she seemed. To this Englishwoman, as to other interviewers, she let on that she was nine or ten years younger than she was in fact, and she invented or exaggerated childhood achievements to adorn the theme of her precocity. She intimated that she had been famous as a child actress: "before she had reached the age of sixteen, she had won for herself a reputation that many an experienced actress of twice that age would have been proud of." When thirteen, she actually had given one or two temperance lectures in Illinois; she now claimed "she was soon in great demand all over the State, and known as the 'Western Temperance Prodigy.' Only eleven years of age! yet earning her own living and doing good work." She never mentioned the great Chicago fire, though it must have been one of her most vivid memories. If she had included it in her recollections, she would have given away the fact that she was born well before 1871, the year of the fire.[4]

Though in appearance "always the same bright, cheery little woman," Loie in reality was far from contented with her lot at the Folies-Bergère. She was getting little material benefit to compensate for her loss of psychic income as her prestige was reduced. Indeed, after the Russian creditor had attached her salary, she and her mother even went hungry sometimes, or so she afterward related, no doubt overdramatizing her life, as she often did. Marchand, she said, saw to it that her dressing room was well supplied with champagne for the entertainment of the distinguished people who came to congratulate her. "But for the manager's wife, who at times sent us things to eat in a basket, I should often have danced on an empty stomach, and have sipped champagne in my dressing room without having had anything to eat at home."

Why Can't I Be Salome?

Home—the apartment adjoining the Folies-Bergère—was losing its charm for her, though her guests found it interesting enough. "Her rooms boast of no costly luxuries, bric-a-brac, or the thousand and one costly trifles which artistes usually surround themselves with," her recent English visitor noticed. "One thing attracts you as you enter the little sitting-room, and that is the bust of her, by the great sculptor Houssin; in her boudoir are also unusual miniature models of stages, and it is by all sorts of experiments on these that Miss Fuller is enabled to judge the effect of any new dance and lighting."

Loie worried about the healthfulness of the apartment, "the sanitation of which," she thought, " was defective." She was particularly concerned for her mother, who was always with her, waiting at each performance to wrap her in a huge cloak as she came off the stage. "Therein, I am certain, lay one of the reasons for the progress of my mother's illness," she later said with regard to the sanitation. Her own health, too, was affected in such a way as to lessen her ability to endure fatigue, she came to believe.[5]

Finally, near the end of the 1893–94 season, Loie decided to leave the Folies-Bergère. Even if she were also to leave Paris, *Le Figaro* commented when announcing her decision, she would nevertheless remain, since she was now in the Grévin Museum, a local waxworks. Her wax figure was illuminated just as she herself was on the stage, giving an effect so lifelike and realistic as to be quite startling.[6]

Loie did leave Paris during the summer of 1894. With her mother, she went to Belgium and the Netherlands, to perform in both countries. At an exposition in Antwerp she did quite well for a while, averaging five hundred dollars a night as a percentage of the receipts—much better than the five hundred dollars a week she had received at the Folies-Bergère before the attachment of her salary.

In Brussels she danced at the British legation as the honored guest of the minister's wife and told a reporter it was "an American monopoly to combine stage-dancing with self-respect." For the Khedive of Egypt she gave a special performance in the great festival hall of a Brussels exhibition, where she faced the largest crowd that had ever seen her presentation. "At its finish I left the platform, & 6000 pairs of hands, with 6000 voices, made me feel what it was to give pleasure to a multitude, & as I stood before it, smiling my thanks & gratitude for its approval, I shuddered at what they could do with a little thing like me if their great force was turned ferociously upon me."

In a more intimate setting—at the Kurhaus in Scheveningen, a seaside resort near The Hague, Holland—Loie danced for Princess Victoria, the sister of Kaiser William II of Germany. The princess rewarded her with an exquisite little watch studded with gems and engraved with a sketch of Loie dancing.[7]

After returning to Paris the Fullers stayed for a while at the Grand Hotel. Then Loie rented a cottage—a "little *châlet*," she called it—just off the avenue Henri Martin in Passy, near the Bois de Boulogne. Passy, with its villas and gardens, was one of the city's choice residential areas, long a favorite of musicians, artists, and literary folk. The Fullers' house, though comparatively modest, seemed a much more pleasant home than the Folies-Bergère apartment had been.[8]

Financially troubled though she was, it seemed unlikely that Loie, after her unhappy experience with Colonel William Hayes, would soon try marriage again—even for money. Nevertheless, it was rumored for a time in New York that she was going to marry an unnamed "wealthy Philadelphian" who offered to pay off her Russian forfeit. "The authority for this is said to be a private letter received by a friend from Miss Fuller herself."

She remained unwed, but matrimony seemed once more to offer a possible solution to her money problems when another rumor of impending marriage circulated in New York. She was now said to have "accepted the attentions of no less highly-esteemed and famous a public man" than Jacob Aaron Cantor, a prominent New York lawyer and state senator. "It being obviously impossible to obtain Miss Loie Fuller's confirmation of a story so delightful to the many friends of both the parties involved, a reporter sought encouragement for it from Senator Cantor himself," the *New York Times* revealed on September 5, 1894. "Mr. Cantor pleasantly parried the question by saying, with characteristic chivalry, that he preferred to let Miss Fuller do the talking."

Why Can't I Be Salome?

Though not Loie's attorney in the Hayes case, Cantor had given her some advice during it. Later he represented her when she was sued for back pay by Isabelle Urquhart and Guy Standing, two members of the ill-fated company that Loie had brought to New York in the summer of 1893.

Cantor was wed within a few years—but not to Loie. Until his death in 1921, he nevertheless remained her adviser, helper, and close friend.

Despite the rumors, Loie was hardly a likely candidate for marriage in 1894 or at any time after that. She had recently been quoted as saying: "Perhaps I demand too much in a man, and probably my definition of a gentleman would be a man who would do just as I wanted him to at all times, providing he did not neglect his business."[9]

Loie aspired to be more than just a music-hall performer, and during the winter of 1894–95 she kept busy preparing a show that she hoped would lift her to a higher level of artistry. It would be, for her, a new and different kind of production, one that told a story.

Her previous performances had not; they were essentially abstractions, though they presumably represented physical objects, such as butterflies, lilies, and the like. Those earlier dances, according to Loie, were largely the results of chance inspiration or a stroke of serendipity. "I've always been working hard on the dancing since the time when I gave a little bit of serpentining almost by accident and it 'caught on' so suddenly," she told an interviewer (whom she impressed as "a charming and unaffected little woman") in 1895. "I've studied and practiced incessantly, and yet my most popular work has come about by accident."[10]

Loie had indeed studied and practiced, and one of the things she studied was the history of the dance. She went to the Bibliothèque Nationale, where she found books with illustrations she could understand even if she could not read the French text. She bought books, some of them in English, such as the one on Herculaneum and Pompeii, with pictures of girl dancers who graced the bacchanalian orgies there. The Bible told of dancing by Miriam, the sister of Moses and Aaron, and by the daughter of Herodias.

"The dance as then given was purely Oriental," Loie came to believe, "and consisted more of the swaying of the body and the moving of the arms than of any motion of the feet." It also involved the manipulation of silken draperies, and if there was then no use of electricity, there was at least the availability of the sun for lighting effects. In other words, those ancient dancers gave essentially the same kind of performance as Loie did. She concluded: "I have only revived a forgotten art, for I have been able to trace some of my dances back to four thousand years ago: to the time when Miriam and the women of Israel—filled with religious fervour and rapture—celebrated their release from Egyptian captivity with 'timbrels and with dances.'"[11]

So Loie thought of herself as already following in the footsteps of the biblical dancer Miriam when she decided to play the part of another biblical (or pseudobiblical) dancer—Salome. The idea came to her from Armand Silvestre, a prolific author who had written librettos for the Folies-Bergère. When Silvestre first saw her do her serpentine dance, he said: "I dreamed of Salome before Herod." "And why can't I be Salome, or whatever her name is, dancing before Herod?" Loie is supposed to have asked upon being told of Silvestre's remark.[12]

The story of Salome dancing before Herod comes from the New Testament (Matthew 14.3–6 and Mark 6.17–22). King Herod had imprisoned John the Baptist, who was denouncing him for unlawfully marrying Herodias, his brother's wife. Herodias wanted John put to death, but Herod held back, fearing John's power as a prophet. At a birthday celebration for Herod, the daughter of Herodias danced for him and so pleased him that he promised to give her anything she asked for. "Prompted by her mother, she said: 'Give me the head of John the Baptist here on a platter.'" The king, reluctant though he was, "sent and had John beheaded in the prison, and his head was brought on a platter and given to the girl, and she brought it to her mother." The name of the girl is not mentioned in the Bible, but she is remembered as Salome.

Salome became a fairly frequent subject of literature and art. Oscar Wilde eventually wrote a play with his own twist to the Bible story. In Wilde's version Herod lusts after Salome, and Salome lusts after John the Baptist. Rebuked and rejected by the saintly John, she demands his head, which she speaks lovingly to when it is brought to her on the platter. Finally Herod has Salome killed also. In 1892 Wilde sent his manuscript to Sarah Bernhardt, in London, and she prepared to stage the play with herself in the title role. She had leased the Palace Theatre, recruited a cast, and begun rehearsals when the Lord Chamberlain banned the play as indecent. However, it was soon published in French (1893) and then in English (1894).[13]

Loie conceived of a Salome drama fundamentally different from either the Bible story or the Wilde play. Her conception guided Armand Silvestre when he, with an American newspaperman, C. H. Meltzer, wrote the libretto for what they called a "lyric pantomime." In this version, as in Wilde's, Herod is hot with lust for Salome, but Loie's Salome is by no means voluptuous or bloodthirsty; instead, she is quite spiritual and essentially chaste. She becomes a follower of John the Baptist and looks to him for protection against the lecherous Herod. Frustrated, Herod orders John's decapitation. Only then does Salome dance for him, and she does it in the hope of dissuading him from carrying out his order. She even offers to yield to him if he will grant John a reprieve. It is too late. The executioner triumphantly presents to Herod the martyr's bleeding head, and at the sight of it Salome collapses in a coma.[14]

The pantomime was to include five dances—Black, Sun, White, Rose, and Lily—which Loie insisted were entirely new in both their choreography and their lighting. For the musical score, she turned to Gabriel Pierné, the organist at Sainte-Clotilde church, a young and promising composer who wrote incidental music for several Bernhardt plays. To design the costumes, she engaged the painter and book illustrator Georges Rochegrosse. She enlisted competent players for the roles of Herod, Herodias, and John. And she found Pierre Berton, manager of the Comédie-Parisienne, more than willing to put on her *Salomé* in his theater.

Not only the pantomime drama but also the stage setting was, for Loie, quite new and different. Instead of the usual bare stage draped in black, there now was scenery, with a painted backdrop showing an exact panorama of Jerusalem and giving the audience the impression of looking out on the city. And the costumes more or less resembled the clothing of the time and place.

By February 1895 Loie was busy overseeing the painters, carpenters, and electricians as they got the theater ready. She was also busy with rehearsals. After watching one of them, a theater critic wrote:

Loïe Fuller is known to almost everybody as the clever skirt dancer, but few know Loïe Fuller as an artist, as a great artist, such as she will reveal herself to the public in a few days' time. As I saw her on the stage of this little theatre—just sufficiently lighted to see the expressions of her face—Pierné at the piano, Armand Silvestre and Pierre Berton following the working of her drama in the wonderful dance—it seemed scarcely believable that this small figure, in her ordinary dark walking dress, without the aid of lights or stage accessories, with no word spoken, could move us to the extent she did.

Her dance to the sun, her religious dance, her dance of desperation, were all remarkable expressions of the mind, and had such an effect upon us that when she fell at the sight of John the Baptist's head, we all rushed toward her and kissed her. It seems extraordinary . . . but it is a moment I shall not easily forget. Armand Silvestre, with her head in both his hands, kissing her on each cheek. Berton at her feet, and all of us with tears in our voices saying, as with one accord, "Que c'est beau!"

Loie, her associates, and local theater critics all anticipated a resounding success for her *Salomé*. She looked on it as the test of a new genre—the possible start of a whole series of similar pantomimes in which she would perform as both an actress and a dancer. She had experience as an actress, after all. She now gave the press to understand that, in her own country, she had starred in many a drama and most notably in *Camille* (which, in fact, she had never played as a professional, if at all.)[15]

Salomé, "a lyric pantomime in one act and five tableaux," opened at the Comédie-Parisienne on March 4, 1895. It was the second and, lasting only about half an hour, much the smaller part of a double bill, which began with *Mademoiselle Eve*, a comedy in three acts. But *Salomé* got much the greater share of attention from theatergoers and critics.

The reactions were mixed. Loie's good friend Roger Marx was, as always, enthusiastic. "To those unacquainted with her past as an actress," he wrote, "Loïe Fuller reveals herself as a mimic second to none, with gestures full of

Loie in Armand Silvestre's Salomé *at the Comédie-Parisienne, March 1895. (Photograph by Langfier.)*

authority, mobile and amazingly expressive features, her face reflecting joy, pity, anger, fright, anguish, one after another and all with startling effect."

One reviewer for *L'Echo de Paris,* a personal friend of the playwright, Silvestre, praised Loie as an excellent "tragic mime." But another writer for the same paper said she was "ignorant of the first step of the choreographic art" and was wholly inadequate as a mime. Still, even this writer was forced to admit that she had "the gift of playing with electricity." A critic for *Le*

Figaro agreed that she was neither a dancer nor a mime—"she mimes like a telegraph"—but deserved applause for the "exquisite effects" she obtained with her veils and lights.

Jean Lorrain, who recently had romanticized Loie as a "beautiful girl" of divine inspiration, was disappointed and disgusted with her in *Salomé*. She now was "heavy, ungraceful, sweating, her makeup running, at the end of ten minutes of little exercises," Lorrain complained to his diary. She maneuvered her veils and draperies "like a laundress misusing her paddle." She was "luminous without grace, with the gestures of an English boxer and the physique of Mr. Oscar Wilde." This was "a Salome for Yankee drunkards."[16]

Lorrain's disillusionment is understandable. Short and fat as she was, Loie hardly had the figure for Salome, who traditionally was pictured as statuesque. And Loie could be seen all too well in the Comédie-Parisienne, an intimate theater with a small stage, where she was close to her audience in a way that she had never been at the Folies-Bergère. Besides, she was now portraying a specific character, following a definite story line, and using a more or less realistic set. Hence she lost that aura of unreality, ineffability, and mystery that had made her seem a creature of poetic charm.[17]

Whether she knew it or not, Loie had made a mistake in presenting a show of this kind. She must have had second thoughts, for she soon abandoned her idea of putting on a whole series of such dance-pantomimes.

Not that her experiment with *Salomé* was a complete failure. For a time, she attracted good crowds and gained their hearty applause, but what appealed to both the public and the press was not the pantomime or her acting in it. The big attraction was her new group of so-called dances, especially the second one, the "Sun Dance," which came to be known as the "Fire Dance." In it she appeared to catch fire and be consumed by tongues of flame as she manipulated her veils to Pierné's music. Was this really dancing? With Loie, it was "more a kind of magic apparition than, strictly speaking, a dance," as one dancing authority declared.[18]

Whatever it was, it continued to please most of her admirers, especially those of a literary or artistic bent. While performing it, she received at least a left-handed compliment from one artistic circle where, at a private dinner, the menu, illustrated by Toulouse-Lautrec, listed one of the dishes as *foie gras de l'oie Fuller* ("fat liver of the goose Fuller").

Why Can't I Be Salome?

There was nothing ambiguous about the adulation of students from the Ecole des Beaux-Arts. They gave Loie one of the greatest ovations of her entire career when she put on a special performance for them on Sunday evening, March 24, 1895. Celebrating her 550th appearance in Paris, the young people pelted her with violets when she came onstage, then showered her with flowers again when she left. "When I was ready to leave the theatre, the students took my horses out of the shafts and drew my carriage themselves," she afterward recalled. "The young men drew my carriage all the way to Passy, where I lived. They conscientiously awakened all the inhabitants with their outcries."

The students had designed a special souvenir program for the occasion. That same evening one of them, J. Henry Friedlander, apparently an American, sent Loie the following note, which she treasured enough to keep for the rest of her life: "Thus ends the fête—and as fair nature cherishes the thought of coming spring—so shall we all of us, disciples of the beautiful and true, cherish the souvenir of our 'Loïe,' symbol of pure charm and grace."[20]

Loie kept going at the Comédie-Parisienne for a total of eight weeks, minus a few days when she was ill and did not appear. Part of the time she omitted the pantomime and presented only the dances that went with it. Finally, on Sunday, April 27, 1895, she gave the last performance of this *Salomé*.

Originally, she had intended to take the play, after its close in Paris, to Great Britain, the United States, and other parts of the world. After resting a couple of months, she did start on a tour, she and her mother, but only with the new dances, not with the pantomime. At the Empire Theatre in Edinburgh the spectators were unanimous in proclaiming her dances far superior to those of any of her imitators they had seen, according to *Le Figaro*. The *New York Spirit of the Times* added: "Loie Fuller continues in the British provinces the successes she has made here and in Europe, and the melancholy Manchesterians and canny Scotchmen are roused to as much enthusiasm by her serpentine dances as the gay Parisians and gayer New Yorkers."[21]

Loie again impressed the British when she had a long stay, lasting until after Christmas, at the Palace Theatre of Varieties in London. She was back in a music hall again, and her "turn" was only one of eighteen vaudeville acts, but it was much the most spectacular. "The measures [dances] themselves, though they implied various natural creations, were reminiscent of everything and convincing of nothing," it seemed to one of those who saw her perform in London. However, "The orgie of colour was so wonderful as to leave objection mute."

A reporter for the magazine *Black and White* went to the Savoy Hotel to interview Loie and found her sitting in a hansom cab, ready to leave for the Palace Theatre. In the course of the conversation Loie brought up her "pantomime dance-play, *Salome*," and said: "I should be happy if London would care to see me in it. Of course. You know I produced *Salome* in Paris, and people liked it." The write-up concluded: "The representative of *Black and White* jumped from the cab to the pavement as the dancer said good-bye; and the cabman drove away without whipping his horse—for he evidently knew that, had he done so, La Loïe, who has an intense love of animals, would instantly have left him without a fare."

Loie never revived that *Salomé*, but she planned to travel much farther with her Salome dances. She was going to take her new repertoire to America—after a visit to the French Riviera.[22]

No sooner had Loie won fame in Paris than she began to cultivate the friendship of other famous people there. Some she got to know as a result of their interest in or association with her on the stage—the art critic Roger Marx, the dramatist Armand Silvestre, the composer Gabriel Pierné—and they became her lifelong friends. Others she deliberately sought out, taking the initiative and communicating with them either directly or through an intermediary. Of these, the most prominent early ones were Camille Flammarion, Alexandre Dumas *fils*, and Sarah Bernhardt.

Camille Flammarion (1842–1925) was the leading French astronomer of his time. In addition to scientific works, he wrote popular books on astronomy and mysticism, among them *The Multiplicity of Inhabited Worlds* (1862) and *The End of the World* (1893). An acquaintance of Loie's, the Polish American actress Helena Modjeska, had a friend in Paris, the exiled Polish countess Wolska, who knew Flammarion. Shortly after Loie's debut at the Folies-Bergère, Countess Wolska called on her and, a little later, took her to meet Mr. and Mrs. Flammarion at their house on rue Cassini.

Loie was taken aback at the sight of the noted scientist, then about fifty years old. "He wore a lounge jacket of white flannel edged with red lace," she remembered. "He had a veritable forest of hair, which formed as it were a bonnet around his head." Mrs. Flammarion explained that his hair grew so fast she had to cut it often, and she used the cuttings to stuff her cushions. Apparently she or her husband spoke at least a little English, for Loie did not yet know enough French to communicate with them in their own language.

The Flammarions were quite taken with Loie. From time to time they entertained her either at their city residence or at their suburban chateau— in Juvisy, about fifteen miles south by railroad from the Quai d'Orsay station. Nicely situated on a hill with a fine view over the Orge Valley, this little chateau had been a stopping place for the kings of France, and Napoleon once stayed there. Flammarion inherited the property from an admirer, a wealthy amateur astronomer (whom he had never met), who had built an observatory on it.

Before long Loie discovered that she and Flammarion had absorbing mutual interests, most notably an interest in color, she for its expression of emotions on the stage, he for what he considered its effects on human and plant life. "It is a fact, for example, that yellow causes enervation and that mauve engenders sleep," she noted, agreeing with him. "In all his work he is ably seconded by his wife."[23]

After Flammarion, Loie's next conquest was the world-famous son of an even more famous father, both of them prodigious novelists and dramatists. Alexandre Dumas *père* (1802–70) is remembered for such enduring works as *The Three Musketeers* and *The Count of Monte Cristo*. Alexandre Dumas *fils* (1824–95) is best known for the equally enduring work *Camille* (*La Dame aux Camélias*), the sentimental story of a courtesan who, too late, finds true love, then dies of tuberculosis. The prototype for this heroine was a well-known Paris woman, supposedly the mistress of Dumas. His grandfather Dumas was the illegitimate son of a black woman in Santo Domingo, and he himself, thus an octoroon, also was illegitimate. Whether because of his background or in spite of it, he concentrated on themes of morality and femininity.

Loie was introduced to Dumas by a prominent Haitian, Eugène Poulle,

Delilah and Loie with the astronomer Camille Flammarion and Mme Flammarion at the Flammarions' summer home in Juvisy. (Courtesy of the Dance Collection, the New York Public Library for the Performing Arts.)

whom she had befriended in Jamaica when she was there as an actress and he as a political refugee. Poulle went home to Haiti after a change in its government. Later he visited Paris along with the Haitian finance minister and went to see Loie at the Folies-Bergère. When she heard that Poulle was well acquainted with Dumas, she told him she would like to meet the great

Why Can't I Be Salome?

man, but Poulle left town before he had a chance to make the introduction. Then, on September 29, 1894, she wrote him:

> I am delighted that you are in Paris once more. You will surely come to see us won't you? And may I hope now to have the very great pleasure to be presented to that dear and great gentleman, Monsieur Alexander Dumas.
>
> How happy you must be to name him among your friends. I am sure one must envy you. For *myself* I am glad he is your friend, because you may perhaps give me the great pleasure to know him. Forgive my *selfishness*.

A few days later Loie and Poulle took the train at the Saint-Lazare station to travel about sixteen miles west to Marly-le-Roi, the old and picturesque little village where the seventy-year-old Dumas lived. On the way, Poulle tried to teach her what to say, in French, when she shook hands with Dumas: "Je suis très contente de serrer votre main" ("I am delighted to grasp your hand"). But when she met Dumas she took both of his hands and said carefully and emphatically: "Je suis très contente de votre main serrée" ("I am delighted with your close-fisted hand"). He responded with a reassuring smile, gesture, and tone. "From this time on," Loie felt, "a great friendship, a great sympathy, subsisted between us, although we were unable to understand each other."

So long as Poulle remained in Paris, he arranged other visits to Marly and served as Loie's interpreter there. After he left again, she was on her own. She worked hard to improve her French and wrote Dumas notes in it that he probably could read, though sometimes with difficulty. She concluded one of her letters: "Thine with great regard.... Pardonnez moi, mis mauvais *francaise*." She ended another: "Votre devotedly.... Excuse my bad *french*." Finally she gave up and began to write whole letters in English, which Dumas apparently could make out if the penmanship was neat enough. She made a special effort to improve her hand, which often was barely legible even for people whose native language was English. "Do you like better my writing small?" she once asked. "It is very difficult for me, but I think it is plainer." And she began to sign herself "Your devoted little friend."

Alexandre Dumas fils *presented Loie with a yellow rose from his garden at Marly-le-Roi, 1894. When he asked what she would give him in return, she gave him a kiss. She kept the flower for years. (Photograph by Prince Primoli; courtesy of the Dance Collection, the New York Public Library for the Performing Arts.)*

On one of her visits to Marly, when Poulle was still present as an interpreter, the conversation turned to *Camille* and the women of the demimonde. Dumas then said something that Loie never forgot: "When we find one of God's creatures in whom we perceive nothing good, the fault is perhaps in us."

A fairly frequent visitor and occasionally an overnight guest, Loie was treated almost as a member of the Dumas family. She brought and introduced friends of hers and was introduced to friends of Dumas. One of these was Prince Primoli, a nephew of Napoleon III and an amateur of photography. One sunny day the prince took a number of pictures of Loie and Dumas in the garden. In one of them Dumas was handing her a yellow rose he had just picked. She kissed him in return.

After opening in *Salomé* she also repaid his hospitality with complimentary tickets for him and his daughter. One evening Dumas and the Flammarions were among the people who crowded into her dressing room after the performance. She noticed that Dumas and Flammarion did not speak to one another. Had the "two most distinguished personalities in Paris" never met? she asked as she introduced them. "Well, Flammarion lives up in the heavens, and I on the earth," Dumas explained. "Yes," Flammarion agreed, "but a little star from out of the West has brought us together!"[24]

After closing in *Salomé* and beginning her British tour, Loie met Sarah Bernhardt. Born in Paris, a member of a Dutch-Jewish family that converted to Catholicism, Bernhardt (1844–1923) achieved a reputation high above that of any of her contemporaries on the stage. She made her first tour of the United States, playing *Camille* along the way, in 1880, and she made five more American tours by 1906. Worshiping the "Divine Sarah" from afar, Loie had attended one of her performances in New York in the 1880s.

In the summer of 1895 both Loie and Bernhardt were performing in Manchester, England. "So I sent word to her that, as I had heard she was anxious to see the dance, I should be only too happy to dance for her after her play was over, if she would come to the theatre," Loie recalled several months afterward. "She came, bringing one or two people in her carriage, and I danced for her just as I would for a crowded house. After it was over she came to my dressing room and took me in her arms and cried over me, assuring me that nothing she had ever seen had so filled and satisfied her imagination."[25]

During Loie's absence in Great Britain there was a wedding in Marly-le-Roi. Less than three months after the death of his mentally ill wife, with whom he had had a miserable marriage, Dumas married a divorcée much younger than he whom he had known since her childhood. From Manchester, Loie wrote him:

> I have read with great pleasure of your marriage. I am very glad to know you both and I hope I have two friends now instead of one, and I hope you will both count me among your sincere and ardent friends.
>
> Some weeks ago—when we were in Scotland—I, by chance, found a little old book that may please you, so I take the liberty of sending it. I meant to wait & bring it to you but "by chance" Madame Sarah Bernhardt is here and has kindly consented to take it to you for me. The names of some of *her* roles are among the first leaves, also John the Baptist Herod & Herodias, and I am sorry I cannot read what is said about them, but *you* can. Then, too, the illustrations when looked at through a glass are marvellous studies in workmanship. I have tried to learn what it all means, & I know nothing. Perhaps someday when I have the happiness to see you again, you will explain it to me.

Loie did not have the happiness to see much more of Dumas, for he did not have long to live. He soon fell ill, grew steadily worse, and wrote to a friend on October 1, 1895: "Assume that I am already dead." He died on November 27, about thirteen months after Loie first met him. As soon as she learned of his death, while she was in London, she sat down to write an account of her visits with him. Her article, "Alexandre Dumas at Marly," appeared in the London periodical *Black and White* promptly on December 7. Years later she recalled: "Among the important men whom I have met few have exercised upon me a charm such as that of Dumas."[26]

Why Can't I Be Salome?

5

The Mistress of Fire

When Loie Fuller revisited the United States in 1896, she scored a much greater success than she had done on her previous visit three years earlier. And when she returned to France in 1897, to reappear at the Folies-Bergère, she regained her former position as its outstanding star. Her rehabilitation was due to the new repertoire of dances that she had developed for her pantomime *Salomé*. These numbers, like those preceding them, depended in turn on her mastery of electric light.

Loie's rise to fame was made possible by the electrification of the stage, the culmination of centuries of development in stage lighting. Most theaters in Shakespeare's time, largely open to the sky as they were, simply depended on daylight. Then, when the buildings were enclosed, the front of the stage was lined with candles or with crude lamps consisting of wicks floating in pans of oil—which caused footlights to be known as "floats." Candles and floats enabled the audience to discern the characters on the stage but dimly, and kerosene or camphine lamps with glass chimneys did little to improve visibility when they came in.

Lighting with coal gas, introduced during the early 1800s and widespread by 1850, was a great improvement. Gas produced a much whiter, brighter, and more variable luminosity. Footlights, border lights, wing lights, spotlights, and house lights could now be centrally controlled, and the auditorium could be darkened while the stage was variously illuminated. Indispensable though it was, gas had serious disadvantages. It gave off unwanted heat, fouled the air (one gas jet consumed as much oxygen as several persons), and constituted a fire hazard.

Supplementing gaslight was limelight, which became common in the 1850s. This consisted of a cylinder of lime glowing in an oxyhydrogen flame. In a lantern with an appropriate lens, the glowing lime yielded a beam that could focus on one area or another so as, for example, to give a moonlight effect or to make an actor or a bit of action stand out. Though powerful enough, the beam was harsh and inflexible.

Competing with the limelight and eventually supplanting it was the earliest form of electrical illumination, the arc lamp. In this, a current passing between two white-hot rods of carbon produced a high radiance at the gap. Originally, each theater had to have its own source of electricity: its galvanic batteries or its steam-powered generator. The arc light was more mobile than the limelight and even more powerful, though also harsh and not easily variable in intensity. It required expert care and handling, its carbon rods needing frequent readjustment.

As early as 1849 arc lamps were used as spotlights for a production at the Paris Opéra. Their designer, M. J. Dubosq, soon began the commercial manufacture of these and other stage-lighting devices. By the 1870s Dubosq was advertising apparatus that could simulate such "physical phenomena" as sunshine, rainbows, lightning, and "luminous fountains." He also sold both electric batteries and "gasometers," which stored and measured out the oxyhydrogen gas that was burned in limelight lanterns.

The incandescent lamp, which Thomas A. Edison invented in 1879, promised to become vastly superior to any existing means of illumination. But the early electric bulb, with its filament of charred thread or bamboo, emitted only a rather dim orange glow. During the 1880s and 1890s theaters in Europe and America adopted incandescent lights, some providing their own electricity, others waiting for the construction of central power systems. Meanwhile, for varying lengths of time, theaters kept gaslight for auditorium illumination and arc lights and even limelights for special effects (spotlights continued to be called "limelights" long after they had ceased to have anything to do with lime).[1]

Loie became an actress during this transitional period in the history of stage lighting. She learned the state-of-the-art possibilities from some of the plays she was in. *Aladdin,* for example, had effected magical transformations when prismatic light was thrown on a curtain of steam while the scenery was being changed. There were also those "sunrise clouds, with yellow, buff, gold, and silver blending." *She* had boasted a storm with thunder and lightning, "vast rolling sea, breaking clouds," and "lurid sunset," and a "cave of the sacred fire of life."

For her own lighting effects as a serpentine dancer, Loie used essentially the same kinds of equipment as her contemporaries did, but she used the equipment in ways that were original and unique. Her "limelight" consisted of an arc light in a box with an opening and a lens, in front of which was a rotatable disk with colored gelatin circles around the edge. This arrangement was common enough; what she contributed were her private formulas for tinting the gelatin and her refined techniques for blending and dissolving the colors when they were projected on her swirling draperies. "How this is done by limelight is my secret," she boasted.

She also used a standard arc-lit magic lantern, or slide projector. "And the magic lantern effects are your own?" she was asked. "Yes," she replied; "nothing that I use in those effects can be bought. I made the slides myself, with a pinking iron, and was years perfecting them." With a double lantern, or stereopticon, she could superimpose one image on another so as to heighten the effect or make a continuous transition between the two.

To protect her gelatins and slides from competition, Loie depended on secrecy, since they were hardly patentable. But she did patent some of her inventions of stage mechanisms. One of these, for illuminating the dancer from below, consisted of the following: a false wooden floor with one or more glass-covered openings, a false floor made entirely of glass, or glass plates over holes in an existing stage floor. An elaboration was a pedestal with a glass top, so arranged that, when lighted from underneath, the dancer "would appear to be mysteriously suspended in air." Another invention was an arrangement of mirrors set at an angle to one another, with a row of incandescent bulbs along each of the joined edges, so as to reflect a "bewildering maze of dancers, skirts, and colors."

According to Loie, she had received her inspiration for under lighting just before she made her debut at the Folies-Bergère. She recalled: "The night I arrived in Paris, as we entered the Grand Hotel, I saw, for the first time, an illuminated fountain. There was a female figure in it, and it was lighted from below. The effect struck me at once. I said to my mother: 'I can use that in my dance.'" She soon persuaded Edouard Marchand to make the necessary alterations in the Folies-Bergère stage, but she succeeded so well without the lighting from underneath that she did not use it for two years or more.

By the time Loie was preparing for *Salomé* at the Comédie-Parisienne, she had a crew of her own to supplement the theater's employees. Heading her electricians was her older brother, Frank, whom *L'Echo de Paris* described as "one of the most distinguished of Edison's students." Loie and Frank together designed the new and more elaborate lighting system that *Salomé* and its dances required. It took the electricians and carpenters fifteen days to get the Comédie-Parisienne ready.[2]

When planning her 1896 appearance at Koster & Bial's Music Hall in New York, Loie did not intend to arrive until a few days before the opening. "Preceding her by a week, however, will come the gang of electricians and stage mechanics who have been with her in Europe, and who will tear up the entire stage of Koster & Bial's and rebuild it so that it will be suited to the numerous complicated dances 'La Loie' has devised since we saw her in the old familiar 'serpentine.'" Loie's younger brother, Bert, was now associated with Frank and was soon to replace him as head electrician.

For her stage effects, Loie dispensed with the traditional footlights, border lights, and other fixed sources of illumination. She relied mainly on her spotlights and magic lanterns, which were hand-held and movable. "Sometimes I use ten lamps, sometimes sixteen, again twenty, and I have used as many as thirty-four in Salome, and it requires a skilled electrician to run each one except the two principal ones, which my youngest brother always manages for me," she explained. Bert, with his two lamps, took a position underneath a glass plate in the stage floor. High in the flies were other light men, one directly overhead and others at various angles from the center of the stage. "Four step ladders of different heights are arranged in the left and right wings nearest the audience, and on each stands an electrician, with his search light in his hand."

Loie meticulously worked out in advance the lights and colors and their coordination with her own movements onstage. She experimented with various successions and combinations of colors until she got what she considered right. "For I began in utter ignorance of what the effect of one color on another was, and had to learn as a painter does what colors gained by union, and what colors were ruined one by the other." Having decided on her choreography and her lighting, she rehearsed her light men with great care.

> When I'm ready to begin, the first thing that I do without any lamps is to teach the men to find their colors and follow me. Then they learn the signals, and the gas man has to be taught when to turn the gas off and on, the stage manager when to ring the curtain up and down, and the man at the back has to learn just when to open the curtain and to come in and

The Mistress of Fire

help me off the stage after I am supposed by the audience to have disappeared into nothingness. And all this must be done so rapidly . . . the idea of mystery must be ever prevalent in the public mind.

During a performance Loie had to give her signals—with a tap of the foot—while busy with the manipulation of her draperies.

These draperies she prepared as carefully as she did the lights and colors. She tested her costumes in advance, after designing and sometimes making them herself. "A little friend of mine stood upon a table as a lay figure for me," she said regarding a costume she had made while still at the Folies-Bergère.

> I draped the silk on her. Then I cut it and put it together, tried it on and experimented with it, saw where something wanted to be taken out here and something put in there. . . . My little friend put on the dress. I went down in the auditorium. I told her just what to do, and she did it, while I watched and studied the dress from every point of view. "Now turn so and so, and do thus and so with your arms," I would say. She would obey. I studied the result, thought, developed and altered the movements to satisfy my imagination. Day after day I lived with that big dress, studying it, becoming familiar with its form, learning all its possibilities, until, when I put it on myself, I knew exactly what I could do with it.

Loie knew exactly what she could do with all her costumes, as she again and again demonstrated in the repertoire she had derived from *Salomé*, a repertoire comprising five dances: "Night," "White," "Firmament," "Fire," and "Lily."

In "La Danse du nuit" she wore a Mother Hubbard of black silk gauze glittering with silvery spangles, over pink tights and a very décolleté bodice. While she waved her arms, clouds of darkness moved with them. Suddenly stars began to twinkle, the moon came out, and then the sky turned dark again. Finally the first streaks of dawn appeared and were followed by the burst of sunrise—by which time the dancer had vanished.

"La Danse blanche" contrasted sharply with the preceding one. Instead of the black gown with its spangles, there was now a more voluminous white robe without any decorations. Instead of a single color of light, there were at least ten hues, ranging from steely blue to warm gray and from opalescent to iridescent. "Sometimes the dancer quickened her step, waving and rolling and tossing her dress, until it fell in thin sheets like falling bits of sky, and sometimes there would be a revelation of a human figure, perfect in outline and delicate in its rush through the air." So said one observer. Loie herself commented that this number was "really a dance." "However much I may give to exterior effects in my other dances, in la Danse Blanche, while the lights are manipulated with great nicety, the result depends on my movements and the handling of the dress."

"La Danse du firmament" reenacted the Creation, the dancer bringing fire and form out of the darkness and the void. For a moment she stood wrapped in the flames, then caused her striped dress to soar and wave as it changed color. The earth appeared. Stars twinkled again, lightning flashed, clouds piled up in pink-tinted heaps, and rows of dark mountains came into view.

In "La Danse du feu" Loie, wearing a white gown and carrying a large and filmy scarf, performed on a glass plate, with the only light coming from underneath and overhead. Flames and smoke swept upward through her rippling silks until, with a great burst of color, the fire consumed the dancer and then flickered out.

"Le Lis du Nile" was the shortest of the five dances but the most difficult to perform. "When I can stand still and give all of my strength to my arm movements it isn't so hard on me, but when I have to divide it between arms and legs it uses me," Loie explained. Her costume for this dance contained five hundred square yards of thin silk, and when it was in motion it extended ten feet from her body in every direction. There was so much of the material that, to keep it all under control, she had to run about the stage while rapidly moving the longer-than-usual wands that were attached to the dress. In the process, she created what looked like a gigantic calla lily.

The Mistress of Fire

For her accompaniment, Loie was no longer using the music that Gabriel Pierné had composed for *Salomé*, nor was she adapting Richard Wagner's "Ride of the Valkyries" to her fire dance, as she had done at one time. Instead, she performed to selected works of recent and contemporary French composers such as Léo Delibes. These pieces served to set the mood, not to provide rhythm, for the dances.

An entire performance lasted about half an hour.[3]

❧

Before bringing her new repertoire to the United States, Loie took it back to France in January 1896. She had a big guarantee for ten performances at the Municipal Casino in Nice during the carnival season. She also had a big guarantee—one thousand dollars a night for ten performances—at Koster & Bial's Music Hall in New York. The terms seemed extravagant for that time, but not all the money was Loie's to keep. She had to pay her own expenses plus the salaries and expenses of the staff of a dozen or so people who accompanied her, not to mention the cost of maintaining and transporting her complicated and cumbersome equipment.[4]

On the steamer *Paris*, with her mother and her two brothers, Loie arrived in New York on February 22, 1896, to be met by her manager and advance agent, Edward A. Stevens, and the music hall's coproprietor Albert Bial. It had been a rough voyage, but Loie seemed her usual sprightly self, with no sign of the physical breakdown that was shortly to come. At the Fifth Avenue Hotel she was given rooms appropriate to her status as a celebrity: they adjoined a suite occupied by former president Benjamin Harrison. To a *New York Times* man covering her arrival, she said: "I don't mind telling you that I am very glad to be back."

And New York was glad to see her again. At Koster & Bial's she opened to as large and boisterous a crowd as the place had ever known. "It was a happy-go-lucky, good-natured, bound-to-be-pleased gathering, out for a good time and determined to have it," according to one of those present, "and composed of men about town, who had tumbled in a hurry from clubdom or Delmonico's to see Miss Fuller's latest dances, and a goodly assortment of business men, actors, sporting men, and a lot of youngsters."

The variety show consisted of ten acts—including comedians, jugglers, and acrobats—and the eager crowd had to wait through several of these numbers before Loie finally appeared. When she did, the crowd was not disappointed.

> Then the curtain fell, the lights went up, Bedlam broke loose, flowers galore, of course, went over the footlights, and after numerous recalls Miss Fuller came forward, kissed her hands to the audience, and executed a peculiar convulsive spasm of her whole frame, expressive of her wildly affectionate emotion upon her reception, and retired. She came forward again and again, and finally with Mr. Bial. In answer to the friends who always yell "Speech!" she said, "With all my heart I thank you," accompanying each word with another convulsive expression of emotion, and the affair was over.

Another member of the audience noted that she made this "speech about her heart without a trace of accent beyond that good old Chicago burr on the 'r.'"

"We suggest Saturday matinee performances for ladies," yet another observer wrote. "There is nothing to be seen like Loie Fuller's dances and the ladies should have an opportunity to see them unattended." But she did not feel up to performing twice on Saturdays, even though she was now omitting one of the five numbers, "La Danse blanche." Throughout her four-week stay at Koster & Bial's she continued to attract a full house six nights a week.[5]

On this visit to her native land Loie had intended to perform only in New York and only at Koster & Bial's. When an anticipated engagement in Europe fell through, she decided to stay in the United States for a while and make a series of one-night stands in several of the largest cities. She ensconced her mother in a little flat with her brother Frank and his wife, then set out with her brother Bert and the rest of her crew. Bert and his electricians would have to improvise their arrangements from place to place as best they could on such short notice.

Things went smoothly enough during the first evening on the road, in

Brooklyn, but not so well at the next stop, in Philadelphia. The Philadelphia Academy of Music was jammed that night.

> Loie had been on the stage for just thirty seconds, when something went wrong with the lights. "Stop the music," said Loie. "Stop that music, I say." The orchestra leader went on calmly playing. "Did you hear me tell you to stop playing? Don't you understand when a lady speaks to you? Here I am begging you to stop playing. If you were a gentleman you would listen when a lady speaks to you." A painful hush came over the house. One or two people started to hiss. Then Loie came to her senses. "Ladies and gentlemen," she began, her voice full of tears, "a fuse has blown out and it must be fixed. It is not the fault of my electricians but of the Academy workers. I cannot give you a satisfactory performance until the wires are fixed. It is not my fault, ladies and gentlemen, and I beg your indulgence for a little while. I—I—I—am very sorry"—and she burst out crying. Then everybody applauded. Not because Loie was crying, but because she was in distress and was a woman.[6]

Clearly, the strain of this hurried tour was already beginning to tell, and Loie was to have no respite for a couple of weeks. Traveling through the Midwest as far as Omaha, she spent from twelve to twenty hours a day in a railroad coach. She would arrive in a city as late as seven in the evening, give her performance, leave at eleven the same night, then travel until the next afternoon.

Finally, when she reached Buffalo on the return trip, she was in such a condition as to worry the physicians who examined her. "She suffered from a terrible lassitude and disinclination to do anything," the doctors found. "If she walked she had an inclination to clutch anything near for support, and she was constantly stubbing her toe—on nothing." Only the exertion of "mere nervous force" had enabled her to dance at all.[7]

After a week of rest, Loie was in Boston to give five evening performances and a Saturday matinee. At the Boston Theatre—"the largest and most magnificent theatre in America," according to its playbill—a vaudeville program preceded her act "because had it followed Miss Fuller's appearance the artists would have played to empty seats." She responded to Boston's warm welcome by offering all the five dances of her repertoire, including the difficult "Danse blanche."

Boston long remembered the occasion. The number and brilliance of the stars who appeared at the Boston Theatre during the 1895–96 season, the theater's historians later boasted, had "doubtless never been equaled in a single season at any other playhouse in the world." The list of stars included Joseph Jefferson, Nat C. Goodwin, Robert G. Ingersoll, Albion W. Tourgée, Maurice Barrymore, Eleanora Duse, Helena Modjeska, Marie Dressler, John Philip Sousa and his band, the Boston Symphony Orchestra, Ignace Paderewski, and Loie Fuller.[8]

Between performances at the Boston Theatre, Loie had spent most of her time resting in bed. Still, she was overdoing her show-must-go-on spirit, and she suffered the consequences. A victim of "nervous prostration," she had to call off an engagement to dance three times a week for five weeks in San Francisco, though her friends thought the California climate would have done her good. "Miss Fuller is completely fagged out by her tour," her manager, Stevens, announced. "She will go to the mountains or the seaside, or wherever she chooses, and a short period of rest will make her all right again."[9]

Taking more than a short period of rest, she was "in a Sanatorium for 6 months," as she recalled years later, without telling where the institution was located. She ceased to get attention in the newspapers from May to September 1896. Somewhere on her recent travels she had met the "Bismarck of Asia," the Chinese prime minister Li Hung-chang, who visited Europe and America that year. Li invited her to come to China and dance for the emperor. Once she had recovered, she arranged to give some performances on her way to the Far East. It was a destination she was never to reach.[10]

By September she was back in the news, scheduled to appear for a week at the Standard Theatre in New York. In a program of "high class vaudeville" she received even more prominent billing than "the world's greatest aerialists, Stirk, Zeno, Anita." Then, on October 7, she went with her attorney to the City Court to defend against a suit that John Kellard was bringing against her. Kellard, an actor in *The Visit,* the play that so quickly bombed in 1893, was now demanding nineteen hundred dollars in salary due him for the six weeks that he had contracted to perform. Loie, denying any liability for Kellard's salary, wished to have the case tried at once. Her lawyer explained: "Loie Fuller will start for Atlanta, Ga., to-night, and from there will go to China, where she will dance at the special request of Li Hung Chang."[11]

A month later the Macdonough Theatre in Oakland, California, announced that Loie would appear there on her way to China. "Every theater on the Coast has been putting forth an effort to secure Fuller on her arrival here," the *San Francisco Chronicle* reported on November 8, but a telegram from her manager indicated that "the great dancer would give Oakland the preference." She was expected to perform there on December 13 or 14.

Before that—on November 23, 24, 25, and 28—she actually appeared at the California Theatre in San Francisco for four evening performances and two matinees. Preceding her on the program were none of the usual vaudeville entertainers but, instead, a succession of local musicians, among them a Trombone Duo, the Treble Clef Quartette, and Prof. Chas. F. Graeber's Banjo, Mandolin & Guitar Club. On opening night the big audience was restless, "tittering through the music and paying no attention to the numbers" that "served as a prelude to the conquering heroine of the evening." She presented her entire repertoire of five dances. "The audience was insistent on a recall, but the last it saw of the dancer she was running about the stage gathering up flowers by the armful, trailing her long white draperies and kissing her fingers, while she cried, 'Thank you, oh thank you!'"[12]

After completing her engagements in the Bay Area, however, Loie did not set sail across the Pacific. Instead, she took a train for Mexico City, where she arrived on January 12, 1897. Her manager informed a reporter from *El Universal* that she would appear at the National Theatre together with the musical-comedy company of the Arcaraz Brothers. She would have time to make only five presentations in Mexico City. "She has to leave immediately for the South of the United States, where she has several contracts pending," the reporter learned; "from there she will go to Australia and then to China, Japan, and other points in Asia."

Loie gave the five scheduled performances and an extra one for charity, utterly captivating the high-society Mexicans who attended the theater. Then she set out on her tour of the southern United States. From Nashville, Tennessee, she wrote to old friends in Monmouth, Illinois, to say she was "now traveling slowly, playing but four nights in the week" on account of her health. Hoping to visit those friends, she gave her advance agent instructions to "bring Monmouth in the circuit," but he did not manage to do so. She no longer expected soon to appear in China or in any other Asian country. Whether or not she herself was strong enough to make such a trip, her mother had become too ill to travel so far, and Loie would not go without her.

So Loie eventually returned to France with her mother—but without either of her brothers, though she had counted on Bert as her head electrician. "When she went to Europe I remained here," he recalled in Chicago many years later, after her death. "She regarded me as something of deserter, for my leaving her caused a coolness to develop."[13]

❧

During her American tours of 1896–97 Loie received a good deal of attention in the newspapers, some of which published fairly extensive interviews with her. She, in turn, paid a good deal of attention to the reports about her, clipping and saving many of them. They generally agreed about her qualifications as a dancer and about her characteristics as a person.

Journalistic critics raised such questions as the following: Was her new repertoire much better than the one she had previously exhibited in the United States? Could her numbers properly be called "dances" now any more than they could before? How original were they? Did she really deserve her fame?

According to a *New York Times* critic, her success showed that it was "a very judicious thing" for a fame-seeking American to go abroad. In Paris "the erstwhile Loie Fuller had become 'La Loie.'" Now, after her reappearance in New York, it was evident "that 'La Loie' is more skillful than Loie Fuller was, that her movements have become, if not quite graceful, yet much more pleasant than they used to be, and most especially of all, that she has secured the services of an exceedingly clever electrician." (She herself was, of course, the clever electrician.)

The most effective of her dances was "Le Feu," the *Times* man believed. "Whoever has seen a great conflagration late at night could recognize the exact, almost startling, verity of the imitation." (Did this comment remind Loie of the great Chicago fire?) Least satisfactory was "Le Firmament," which "contained some stereopticon effects—flowers, faces, moons, stars, and the like, thrown on the waving skirts—that had an unpleasant cheapness and were in questionable congruity with the other effects."

"There is more of the poetry of color than of the poetry of motion in Miss Fuller's dances," said a writer in the *Critic*. "A dance of this artistic sort has its own limitations and conventions, and a certain amount of good-will and imagination on the part of the spectator is necessary, here as in every other art, if he is to receive the desired impression. But, at times, as in the Fire Dance, the picture is realistic enough to be recognized by the most matter-of-fact spectator."

"The serpentine dance, as Loie Fuller dances it, is something utterly sui generis; with the skirt dance it has infinitely little in common," a Boston critic declared.

> Looking back in our memory, the only thing we can find in the least like it is what used to be called—if we remember aright—the "prismatic crystal fountain" in the palmy days of the "Black Crook." A fountain of real water used to play in the center of the Boston Theatre stage, and a lime-light was thrown upon it through a prism, producing a most wonderful play of color, while the orchestra played sensuous music.

In the skirt dance, the Boston writer went on, the swing of the skirt served to emphasize the "graceful bodily movements" of the dancer. In the serpentine dance the drapery and what is done with it—"it is too voluminous to be called a skirt"—is all important in itself; the performer's body is seldom seen. "The serpentine dance belongs properly more to pyrotechnics than to the art of dancing. It is a sort of living fire-works."

Another observer agreed with the Boston critic—except as to Loie's

Loie dancing "The Butterfly," 1896. This picture well illustrates her use of wands or rods that enabled her to toss vast quantities of fabric so as to create flowers, fire, and other effects. (Photograph by Samuel Joshua Beckett.)

invisibility while performing. "Through it all the young woman is as distinctly visible as though she were in her bath," wrote Hugh Morton in the *Metropolitan Magazine*. She was indeed a mistress of electric effects, Morton thought.

> "But she doesn't dance," said an envious *première danseuse* who was watching her one night.
> "My dear," put in someone who was sitting close by, "do get her to tell you how she learned not to."
> She does not trip to any set measures [Morton conceded], and her feet do not meet and leave the stage with the rhythmic precision observable in almost every other dancer that has ever lived. The beauty of motion that she displays and with which she amazes all beholders is produced by a marvelous trick of manipulating hundreds of yards of web-like fabric and amid the fiercest glare of light that has ever been projected upon the stage.

Morton concluded: "She is a spectacle that is scarcely equalled by rainbows, torchlight processions, Niagara Falls, or naval parades."[14]

Loie had a way with most newspapermen and newspaperwomen, and if she struck them as a fiery spirit when performing, she impressed them as a winsome little thing when being interviewed. "La Loie off the stage is a cheerful, blue-eyed, soft-voiced creature, frank, honest and real, devoid of affectations, full of imagination, and extremely American," a *Boston Herald* reporter gushed (much as English journalists had previously done). "There is nothing theatrical about Miss Fuller. You can easily believe when she puts a slight, sensitive hand into yours and looks right into your eyes that she is a loyal friend and the devoted daughter that her friends all know her."

A devoted daughter she certainly was—and was proud to be—but she did not like the inference that was drawn from the fact. She protested:

> I often see it in print that I go nowhere without my mother, and the inference is that I am perhaps prudish and take that stand for the sake of appearances. Not at all. If a boy invited

me to supper, if I were willing to go at all, I would as soon go alone with him as any way. But that is not the reason that, when I was in Paris, and she was able to go, I never went without her. We were two women alone together. If I went without her she was lonely. Every one who met me knew I had my mother with me; that we were strangers in a foreign country. Now any one who was selfish enough to ask me without asking my mother might go hang. I couldn't go out and eat a good supper thinking that she was taking a cold bite alone. There was no idea of impressing any one with my notion of propriety. I am never bothered by ideas of that sort.

Delilah fully reciprocated her daughter's affection, as a *San Francisco Chronicle* writer noted when interviewing Loie. The dancer possessed "autographs of all the celebrities and gifts from princesses and archduchesses and earls. But her mother, who is always with her, slips an arm about her neck and says, 'Above all, she's a dear girl.'"

Loie did not object to being described as naïve and natural, nor did she disagree when the *Chronicle* reporter said she was "not a sylph." Indeed, she thought she owed her success largely to her build. "If I hadn't been 'stocky,' like my father, I could never have done it," she said. In describing her, the reporter went on to say she wore no jewelry, though "loads" of it had been given to her. "She is simple in her tastes and dress, indulging only in an intoxicating odor that floats around her." She has a "plain face" but "a clever brain and a tongue nimble as her toes." "She knows most of this world's people who are worth knowing, and she takes an unaffected pleasure in talking about them." (Apparently she managed to avoid sounding like a name-dropper.) "She curls herself in her chair like a cat, and she catches your hand impulsively as she talks, but behind her wide-open eyes there is a faculty of analysis—New Englandese in its keenness." She talks so fast that now and then she has to stop to catch her breath, and sometimes she stutters a bit.

According to the *Chronicle* interviewer, Loie was basically "a plain, plucky American girl," but she had acquired a "Parisian veneer" and some "little un-American ways." According to most of the journalists, however,

The Mistress of Fire

she was notable for her unadulterated Americanness, and to some she was an inspiration to national pride, if not to downright jingoism. "Our object is to stand up for art in general and native art in particular, and with this patriotic purpose we mean to say good words for Loie Fuller, who, although a Chicago girl, has won the applause of Europe," the *Chicago Press* editorialized. "Blood is thicker than water, and however indignant the Anglomaniacs, the Franco-maniacs and Italo-maniacs may be, we intend to argue that there is some good in America."[15]

But Loie certainly did not act the part of a Yankee chauvinist when she visited Mexico. She succeeded in captivating the press and the public there as effectively as in her native land. Deliberately cultivating "the boys" ("los chicos") of the press, she was rewarded with plenty of favorable publicity.

As *El Universal* reported, Loie was both charmed and charming when a military band appeared in the patio of her hotel to serenade her. She commented on the band's numbers in such a way as to show that she was a great admirer of good music. After the band played "Home, Sweet Home," she said her reception here was so warm and friendly that Mexico seemed like home to her. At the end of the program she was awarded a medal and was asked for her autograph, which she willingly and repeatedly gave. Then she brought down from her rooms her own autograph album—with its signatures of statesmen, inventors, scientists, and artists—and had the bandleader put his name on the same page where Giuseppe Verdi, the composer of *Aïda,* had signed. Finally, she directed that the musicians be treated to beer, cognac, champagne, pastries, and sandwiches, and that they all be given passes to her first performance, which was scheduled for that same night.

According to *El Universal,* Loie received 40 percent of the National Theatre's net receipts during her appearance there. "She made five thousand pesos and spent four thousand on jewelry in various Mexico City shops." Presumably, she was not going to wear these gems.

Before departing from the city, Loie showed her "keen intelligence" when she asked a couple of public officials: "Proportionally, how does crime in Mexico compare with that in my country?" The two officials maintained an "ignominious silence," and Loie, "better informed" than they, answered her own question: "Well, gentlemen, according to the statistics that I have seen, there are 50 percent fewer crimes in proportion to population in Mexico than in the United States."[16]

In her dealings with press and public during her tours of 1896–97, as in her previous relations with press and public, Loie seems to have been rather artful in her artlessness, rather shrewd in her affectation of naïveté. She was, perhaps, almost as good a performer off the stage as on it.

~

The French had always taken Loie more seriously than the Americans had, and they did so again after she reappeared at the Folies-Bergère on October 21, 1897. Since her first triumph in Paris five years earlier, *Le Monde illustré* now recalled, she had maintained her fame by constantly adding something new to her work, as when she performed inside a semicircle of mirrors and caused her image to be reflected infinitely. True, she had "lost the charm of mystery" with her *Salomé*, but with her latest creations, especially the fire dance and the lily dance, she was again enthralling the Paris public. Indeed, she was proving herself more of a "mistress of fire" than ever, according to *L'Echo de Paris*.[17]

Even Jean Lorrain, who had compared Loie to a flailing and sweating washerwoman in *Salomé*, had nothing but praise, at first, for her performance in the new repertoire. Writing under his pseudonym Raitif de la Bretonne, he noted how the Folies-Bergère shook with applause when the "living flower" faded away and Loie Fuller materialized in a beam of light. As she came forward, tired but smiling, "her face with her blonde curls" looked lovely among the great bunches of chrysanthemums that her fans and devotees had sent.

Once more Loie enjoyed top billing at the Folies-Bergère. Her sexy rivals of 1894—Emilienne d'Alençon, the Barrison Sisters, and Caroline Otero— were no longer on the program. As usual, the manager, Edouard Marchand, kept changing the bill in 1897 and 1898 while Loie remained the star. Her fellow performers included bicycle acrobats, the Spanish dancer and singer La Tortojada, and the ballerinas of *The Rape of the Sabines*, which was hailed as the most beautiful ballet ever offered at the Folies-Bergère. But none of the other acts won anything like such popular acclaim as Loie's did.

The Mistress of Fire

Though Marchand continued to search for new attractions—not only for the Folies-Bergère but also for the other two theaters he managed, the Scala and the Eldorado—he found nothing to put ahead of Loie's repertoire during these years. She was in a strong bargaining position, and he in a generous mood, when he reengaged her in 1898. She asked him for a dozen electricians, and he gave her eighteen. For the time being, she did not have to maintain her own electrical crew.

According to one report, it took not eighteen but thirty-eight electricians to transform Loie from a plain and even grotesque creature into something immaterial and splendid. "Anyone meeting her in the afternoon—with her violet velvet sack coat, her unfashionably short wool dress, her boater perched on her tight bun, her gold-framed pince-nez—would hardly suspect that she was the woman of genius who had made herself the mistress of fire."[18]

In the eyes of her American admirers this woman, so plain offstage, became onstage a high-class and even an artistic performer. In the eyes of her French admirers, her transfiguration went further than that. She became a truly great artist, one worthy of discussion in the context of her leading contemporaries in literature and music as well as art.

"*La Loïe Fuller!* The very name evokes the ideal that reality denies us; with her, Art itself finds a place on the stage." So wrote the art critic Raymond Bouyer in the autumn 1898 issue of *L'Artiste*. Bouyer quoted in full the Belgian poet Georges Rodenbach's fifty-eight-line ode to Loie, beginning: "Déchirant l'ombre, et brusque, elle est là: c'est l'aurore!" ("Brusquely tearing the shadows, she appears: she is the dawn!") Linking her with another Belgian poet, Fernand Séverin, Bouyer said that both of them were "artists of silence," great musicians whose "mute harmony" lingered in the mind. She was a poet as well as a musician. "Miss Loïe, your magic originality is both poetry and dance," Bouyer rhapsodized. "You are both ancient and modern. Bold heiress of the ancients, sister-soul of our souls, you are dream, dragonfly, fire, light, flower, star."[19]

For the rest of 1898 Loie kept pretty well to her grueling schedule of seven nights and two or three afternoons a week at the Folies-Bergère. She managed to avoid another physical breakdown, though she did miss several performances after injuring a wrist while rehearsing.

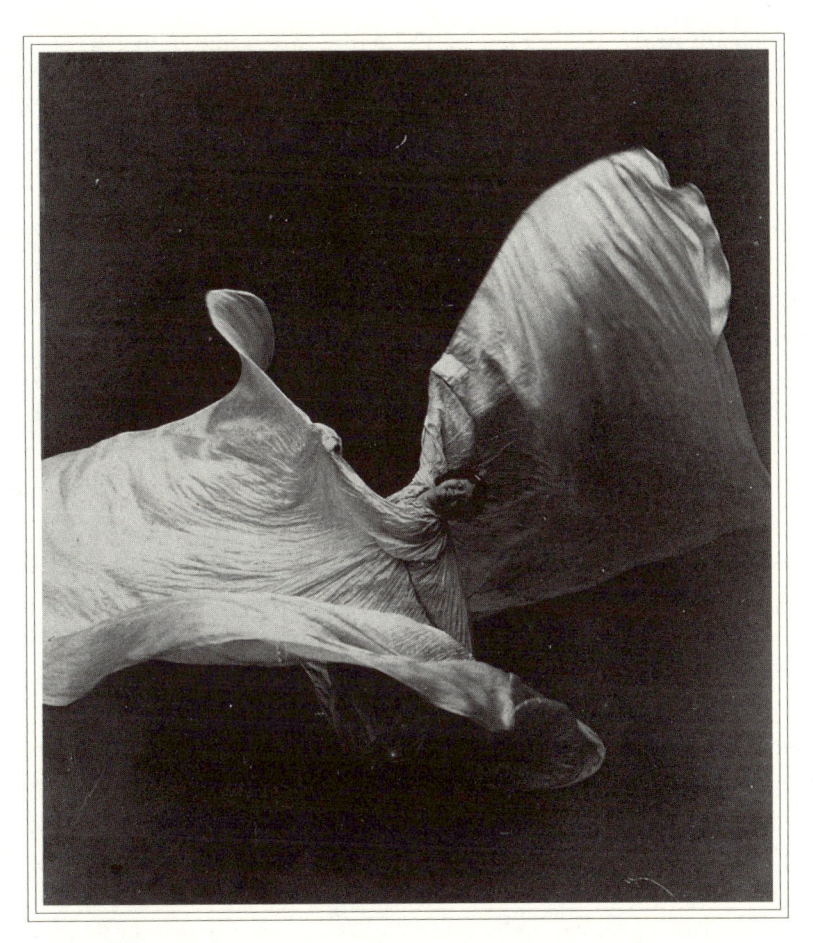

"La danse du Lys," 1900. (Photograph by Isaiah W. Taber; courtesy of the Musée d'Orsay, © R.M.N.)

She even had time and energy to perform for the diplomats who met in Paris to draw up a treaty ending the Spanish-American War. On October 12 (Columbus Day) the peace commissioners attended a reception as guests of *Le Figaro* at the newspaper's office. They were entertained first by three Spanish performers, among them the "greatest Spanish actress" of the time, and then by Loie. Finally, addressing the American delegation, she took it upon herself to recite some verse she had written for the occasion to plead

The Mistress of Fire

for an early peace, the last line of which ran: "May arbitration win the day." According to a news report, "The Spanish commissioners applauded loudly, but the American commission received Loie's impertinence with stoney silence."

February 1899 found Loie fulfilling an engagement in London, where she danced between the acts of *Little Miss Nobody* at the Lyric Theatre. On the playbill her name was in type as large as the title of the play, and in the London press she was greeted as both a remarkable person and a true artist. "She is not merely the heroine of a few glittering moments during which she occupies the stage of the *Folies-Bergère* each night, for she holds in addition a conspicuous place in that society which includes those Frenchmen who in science, art, and letters are adding to the intellectual dignity of the human race." Such was the report of *The Poster,* which added: "It is Loie Fuller's crowning merit that she does nothing in her dances which is unintelligent, nothing which is intended merely to provoke the wonder of the vulgar."[20]

Jean Lorrain expressed a very different opinion later that same year, after Loie had returned to the Folies-Bergère and put on a new mirror dance. Constantly changing—if not always improving—her repertoire, she had invented and patented an elaboration of her mirror arrangement. Added to the semicircle of mirrors was a sheet of clear glass at the front. When the auditorium was dark and the dancing figure illuminated, the clear glass served as an additional mirror, one that the spectators could see through while it reflected both the dancing figure and her reflections in the other mirrors. The object was to increase the already seemingly infinite number of images.

When Jean Lorrain saw the new mirror dance, he was again disappointed in Loie, as he noted in his diary on December 10, 1899. The glass cage struck him as an aquarium, inside of which Loie was cut up and her fragments parceled out, to bustle about in the aquarium's several compartments. "The best is the enemy of the good, and she has tried to do too well." She had also fallen short with other new effects, it seemed to Jean Lorrain. There were hanging things of grayish cloth that were supposed to look like stalactites but looked, instead, like elephant trunks. Then there was her "trick of the Archangel," in which she seemed to be sitting in her nightgown on top of something—to represent, perhaps, a sitting hen on the nest. Whatever it was supposed to be, it was hideous.

> Poor Loie! But there is her mother. Yes, in an ermine cape, with the look of an Ingres portrait, stiff and straight, she comes every evening to rest her elbows on the edge of a box right in front of the stage. She has quite a following of clergymen and young ladies, who make one think of the Salvation Army. And there, pale, her lips discolored, looking as distinguished as an English peeress, though almost ghostlike, she follows Loie's dances with big wide eyes. Then, at the end of the show, she slowly gets to her feet and throws kisses at Loie. And La Loie, who dances only for her, leans forward, wrapped in her long white robes, and, from her high pedestal, nicely returns her mother's kisses. Now, isn't that touching?[21]

Jean Lorrain has been described as an "aesthetic dictator" who could make or break reputations despite his "outrageous exhibitionism and openly decadent tastes—drugs, sado-masochism, and aggressive homosexuality." His journals were published, exposing his spontaneous as well as his considered judgments, but whether he flattered Loie or ridiculed her, he had no lasting effect upon her fame.[22]

To be attacked by burglars was the last thing Loie expected when she and her mother moved into the house of their dreams. They had been living in a flat near a railroad, where the continual "tooting of the engines" bothered both of them and especially Delilah, ailing as she was. They longed for a quiet location and a large yard, and after weeks of searching they found just the place at 24 rue Cortambert in fashionable Passy. The house, though once described as a "dainty little Paris 'hotel,'" was more than roomy enough for the two of them and was set in spacious grounds that were surrounded by a high wall.

After leasing the property and moving in, Loie held a housewarming, to

The Mistress of Fire

which she invited a hundred people, most of them notabilities. Among those accepting her invitation were the sculptor Auguste Rodin, the painter Benjamin Constant, the novelist Anatole France, and the journalist and art critic Victor Henri Rochefort. One of the guests recalled that "the last word of *chic*, the final *cachet* that stamped you in those days of grace, before 1900, as being in the inner circle of things Parisian was to get an invitation . . . to dine at Loie's." So it was on this occasion in 1899. "Many of these celebrities had met each other there for the first time, they stood a little on their dignity, but who could be stiff and severe when Loie Fuller was hostess?"

It was a pleasant May evening. After dinner Loie had to leave for her usual appearance at the Folies-Bergère, and when she came back at midnight she found the guests waiting expectantly. She invited them to the garden while she hurried upstairs to her bedroom to change her clothes. "Presently a cherubic-looking figure, dressed in vaporous garments, seemed to float downstairs." On the lawn, in the light of a pale moon and yellow Chinese lanterns, she improvised a dance while an American woman friend played a violin for accompaniment. When Loie finished, the spectators bravoed and embraced her, Benjamin Constant giving her "a couple of sounding kisses on the cheeks."

Loie was ready with a spontaneous encore. Back in the house she stood on a chair and, "like a little girl," recited the verse she had once recited when she was indeed a little girl—"Mary had a little lamb." Only this time she did it "in a sort of pidgin French, all charming." Delilah did not feel like coming down for the party, but she enjoyed what she could hear from her bedroom and what Loie regaled her with afterward.[23]

Despite this auspicious beginning at 24 rue Cortambert, the house did not prove to be an entirely happy place for the Fullers. Their worst experience there occurred less than a year later, on March 16, 1900. That night, after dismissing her maid, Loie was alone in her room preparing for bed when two masked men stealthily approached. They had scaled the wall and entered the house through a ground-floor window. Before Loie knew they were in the room, one of them grabbed her by the throat and ordered her to keep still. Instead, she let out a scream. Beating her with his fists, the burglar knocked her to the floor, where she lay unconscious while he and his accomplice searched for valuables. There was only a little money in her purse, and her collection of jewels was safely in a bank vault, but the men took whatever of value they could find. They were gone when Loie came to.

She wakened her maid, who telephoned her physician. After examining her, he said she was suffering from shock as well as bruises and would not be able to appear in public for at least six weeks. She would recover barely in time to get ready for the Universal Exposition, at which she was to shine.[24]

6

A Theater of Her Own

The approaching turn of the century was to bring both new career triumphs and new relationships to the life of Loie Fuller. Concurrent with Loie's rise to fame in 1890s Paris, a fresh decorative style, known as Art Nouveau, was flowering in France and throughout Europe and the United States. Purely by chance, the dancer was to emerge as its personification. It has been said that she might well have claimed precedence over Hector Guimard and Samuel Bing as an initiator of Art Nouveau in France.[1] She was to be celebrated for that influence at the Paris Universal Exposition of 1900, where she had her own theater, a proclamation of the new style in every respect.

Loie's longtime friend Roger Marx, one of the organizers of the exposition, was to play a key role in Loie's success there. On a personal level, he also deserves credit for helping her acquire two of her most intimate friends: her lifelong companion, Gabrielle Bloch, and the greatest sculptor of the era, Auguste Rodin.

Ever since Loie's first meeting with Marx, soon after her original debut at the Folies-Bergère, he had continued to praise her performances from an artistic standpoint while steadily growing in authority as an art critic. She, for her part, became more and more intimate with the Marx family, which included two boys, the older of whom was named Claude. "They were regular habitues of my matinees & my devoted admirers," she recalled, "—so when Claude got to be 8 or 9 years of age, he wrote poems about me, made little Loie Fuller statues [of wax], and turned into a little Loie Fuller himself. I gave him a dress & before long he was creating dances all his own."[2]

Gabrielle Bloch was a cousin of Mrs. Marx, who no doubt facilitated Gab's introduction to Loie. Gab had worshiped Loie from afar after attending one of the earliest Folies-Bergère matinees as a girl of fourteen (she was about sixteen years younger than Loie). "Soul of the flowers, soul of the sky, soul of flame, Loïe Fuller has given them to us," that matinee moved Gab to write. "She has created the soul of the dance, for until Loïe Fuller came the dance was without soul!"

Not long after that, when only thirty-seven, Gab's mother died. "Gab loved her dearly, & she was devoted to Gab," as Loie later wrote. "She saw little or nothing of her father, & lived the life of a hermit, until she met me." After meeting Gab, Loie gave her a photo of herself, on which she had

Loie gave this portrait to Gab Bloch, inscribing it "To my dear little friend." It is an early memento of a relationship that lasted more than thirty years. (Photograph by Langfier; courtesy of the Dance Collection, the New York Public Library for the Performing Arts.)

written: "To my dear little friend, souvenir of Loïe Fuller." This was the "little friend" who served as Loie's lay figure, trying on costumes and trying out movements while Loie experimented with dance elements and lighting effects. But Loie did not realize how fond of her Gab was until they had been acquainted for two years or more.

Gab did not readily communicate her innermost feelings even to Loie, but seemed at times inscrutable and almost pathologically shy. In this respect she was quite different from the gushing, outgoing Loie, and quite different also physically, being black-haired, dark-eyed, and slow and sinuous in movement. But she was approximately the same height, so Loie thought of her as neither tall nor short. The French girl spoke English in a way that Loie considered quaint—"Ah! I have look in ze glass!" Loie once quoted her—but she spoke and wrote English vastly better than Loie did French, and so English was their medium of communication.[3]

Loie and Gab were already close by the time Loie met Rodin (1840–1917), who, once controversial, had become world famous, hailed by his admirers as the greatest sculptor since Michelangelo, if not the greatest ever. Stocky, heavy-featured, black-bearded, still vigorous and lustful in his fifties, Rodin had developed a fondness and a fascination for women. He "precipitated himself on every woman he met," according to the American-born duchess of Marlborough. "You know—hands all over you." While living with his longtime mistress Rose Beuret, he had numerous affairs, the most serious of them involving his student and lover Camille Claudel, a talented sculptress who broke with him because he would not leave Rose for her, and who was eventually committed to an asylum. But he did not precipitate himself on Loie; his relationship with her was entirely platonic.[4]

Roger Marx had long been a friend, defender, and trumpeter of Rodin. After Loie's reappearance at the Folies-Bergère in the fall of 1897, Marx invited him to one of her performances and he declined. A little later Marx and his wife took Loie to Rodin's atelier, but there was some misunderstanding about the time, and Rodin was gone when his visitors arrived. He sent his regrets at having missed the Marxes and also "the lovely modern tanagra, the beautiful Loïe Fuller."[5]

By the summer of 1898 Loie had made Rodin's acquaintance, and during the next two years she assiduously cultivated his friendship. When she

Loie presented this photograph of herself to Rodin and Rose Beuret some time after 1897, more than fifteen years after it was taken in Chicago. (Photograph by Rider; courtesy of the Musée Rodin.)

opened for another season at the Folies-Bergère, she invited him to the dress rehearsal as her guest. Later, when she debuted at the Olympia, she presented him tickets for two loges and asked three of his distinguished friends to join him. She entertained him as hostess at her house and called upon him and Rose Beuret at theirs, always treating her with the respect due his wife. Since he did not speak or read English, she communicated with him as best she could in his language, though she now had a bilingual secretary who wrote some of her letters for her. Loie addressed him at first as "Cher Amie [Ami]" ("Dear Friend") and later as "Cher Maitre" ("Dear Master"). Her French was still full of errors but was more or less understandable, as when she inquired: "Avez vous recoir ma lettre de semaine passez?" ("Have you received my letter of last week?").[6]

Loie wanted Rodin to make a statue of her, and supporting her was a woman who had joined his circle at about the same time. This woman, Emilia Cimino, was an aspiring artist a few years older than Loie, born in France to Neapolitan parents in exile there, and fluent in French, English, Italian, Spanish, and German. Cimino was quite willing to intercede with Rodin in Loie's behalf. While a rival of Loie for his attention, she was also a rival of Gab for Loie's attention. She wrote to Rodin on October 26, 1898:

> I saw Loïe Fuller yesterday. She was charming as hostess and looked ten years younger without that ugly hat that hid her pretty forehead. She is first-rate, I think. She is certainly going to beg you to make a tanagra of her, a large one. I see a lovely thing there. And when she is posing for you, you will like her even more than when she was visiting you.
>
> She introduced me to her mother, a very, very good person. She [Loie] is not so eccentric as she gave the impression of being when at your home, but is much better than that, though perhaps her genius is not quite so remarkable as my feeling for her has led me to imagine. But I like her very, very much, and she is fond of you—which adds to her charm.

Loie let Rodin know that she would like for him to make a head of her and another of her mother, but he held off, while Cimino told him she was avoiding Loie. "Saturday I dined at Loie's with Mlle Block [sic], with whom she is absolutely smitten, so much so that I now flee from her (Loie) as soon as she comes near." Months passed and, jealous though she was, Cimino did not lose interest in either Loie or the question of a Loie sculpture. "Loie doesn't write to me any more, and I don't know whether she has posed for you," Cimino confided to Rodin, and she asked him to intervene in her behalf: "Would you tell her that she is badly neglecting me and that I am losing sight of 'my star'?"

Cimino was eager to sketch Loie, and Rodin's estranged lover, Camille Claudel, also seemed interested in sculpting her, after Loie had paid Claudel a visit, with Roger Marx again serving as intermediary. Finally, by early 1900, Rodin himself was ready to make a Loie sculpture. What she had in mind is suggested by the comments she made about one of his sculptures of a female figure. That statuette was a "feminist preachment," she thought. "It represents the free, straightforward, energetic woman who absorbs the inert man lacking those qualities." She pressed Rodin to get her own statue done in time for it to be exhibited in her theater at the Universal Exposition, which was about to open.[7]

Rodin's photographer, Eugène Druet, took a series of pictures of Loie dancing, these to be used as supplementary models for the sculptor. She also began to pose for him but soon was so preoccupied with the construction of her theater that she could not keep up with the modeling. "Loie wishes for me to express her regrets," Cimino wrote Rodin, "for interrupting the poses when you are willing to work for her despite your pressing engagements." Meanwhile a visitor to Rodin's atelier was impressed by what he saw: "You might be inclined to smile on entering the statuary warehouse, rue de l'Université, where Rodin is making a statue of Miss Loïe Fuller, to see the two of them conversing, he in his large white smock, she in her black raincoat, in the midst of the marbles and plasters. But you quickly become serious when you hear the warm and earnest discussion, in which the dancer holds her own with the sturdy and shrewd sculptor." For the present, however, Loie was too busy to spend enough time with Rodin for him to finish the job.[8]

Loie's appeal to Rodin to make a sculpture of her was a unique act for her. From the moment of her debut at the Folies-Bergère, she had been besieged by other artists wanting to capture her performance. It was said at the time that "she may well have been portrayed by more distinguished artists than

Rodin's photographer took a series of pictures of Loie for possible use by Rodin in making a sculpture of her about 1900. (Photograph by Eugène Druet; courtesy of the Musée Rodin.)

Loie's embodiment of the spirit of Art Nouveau is seen in this "flower" she created in 1896. (Photograph by Samuel Joshua Beckett.)

any other woman in modern history."[9] Even before the end of the 1892–93 season, probably no performer in contemporary times had had "her features more often reproduced than has the serpentine dancer of the Folies-Bergère."[10]

 The dancer's timing in 1892 Paris was perfect in that it coincided with the emergence of Art Nouveau. Largely an uprising of young and creative spirits against the base standards of nineteenth-century French commercialism and materialism, the movement was feminine in spirit, even though it was dominated by men. Its lines were flowing and sinuous; its subjects, often influenced by the influx of Japanese art into Paris, were drawn from nature. Flowers with long, bending stalks; vines and trailing tendrils, elongated women with undulating hair—these and other themes were expanded to include the metamorphosis of the human into the natural: woman-flower, woman-butterfly, woman-bird. Also frequent was the impression of movement caught, suspended in timelessness. Often the design was so abstract as merely to suggest the subject.

Loie embodied Art Nouveau through her unique combination of light and motion. "Hidden in swirling diaphanous veils of painted silk gauze, mysteriously emerging from shadow into colored light, and crowned with a mane of fire-red hair, she epitomised their exotic visions of Woman as a sensuous but intangible dream metamorphosing into a flame, a cloud, a moth, or a flower. For this was a style dedicated to women and flowers." For the artists, she was a true synthesis of the performing and the visual arts and a combination of music, color, and movement.[11] "When she danced, 'sculpted by the air, the cloth rose and fell, swelled and contracted . . .' [she was] recalling the fluid, tenuous lines of art nouveau designers with their predilection for goblets shaped like tulips, grills like ramblers, and frames of desks and screens like espaliered trees."[12] Using the serpentine dance, the lily dance, and other nature-inspired themes, Loie's dancing was the Art Nouveau of choreography.[13]

No one knows either the number of artists who did representations of Loie or how many works each of them created of the dancer. More than seventy artists from about ten countries have been identified as having done lithograph posters; oil, pastel, or watercolor paintings; sculptures in bronze, terra-cotta, or glass; ceramic or porcelain works; and gold and silver jewelry and medals. (A comprehensive listing of known pieces is provided in an appendix at the end of this biography.) Some of these and other Loie images have disappeared over the years, perhaps going into private collections or possibly being destroyed during World War II.

Beyond the pieces, some one of a kind, others produced in volume, that can be identified specifically as representing Loie herself, it is impossible to estimate the number of Art Nouveau works that would be influenced by her. A prime example is Agathon Léonard's series of fifteen unglazed porcelain dancer figures, manufactured by Sèvres, which was to be one of the most popular entries in the Paris Exposition of 1900.[14] At the same exposition, René Lalique was to pay tribute to Loie by installing in his window display a grille of butterfly women.[15] In recent times, a vermeil and plique-à-jour necklace featuring a dancer with veils swirling above her head has come to light in New York, along with a silver pendant with a similar motif in London. When viewing an Art Nouveau piece, one is tempted to identify every item that features a butterfly-woman or a woman-flower as being Loie herself. Yet one is unable to say whether it is Loie or not because Art Nouveau and Loie Fuller are inextricably interwoven. Few of the artists made literal representations of the dancer; rather they sought to capture the swirling draperies and the rapidly changing colors produced by her special effects. "To express the ethereal qualities of the moving image, artists idealized the figure. It was not Loie Fuller as a person who was the Art Nouveau dream but rather the vision she created."[16]

To advertise that vision, Loie commissioned and paid for at least thirty color lithographic posters for her performances at the Folies-Bergère and at various Parisian theaters and music halls. Among the best were those by Jules Chéret, a pioneer painter, designer, and lithographer who produced more than a thousand poster images between 1866 and 1900. "With excellent judgement she went to Chéret—Chéret the master of gorgeous and fantastic color—to herald her earlier performances in that metropolis to the gaiety of which his posters have added so materially," commented the editor of the English magazine *The Poster* in February 1899. "In his long career as an *affichiste,* Chéret has produced nothing more successful than his series of designs for Loie Fuller."

He produced three posters for Loie, with the *Folies-Bergère/La Loïe Fuller* (1893) being the most famous and also the most reproduced in Art Nouveau reference works. Printed in four different color combinations, it is highly prized in the dark green background version with the dancing figure in orange, yellow, and celadon green. In 1897, the artist recreated a smaller image of this poster for inclusion in the series *Les Maîtres de l'affiche.* Chéret deviated from his usual style in all four of the images of Loie in that he set off the central figure, as on the stage, "by the dark background and the splashes and strokes of color [that] came as close as was possible in a static image to reproducing the illusion of swirling draperies."[17]

Pal (Jean de Paléologu), a Romanian working in France, was also effective in capturing Loie's movement in the ten or more posters he designed. Less mobile is Georges Meunier's portrayal of the dancer. Though a student of Chéret, he has been criticized for making the piece inappropriately heavy. Even so, this is considered to be the rarest of Loie Fuller posters and is highly sought by collectors both for that reason and for its capture of the fire dance's spirit. Also rare is the work by Bac (Fernand Sigismond Bac), a German working in France, who made her very first poster in Paris (1892).[18]

One of the most famous of the period's poster artists, Henri de Toulouse-Lautrec, was never commissioned to do a poster of Loie Fuller, nor did she own one of the lithographs or oils he did of her:

> At the Folies-Bergère, Lautrec like all Parisians was fascinated by the dancing of Loie Fuller. . . . He would, no doubt, have liked to have been among those who did posters of her, but the dancer did not really appreciate his lithograph, even though it had success within a limited circle, for it went on sale in February–March 1893 and was reproduced in *L'Echo de Paris* on 9 December 1893. The meeting of the minds between Loie Fuller and Lautrec never really happened. Why?

The explanation is given by a modern-day French cataloger of Lautrec that the artist sought to find the "real person" and then interpreted that with a facial expression or a characteristic body pose. With Loie that was difficult because once onstage "she tended to become an impersonal goddess communing with the forces of nature." The symbolist Camille Mauclair in *Les Idées vivantes* explained Loie's work: "The realism does not speak to the soul but it completely satisfies the intelligence. In it there is no spontaneity, no free improvisation, no individual fantasy, but a profound skill, an 'execution' achieved with disconcerting perfection."[19]

An American cataloger of Loie Fuller skips over her and Lautrec's failure to "share a kinship in artistic sensitivity" and possibly hits closer to the reason for no poster commission: "She [Loie] probably did not like it [the lithograph series], since it was almost a caricature and thus may have offended her."[20]

Despite Loie's feelings about the lithograph series of fifty prints, each hand colored and dusted with gold, silver, or bronze powder, the images, which verge on the abstract, have captured her "remarkable floating movements as well as the changing light effects that Fuller achieved by using glass plates, large lantern projectors, colored gelatins, and other inventive devices."[21]

Equally impressive was the wide range of works created by the sculptors of Loie in bronze, marble, ceramic luster, pâte de verre, and terra-cotta. Pierre Roche (Fernand Massignon), a longtime friend of Loie's, produced the greatest number and variety of pieces, also doing oils, medals, and gypsographs (painted bas-reliefs in paper), a process he is credited with inventing. He was one of the few artists whose sculptures of Loie were portraits. "They were flattering to both face and figure. Roche made most of his portraits early in her Paris career, images that he continued to use for years afterward—providing a perpetual youthful image of the dancer."[22]

The *Revue blanche*, May 15, 1899, exclaimed: "How one would like to contemplate for a long time, for a very long time, Pierre Roche's 'Loïe Fuller,' that marble gem sculpted to the glory of the capering magician!" (Loie—or somebody—gave a copy of this and similarly effusive clippings to Rodin, perhaps to suggest her worthiness as a subject for him.)[23]

Also paying tribute to Loie with noteworthy works was the sculptor Edouard Houssin, who, among other things, sculpted a small white marble head, one of the few pieces that actually looks like the real Loie. François Carabin used bronze and ceramic luster to portray the dancer in a series of poses, most of which show her in the shorter skirts, without wands, that were typical during her early career in Paris. One of Loie's favorite sculptors was her close friend Théodore Rivière, who in addition to producing a marble of the lily dance, made many small sculptures of the dancer. It was easy for her to obtain copies of his work, and even after his death in 1912 she continued to order his sculpture from both his widow and his foundry until the 1920s.[24]

Of all the sculpture produced of Loie, the pieces that continue to be the most popular in present-day exhibits and cited in key Art Nouveau reference works are the bronze table lamps that were created by François-Raoul Larche. With at least four variations of this figural lamp of the dancer,

Larche combined "the swirling movement and excitement of Loie Fuller's dance that also suggest the bustling ambiance of Paris, and the busy array of pavilions at the 1900 Paris Exposition. Also apparent is the sensuous undulation of her draperies, typical of the Art Nouveau line. She has become the ubiquitous fin-de-siècle femme fatale. Finally, Larche also ingeniously included the new scientific wonder of the late nineteenth century—electricity."[25]

Sarah Bernhardt, Loie's famous friend who had a box at the Folies-Bergère during the dancer's second season, owned one of the Larche lamps; it is pictured in Miss Bernhardt's apartment on the mantle in a photograph taken about 1900.[26] At the same time, the subject of the lamp had displayed in her studio one of the loveliest of Alphonse Mucha's posters of the Divine Sarah—*La Dame aux camélias*.

In addition to the artists such as Larche who used Loie as a model, the dancer's performance exerted a broad and pervasive influence on other designers both in Europe and in the United States. The master glassworkers—Emile Gallé, René Lalique, and Louis Comfort Tiffany—especially mirrored her effects. After attending one of her shows at the Folies-Bergère, Gallé had written rapturously of "this magician" with her transformations of color and light, which made him think of "metempsychoses," the transmigration of souls. He acquired a Carabin sculpture of Loie, which remained a constant reminder of her performance. Later he admitted that "he was led to seek new colorings by seeing the beautiful light effects invented by Loie Fuller." Lalique similarly employed motifs and tints that were suggested by her dances. Tiffany, an American who had studied painting in Paris, fashioned glass in forms that also derived their inspiration from her technique. "Loie Fuller must have produced the effects of a moving, iridescent, illuminated Tiffany vase," an authority on Art Nouveau has aptly observed, "whereas Tiffany's slender, soaring spiral vases seem to be veiled dancers frozen into glass."[27]

Art Nouveau, with Loie as its personification, had its supreme moment at the Paris Exposition of 1900. Not that the style predominated there in the architecture; only a handful of buildings were reflective of the modern design, with most of them falling into the category of heavy and traditional edifices. Not even Rodin's pavilion, which was located near Loie's, resembled

Time-release photograph of Loie dancing in her studio about 1910. The two oil paintings by Lerolle and the two marble busts are now lost. In the shadow at the left is Alphonse Mucha's poster for La Dame aux camélias, *starring Loie's friend Sarah Bernhardt. (Photograph by Harry C. Ellis; courtesy of the Musée Rodin.)*

the new style, either in the design of the building or its artistic contents. In effect, her spirit was more in evidence than the world-famous sculptor's. "Instead of the 'Parisienne' [female symbol of Paris], stiff as a dressmaker's dummy, an effigy of Loie Fuller should have crowned the Porte Binet [main entrance]. Her image, or rather her quality of movement, could be found reflected in all the truly modern parts of the exhibition, in bronze, in fresco or in terracotta." Her statue was prominent not only on her own building; a plaster effigy of her in a swirling gown was also poised high above the Palace of the Dance.[28] It is interesting to note that of all the famous female entertainers in 1900 Art Nouveau Paris, including Sarah Bernhardt, Cléo de Merode, Caroline Otero, Liane de Pougy, and Emilienne d'Alençon, Loie Fuller was the only one to have her own pavilion at the exposition.

One of the Beaux Arts students at that time, Henri Sauvage, became the architect of Loie's theater in 1900, when he was just turning twenty-seven. Sauvage was a friend of Rodin, who no doubt recommended him to Loie, and who also, along with Roger Marx, probably encouraged her to set up a theater of her own. The building, like nearly all the exposition structures, was to be only temporary, and so the architect could expect to enjoy considerable leeway in designing it. But, of course, he would have to take into account the wishes of his client, who held strong opinions as to how the theater should be built.

Loie was soon at odds with Sauvage. She rejected one of his plans, changed her mind about another after construction had begun, and was dissatisfied with the way the third was carried out. "It seems that architects were not making estimates in Paris," she later gave an American newsman to understand. "It was too hard to get regular workmen, and materials ran up to unconscionable prices and none could tell on one day what architectural complications the next day might bring forth." She had expected the whole job to cost no more than ten thousand dollars. After signing checks for about fifty thousand dollars, she refused to pay any more and took the matter to court, where it was left to arbitrators to decide the real value of the labor and materials she was being charged for.[29]

Loie closely watched the construction, which was late in getting started. As Arsène Alexandre, a prominent art critic and another of Rodin's close friends, wrote soon afterward,

The ditchdiggers arrived on the eve of the exposition's opening [in April], the carpenters later, and the masons after everything was open. Everybody said: "This is ridiculous! It will be ready in November—if they hurry up."

People don't know Loie's energy, her get-up-and-go. She is what is called *a very pushing woman*. According to the experts, the construction would take six months; actually, it took six weeks. During that time Miss Fuller was architect, painter, decorator, mechanic, electrician, manager, and everything else.

There was nothing more amusing and charming than to see her on the construction site, running around to supervise the work or to correct a mistake, her plum-colored dress disheveled, her hair in wild disarray. One minute she was half-dead from fatigue; the next minute she suddenly came to life and greeted her friends in the midst of her construction (or her ruins—it's hard to say which) with all the vivacity and affectionate graciousness that she knows how to put into her slightest gesture and the slightest word of her fractured French.

Then, all at once, she disappeared, leaving her workers in the lurch and her architect bewildered. She had gone off to buy material at some distant department store, or to contend with a ferocious prefect of police, or to mollify one or another stubborn functionary.

She wore out two or three secretaries, though she wrote more letters than any of them. For carrying on this trade—or, rather, these hundred trades—she found the means by dancing at the Olympia in the evenings and also, I believe, often in the afternoons. It almost seemed as if it were her ghost that danced and her real self that thrashed about at the exposition, under some torrential downpours, among the carpenters, teamsters, and interior decorators.[30]

While in the midst of this hectic activity, Loie found time to help a stranger who came from Monmouth, Illinois, her hometown of a quarter

Art in Loie's likeness made by Pierre Roche for her 1900 theater. The statue in the foreground stood on the roof, above the main entrance. The plaster casts at the lower left and right represent Loie as Drama and Comedy.

century earlier. Her caller was Will Nicol, a youth who aspired to become a magician and who, under the name of Nicola the Great, eventually achieved some success as one. She spent three hours with young Will, watching him do some of his tricks, advising him how to secure engagements in Paris, and suggesting that he make a clown costume from a U.S. flag.[31]

The completed Loie Fuller Theater, a strange little building, had an air of narcissism about it, totally devoted as it was to the dancer and her reflection in art. Its façade was wrapped in folds of plaster that called to mind her draperies in motion, and it was topped by a life-size Loie statue, which looked like a great bird about to take flight. All this was the work of Pierre Roche, and so were the curved bas-relief figures of two dancing girls that entwined the entrance. At night the white stucco exterior became ablaze with light, shining up from below. Inside, during the day, sunlight streaming through stained-glass windows gave a kaleidoscopic effect. In the evening, a similar effect was created by electric lights. The stage was quite small, with the auditorium having room for only two hundred seats.

This being a Loie Fuller museum as well as a Loie Fuller theater, the foyer served as the art gallery. It was filled with statuary, paintings, sketches, and other art objects, none of which had been originally commissioned by Loie. Having purchased reproductions of some of the smaller items, she resold these copies to fairgoers and also presented them as gifts to friends.

The dancer did commission a poster to advertise her rue de Paris performances at the exposition. Designed by Manuel Orazi, an Italian who worked in France and made Sarah Bernhardt's first poster in Paris, the work is considered to be one of his three best creations. Other than having Loie's signature chestnut hair, the sylphlike central figure bears little resemblance to the real Loie Fuller. Rather, it captures the movement and spectacle of the dancer's performance.[32] Martin Battersby has noted "a very marked Japanese influence . . . in this poster, the elongated shape being similar to that of a *kakemono* [scroll]."[33] A further oriental touch is the use of conventionalized Japanese emblems or crests on the image, golden details that were also used by Massier and Lévy-Dhurmer on their luster glaze ceramic charger depicting Loie Fuller.

At the same time, the theater building itself served as a large-scale poster, a more than sufficient advertisement.[34]

Entrance to Loie's theater at the Universal Exposition of 1900. The theater was located on the rue de Paris, which was on the Right Bank.

Loie's name was popularly associated with the novelty and wonder of electric lighting, and the Universal Exposition of 1900 featured electricity even more than the one of 1889 had done. The Palace of Electricity, "the active soul of the Exhibition," poured forth the magical, mysterious fluid that gave light and life to the entire show. Here was a fluid energy that seemed synonymous with the flowing dynamic of Loie's dances.[35]

Recalling her theater and its display of art a few years later, the *Architectural Record* gave her a flattering write-up, even though it might "seem strange to see Miss Loïe Fuller spoken of in a magazine devoted to architecture and decorative art—a music-hall star taking the place of a skyscraper, a baroque house-front or a piece of furniture."

Miss Fuller has revealed to artists the magical effects produced by the traversing of substances by light and color. It is possible to trace the same influence to furniture decoration and even in architecture.

Taken at the best, what effect has "art nouveau" had? That of relaxing the rigid lines of the decorative styles, which had got to exist entirely as formulae and senseless imitations of the past. That there have been many exaggerations, many mistakes and many absurdities committed in the name of "art nouveau" nobody will deny. There is no need, however, to be alarmed at that. Only those who stand still can be sure of not tripping, but immobility is akin to death. Well, the taste shown for sinuous forms in furniture and nick-nacks undoubtedly has its analogue if not its origin in the skirt dance. This achievement is somewhat analogous to what Miss Fuller has brought about in the art of dancing. . . .

Thus Miss Fuller's impression upon the world will not have been a transient one. What mark has been left by the great dancers of former generations—Taglioni, Fanny Essler and others? None at all. Something will, however, remain to recall the memory of Loïe Fuller. She has contributed towards the creation of a new style: she has come upon the scene at the right moment.[36]

The next year, 1904, Roger Marx and Pierre Roche dedicated to Loie a masterpiece of Art Nouveau and gypsography: a portfolio with twenty-seven unbound pages, fourteen of them and a paper wrapper illustrated with Roche's embossed color prints. The text, an essay by Marx, amounted to another of his paeans to Loie. "What lessons may artists yet learn from the way her flying draperies fold and flow!" he exclaimed. "Not only can an ornamenter, seeking a style for the future, derive original decorative themes from it; but all poets of design, all those who bring inert materials to life, can benefit from its refreshing hints as to shape and hue."[37]

In fact, Art Nouveau had already begun to decline. All along, as the *Ar-*

chitectural Record noted, many exaggerations, mistakes, and absurdities were committed in its name, and with the passage of time the number of such distortions multiplied. Only a thin line had separated the worst of Art Nouveau from kitsch, and the line tended to disappear completely as more and more of the works were plagiarized, debased, and mass produced. Within a decade the new style was old hat, and Loie's contribution to its development was pretty much forgotten, until rediscovered years later by art historians.

※

"Le Théâtre de la Loïe Fuller" was located near the Place de l'Alma, at one end of the rue de Paris, which paralleled the Right Bank of the Seine, across the river from most of the exposition.

The rue de Paris, a temporary street, contained other small theaters, which were quite different from Loie's, most of them ranging from the tawdry to the sleazy. Among them, the Tableaux Vivants featured "a wretched troupe of tiny Spanish boys and girls" who danced and sang as best they could. The Grand Guignol, a poor imitation of the real Grand Guignol in Montmartre, provided one-act horror plays. La Roulotte offered, among other things, a "wearisome revue." In front of these establishments, barkers delivered their noisy patter, sometimes with the aid of drums, tambourines, and samples of the performances inside. Fairgoers thronged the street—which at night was festive enough with Japanese lanterns hanging in the trees and was alluring enough with painted prostitutes plying their trade—but comparatively few of the fairgoers were willing to pay even the modest admission to the shows.

Also on the rue de Paris stood the Palais de la Danse, with the statue of Loie at the top. This building housed wax figures of ballerinas and was the scene of continual ballet dancing, quite conventional except for a troupe of Russians who were "marvelously agile" and "full of a wild humor." Various other nationalities presented their typical dances in pavilions that foreign governments sponsored in the main enclosure on the Left Bank. But none of those histrionic or terpsichorean entertainments could compare with what Loie had to offer.[38]

She was again functioning as both a performer and an impresario. Wanting something fresh and provocative for jaded Parisians, she was confident she had found it when she heard about a troupe of Japanese who were playing in London after a rousing success in New York. Negotiating with them through the Japanese minister in London, she succeeded in engaging them and bringing them promptly to Paris.

The star of the company was Sada Yacco, a tiny, Tokyo-born, twenty-eight-year-old former geisha. She and her husband, Kawakami, took the leading roles in a one-act playlet, *The Geisha and the Knight*. They and the rest of the actors spoke their parts in Japanese, but they mimed so actively and so cleverly that Westerners had little difficulty in following the plot, which, in any case, was simple enough to be easily understood.

In the play the geisha Katsouraghi (Sada Yacco) falls instantaneously in love with the Samurai Nagoya (Kawakami) when he visits the geisha quarter. Another samurai, Banza, who is in love with Katsouraghi, grows jealous and challenges Nagoya to a duel. She steps in and heads it off, but discovers that Nagoya is already engaged. Now *she* is consumed with jealousy. To protect Nagoya from her, his betrothed sneaks him into a Buddhist temple where women are not allowed. Katsouraghi, by charming the priests with her dancing, gains entrance and falls upon the hiding couple with curses and blows until she is stopped by a temple guard. Then she dies of a broken heart in the arms of the man she loves.[39]

Loie's theater was scheduled to open with this play and with dances of her own on June 25. She invited, as her guests, Rodin and a number of other Parisians prominent in artistic or theatrical affairs. Among the guests was Jules Clarétie, a leading drama critic and the director of one of the city's most distinguished theaters, the Comédie-Française, whom Loie now met for the first time. She expected an abundance of free advertising to result from these invitations, and she was not to be disappointed. As for Clarétie, he and his wife became intimate friends of Loie's, and years later he was still giving her valuable publicity.

Loie's printed invitation cards were decorated with crossed flags, French and American, symbolizing the Franco-American spirit of opening night. Her theater was filled with friends, old and new, at least half of them Americans. Among them were college boys vacationing in Paris, who made a patriotic display of U.S. flags.

"Then I turned Sada Yacco loose," Loie recounted a little later. "I never saw anything like the way those critics went wild with enthusiasm." On the whole, the critics did indeed react enthusiastically to both the first and the subsequent performances of the Japanese, especially Sada Yacco. Jules Clarétie glorified her, and so did Jean Lorrain. While dismissing the plot as childish, Lorrain raved about the acting—the strange poses, gestures, and facial expressions—which had a hallucinating effect on him, like an opium nightmare, he said. Throughout the summer and fall, as long as the exposition lasted, the "minuscule" Japanese woman kept on winning tributes from "the princes of literature, art, and the theater."

Among the experts there was, however, some difference of opinion about the effectiveness of Sada Yacco's death scene. "This Sada Yacco knows how to die—like Sarah herself," Lorrain said. One Paris journalist thought she did even better than Sarah Bernhardt. "Among us, it appears, actresses no longer know how to die." But an American commentator declared it nonsense to say that "Sarah Bernhardt herself never did better or even as well." In this critic's opinion Sada Yacco, though otherwise excellent, left something to be desired when it came to expiring. "Her death, with its queer winkings and shudderings and upheavals of breast and stomach, is the danse du ventre de la mort [the belly dance of death]."[40]

Rodin was fascinated by Sada Yacco, death scene and all. When asked what he considered the main attraction at the fair, he said he got the "liveliest impression" from the Far Eastern exhibits. "And then the exotic dances, above all at Loïe Fuller's, and with her this Sada Yacco, of lively and wonderfully perfected art." Rodin recommended the show to his friend Léon Maillard. "I must tell you that I have finally been able to see Sada Yacco and that I am most grateful to you for having called my attention to this marvelous dispenser of life," Maillard responded. "And that superb death! how well she shows that all creatures are of the same origin.!"[41]

Sarah Bernhardt did not think she had anything to learn from Sada Yacco, but the latter expressed some curiosity about the former. So Loie took her to see Bernhardt, who was playing in Paris in *The Eaglet*. "She watched the play in that imperturbable way of hers, and after it was over I asked her what she thought of it," Loie reported. "'Think European acting very much speak words; Japanese acting very much act things,' she said, and that was all I could get out of her."

The Loie Fuller Theater proved a popular as well as a critical success. Day after day the demand for seats exceeded the supply, and before long Loie was able to raise the admission price from one to five and even ten dollars (in francs). "It was all a personal triumph for the little Japanese woman," she confessed. "I gave ten-minute dances three times a day, but I just danced any old thing. I wasn't it." No matter how narcissistic the theater itself might seem, Loie was disarmingly modest about her own performance in it.

She fell far short of doing herself justice, to judge by the encomiums of some the critics and particularly Camille Mauclair, one of the most illustrious of all. First, Mauclair lauded Sada Yacco as a tragedian of the very highest quality, one who understood to perfection the basic principles of drama. He said she expressed the entire range of feelings that could be expected of an amorous and jealous courtesan, and she did it with an amazing ease of transition. Then he praised Loie as the "priestess of pure fire," more admirable now than ever. Sada Yacco's was a hard act to follow, and Loie, a great artist, proved herself still greater by daring to follow it. Wonderfully, the juxtaposition of two such extreme opposites—the Japanese realism and concreteness, the American idealism and abstractness—intensified the dramatic effect. By this fortunate coincidence, Mauclair said, the exposition was able to offer, as a bit of compensation for its inevitable boredom and banality, a rare lesson in the art of the drama.[42]

Besides performing under rather difficult conditions, Loie had to direct the entire show, under conditions even more difficult. She fired one manager and then another before finding a third with whom she could get along. "Then I thought I'd run a theatre in American fashion," she later revealed. "Do you suppose Paris is going to allow any foreign whipper-snapper to step in and show it tricks?" In particular, she wanted to hire boys as ushers, dress them in neat uniforms, pay them adequate wages, and have them give away programs. But it was the custom in French theaters for "little old women in rusty black" to do the ushering and to take tips, sell programs, "and never give back the change." Disgusted, Loie had to yield to tradition.

A Theater of Her Own

Loie's twofold duty as performer and director was strenuous. "The plump little woman, bustling, lively, drolly and naïvely dowdy, becomes the marvelous dream creature that you know, dancing to distraction," one of her admirers wrote. Then, "exhausted by fatigue—but imagine fatigued steel—she becomes between the scenes the active, intrepid director."[43]

While performing with the Japanese troupe, Loie celebrated her thousandth appearance on a Paris stage. Before the close of the exposition, she and the troupe received a special honor when they were invited to perform at the Palais de l'Elysée, the official residence of the president of the French republic. The occasion was a fête for the awarding of prizes for exposition exhibits.[44]

In sum, Loie enjoyed a double triumph at the exposition, her theater being memorable both as a prime expression of avant-garde art and as the scene of the most original and artistic entertainment. Incidentally, she also helped to advance the cause of women's rights. Women had been legally excluded from the stage in Japan, where male actors traditionally played female roles. The Japanese government finally opened the acting profession to women because of Sada Yacco's brilliant success in New York, London, and above all, Paris.[45]

Loie's instant stardom in Paris led A. Hamburg to compose the *Loïe Fuller Gavotte,* publicly sold sheet music with arrangements for either piano or orchestra. The dancer's approval of the music was evident in a Folies-Bergère program for Thursday, November 30, 1893, which featured Loie performing her "new dances" to this gavotte that evening, as well as during the "family" matinees that week. (Photograph courtesy of Bibliothèque Nationale de France, Music Collection)

To honor Loie and commemorate her 550th performance in Paris at a special fête on March 24, 1895, students of the Ecole des Beaux-Arts presented her with twenty-three of their watercolors. *La Loïe Fuller/Vivante Fleur* by J. Girard is one of the more unusual of those pieces, which ranged from *Salome* images to nudes dancing with flowing scarves (Loie never danced nude) to Notre Dame and the fountains, probably last-minute generic tributes. (Photograph courtesy of the Dance Collection, the New York Public Library for the Performing Arts)

𝒫ierre Roche (Fernand Massignon) produced the greatest number of Loie pieces of any of the more than seventy artists who depicted her. His critics have lambasted his "perpetual youthful image of the dancer": the oil painting at top, done in 1894, is quite similar to the gypsograph (painted bas relief) produced in 1904 for *La Loïe Fuller,* Roche's collaboration with Roger Marx. In 1900, however, Roche created pieces such as Loie as *Drama* and as *Comedy,* depicting the dancer as closer to her true age of forty. (Photograph at top courtesy of the Maryhill Museum of Art)

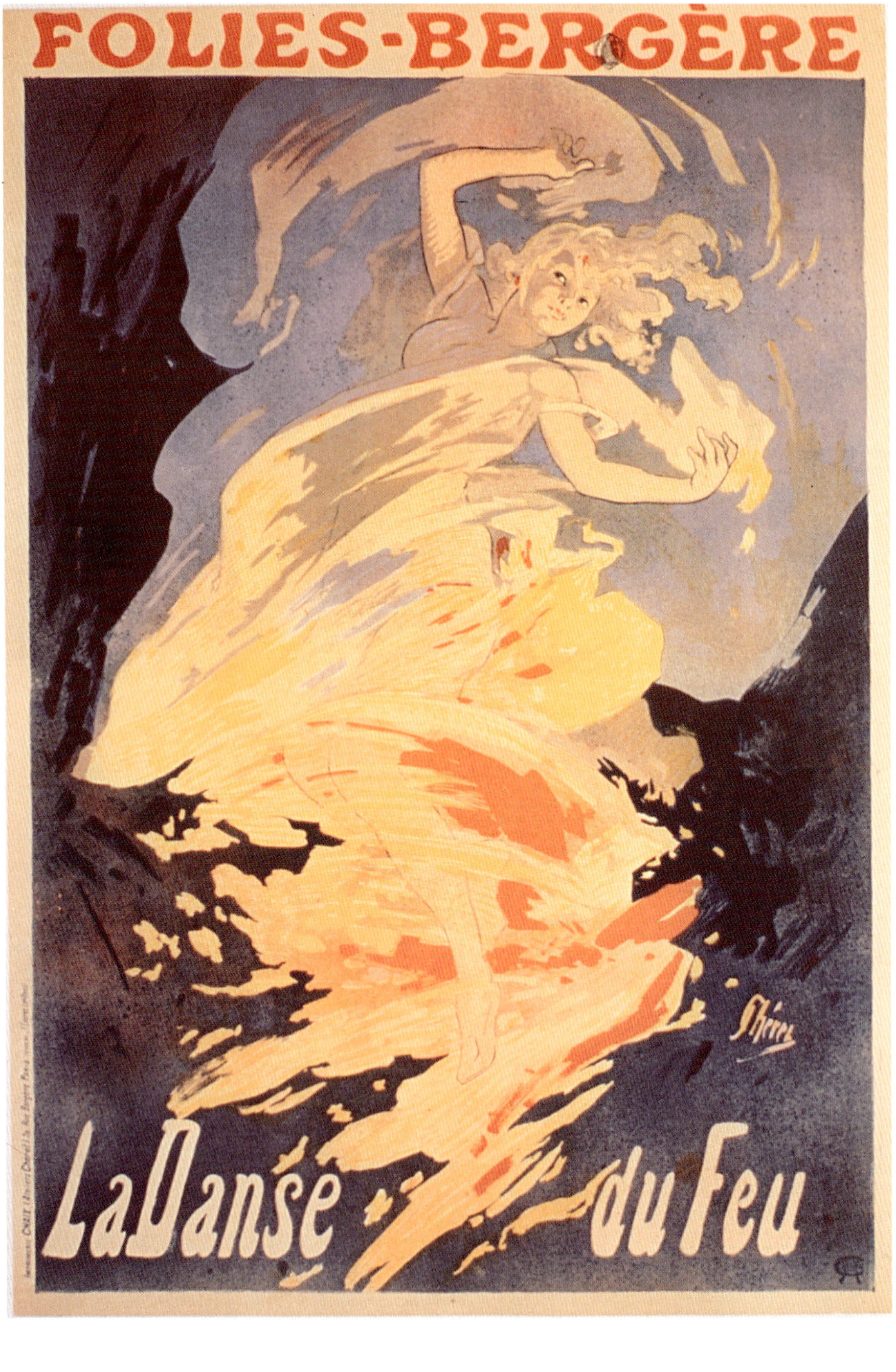
FOLIES-BERGÈRE
La Danse du Feu

The Fire Dance, in which Loie used billowing silk and spectacular colored lighting effects, was a favorite of both Parisian audiences and artists. Pierre Roche created a bronze sculpture of the dance about 1897. That same year a color lithographic poster, shown at left, was done by the father of French poster makers, Jules Chéret. One of his students, Georges Meunier, produced in 1898 what eventually would become the rarest of all Loie posters (top right). It is considered to be his rejection of Chéret's influence, with French critic Crauzet blasting its turbid shadows and heavy fabric when all in this dance is "luminous, transparent, and light." PAL's (Jean de Paléologu) image of Loie (below right) is more vivacious, and the viewer can almost feel the realistic licking flames. (Photographs courtesy of the Musée de la Publicité, UCAD)

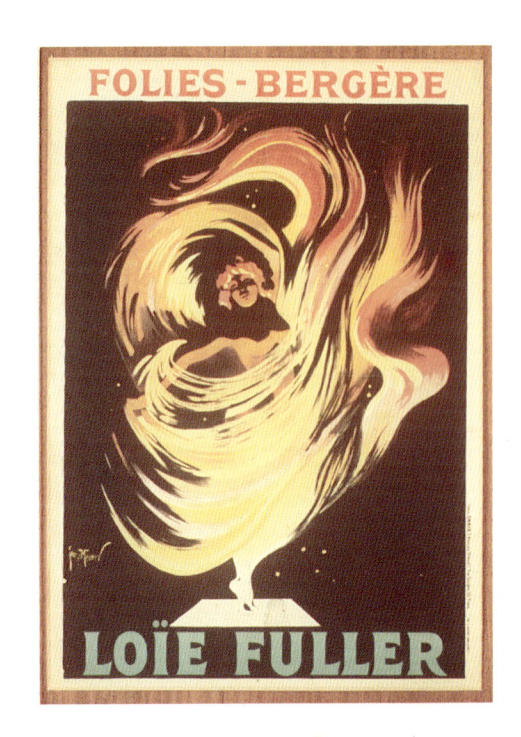

The work of François-Raoul Larche, a French sculptor who died in 1912, has been highly instrumental in perpetuating Loie Fuller's name and accomplishments among art aficionados. Each of these four gilt bronze table lamps offers a study in how the dancer so effectively used huge quantities of silk to create movement and also shapes that occur in nature. The lamps are highly prized because they provide the additional element *light* so revered by Loie. The two lamps in the center are apparently the rarer of the four because they are not commonly seen in U.S. museums or at auction. At bottom left, the

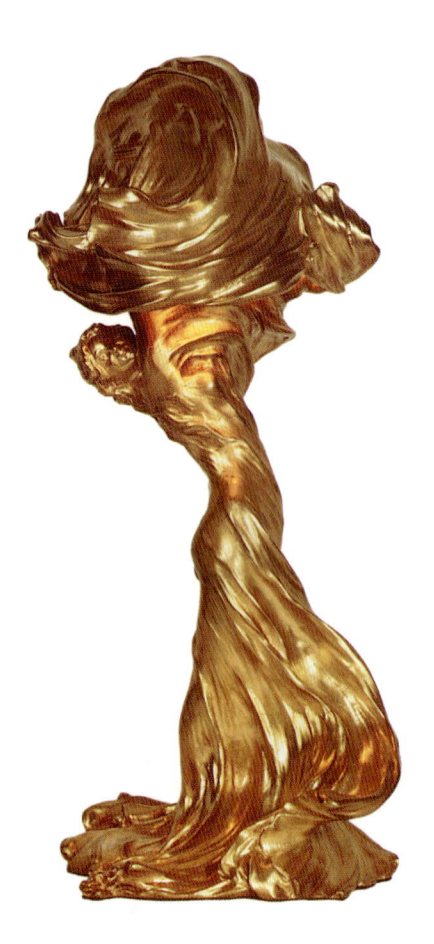

bronze both offers a beautiful view of the dancer's back and recreates the sinuous Art Nouveau line. The lamp most often reproduced in print and also exhibited is at lower right. This piece is featured in several important museum collections in the U.S. and Europe.
(Two center photographs courtesy of the Macklowe Gallery, Ltd.; photograph at lower right courtesy of Sotheby's, London)

The Romanian poster artist PAL (Jean de Paléologu) was one of the most prolific of the Loie artists, as he created at least nine other Loie color lithographic images in addition to his *Fire Dance*. These two posters, both made about 1897, are especially adept at portraying the exuberance and grace of Loie's dance. Like most other of her posters, they show her performing against the dark background which in real performances was usually black velvet. (Photograph at top courtesy of the Musée de la Publicité, UCAD)

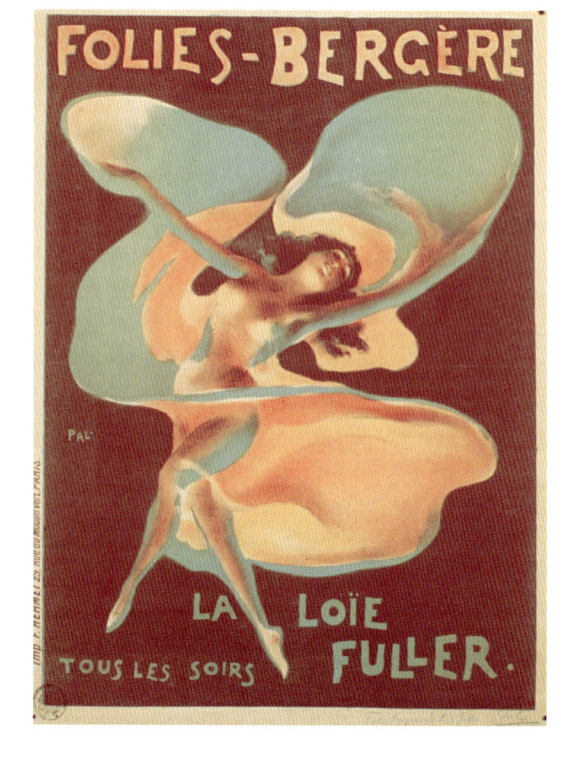

Henri de Toulouse-Lautrec's artistic renderings of Loie were created from afar; he and the dancer did not enjoy a relationship such as Loie had with several other artists. Lautrec took his observations of Loie's performances at the Folies and turned them into a series of fifty lithographs, all with the same black line image. Using subtle and vivid watercolors, sprinkled with gold, silver, or bronze powder, he recalled the special lighting effects so much a part of Loie's presentation. These two pieces from that series are representative of the dramatic results that can come from relatively simple techniques. (Photographs courtesy of Bibliothèque d'Art et d'Archéologie, Fondation Jacques Doucet)

$\mathcal{L}$ittle is known about the sculptor of this untitled, though obviously Loie, bronze figure except that it was produced about 1903 by Clara Pfeffer, an American artist. This is probably a one-of-a-kind piece, unlike many of the objects produced by Carabin, Larche, and other Loie artists. As part of a private collection, it must be enjoyed by the public only in photographs. In the fall of 1995, art lovers were treated to a highly unusual display when the Museum Villa Stuck, Munich, used this piece to recreate the mirror effect that Loie used with some of her dances, thereby multiplying Pfeffer's lovely bronze image into countless Loies. (Photograph courtesy of the Macklowe Gallery, Ltd.)

This bronze by the Düsseldorf native Hans Stoltenberg-Lerche is the only known vase to have been made of Loie. Inspired largely by oriental art, as were many of the Art Nouveau artists, and a student of Eugène Carrière, a lithographer and painter influenced by the Symbolists, Stoltenberg-Lerche expanded beyond media on paper and canvas into stone, glass, precious metals, and bronze. Later in life, he retired to Italy where he did another famous bronze, Pope Leo III.

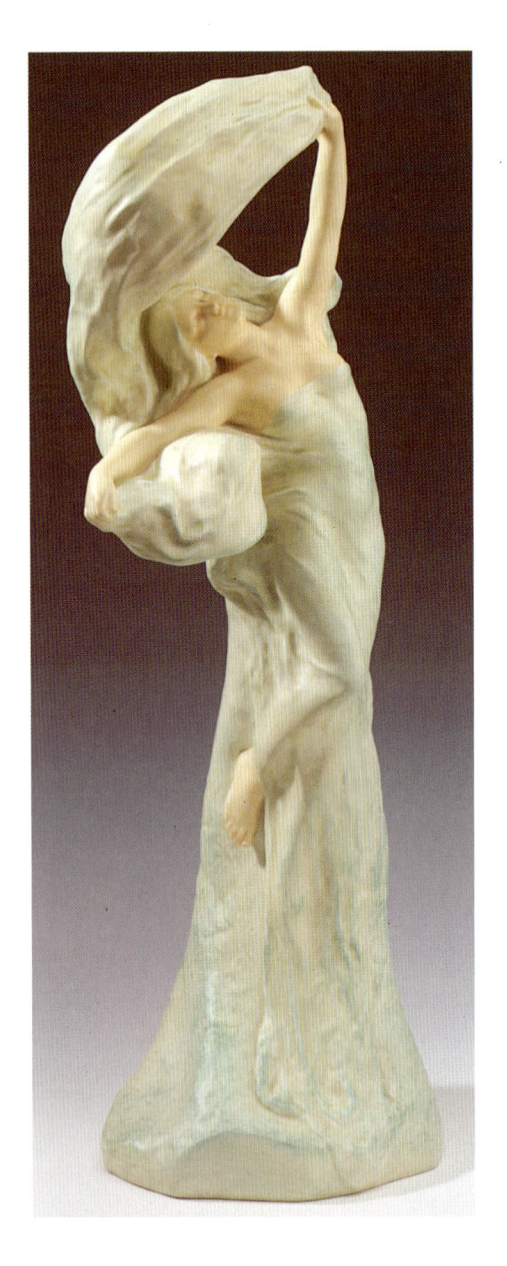

This delicately detailed porcelain lamp, date unknown, by the Austrian Paul Teresziuk (Tereszizck) was produced by A. Forster and Co. in Vienna. It is a testimony both to Loie's popularity throughout Europe and to the desire of the artist to capture the dancer's performance forever. Teresziuk also created a bronze of Loie about 1897 which does not resemble the lamp physically, but like it conveys with its magnificent form much of the beauty Loie brought to the stage. (Photograph courtesy of Historical Design Collection)

$\mathcal{A}$s was Toulouse-Lautrec, the two artists Clément Massier and Lucien Lévy-Dhurmer were very successful about 1895 in recreating the performing Loie. This untitled stoneware piece, a charger, effectively uses its iridescent glaze and undulating lines to convey an impression that the dancing

figure is actually moving. Another unique feature of the charger is the artists' use of gold emblems, seals, or crests so evident in Japanese art and culture. Of all the known Loie artwork, only one other piece, the next color plate by the poster artist Orazi, contains these symbols. (Photograph courtesy of Historical Design Collection)

$\mathcal{M}$anuel Orazi, an Italian who worked in France, was selected by Loie to create what was probably the most important poster of her career—*Théâtre de Loie Fuller, Exposition Universelle*. Advertising her performances at the Exhibition of 1900 in Paris, the color lithograph was printed in three editions in three different color schemes. At left is pictured the piece with full ad, and at right the same image with only the words "Loie Fuller." The posters' gold emblems or seals, which indicate the influence of Japanese culture, were especially appropriate when one recalls that Sada Yacco and her oriental troupe were introduced at this exposition and became a major attraction at Loie's theater. (Photograph courtesy of the Musée de la Publicité, UCAD)

One of the last posters done during Loie's lifetime was by Paul Colin, perhaps the most famous of French Art Deco poster artists. The image *Champs Elysées Music Hall, Les Féeries Fantastiques de la Loïe Fuller* (1925) is a marked departure in two respects from the Art Nouveau posters of Manuel Orazi, Jules Chéret, PAL, and other *fin-de-siècle* artists. The obvious difference is that Nouveau is "out," Deco "in," the sinuous female figure replaced by the controlled geometric design. Not apparent in Colin's finished product is that he designed this poster without having ever met Loie and probably without having seen her perform on stage. This is a distinct contrast to Loie posters created during the Nouveau period of her career, which she usually commissioned from the artists she knew well, with the light, movement, and color of the posters echoing her on-stage performance. (Photograph courtesy of the Bibliothèque Nationale de France, Poster Collection)

Loie's influence on fine jewelry making at the turn of the century is much more difficult to measure than her contributions to painting, sculpture, glass making, and color lithography. Today there exists no publicly displayed, monumental piece of jewelry titled "Loie Fuller." In the *untitled* but *inspired-by-Loie* jewelry category, three pieces merit mention. The first, pictured here, is a finely wrought vermeil and green plique-à-jour necklace that features a large and two small dancers with veils swirling above their heads. This item exhibits the three Loie trademarks of motion, color, and light to a greater degree than the other two pieces. There is mention in reference works of an untitled bracelet of linked dancers, ca. 1900, by the French artist Henri Téterger, but its location is unknown. Also, an anonymous artist produced an untitled gold brooch with precious stones that is a nude with butterfly wings; in a private collection, this piece is considered to be so sufficiently inspired by Loie that it was included in a major public exhibit of Loie Fuller art. (Photograph courtesy of Historical Design Collection)

7

Sada, Isadora, Marie, the Curies, Rodin

She would lose money on Sada Yacco, feel betrayed by Isadora Duncan, and, much to her regret, have a falling-out with Rodin. But she would gain new and important friends in the Curies and discover a veritable idol in Princess Marie of Romania. All this would happen during the three years following the Universal Exposition of 1900, while Loie would manage to maintain and even enhance her reputation as an incomparable dancer and an admirable human being.

"Take my advice. Don't try to build and run a theatre at the next World's Fair. I'm a wreck." So Loie said to a reporter on her arrival at New York in January 1901. "I'm going to Japan to rest from French architects and managers and ushers. Sada Yacco was eager to have me dance in Japan."

Sada Yacco, Kawakami, and their company, who had done so well for Loie at the exposition, seemed to her worth taking on a year-long tour. She thought that, after visiting Japan with them, she would introduce them to Germany, Russia, and other countries on the Continent. But her European plans were uncertain, and because of her mother's recent relapse she kept postponing the Japan trip.

While waiting, Loie was, "twice a day, amusing a large and tumultuous group of spectators" at Koster & Bial's Music Hall in New York. "So artistic and lovely is Miss Fuller's mirror and fire dances that it seems a pity that the management should deem it necessary to have well-dressed persons before the footlights to call out 'Great! I saw her in Paris!' and to rise to their feet and shout uproariously," one of the spectators reported. "Miss Fuller's performance is given in a darkened house, and a conspicuous feature of the entertainment is the lighting of matches by belated comers in order to find the seats assigned to them."[1]

By the time her mother was well enough to travel, Loie had received from England an offer so attractive that she put off indefinitely her departure for Japan. (Her Japan trip, like her earlier China trip, was never to materialize.) She and her Japanese company performed in London during the summer of 1901, in Paris during the autumn of that year, and in various other European cities during the winter of 1901–2.

Sada Yacco and Kawakami had enlarged their repertoire to include several mimed playlets in addition to *The Geisha and the Knight*. Among these, *The Shogun: A Tale of Old Japan*, dealt with fourteenth-century struggles for power. *Saikoku* was a Japanese version of the trial scene from *The Merchant of Venice*. In *Zingoro* a sculptor, the Japanese Pygmalion, falls in love with a statue he has made, and a disgraced warrior commits hara-kiri in *Kesa*.

An evening's show usually consisted of two of these playlets with Loie's performance sandwiched between them. While Sada was everywhere acclaimed, Loie received an equal if not a greater share of praise from the critics. One of them in London thought Sada a "singularly restrained and charming actress," though she and her fellow players relied too much on a "disconcerting employment of quaint gesture, naïve pantomime, grotesque realism." Another London critic said Loie's performance was "delightful to the eye, the combination of light, color, pose, and movement being exceedingly ingenious and extremely picturesque. Nothing could be better in its way."

As always, Loie kept freshening her act with new variations. For example, she elaborated on her fire dance to recreate the melodramatic scene from the play *She* in which the young and pretty Ayesha twice goes into the flames and emerges the second time as an ancient hag. Loie also introduced "two new bits of picturesque posing, in one of which she makes use of a moving background, open to view, and, therefore, unlike the gloom amid which she usually disports herself."[2]

When a Paris reporter wanted to interview Sada and Kawakami, Loie obligingly served as interpreter, translating their broken English into her broken French. Laughingly, she then related some of the difficulties she had run into as impresario of the troupe. Several Paris hotels had refused to accept the Japanese as guests, being fearful of these strange people with their exotic garb and their huge trunks of woven straw. Finally, one hotel agreed to accommodate them, much to Loie's relief, but the next morning she found the whole group assembled in her yard, waving their arms and shouting: "Hotel! Never again!" She had to turn her house over to them and find somewhere else to stay for the time being.[3]

If the Japanese performers sometimes struck the French as strange, the French and other Westerners, including Loie, seemed equally peculiar to Kawakami and his five-year-old son. The boy once showed Loie some drawings he had made of people with eyes popping out of their heads like billiard balls. This was "an odd way to draw eyes," she suggested to the boy's father. "Yes," Kawakami replied, "but it is because the European eye is quite like the eye of a fish." She then asked him just what did Europeans look like to the Japanese. "All Europeans," he said, shifting his zoological comparison, "resemble pigs."

As the impresario, Loie incurred heavy expenses not only in paying salaries but also in providing food, lodging, and transportation for the troupe of thirty people. "These thirty cost me more than ninety of another nationality would have done," she ruefully recalled. For them, she had to attach to each train "an enormous car laden with Japanese delicacies, rice, salted fish, mushrooms, and preserved turnips." Most of the time her revenues barely equaled her expenditures, and they fell far short when a theater manager in Vienna broke his contract with her. The tour as a whole proved to be another of her money-losing enterprises.[4]

Costly though this European tour was, it had momentous consequences for Loie. It involved her with two women who were to figure significantly in her public career and her personal life, one of them as a rival if not an outright enemy, the other as an idol if not an actual goddess. These two were Isadora Duncan and Princess Marie of Romania.

After crossing the Atlantic with her mother, sister, and brother in a cattle boat, the California-born and -bred Isadora Duncan, a twenty-two-year-old aspiring dancer, had arrived in Paris in time for the Universal Exposition of 1900. There she attended Loie's theater night after night to watch Sada Yacco and be "thrilled by the wondrous art of this great tragedian." She also explored Rodin's pavilion and "stood in awe" of his wonderful works.

Haunted by "the sense of Rodin's genius," Duncan eventually made her way to his studio, where he demonstrated his genius by quickly molding a lump of clay into a woman's breast. Then, after inviting him to her studio, she demonstrated her genius by changing into her filmy white Grecian tunic and dancing for him. As soon as she stopped, he moved on her. "He ran his hands over my neck, breast, stroked my arms, and ran his hands over my hips, my bare legs and feet. He began to knead my whole body as if it were clay, while from him emanated heat that scorched and melted me. My whole desire was to yield to him my entire being and, indeed, I would have done so if it had not been that my absurd up-bringing caused me to become frightened and I withdrew, threw my dress over my tunic and sent him away bewildered. What a pity!"[5]

Later Duncan danced for Loie. The "Western Nightingale," Emma Nevada (Emma Wixom), Duncan's fellow Californian and Loie's close friend, was singing in Paris. One night Loie went with Nevada to Duncan's studio to meet Duncan and watch her perform. "She danced with remarkable grace, her body barely covered by the flimsiest of Greek costumes, and she bade fair to become somebody," Loie thought. "In her I saw the ancient tragic dances revived. I saw the Egyptian, Greek and Hindoo rhythms recalled."[6]

Indeed, Loie was so deeply impressed that she then and there invited Duncan to join her traveling company. The company was leaving Paris the very next day, but Duncan could catch up with it in Berlin. She readily accepted Loie's invitation, glad for an opportunity to perform under the auspices of such a well-known star and to appear on the same stage with the wondrous Sada Yacco.

On arriving in Berlin, Duncan was startled to find Loie "surrounded by her entourage" in a sumptuous hotel suite. "A dozen or so beautiful girls were crowded about her, alternately stroking her hands and kissing her." As the company traveled from Berlin to Leipzig and Munich, Duncan took particular notice of Gabrielle Bloch:

> In the midst of these nereids, nymphs, iridescent apparitions, there was a strange figure in a black tailor-made. She was shy, reticent, with a finely moulded yet strong face, black hair brushed straight back from her forehead, with sad, intelligent eyes. She invariably held her hands in the pockets of her suit. She was interested in art, and, especially, spoke eloquently of the art of Loie Fuller. She circulated around the bevy of brightly colored butterflies like some scarab of ancient Egypt. I was at once attracted by this personality but felt that her enthusiasm for Loie Fuller possessed her entire emotional force, and she had nothing left for me.

Sada, Isadora, Marie, the Curies, Rodin

One night Duncan was awakened by a red-haired girl kissing her passionately and, another night, was awakened by the same girl threatening to strangle her.

For Loie, so far as her performances on the stage were concerned, Duncan had nothing but praise, being "dazzled and carried away by this marvellous artist." "What an extraordinary genius!" "That wonderful creature—she became fluid; she became light; she became every colour and flame, and finally she resolved into miraculous spirals of flames wafted toward the Infinite." Despite her admiration for Loie's art, Duncan began to ask herself what she was "doing in this troupe of beautiful but demented ladies."[7]

Loie reciprocated Duncan's attitude, finding Duncan much more attractive as an artist than as a person. She expected her to be a grateful protégée. To launch her, Loie hosted an afternoon party at her hotel in Vienna, to which she invited artists and art critics, theater managers, the British and American ambassadors and their wives, and the princess of Metternich. When the time came for Duncan to perform she was not ready, and Loie "begged her to hurry, explaining that she ran the risk through her negligence of offending the audience that would definitely give her a start." But Duncan persisted with her leisurely preparations. Loie later recalled:

> All at once she made her entrance, calm and collected, looking as if she did not care in the least what our guests thought of her.
>
> But it was not her air of indifference that surprised me most. I could hardly refrain from rubbing my eyes. She appeared to me nude, or very nearly so, to so slight an extent did the gauze which she wore cover her form.
>
> She came to the front, and while the orchestra played a prelude from Chopin she stood motionless, her eyes lowered, her arms hanging by her side. Then she began to dance.
>
> Oh, that dance, how I loved it! To me it was the most beautiful thing in the world. I forgot the woman and all her faults, her absurd affectations, her costume, and even her bare legs.

As a result of Loie's efforts, Duncan secured an engagement to perform in Vienna.

In Budapest, when Loie put on another entertainment to introduce her protégée, she found at least one theater manager interested in engaging her. But Duncan and her mother, who was now with her, abruptly left Budapest and returned to Vienna for Duncan's performance there. Hearing that they did not intend to come back, Loie telegraphed to ask if Duncan was planning to rejoin the troupe. She replied by wire: "Only in case you will deposit to my credit ten thousand francs in a Viennese bank before nine o'clock tomorrow morning." Now that she was well started, Duncan no longer had any use for Loie, or so it seemed to her.

So far as Loie was concerned, Bucharest more than made up for Vienna, Budapest, and all the exasperations of the tour. On the evening of her first appearance in Bucharest, the prince and princess of Romania were in the theater's royal box. After the performance she received a message from Princess Marie congratulating her and asking her to give a matinee so their children could see her dance. The next day she sent Marie a note to thank her and to say she would be glad to perform at the palace. Back came a "charming letter" in which Marie accepted the proposal and invited Loie for a visit.

At the palace an official conducted Loie up a grand staircase and into a "most delightfully arranged room," where a "young woman, tall, slender, and extremely pretty," came forward, smiling, and extended her hand. Loie was enraptured. "I actually forgot where I was, and I fancied myself in the presence of a legendary princess in a fairy-tale chamber."[8]

Marie was more than "extremely pretty": she was beautiful. Twenty-six years old, the granddaughter of Queen Victoria of Great Britain on one side and Czar Alexander III of Russia on the other, she had been born and brought up in England and was thoroughly English at heart. Her husband, Prince Ferdinand, was German, a member of the imperial Hohenzollern family, by whom she already had four children (and was to have two more). Though a dutiful wife, she was not always a happy one; "there were times during these early years," she remembered, "when I absolutely wallowed in my misery." Ferdinand displayed a "painful anxiety to prevent any friendship" between her and others at the court. "This made life exceedingly lonely and was one of the reasons why I took a long time in becoming a really good Roumanian." Gifted with artistic and literary talent, she found solace in painting, decorating, and writing.[9]

After shaking hands with her, Loie realized that Marie was by no means a remote creature from a dream world—or even quite a stranger—but a person with whom she could talk as with a longtime friend. Marie proceeded to show her around the palatial apartment. Here, among other things to see, was a large photograph of the princess in a Romanian folk costume. "It seemed that the picture was tinged with sadness," Loie recalled, "and I wondered whether the princess would not someday regret her enforced exile." And here was a "large portfolio in which she had painted some flowers. One of these pictures represented some Chinese plants drooping in a melancholy fashion." Marie explained: "I painted them one day when I was feeling very blue."

That evening a stage was improvised in the palace dining hall, and Loie's two electricians were on hand to man the lights. She had expected to perform for Marie alone, since they had agreed that the children would not be present, but awaiting the performance was a large crowd consisting of the king, the queen, and all their retinue. To the music of the court pianist and also that of an orchestra conducted by her own director, Loie "must have danced at least twenty times," responding to the enthusiastic and persistent applause. Afterward the king, the queen, the princess, and many others congratulated her "in a most charming way."

When the time came for Loie to depart for Rome, she found herself embarrassingly short of Romanian money. The only person she knew well enough to turn to was Marie, who received her in her boudoir at nine o'clock in the morning. "She was in her night-robe, and had put on a dressing-gown of white silk over which her beautiful dishevelled hair hung," Loie recalled. When she explained her predicament, Marie rang a bell and gave an order that would lead to the cashing of Loie's check. The two women sat and chatted awhile, and when Loie got up to leave, Marie kissed her.

Loie took away from Bucharest a memory and a memento that she was to treasure for the rest of her life. She held a photograph of the princess on which were written these words: "One of your most ardent admirers. In souvenir of a delicious evening with which you rejoiced all my love of Art! Marie, Princess of Roumania, Princess of Great Britain & Ireland, 1902." On the back of the picture Loie had written in words a bit jumbled by emotion: "My mind's eye looked so hard that tears came into my soul, tears of gladness and of joy to be remembered ever. In remembrance of an artist soul I met in the world's wilderness and saw in the sunshine of truth. Loïe Fuller, March 24, 1902, Bucarest, Roumania."[10]

"*Radium*—very interesting," Loie mused after spending a morning with the Curies at their Paris home. Pierre and Marie Curie, husband and wife, were already well known as the discoverers of radium, were continuing to investigate its properties, and were soon to receive the Nobel Prize in physics for their work.[11]

Their work had attracted Loie's attention when she read in a newspaper that radium was luminous. Why not apply it to one of her dresses and create a sensational radium dance? To find out more about the new and strange element, she wrote to the Curies, who let her know that the substance was much too dangerous for what she had in mind. Loie was pleased and flattered that they had even bothered to reply. To show her gratitude, she offered to put on a special performance for them—at their home.

> Pierre and Marie accepted. An odd, badly dressed girl, with a Kalmuck face innocent of make-up, her eyes as blue as a baby's, came to the door, followed by a troop of electricians laden with material. A little worried, the couple left the room to the invaders and went off to the laboratory. And Loie labored for hours, tried different combinations of light, and arranged the curtains and rugs she had ordered to reconstruct her enchanting spectacle in the narrow dining room of the two professors.
> The severe little house with the well-guarded gate thus welcomed a goddess from the music halls.

Sada, Isadora, Marie, the Curies, Rodin

That, at any rate, is the way the Curies' daughter Eve remembered the event three decades later.

After Loie's performance at the Curies', she and they soon were visiting back and forth, and she could add them to her already impressive list of famous friends. With her penchant for introducing celebrities, she was glad to comply when the Curies asked her to introduce them to the notability whose friendship she valued the most—Rodin.[12]

Loie had continued to cultivate him, and when she appeared in Paris with her Japanese players in the fall of 1901, she invited him to attend on opening night and, along with him, three of his distinguished associates. These were Eugène Carrière, a painter and lithographer who made several portraits of Rodin; Eugène Druet, the photographer who worked with him and who took numerous pictures of Loie; and Octave Mirbeau, a journalist, novelist, and dramatist of whom Rodin made a bust. Now on good terms with Loie once more, Rodin's interpreter and adorer Emilia Cimino urged him to arrive early for Loie's (not Sada Yacco's) performance, which was to begin at eleven o'clock. "Her tableaux last so short a time that if you are a few minutes late you will miss her completely." And Rodin's presence there, she thought, "will be a great glory for her."[13]

Loie also continued to make Rodin acquainted with visitors from the United States, whose presence must have been a nuisance for him at times. After she arranged for her house guest Alice Weston to go with Delilah to see his atelier on an October day in 1901, Alice asked him to change the agreed-upon date, and he obligingly did so.[14]

In addition to his atelier at 182 rue de l'Université, Rodin possessed a workshop in the village of Meudon, a few miles south of Paris. Here, on a hilltop with a splendid view of the Seine, stood the rather modest and sparsely furnished villa that he owned and, with Rose Beuret, had occupied for several years. The house had as yet no electricity or plumbing but did have a studio that the previous owner, a painter, had added. In 1901 Rodin bought an adjoining plot and arranged for his Universal Exposition pavilion to be reerected there. Now, for the first time, he enjoyed ample space and, for the first time, began to welcome guests.[15]

One of his more frequent guests was Loie, who felt like leaping for joy whenever she approached his place. At the gate she would meet a dog that came running to give her "a most joyous welcome," and then Rodin, who would follow more slowly but with just as hospitable a greeting.

> In his rather unwieldy body and his features, which are trifle heavy, great kindness and sweetness of disposition are evident....
>
> He receives you by extending both hands, very simply and with a friendly smile. Sometimes a movement of the eyes and some words to which you pay no great attention may hint that the moment has perhaps not been well chosen for a visit, but his instinctive good nature gets the upper hand. He places himself by your side and shows you the path that leads to the top of the hill.

On a Sunday afternoon in April 1902, after returning to Paris from Bucharest, Loie took a carriage ride to Meudon with her friends Pierre and Marie Curie—he "brown, tall, and thin," she "slight and blonde"—to call on Rodin. "When I introduced them not a word passed," Loie afterward related. "They grasped each others' hands, and looked at each other." Silently, Rodin led the visitors through the three studios of his newly reconstructed pavilion, his "temple of art," where he proudly displayed his sculptures, "fondling the marble" of one of his favorites. "We left. In the carriage that took us back I asked my friends if they could describe their impressions, their sensations. They replied in the negative. Yet on their faces there were evidences of great happiness, and I knew they had appreciated and understood Rodin."[16]

Though the kindly advice of the Curies had deterred Loie from using radium, it had not discouraged her from trying to get a similar effect with other chemicals. She built a little laboratory behind the house at 24 rue Cortambert, obtained the help of several people, including a chemist, and experimented with ways of producing phosphorescent salts and applying them to cloth. One of the experiments resulted in an explosion. "When we came to our senses we found that none of us were hurt but everybody had

Sada, Isadora, Marie, the Curies, Rodin

lost his eyelashes & his eyebrows and all of our clothing was damaged, and the phosphorescent dress had disappeared in smoke."[17]

Had she known it was going to result in the loss of Rodin's friendship, Loie surely would not have done what she did. All along, she had the best of intentions. She wanted to introduce the master's work to the American public and at the same time show off some representations of herself in art. On her next American tour she would take along her own collection, which contained a few Rodin pieces, and she would borrow additional ones from him. Before embarking at Cherbourg with a big entourage that included Gabrielle Bloch, she sent him a note to say her agent H. Hamburg would call on him to arrange for the later shipment of the "collection 'Rodin.'" Rodin probably thought she had a one-man show in mind.

Loie's venture got off to a rather inauspicious start. She was scheduled to begin her tour at Hyde & Behman's Music Hall in Brooklyn on the afternoon of February 2, 1903. But her ship, the *Saint Paul,* due two days earlier, did not dock until that very morning. So her matinee was canceled and her evening appearance hastily arranged, with only one trap in the stage floor and time to put up only four lights. "Despite all these drawbacks, Miss Fuller pluckily agreed to go on." And she did fairly well, especially with the last of her four numbers, when she performed on a pedestal five feet high and appeared to be suspended in midair, thus "producing a weird and sensational effect."[18]

While continuing her performances, Loie looked forward to presenting her art exhibition, which was to be held at the National Arts Club on Thirty-fourth Street in New York. The club, with more than a thousand members, including some of the most prominent artistic and literary Americans, enjoyed a reputation for sponsoring and displaying the "highest and best in all the arts."

Though ideal for Loie's purposes, the National Arts Club kept delaying to set a date for her exhibition to begin. On March 17, a month and a half after her arrival in the United States, she cabled H. Hamburg, her Paris agent, that the date would be April 27 and that Rodin's works should therefore be sent by April 10. In reply, she received a letter from Rodin himself saying that, after thinking the matter over, he did not wish to send the works at all. To Loie's relief, he soon changed his mind again, and when the exhibition was postponed until May 6, she had more than enough time to get ready for it.

Part of this time she spent visiting an old friend, the *New York World* reporter Nellie Bly. Bly's real name was Elizabeth Jane Cochran; her pen name was bestowed on her by an editor who got his inspiration from the Stephen Foster song. By dint of boldness, ingenuity, and hard work, Bly had made her way upward in the man's world of journalism. She and Loie had much in common and, no doubt, much to talk about.[19]

Loie also ran into an acquaintance whom she was less fortunate to see—Emilia Cimino, who happened to be in New York on business of her own. Cimino was about to turn into an enemy, stirring up trouble between Loie and Rodin, to whom she sent frequent reports.

At first, Cimino had quite favorable things to tell Rodin about Loie: "She is a very able businesswoman." "I'm glad to see that Loie is in an artistic relationship with such an honest and perfect artist [i.e., Rodin]." But Cimino changed her tune after she invited Loie to a gallery exhibiting her own paintings and Loie did not bother to respond or attend. Loie's indifference, Cimino felt, showed that the woman was "hostile to true art," an attitude that might cause her to lose a "valuable ally." Cimino was further antagonized when she beheld Loie's National Arts Club exhibition, which ran from May 6 to 16, 1903.[20]

Some of Rodin's major works in plaster, bronze, and marble were on display. Equally conspicuous, however, were representations of Loie, most of which she had exhibited at her Universal Exposition theater in 1900. There were life-size portraits, marble statues, bronze statuettes, glass pieces, pottery, an ivory figure, a fan, a case of medals, and whatnot—all of them depicting the serpentine dancer in one way or another. They were by such artists as Roche, Rivière, Massier, Gallé, Constant, Gérôme, Rochegrasse, Lerolle, Kromberg, and Nocq, who thus shared honors with Rodin. Loie herself, according to one newspaper report, was a "glorious object of art" as she "glided and floated in diaphanous drapery" while dancing among the other art objects at the exhibition.

Sada, Isadora, Marie, the Curies, Rodin

This was "an exhibition of statuary and paintings belonging to Miss Loie Fuller," according to the printed invitation cards that were sent out. The *New York Times* reported that the National Arts Club had "taken advantage of the visit of Miss Loie Fuller to New York in order to exhibit her collection of sculptures by Rodin and others." These others were interesting enough, according to the *Times*. "It is the exhibition of Rodin sculptures, however, that makes Miss Fuller's collection particularly interesting, for on the one hand, never before have so many been shown here at the same time, and on the other Rodin himself is the sculptor most discussed, most condemned, most admired, and most copied at the present day." Some papers gave the Loie representations as much attention as the Rodin works, and one paper praised the former at some length but did not even mention the latter.[21]

Cimino promptly sent Rodin some clippings of such articles, one of the invitation cards, and a letter elaborating on Loie's misdeeds. When Cimino volunteered a lecture on Rodin's art at Loie's exhibition, Loie refused to let her send out invitations. Worse than that:

> People find it hard to understand how she acquired such an extensive Rodin collection. She likes to give the impression that you are older than you are and that, because of a senile passion, you are working day and night for her. According to her, the plaster figures are some of the works that you are busily making for her in marble. But she does not press you, "poor old dear," because she realizes that you can only carry out your projects slowly. . . .
>
> [P.S.] Don't show this to Loie when you see her, but try to remember that she is the enemy of art—that she is a hard and greedy woman who knows only her own interests.

Indirectly, Loie heard about Cimino's displeasure, and she and Gab attributed it to jealousy, believing that Cimino was put out because her paintings had not been included in Loie's exhibition. Loie wrote her several letters in the hope of convincing her that, from first to last, she had been devoted to Rodin's interests and had served them at *"enormous sacrifices"* to herself. While aware of Cimino's discontent, Loie had no inkling of its depth or of the venom with which it was being communicated to Rodin, whose amour propre was all too easy to offend.[22]

After Cimino had left for France, Loie arranged to lend a number of Rodin's and others' works to the Metropolitan Museum of Art. She asked Rodin for his permission, telling him that the Metropolitan, the "national museum here," had offered to exhibit his bronzes and marbles for a year. Should she accept? "Don't accept," he immediately replied by wire. "Return everything at once."[23]

Instead of returning everything, Loie held back five of the choicest items: a marble of *The Tempest* and bronzes of *The Thinker, Head of Balzac*, and *Head of Saint John the Baptist on a Platter* by Rodin and a bronze of the *Bust of Rodin* by Camille Claudel. These were priced at a total of 24,000 francs (about $4,683), which she proposed to pay in a few installments. (She made the first payment with a New York bank loan, pledging the pieces themselves as security.) The pieces, she assured Rodin, would be put in the museum, where they would be kept in a separate glass case, would be marked with Rodin's name, and would not be identified as belonging to Loie—though one of the tags prepared for the exhibit read "'The Thinker' by Rodin. Loaned by Miss Loie Fuller. June 26th, 1903."

Loie thought Rodin was making a serious mistake in recalling the rest of his pieces, one of which was a small plaster model of the *Tower of Labor*. This he had finished when he was appointed to design and supervise the construction of a great monument to the glory of work, to be erected for the 1900 Universal Exposition. The cost having proved prohibitive, the maquette was all that remained of the project. Loie, who dreamed of carrying it out, now wrote to Rodin, struggling to express herself in French:

> I am sorry you did not leave your plasters here, because I think that, with the influential friends I have here, I would eventually have been able to arrange for [the construction of] the Tower of Labor. Pierrepont [sic] Morgan has just returned, and I would like to see him about it. But I can't even show him the model, since I have sent it back to you. I am quite miserable, my heart broken. All my efforts for nothing!

Sada, Isadora, Marie, the Curies, Rodin

All your *true* friends will tell you, I believe, that it is unfortunate the plasters were returned. . . .

(Pour ecrire en francaise est si difficile pour moi.) Excuse mes errors a bien tot. Your devoted friend [in English] Loïe.[24]

After the close of her National Arts Club exhibition, Loie had resumed her stage performances. The Saint Nicholas Garden engaged her "at one of the biggest salaries ever promised a vaudeville performer in America"— "$1,500 a week for two weeks"—to present four "all new" numbers, one of which was a phosphorescent dance. She continued through July to perform at one theater or another as "one of the important summer attractions in New York. Her dances seem still to have the power to attract the public." She "carries with her a remarkable retinue, including a maid, a companion and a private secretary." She "is said to be worth nearly $200,000" (a fortune for that time). In fact, Loie was, as usual, short of funds, and a landlord was having difficulty collecting five dollars from her for one month's rental of a basement on West Twenty-sixth Street, where presumably she had stored some of her artworks or theatrical properties.[25]

In August, after returning to Paris, Loie sent Rodin a check and a promissory note in partial payment for the works of his that she was leaving at the Metropolitan Museum of Art. For the time being, she assumed that she was still on good terms with him, and she continued to send American acquaintances to visit his atelier. But she gradually came to realize that he was displeased with her and was steadily becoming more so.

Rodin was still hearing bad things about her from Cimino, who took it upon herself to act as a peacemaking—in reality a troublemaking—intermediary between the two. She told him, among other things, that Gab was going to mortgage some property of hers to raise money for the purchase of additional Rodins, which Loie would ship to the Metropolitan. After these had been on exhibit there for a year, she would sell them at a handsome profit, having thus evaded the 60 percent customs duty on artworks. "I think you have nothing to gain from all this," Cimino advised Rodin. "Keep this letter to yourself, but please be on your guard, and remember that Mme Roger Marx is a Jewess and a cousin of Gabi and that Marx also is of that persuasion. Gabi is quite the big businesswoman when she is directed by Loie."

Theatrical trunks, bearing her name, surround Loie here. From time to time her baggage was impounded by landlords or theater managers, usually for debts or contractual disputes. (Courtesy of the Dance Collection, the New York Public Library for the Performing Arts.)

⁂

Other critics of Loie were also in touch with Rodin. John W. Simpson, a New York lawyer and art collector, provided information about the state of affairs at the Metropolitan. He corresponded with his wife, Kate, who was in Paris with their daughter Jean while Rodin made a bust of the one and sketches of the other.[26]

For some time Loie persisted in believing that, if she had a chance to talk

Sada, Isadora, Marie, the Curies, Rodin

freely with Rodin, she would be able to explain everything to his complete satisfaction. But she kept postponing a conference with him because she was preoccupied with rehearsals. By the time she had a definite appointment with him, at Meudon, she was no longer quite so confident. She wrote him, again laboring with her French, a letter that amounted to a cri de coeur:

> Dear Friend
>
> I have received word from your secretary that it is to be Tuesday after breakfast—that is, after your meeting with Mrs. Simpson. I want to put an end to this question. I would like for you to explain to me what you really think about it. You must tell me the truth, frankly and absolutely. If anyone has anything to say about me, they should be honest enough to say it *in front of me* exactly the same as to you alone. Because in this affair you have not acted like the friend of mine that you have always been in the past, and as I have done nothing wrong, there is certainly an evil spirit somewhere. And I beg to insist on a frank explanation from you, *in front of me*, for terminating our friendship once and for all. We are, or we are not, friends. As for me, I am the same as always, and you are not. Why? This matter must be cleared up. Your talent, your works, your friendship, these I have valued with all my heart as an artist and as a human being, and everything I have done is a result of that, and if you misunderstand me it is the result of some outside influence that doesn't know the truth, and Tuesday you must realize this.
>
> Your sincere friend
Loïe Fuller.[27]

Apparently the Tuesday meeting resulted in some degree of reconciliation, but this did not last long. Loie left for London, to perform for a couple of months at the Palace Theatre, where she pleased the crowds with "some new experiments in her remarkable skirt dancing." In mid-October, while she was in London, the promissory note she had given Rodin, and he had deposited in his bank, fell due and was not paid. The bank notified him that he owed the face amount, nearly 10,500 francs, plus a penalty of 71.95 francs. He now demanded from Loie the return of the pieces of his that she had left at the Metropolitan. He soon recovered those things but did not so soon recover his regard for Loie. He and she remained at outs for almost three years.[28]

The world knew Loie well as a dancer, but not so well as a person, it seemed to her old friend the critic Jérôme Doucet. He therefore interviewed her and wrote a long article about her personal side, an article that appeared in the widely read Paris periodical *La Revue illustrée* on November 1, 1903, just after her estrangement from Rodin. Doucet's essay gave intriguing glimpses of Loie at the age of forty-one, both as she really was and as she would have liked to be seen.[29]

People often laughed, Doucet pointed out, at the way Loie dressed—at her black rubberized raincoat, her outmoded hat, her thick veil. Deeply concerned though she was with her dancing costumes, she did not care in the slightest about her street clothes. Anyhow, she needed the heavy veil to shade her poor eyes.

Her eyes had suffered from exposure to the bright lights she used in her performances, and for a time she feared she was going blind. When eye doctors failed to help her, she turned to a Christian Science practitioner and then to a mystic healer. "I allowed my eyelids to be stroked and my temples and head to be manipulated," she said, "and when I left the healer's hands I felt just as if I had been electrified." Whether because of these treatments, or because of long periods of rest in a darkened room, her eyesight ceased to deteriorate, but it remained somewhat defective for the rest of her life.[30]

Growing heavier as she grew older, Loie had reason to be concerned about her weight, since it was a rather serious professional handicap. It was a subject she could handle with a light touch, as when she told about the three-year-old who was brought to her dressing room to meet her but shrank away as soon as she saw her. "What is the matter, dear?" the girl's

Sada, Isadora, Marie, the Curies, Rodin

mother asked. "This is Miss Fuller, who danced for you so prettily a few minutes ago."

"No, no," the child objected. "This one here is a fat lady, and it was a fairy I saw dancing."

But Loie could not always dismiss the matter so easily. For a while she had a recurring dream in which "she saw herself growing obese until she had assumed the shape of a balloon. Then came a crash, and she saw herself falling through the glass plates upon which she danced."[31]

Harmful though light was to her, Loie praised it as an agent of good, waxing quite philosophical about it. The Great Light and the Great Truth are identical, she believed. As she explained her theories on this and other topics, she spoke in a kind of French that Doucet considered often odd but always vivid and expressive. She thought of herself as using light in much the same way that a musician used sound, and she predicted that a time would come when light with all its rhythms, tones, and harmonies would be played on an instrument just as music was.[32]

According to Loie's philosophy, one should always follow one's instinct, for doing so would result in spontaneity and sincerity. This, she said, was what she had done in developing her distinctive style of dancing: rather than setting out to revolutionize the art, she simply did what she *felt*.[33]

Quite different was Isadora Duncan, who recently had performed at the Sarah Bernhardt Theatre in Paris. Duncan repeatedly announced her mission, which was to reform the dance by driving the present performers out of the Temple of Terpsichore and replacing them with her pupils, who would restore the choreographic style of ancient Greece and Rome. "Since she has told us so many things," wrote Doucet, no doubt making Loie's opinion his own, "why hasn't she told us that Loïe Fuller was her teacher and taught her those tanagra-like Botticellian poses, those Leonardo da Vinci cadences, and those Filippino Lippi looks?"

"La Loïe could become a millionaire, as Sarah has done, but she does not love money except for the means it gives her to do her work, to prepare new surprises, to compose new fairy stories." Only the largest theaters could afford the luxury of Loie. Yet, despite the cost to them, she netted little profit, since she bore such tremendous expenses. She kept up the experiments in her backyard laboratory, maintained her large and well-paid staff of stagehands, electricians, and others, and had to transport them and tons of baggage wherever she went with her show.

Generous, kindhearted, she not only took loving care of her old mama but also looked out for strangers and strays that came her way. There was, for instance, the blind man who tried to make a living with his accordion and who, with his wife, dined once a week as Loie's guest. There was the mangy dog that she took in and cared for despite its interminable barking. There was the occasion when she called off a carriage ride because the weather had turned bad, the cobblestones were slippery, and she feared for the safety of her horses.

Exemplary though Loie's conduct was, some malicious tongues circulated malicious rumors about her, Doucet continued. Rejected friends (such as Emilia Cimino?) intimated that her love of the dances of ancient Greece inclined her to the moral standards of that age. But to those who really knew her, she was a paragon of morality. "Like the apostles, she is above the weaknesses of life."

When Doucet asked her if she had not been proposed to many times, her baby-blue eyes opened wide and she said: "People love my dances but I don't know if they always love me." And when he suggested that a young man who was crazy about her was afraid to tell her so because she was a great artist and he merely an unimportant painter, she replied: "So far as I am concerned, it's not a question of the great artist, but of great hearts. I don't dream of either a name or glory. I would marry a man of merit—like Zola—but there are perhaps a thousand unknown Zolas, whom luck has not favored." Once, when someone mentioned a man's having left his wife, Loie (remembering Colonel Hayes?) remarked: "I don't understand how a married man can pursue another woman, just as I can't understand how anyone in love with one person can marry another."

Loie told Doucet she was born on January 22, 1869—exactly seven years later than her actual birth date. "Why should I hide my age? What is there to be ashamed of?" she innocently asked. "It seems to me it would be glorious, when I am forty, to have kept my suppleness and vitality. What would be shameful would be to have been born in 1869 and never have accomplished anything yet."

Sada, Isadora, Marie, the Curies, Rodin

8

Wanderers in Glory

The house at 24 rue Cortambert, Paris, with its spacious, walled-in grounds, was the nearest thing to a real home that Loie Fuller had known since leaving Chicago some twenty years before. Ever since, hers had been a transient life, and even during her five-year lease of the Cortambert place she spent most of her time traveling and staying in hotels. After the lease terminated, in the spring of 1904, she made her Paris residence the Hôtel de la Cité du Retiro, a "maison de famille" with a female hotelier, near the Place de la Madeleine. She continued to spend a great deal of time on the road, stopping at one hotel after another.

For several years her travels avoided the United States, and temporarily she was almost forgotten there. "Were you not very much interested in the sale at the Knickerbocker Art Galleries of the life-size plaster casts of Loie Fuller?" a New York columnist asked readers in July 1905. "I was, and at the same time I wondered how many artists of to-day were painting her portrait or how many sculptors were sculpturing various members of the Fuller anatomy." Until recently, she had been "a fad as well as a big money-making star," and editors had been "constantly on the watch for news stories" about her. "During the past two or three years Miss Fuller has not been very prominent in the public eye in this country, although she can make plenty of money on the Continent and in South America."[1]

Loie did perform in South America during the summer of 1904 and in Germany during the winter of 1905–6, but whether she made "plenty of money" is questionable. The South American itinerary included Buenos Aires, Montevideo, São Paulo, Rio de Janeiro, and Santos. The tour brought its discouragements, one of which prompted Loie to jot down the following thought while in Montevideo:

> "Come what come may,
> Time & the hour runs
> Through the roughest day."
> (& *also the others too*).

In Germany, likewise, Loie and Gab were "not having a very good time," according to what a Paris friend of theirs read in a newspaper. One of the less happy moments was occasioned by an automobile accident. Eager as always

Loie, who was usually chauffeured around Paris, here acts as her own driver in an automobile that appears to be about a 1918 or 1920 model. (Courtesy of the Dance Collection, the New York Public Library for the Performing Arts.)

to keep up with technology, Loie had acquired her own car long before the horseless carriage replaced the horse-drawn kind. This car she took along with the rest of her baggage on the train, so that at every stop her mother could ride in comfort and in style. Apparently Delilah was not with Loie when the latter and some companions had a "miraculous escape" while driving out from Berlin. "Her automobile was going at forty miles an hour, when it ran off the road down a bank and overturned. The machine was hopelessly wrecked and Miss Fuller and six other occupants were thrown out. Luckily the ground was very soft and none of the party was seriously injured."[2]

One of Loie's happier moments occurred on this tour when she had a bit of time on her hands while stopping at the Hotel Royale in Hanover. Gab was staying at the same hotel, and Loie could have expressed her sentiments in conversation with her but, instead, whimsically sent her a series of postcards, three of which she mailed one day and a fourth the next. On a card with a picture of the Nicolai Kapelle (Englische Kirche) she wrote:

> Souvenir of our visit here when we were wanderers in glory over the face of the earth, and restless for quiet, peace and a home with the time ours to stay in it. My life friend dear Gab.
> Thy Loïe

Next on a card with a reproduction of one of the paintings in the Provinzial Museum, Hanover:

> Equality's the thing. Therefore make thyself worthy to be any man's equal!
> Loïe Fuller

Then on a card picturing the Hotel Royale itself:

> Dear Gab.
> How funny we are. I was just thinking of our lunch. You ate all the meat, I all the vegetables, you all the cheese, I all the radishes, you the consomme or bouillon & I all the fruit & then you scolded because I couldn't sit any longer. You know I can never bear to be a long time at the table unless some special talk is going on that makes me forget I am there, and besides I always get stiff if I sit any where long. You take all the beer & I all the water, & very little of that, these bottles are so small here.
> Yours tenderly, my dear, strong girl, Gab.
> Loïe

And finally the following, again on a Hotel Royale postcard:

> My dear, dear Gab
> What opposites we are, you and I. You want to sleep from 12 to 12, and unless you do so you are *so so* sick whereas I am

sick if I do, for only seven or eight hours suffice for me. You don't take morning coffee & I do. You always take black coffee after meals & I don't. You never touch fruit & I never can get enough. You like sweets & I hate 'em. You love pate de fois [gras] & I can't bear them [sic]. You can't eat vegetables boiled in water & I like 'em best that way. You hate to walk & I love it. However we do get on so well together & I'm old & you're young. It is so strange my dearest Kiddie.

Loïe[3]

Things Japanese fascinated Loie, and despite her disillusionment with Sada Yacco she took on the responsibility of fostering another former geisha from Japan. Through this experience she again lost money, yet she was more than compensated, for through it she also regained the friendship of Rodin.

A troupe of Japanese actors, dancers, musicians, and acrobats had been performing at the Savoy Theatre in London during the winter of 1904–5 while Loie was staying at the adjacent Savoy Hotel. As she watched them on the stage, she was particularly impressed by one member of the troupe, a woman about thirty-seven years old and not quite four feet tall but "pretty withal, refined, graceful, queer, and so individual as to stand out." Convinced that this woman ought to be made the star, Loie rechristened her Hanako (instead of Hisako Hohta) and composed a miming play in which, like Sada Yacco before her, she was called upon to die. Her death scene was at least as effective as Sada's, according to Loie's description of it:

> With little movements like those of a frightened child, with sighs, with cries of a wounded bird, she rolled herself into a ball, seeming to reduce her thin body to a mere nothing so that it was lost in the folds of her heavy embroidered Japanese robe. Her face became immovable, as if petrified, but her eyes continued to reveal intense animation. Then some little hiccoughs convulsed her, she made a little outcry and then an-

Wanderers in Glory

other one, so faint that it was hardly more than a sigh. Finally with great wide-open eyes she surveyed death, which had just overtaken her.

It was thrilling.

Loie secured an impresario for Hanako and the rest of the company, and they set out on a nine-month tour of Europe. They were enthusiastically received everywhere, and especially in Helsinki, the Finns being decidedly pro-Japanese at this time of the Russo-Japanese War, when Czar Nicholas II was depriving them of their traditional rights of home rule in his Grand Duchy of Finland.[4]

Eventually Loie herself took charge of the Japanese entertainers and traveled with them for several months, taking them in the summer of 1906 to Marseilles, where a great Colonial Exposition was being held to celebrate the glories of French colonialism. Performing there was a group of dancers from Cambodia, then one of the French colonies. Having seen and admired the Cambodian dancers in Paris, Rodin followed them to Marseilles, where he busily made sketches of the women. Having heard of Hanako, he was also interested in using her as a model. So he looked forward to meeting her and Loie in Marseilles and was even willing, at last, to make a sculpture of Loie too.

From Zurich, Loie wrote to Rodin on August 4, 1906: "I expect to be in Marseilles on the 10th or the 12th. But are you sure that this will not inconvenience you—because we can arrange another time. I would not, for all this world, want to have you quit your present work to make a statue of me." Still self-conscious about her French, she once again apologized for it. "I've never had time for the necessary study," she explained. "Never a single lesson in reading or writing. I've been so busy that I had to do it all by ear, and I'm sure that you can read it only with great difficulty." She lapsed into English to conclude the letter: "devotedly your friend / dear Artist, dear friend."[5]

At the Marseilles exposition Loie had a joyous reunion with Rodin, an occasion memorialized by the two of them having their picture taken in rickshaws, those symbols of colonialism, drawn up side by side. Rodin was as completely bewitched by the tiny Hanako as he could have expected to be.

LOIE FULLER

Auguste Rodin and Loie Fuller in rickshaws at the Colonial Exposition in Marseilles, 1906. (Courtesy of the Musée Rodin.)

Loie as well as Hanako shone at the fair. On the same outdoor stage where she and Rodin watched the Cambodians perform, she herself danced before tens of thousands of people, the largest crowd she had ever appeared before. On a starlit night she stood in darkness when she finished her dance and the lights went out. "The roar of applause became something fantastic in the dead of night. It was like the beating of a single pair of hands," it seemed to her. "That day I had the feeling that the crowd was really the most powerful of monarchs."

One of the monarchs at the exposition was an African king—that is, a man who would have been a king if the French government had not taken away the throne of Senegal. He was, Loie thought, "a magnificent negro,

Wanderers in Glory

six feet high, who looked like some prince from the Thousand and One Nights," and in his presence she remarked to some friends in French: "What a handsome savage; I wonder if they are all built on this model in Africa." When she was presented to him, she was embarrassed to hear him say in polite and excellent French that he had been educated in Paris and had often applauded her performances there. Later, engaging him in conversation, she learned that he had four wives, none of whom would ever be jealous of a white woman. "If a white woman with long blonde hair should suddenly appear in your country, among your black women, would she not be taken for an angel?" Loie asked. "Oh, no," he replied. "She would be taken for a devil. Angels are black in our Paradise." Afterward Loie reflected: "It had never before appeared so clear to me that men make their gods in their own image, rather than that the gods make men after theirs."[6]

For Loie and her troupe, Marseilles was the end of the line. "Poor Loïe Fuller must have a lot of debts," the Cambodians' manager, Eugène Raguet, told Rodin. "I think she is going to lose plenty of money and won't be able to organize the Swiss tour that I had expected for my Laotians." Loie's group now broke up, and Hanako offered to join Raguet's company. "The Japanese are the worst ingrates that I know of," Loie complained to Rodin. "All I have known are that way, both with me and with others. I think my Japanese are like children, like bad pupils."[7]

When Loie next heard about Hanako, she let bygones be bygones and determined to rescue her. Hanako, it seemed, was working in a "cheap concert hall" in Antwerp, where she felt almost like a prisoner, since she could not afford to leave. To fetch her, Loie sent her female secretary and one of Hanako's recent fellow actors, Kaoru Yoshikawa (whom Loie called Sato), to Antwerp. Loie then got together with Hanako, Yoshikawa, and two other Japanese actors; she arranged a series of engagements for them and prepared several dramas for them to mime, each with its obligatory death scene.[8]

While Hanako was acting in Loie's plays, she lived with Loie for a time at the Cité du Retiro, and Loie arranged with Rodin again and again for Hanako to pose for him. She herself posed for him occasionally. "Hanako will come to you at two-thirty and I at five o'clock," she wrote him on May 29, 1907. On another occasion: "Hanako and I thank you for your lovely gifts.

You are too kind! We are most fortunate. Loïe and Hanako." Again: "A thousand-thousand thanks for your beautiful little head of Hanako. It is superb, and I love you with all my heart." This was one of fifty-three heads of Hanako, each with a subtly different expression, that Rodin ultimately made—a larger number than he ever made of anyone else, so fascinated was he with her mobile features. He also sculpted a head of Loie, which he signed and dedicated "To that admirable, inspired artist Loïe Fuller."[9]

With Loie serving as matchmaker, Hanako and Yoshikawa were married, and their company went on a tour of the United States. After their return to Paris, Hanako was hailed as a rival of Sada Yacco. Loie asked Sada to appear at a private function, and Sada promised to do so. "But these Japanese are irresponsible," Loie cautioned the prospective hostess, and she offered to send Hanako in Sada's place if necessary. Between the two Japanese celebrities, Loie now favored Hanako. "Sada has arranged to play at the *Modern!!!*" she confided. "And I think that *Hanako is going to play in a better theatre.*"[10]

Loie was by no means losing her powers of creative imagination, as she amply demonstrated during 1907. Having invented a substitute for stage properties—a kind of "magic-lantern scenery"—she used it in putting on a larger-scale dance spectacle than any she had previously attempted. As a playwright, she advanced from pantomimes to spoken drama, authoring a play that was produced in London. And turning again to the Salome theme, she gave it a different twist in a show that was even more spectacular and terrifying than the one she had presented thirteen years before.

In her newly invented setting, a thick white cloth was hung at the back of the stage. At the front, just behind the footlights, was stretched a curtain of thin white gauze. Slide projectors sent pictures through the gauze and onto the back, thus creating scenes in which a dancer or dancers could perform. This kind of projected scenery might eventually do away with painted scenery, Loie believed. At any rate, it proved highly effective for her purposes.[11]

This technique was put to use when, in January, Loie staged an elaborate show, with 120 supernumeraries, at the Paris Hippodrome. A vast indoor arena, well suited for her bigger-than-ever effects, the Hippodrome usually featured types of entertainment—such as horse races, dwarves riding camels, or a brass band mounted on elephants—that had little appeal for the well-bred or the well-dressed. Loie, with her novel creations as with her earlier ones, attracted a very different kind of crowd, which on opening night included, among other celebrities, Jules Clarétie.

Accompanied by her 120 acolytes, who kept moving and swaying in the background, Loie presented six tableaux at the Hippodrome. In these scenes, lost souls wandered like ghosts through the heavens. Clouds took various shapes, stars shone brilliantly, divine spirits appeared, and butterflies and living flowers unfolded. Loie led her followers—and the spectators—down into the depths of the sea, where strange vegetation floated and monstrous fish swam by. Finally, everything turned red as she evoked the devil and the flames of hell consumed the damned.

Reviews were favorable. "La Loïe Fuller has put into practice her theory of the orchestration of light; indeed, she plays what are literally chromatic scales, harmonizing multifarious hues," one critic declared, comparing her to a musician and then to a painter. "With the imagination of an artist and a poet, in her six tableaux she paints pictures by means of light."

Another critic was even more enthusiastic, though he could not help contrasting the stage Loie, seen from afar, with the real Loie whom he remembered having once seen close up.

> She had just come from performing her serpentine dance. Backstage, the chorus girls of the revue that would conclude the show were waiting, half nude and exaggeratedly made up, for the curtain to rise. I had to make my way through that smiling, vulgar mob to get to the nook where the ideal dancer had taken refuge. She was stretched out on a common sofa. Some young friends were worshipfully wiping the sweat from her forehead and cheeks. Breathless, damp, exhausted, she had put on her gold-frame glasses, which made her look like some scholar who had come from Germany to deliver a boring lecture. She moaned with fatigue while, kneeling around her, faithful to their instructions, the girls murmured ten-

derly, soothingly, the word "Darling! Darling!" It was familial and touching.

I felt out of place. It is wise to keep one's distance from those whom one admires. . . . I have seen the long batons that give motion to the sheer materials, and I have also seen the person who is linked to the long batons. I wished that she was ethereal like the visions she offered us. I was such a fervid fan of hers that I had expected to meet not a woman but some kind of mythological creature.

And now, the critic went on, "thanks to the projectors that create a changing and unreal decor around her, thanks to the supernumeraries who evoke mysterious and supernatural throngs," Loie reigned over space and over the deep—the sovereign of the infinite.

> This is not a dance but a witchery, almost a religion. . . . La Loïe Fuller . . . has also reminded us that the dance is not an exercise in acrobatics; she has inspired us to disdain pointes and ballerinas in pink tights and gauze skirts. She has restored our admiration for simple and harmonious poses, and her gestures have often made us think of ancient statuettes. She has prepared us to appreciate the art of Isadora Duncan.[12]

Though a critical success, Loie's set of tableaux did not have a long run at the Hippodrome. Soon, while working out pantomimes for Hanako and company, she tried her hand at spoken drama, writing a one-act play, *The Little Japanese Girl*. In it the title character, a maidservant, happens upon the toilet accessories of a princess, who has left them temporarily in the woods. The maid experiments with the beauty aids, rearranges her hair before a looking glass, and puts on a kimono that the princess has left. When the prince comes upon the maid, he assumes that she is the princess, and when she hides her face and refuses to acknowledge him, he angrily departs. When the maid's lover arrives and the prince returns to find the two of them embracing, he is seized with a jealous rage and stabs the little girl in the back. And when the princess reappears, he realizes his terrible mistake and is overwhelmed by remorse as the maid writhes in the throes of death.

In the summer of 1907 the Savoy Theatre in London produced *The Little Japanese Girl* with an English cast as a curtain raiser for the long-running *Brewster's Millions*. While her play was on, Loie visited London and, to advertise it, was photographed wearing a Japanese costume. Critics assumed that she had translated or adapted the play from a Japanese original, and their reaction to it was mixed. "Miss Pauline Chase . . . plays the death-scene with a touch of real pathos," one of them said. "And the little piece is quite beautifully mounted and more worthy of attention than are curtain-raisers as a rule." Others wondered why the dialogue was "mostly in pidgin English—of the sort that might be used by the Chinese laundrymen in San Francisco"—the sort that consisted largely of adding "ee or ey to various words."[13]

Already Loie was preoccupied with a much more serious enterprise, one that no less an authority than Jules Clarétie had recommended her for. After seeing her performance at the Hippodrome, Clarétie had suggested publicly that she reappear "with some new invention, some fairyland setting such as one dreams of for 'Salome.'" Salome was beginning to get a good deal of attention in Paris. During the spring of 1907 an operatic version of the Oscar Wilde drama, with a German orchestra playing music by Richard Strauss, was offered at the majestic Théâtre du Châtelet. Meanwhile Maud Allan presented her own sexy interpretation, *The Vision of Salome,* at the Théâtre des Variétés, a vaudeville house.

Born in Toronto in 1873, brought up in San Francisco from the age of six, Maud Allan was studying piano in Berlin when her beloved brother was hanged for the murder of two young women in San Francisco's Emmanuel Baptist Church. His fate shadowed the rest of her life. After developing her own style of free-form dance, she toured for a time with Hanako and others in Loie's troupe until it broke up in Marseilles in 1906. Maud did not appreciate that Loie had done her a good turn in taking her on, or that Loie was losing money on the tour. According to Maud's story, Loie and Gab deliberately cheated her and then told her she would have to sue them if she thought they owed her anything. A little later she debuted in Vienna in her seminude version of Salome, which she afterward brought to Paris.[14]

Loie planned to present her own spectacular show, *The Tragedy of Salome*, once it was ready in the autumn, at the Théâtre des Arts, a much more high-toned place than Maud's Théâtre des Variétés. Preparations for Loie's show took an extraordinary amount of time and effort. While the poet Robert d'Humière devised a plot for the pantomime and the composer Florent Schmitt wrote the accompaniment, Loie busied herself with choreography, costumes, stage design, and lighting effects. So complex were the arrangements that she had to postpone the opening date again and again. While taking care of the final details, fatigued though she was from all the work, she made a quick trip to London to get a new and improved projector that an electrician there had made especially for her.[15]

On the day before the dress rehearsal Clarétie attended a private rehearsal at Loie's invitation. He later wrote for *Le Temps*:

> There, on that evening when I saw her rehearse Salome in everyday clothes, without costume, her glasses over her eyes, measuring her steps, outlining in her dark robe the seductive and suggestive movements, which she will produce tomorrow in her brilliant costume, I seemed to be watching a wonderful *impresaria*, manager of her troupe as well as mistress of the audience, giving her directions to the orchestra, to the stagehands, with an exquisite politeness, smiling in the face of the inevitable nerve-wracking circumstances, always good-natured and making herself obeyed, as all real leaders do, by giving orders in a tone that sounds like asking a favor.
>
> "Will you be good enough to give us a little more light? Yes. That is it. Thank you."
>
> Then I had the immense pleasure of seeing this Salome in everyday clothes dance her steps without the illusion created by theatrical costume, with a simple strip of material, sometimes red and sometimes green, for the purpose of studying the reflections on the moving folds under the electric light. It was Salome dancing, but a Salome in a short skirt, a Salome with a jacket over her shoulders, a Salome in a tailor-made dress, whose hands—mobile, expressive, tender or threaten-

ing hands, white hands, hands like the tips of birds' wings—
emerged from the clothes, imparted to them all the poetry of
the dance, the infernal dance or the dance of delight.[16]

On opening night, November 9, the theater was filled with a "wonderfully interesting assembly of representatives of all that [was] brilliant in the artistic and literary life of Paris," besides some of what was most prominent in political life, including Georges Clemenceau, the premier of France, and Aristide Briand, a leading member of the Chamber of Deputies. As soon as the curtain fell, Briand sent Loie his card with a penciled message of congratulations. "She came to the footlights, held the card in the air, kissed it, waved her fingers to the box where the ministers sat, and withdrew amid laughter and cheers. Briand blushed like a girl."[17]

Night after night, women shrieked in terror at some parts of Loie's performance, and no wonder. The "Dance of the Pearls" was mild enough, and so was the "Peacock's Dance," in which she wore a long-tailed costume made of forty-five hundred peacock feathers. Then, in the "Dance of the Serpents," she was a witch in shiny green scales playing with two (prop) snakes six feet long. After she set them down, they writhed about on the floor, "darting out their heads horribly," while she capered around them "with hideous glee." In the "Dance of Steel" she was struck by harsh, metallic, knifelike flashes of light as she moved about in semidarkness. She seemed to disappear beneath the sea, then rose up to perform the "Dance of Silver" while robed in sheets of silver and gold bedecked with glittering jewels.

> A negro executioner appears with John's head upon a charger. Salome takes it, dances, and then, suddenly stricken with horror, throws the head down into the sea, which flames blood colored. Salome falls fainting to the ground.
>
> A storm springs up and in a shaft of light the head of John appears to Salome. This dance, the Dance of Fear, was the most wonderful of all . . . whichever way she turned, the head confronted her.[18]

Loie's performance drew warm to glowing reviews from English and American as well as French critics. "She has offered us some more curious

Poses from the 1907 production of Robert d'Humière's Salome, *including dances of pearls, serpents, steel, silver, peacocks, and fear.*

and various dances, together with ingenious and artistic lighting effects, with which we are familiar and of which we never tire." "The dances surpass all Miss Fuller's previous efforts in the way of bizarre saltation." She has "achieved the triumph of her long career."

Especially enthusiastic was the feminist magazine *Femina*, which ran a flattering article with several photographs of Loie wearing her various Salome wigs. She "personated a new Salome with great success," *Femina* proclaimed. Her facial expressions were remarkably "diverse and gripping." Dancing before Herod, she "brought to bear all the seductive resources of a woman, in turn loving, humble, treacherous, scornful."[19]

Like the writer in *Femina*, Clarétie in *Le Temps* viewed Loie's Salome as a triumph of feminism. After watching her rehearsal, he had

> a vision of a theater of the future, something in the nature of a feminist theater.
>
> Women are more and more taking men's places. They are steadily supplanting the so-called stronger sex. The courthouse swarms with women lawyers. The literature of imagination and observation will soon belong to women of letters. Despite man's declaration that there shall be no woman doctor for him, the female physician continues to pass her examinations, and brilliantly. Just watch and you will see woman growing in influence and power; and if, as in Gladstone's phrase, the nineteenth century was the workingman's century, the twentieth will be the women's century.

Loie's Salome may or may not have portended the women's century; in any case, it hardly proved to be a model for the theater of the future. It did not last through the 1907–8 season, nor did it have any descendants.[20]

❧

Loie managed to remain a busy hostess and to enjoy an active social life even though her home now was only a hotel suite, her shows took much time and energy, and illnesses again and again enfeebled her. Almost every

Loie used a fractured French in both speaking and writing. In this letter to Rodin she invites him to lunch, changes her mind about the date, crosses it out, and substitutes another day, instead of rewriting the note.
(Courtesy of the Musée Rodin.)

winter she was laid low, for days or weeks, by respiratory disease—by the cold she said she was born with and never got over. While scheduled at the Hippodrome, she rested in bed day after day to conserve her strength, getting up only to go onstage. Even so, she had to miss several performances. "I've really caught it this time, and my room is a furnace because nothing but heat will make me well, so I'm not receiving anybody," she confided to one of her cronies. "I'm waiting for the summer and sunshine for a cure—but God knows when I will recover from this bronchitis and congestion of the lungs."[21]

While in Paris, living at the Cité du Retiro, Loie usually did her entertaining at that hotel or at the Bedford, on the other side of the Place de la Madeleine, or at some friend's house. While on the road, she received her guests wherever she happened to be staying, as when, "in her glory," she "had quite an 'At Home'" at the Savoy Hotel in London. She once invited Rodin, a day ahead of time, and offered to send a car to take him to an impromptu garden party at the home of an American socialite who resided in the ultrafashionable Bois de Boulogne.[22]

Keeping on excellent terms with Rodin, Loie not only provided him with Hanako as a model but also offered him choice seats at the Hippodrome show and at the Salome pantomime. When he failed to appear at the Salome dress rehearsal, she appealed to him: "Can't you ever come to see me in Salome? It's not very interesting, but I would like to see you, and I am ill." She continued to take friends and acquaintances to visit him.[23]

One of these was Marie Curie, whom Loie helped to comfort after Pierre Curie, walking absentmindedly in a Paris street on a dark, rainy April day in 1906, was run over by a dray and killed. "We—Madame Curie and I—are coming to see you on Monday, July 15, at 3:30 at 182 rue Université—to hug you and ask your advice," Loie wrote to Rodin on July 12, 1907. "Please *telegraph* me if this date is suitable—and if not, set another time for our rendezvous." Mme Curie gave Loie a signed copy of her book *Researches on Radioactive Substances,* which Loie kept but never read (the pages remained uncut).[24]

One day Loie and Gab went to Rodin's atelier with a distinguished group—a singer from the Opéra, the music critic of *Le Temps,* and the directors of two Paris theaters—only to discover that the sculptor had departed for London that very morning. "Alas!" thought Loie, but she had the consolation of knowing that she was about to leave for London herself (to see her Japanese play at the Savoy Theatre), and she arranged to meet Rodin there.[25]

Besides Rodin and other notabilities, Loie invited to one of her dinners the most famous of living French novelists, Anatole France, with whom she had been acquainted for some time. "Twice I have passed by your place hoping to see you for just a moment," she wrote him later, while her *Salome* was on. She enclosed in her letter a handwritten note that would entitle him to a loge at the final matinee. "It would give me so much pleasure to see you again."[26]

Sarah Bernhardt reentered Loie's life when she sent her business manager to ask Loie to come and give advice about the lighting of her new play, *La Belle au bois dormant*, which was to be staged in Paris in 1907. "I was ill enough to be in bed," Loie recalled, "but I arose to receive him. I promised him that I would go to see Sarah the next day." Bernhardt gathered from her manager that Loie was coming the same day. "When she learned that she could count on me only for the next day, she declared that I had fallen ill very suddenly. This thing wounded me to the quick, for I still loved Sarah. Next day I went to her house and she saw that I was suffering, for I could not utter a word. She took me in her arms and called me her treasure. That was enough."

Later Bernhardt came to Loie's theater to look at her lighting arrangements. Still later, when Loie asked her which apparatus she would like to use, the actress replied that her own electricians could do whatever she needed to have done. "Besides," they said, "it is only a matter of a gauze curtain and a revolving lamp." Disillusioned, Loie concluded that Bernhardt, though "an inspired artist," was "also a woman"—but "she remains my divinity just the same."

After Loie invited the Claréties to see Hanako perform, they invited her and Hanako to lunch. "Hanako appeared to be quite unaware that she was going to lunch with a celebrated writer, and experienced no excitement at the idea of paying a visit to the director of the world's first theatre." Appreciating Hanako more than she did him, Clarétie stated in his newspaper column: "It is delightful to see at close hand and in so attractive a guise this little creature, who looks so frightful when, with convulsed eyes, she mimics

Wanderers in Glory

the death agony." He also wrote that he would like to hear from Loie "how she first conceived these radiant dances," which she had "just begun again at the Hippodrome." In a letter to Loie he suggested that she write her memoirs, and at an afternoon party Mme Clarétie and her other guests encouraged Loie to do so. At the *Salome* rehearsal he attended, Clarétie repeated the suggestion and urged her to follow it. So she began to think of writing a book.[27]

※

Then Félix Juven, a well-known Paris publisher, offered her a contract. She realized she "was not born with literary qualities," but she began to "search through the archives" of her memory to see if there was sufficient material there. "There were interesting people to talk about certainly, so why not write about them?" she wondered. Indeed, there were all those famous and royal personages—Dumas, Bernhardt, Rodin, Anatole France, Princess Marie, and the rest—and she concluded, without concern that it might seem more like name-dropping than modesty: "ah yes I might be able to fill a book without talking too much about myself."

She soon regretted signing the contract. It obligated her to deliver the manuscript, in both English and French, on or before December 31, 1907, which was less than two months away! She nevertheless sent Juven a list of chapter topics, which he approved. Except for a chapter on her "stage entrance" (her birth and infancy), the book would concentrate on the years since her invention of the serpentine dance, 1892–1907. It would be titled *Quinze ans de ma vie* (Fifteen years of my life).

By December 1 not much of the manuscript was ready in English, and the translation had not even begun. Fortunately, Loie numbered among her friends the Princess Karageorgevich and her son, Prince Bojidar, of the Serbian royal family. The prince, who had written a book on India in beautiful French, agreed to serve as Loie's translator.

> But [she recounted not long afterward] I was not well and my cough got worse till nearly all my days were spent in bed, only leaving it at night just long enough to drive to the theatre for

> my performance of Salome, the exertion of dancing augmenting my cough more each night, & return home again only to take to my bed till it was time for the next performance. But I kept on writing & sending my chapters to the Prince for translating.
>
> About a week before the expiration of time stated in the contract, I rec'd a letter from the editor [i.e., the publisher] saying that if my mss was not forthcoming on or before Dec 31 he would be obliged to hold me for damages as he had [to] keep his press open for the printing of my book. So I dictated to a lady stenographer while I was dressing at the theatre for Salome, and gave notes to a man stenographer for an hour or so after I got dressed & was waiting to rest so that I should not go out into the cold over heated from the dancing. And during the day and night I sat up in bed whenever I was able to do so & wrote all that I could myself.

The pages piled up too fast for the prince, who had to do most of his translating at night, since he worked during the day making jewelry. Other friends of Loie's gathered on December 30 to work all night and finish the job in hasty and imperfect French, which the prince could redo later. Thus the deadline was met, but the publisher then demanded fifty additional pages, and Loie was still working on these at the beginning of February 1908.

> Just then my mother, who heretofore could sit up for some little time during the day, was now confined entirely to her bed which was in the room next to mine, & by her cough I knew she had an attack of acute bronchitis coming on. And I grew worse with a bad sore throat, which the doctor said was catching & I must not go near her. Soon however I could feel that she was not receiving proper attention, so I left my bed, dressed myself and started in to nursing her . . . for, although my poor mother paralyzed as she was could only say Yes & No, I discovered that . . . she had been neglected [by the nurse]. . . . During the nights I sat with her I kept at the book.

Wanderers in Glory

Loie with her mother, Delilah, about 1906. (Photograph by Harry C. Ellis; courtesy of the Dance Collection, the New York Public Library for the Performing Arts.)

In desperation, Loie appealed to one of the world's greatest authorities on microbes, the Russian-born scientist Elie Metchnikoff, who had succeeded Louis Pasteur as head of the Pasteur Institute. Metchnikoff, himself suffering from a cold, agreed to consult with Loie either at the institute or at her hotel, but was unable to save her mother. "Pneumonia set in & 24 hours afterward she passed through that protracted and stifling death." Loie had finished the last chapter of her book the previous night.[28]

"I have just lost my mother & we have cremated her," Loie wrote in English to her "Dear dear friend" Mme Jules Clarétie. Loie was fond of Mme Clarétie's mother. "Kiss her a hundred times for me. Kiss her dear hands & love her tenderly! The parting will be so hard when it comes," Loie counseled. "I am still ill with bronchitis, & must wait for the summer to reestablish me in health & spirits."

As soon as she felt like traveling, Loie went to Berlin and spent twelve days there to see about publishing her memoirs in German. After her return to Paris her friend Gladys Thomas invited her, Rodin, and Roger Marx to breakfast at the Hotel Bedford. "We have a lot to tell you," Gladys wrote to Rodin. "Loie is improving and is bearing the loss of her mother better than we could have expected." But Loie gave a rather different impression to one of her French cronies. "Our great friend Bojidar Karageorgevich, who translated my book, died yesterday, and I myself am suffering very, very much," Loie confided to this woman. "With my mother gone and all the rest, I am almost dead myself, and all my nerves are hurting." She sought solace from Gab by asking her how she had felt when her mother died.[29]

Quinze ans de ma vie came out in the fall of 1908. No German edition appeared, but a condensed version in English soon ran serially in the *Chicago Record-Herald* and the *New York Herald,* while excerpts were printed in other American papers. Five years later, in 1913, a different English translation of the entire book, under the title *Fifteen Years of a Dancer's Life, with Some Account of Her Distinguished Friends,* was published in London and Boston. Once Loie's words had been turned into French and then back into English, they seemed more like those of a cultured English lady than like her own. The difference can be seen in the opening passages of the book as she originally wrote or dictated them and as they eventually appeared in print:

Wanderers in Glory

"Why whose baby is it?" "I don't know." "Well in any case don't let's have it here, take it up and fetch it along."	"Whose baby is this?" "I don't know." "Well, anyway, don't leave it here. Take it away."
Whereupon, one of the two men who were speaking picked up the little thing and carried it off down into the ball room. He held it sitting upright on his arm.	Thereupon one of the two speakers seized the little thing and brought it into the dancing-hall.
It was a funny little bundle of humanity. Its hair was very long and black and curly and it weighed about six lbs.	It was an odd little baggage, with long, black, curly hair, and it weighed barely six pounds.
The two gentlemen passed into the ball room and began to ask every woman there whose baby it was, and nobody knew.	The two gentlemen went round the room and asked each lady if the child were hers. None claimed it.

The memoirs were more interesting and more rewarding than was to have been expected from the hasty and haphazard way in which they were put together. Without them, many incidents of Loie's life would have been lost to posterity. One chapter, "Light and the Dance," gave a good exposition of her theory that light and color could be played like music and that "there is as much harmony in motion as in music and colour." Motion conveys emotion better than language does, she argued. "In the dance, and there ought to be a word better adapted to the thing, the human body should, despite conventional limitations, express all the sensations or emotions that it experiences."

On the whole, however, the book consisted of a rather miscellaneous collection of anecdotes. It lacked continuity and a sense of chronology, Hanako being treated before Sada Yacco, for example, though Sada arrived on the scene several years earlier. There were gaps in the story (Colonel William Hayes was not even mentioned), errors due to lapses of memory, and instances of deliberate misinformation. Among the last was the falsifying of the author's age. "I had then just passed my twentieth birthday," she wrote in regard to the winter of 1891–92, when she was first developing her serpentine dance and was actually going on thirty. Relying on *Fifteen Years* as their main or only source, many later writers of biographical sketches have been misled.[30]

While working on her memoirs, Loie had requested a statement from Clarétie giving his views on a series of weighty questions, such as "What is Justice—or the difference between the justice of man and of Nature?" To remind him of her request, she appealed to Mme Clarétie: "A letter from him would make my book so interesting and I would be so very grateful." The book, as things turned out, did not contain any such letter, but it did include an extensive quotation from Clarétie's recent long and flattering article about Loie in *Le Temps*.

Rodin responded with a letter from Meudon on January 19, 1908, and she happily quoted it in the book. "Mme Loie Fuller, whom I have admired for a number of years, is, to my mind, a woman of genius, with all the resources of talent," Rodin had written (in French, of course). "Her talent will always be imitated, from now on, and her creation will be reattempted over and over again, for she has re-created effects and light and background, all things which will be studied continually, and whose initial value I have understood."

Anatole France did even better, providing a handsome introduction for the book. He began:

> I had seen her only as she had been seen by multitudes from every corner of the globe, on the stage, waving her draperies in the first light, or transformed into a great resplendent lily, revealing to us a new and dignified type of beauty. I had the honour of being presented to her at a luncheon of the *tour du monde* at Boulogne. I saw an American lady with small features, with blue eyes, like water in which a pale sky is re-

flected, rather plump, quiet, smiling, refined. I heard her talk. The difficulty with which she speaks French adds to her power of expression without injuring her vivacity.

The famous novelist went on to describe Loie as a "brilliant artist" with a "marvellous perception of spiritual values" and a "considerable theory of human knowledge and philosophy of art." He thought she was "profoundly religious," "marvellously intelligent," and "even more marvellously instinctive."[31]

9

*La Loïe
and
Her Muses*

*A*fter fifteen years as a famous dancer, Loie Fuller entered upon another phase of her career. Not that she ceased to play with light and color, nor did she soon give up her solo performances of the serpentine and its successors, but she began to concentrate mainly on teaching others, and what she taught them was something she considered both new and ancient in the terpsichorean art. She called it "natural dancing." Founding a school, she took girls of all ages (and on one occasion a man) as her pupils and performers, her "muses." Thus she came more directly than ever into competition with Isadora Duncan, who already had a troupe of girl dancers in the field.

In the summer of 1908 Loie was rehearsing some of her girls for a performance in London, where she thought of locating her academy until she failed to find a suitable place. At the Savoy Hotel a woman introduced her six-year-old daughter, who "began humming her own music and dancing to it" for Loie's benefit. This was just the kind of natural dancing that Loie now advocated, and she readily accepted the child as one of her pupils, who eventually numbered about fifty, ranging in age from five to twenty-nine. "I have heard it from Miss Fuller first hand that both Isadora Duncan and Maud Allan repaired to her in the early stages of their development for advice and instruction," a London correspondent of the *Chicago Tribune* reported, "and the American dancer is still carrying on the good work." Loie was exaggerating, of course, when she thus gave the impression that she had taught Duncan and Allan how to dance.[1]

Busy though she was with rehearsals, Loie as always had time for socializing and for collecting celebrities. She was especially pleased to meet Ellen Terry, who had long been considered the greatest actress on the English stage, and who now, though well past her prime at sixty, struck Loie as "that wonder & marvel of artist & womanhood!" (One of Ellen Terry's two illegitimate children became the father of one of Isadora Duncan's two illegitimate children.)[2]

Loie presented her pupils in the *Ballet of Light* at the London Hippodrome in September. "It was altogether a dazzling and clever performance and was well received by the audience," according to one of those present. "To obtain the extraordinary light effects 1,000 amperes of electricity are used at each performance—sufficient to light a whole town of 30,000 inhabitants." "The lighting effect is very pretty," another viewer conceded, but went on to comment: "There are twelve girls in the act, badly drilled besides dancing poorly."[3]

In any event, one American visitor was fascinated by both the lighting and the choreography of Loie's new act. Henry Russell, director of the Boston Opera House, invited Loie to Boston to give advice on the lighting arrangements of his new building, which was under construction. He also wanted her to present a program of dances there as soon as the building was completed.

After a November reappearance in London—this time by herself, to present some "Mysterious Dances" on a vaudeville program at the Palace Theatre—Loie continued to develop her pupils and their repertoire in Paris during the winter of 1908–9. She boasted of some promising performers, among them a girl who could do a Salome dance on her hands, with her feet in the air. "Another little girl I have crawls marvelously. She does all her dancing on the ground," Loie said. "Still a third dances only with her hands. These dances of the hands are a new idea of mine."

For their Paris debut, Loie's girls presented her interpretation of Felix Mendelssohn's incidental music to *A Midsummer Night's Dream* at the Théâtre Marigny on February 28 (after a week's postponement because of another of her bronchitis attacks). Auguste Rodin and Jules Clarétie, present as her guests, were enthusiastic. Afterward Rodin wrote her that "nothing in all antiquity" could have been more beautiful.[4]

Looking "remarkably well and sprightly," Loie, along with Henry Russell, landed in New York on March 31 to spend several weeks in Boston and offer her counsel on the lighting system of the new Opera House there. She recommended omitting footlights entirely and relying instead on lamps strategically located throughout the building. She also proposed to make the proscenium twice as high as usual, to accommodate two stages, one on top of the other, separated by a glass floor. And she urged the adoption of her kind of projected scenery to supplement if not supplant the ordinary painted stage props.

To inquiring reporters in New York and Boston, Loie meanwhile explained what she meant by "natural dancing," the kind she expected to present at the Boston Opera House the next season. "It is a new idea in a ballet," one of her interviewers gathered. "The old-fashioned toe-dancing, simpering, skipping lady of uncertain age" would have no place in it. It would be divided into parts comparable to the singing parts in an opera. "One girl may dance but a single bar of the music. Another will dance a line or two. There will be dancing duets, trios, and choruses." And each girl would present her own interpretation of the dance. Loie explained further:

> By no means is my kind of dancing like Isadora Duncan's, although there are one or two points in common. The two kinds are as different as night and day. Miss Duncan's dancing is essentially a cultivated art—a learned kind of dancing that takes much practice—whereas mine is natural, inspirational, and spontaneous. Miss Duncan imitates the movements of dancers as represented on Greek vases and her pupils copy her. I and my pupils give the original natural expression and movements which inspired the Greeks when they made their vases. . . .
>
> I have had three different phases in my career since I first began. The first was devoted to the "Serpentine." In the second I took to more legitimate and dramatic dancing. The third has brought me to what I call natural dancing—the dancing inspired by nature.

"Miss Fuller has an unusual mind," one of her interviewers was moved to remark. "She is an admirable conversationalist, who speaks with extraordinary fluency, and—be it said without discourtesy to the brilliant woman—that she carries much more the manner of a Boston school mistress than she does of a dancer who has set two continents wild."[5]

After her return to Paris, Loie met a man who provided an even more attractive offer than the one from Russell of the Boston Opera: Otto Kahn, a member of the investment banking firm of Kuhn, Loeb & Company, who had recently become chairman of the board of New York's Metropolitan Opera, and who happened to be traveling in France with his wife. At his instance, Loie signed a contract for the appearance of herself and her

The Muses with Loie in the garden of the countess of Choudais, Paris, about 1911. (Photograph by Harry C. Ellis; courtesy of the Musée d'Orsay, © R.M.N.)

troupe at the Metropolitan in the fall. She then took the Kahns to meet Rodin and view his statuary at Meudon.[6]

While preparing to take her pupils to America, Loie showed them off to friends in a series of private performances during the summer. On Bastille Day, July 14, the girls performed on the lawn at the astronomer Camille Flammarion's chateau in Juvisy, where "staid academicians and mathematicians delighted in their fluttering Greek draperies," and Flammarion himself declared that, on this occasion, "the new choreography had its birth."

Next, the girls appeared at Mrs. T. Alexander Clarke's estate in the fashionable Bois de Boulogne. Very likely, it was Mrs. Clarke whom Loie had had in mind when she asked a group of her colleagues to excuse her from a breakfast date: "Because I have promised to have breakfast with a friend, a charming woman who has only one fault—she has too much money!" A leader of American society in Paris, Mrs. Clarke certainly had plenty of money, and she was now using some of it to finance Loie and her troupe.

La Loïe and Her Muses

At the garden party in the Bois de Boulogne, the girls "danced on the lawn in the moonlight, in and out of the shadows of the trees, like fairies or spirits of the air," as one of the guests declared. Another, the composer Jules Massenet, was so pleased that he offered to let Loie use some of his music free of charge.

Later Rodin sent Loie an invitation in a letter that Henry Russell carried to her. "You will let me come with all my girls?" Loie responded in a note to Rodin. "*All* of them want so much to see Meudon!" There, on his spacious grounds, the old sculptor presented them, with unstinted praise, to a crowd that included many distinguished people, if fewer aristocrats than had attended Mrs. Clarke's party.

Then, from time to time, Loie and her girls were guests of Prince Paul Troubetzkoy, a member of the Russian nobility, at his country place near Paris. The forty-two-year-old prince was not only an ardent vegetarian but a thoroughgoing health faddist. "His great discovery," according to a newspaper account,

> is the medical value of the radium-effluvia of the earth—obtained by sleeping out.
>
> "The living body breathes through a billion pores," he says. "The whole skin must bathe in air. We must absorb the radiations of mother earth and palpitate in the bombarding ions of our father, the sun."
>
> Loie Fuller, who is naturally drawn to every crank she meets, became a hygienic disciple of Troubetzkoy at first sight.

Princess Troubetzkoy often danced with Loie and her girls in the open fields, and it was said that Loie had received her inspiration for natural dancing from the Troubetzkoys and their pet wolves.[7]

In her school Loie taught natural dancing by a natural method. "I do not teach these children," she said. "They teach me." She merely asked them to express, each of them in her own way, an emotion such as joy, fear, or sorrow, or to imitate some activity such as chasing a butterfly, or to impersonate some imaginary being. But she pointed out:

Just as in the best acting, the dancer for the time must be the creature she is representing, and it must be remembered that in the dances that stir the public this creature is no ordinary mortal. She is some creation of a poet, some spirit of music, a dream of mythology, a woman of a remote period or fantastic time, a being of high romance or drama. To make her live, the dancer must understand her. It is desirable to this end to read old literature, to think, dream, imagine oneself a woman of any age or status. Not until a dancer does this is she able to uplift an audience into the feeling that this is the expression of a woman's soul; that it is not pantomime, but life.

Loie's school building was one of a number of churches that had been abandoned for religious uses and had become available at a low rent when the French government discontinued its church subsidies. While she gave such choreographic instruction as she thought appropriate, tutors provided lessons in the ordinary school subjects for the younger members of the troupe.

By the end of the summer Loie considered her repertoire and her performers well prepared for the American tour. She and the group as a whole would take part in the *Ballet of Light,* which in its developed form included the following scenes: "The Sea," "Snowstorm," "Typhoon," "Volcanoes," "The Sweeping Fires," "Falling Stars," "Aurora Borealis," "Angels," and "The Unfolding Spirit." Several grown-up members of the troupe, experienced dancers, would perform solos, interpreting various familiar pieces of music. The outstanding young soloists were the Italian Rita Sacchetto, the Germans Gertrude von Axen and Irene Sanden, the Russian Thamara de Swirsky, and the American who went by the name of Orchidee. A "man muse," the Boston socialite Paul Jones Chute, who assisted Loie as an instructor, could also be called upon as a performer.

Loie herself was ready with her "Dance of the Hands," which she said Rodin had inspired with the following observation: "The soul expresses itself through each and every part of the human form. A hand separated from the body can express its joy, its sorrow, its grief with as great perfection as the complete form of man." In this dance Loie's hands were seemingly separated from her body, they alone being visible in the spotlight. With them she could interpret Massenet's "Eau courant," Gounod's "Ave Maria," or Schumann's "Träumerei."[8]

Since Loie and her troupe had been so well received at their private performances in France, she was confident they would prove a hit in the United States. "I think my Muses will be appreciated there, if anywhere in the world," she said before embarking. But her cheery attitude was belied by her financial trouble. "In fact," the *Musical Courier* reported,

> Miss Fuller was almost unable to leave Paris, having been threatened with the seizure of her trunks and other accessories for personal debts. At the last moment Mrs. T. A. Clarke, who is well known in financial circles in Paris, advanced a large sum of money. She refused today to state the exact amount, but the total of debts she assumed is supposed to be about $20,000.
>
> Mrs. Clarke said this was not the first time she had helped Loie Fuller, but it would be the last.

Paul Jones Chute and several of the dancers were stranded in Paris for a few weeks while waiting for expense money and steamship tickets.[9]

On arriving at the Astor Hotel in New York on September 1, 1909, Loie displayed a curious little object for a reporter's edification. She said it was a spinthariscope (a word that neither she nor the reporter could spell correctly). Looking into the thing, one could see tiny sparks that were produced by the disintegration of radium. "You know there are 3,000,000 atoms in a molecule," Loie remarked authoritatively. The reporter was impressed. "La Loie Fuller is more than the foremost dancer in the world," he wrote; "she is a scientist of ability and extended acquaintanceship."

Despite this send-off, Loie was heading toward something between anti-climax and catastrophe, as she had done on previous American tours. This time she had come with several engagements in addition to those at the Metropolitan and the Boston Opera House, but she was depending mainly on her performances at those two places. Before long, however, the Metropolitan both postponed and shortened her prospective stay there, thus violating her contract. Though she was paid an indemnity, this was not enough to make up for what she had lost, nor were the new engagements she managed to obtain on short notice. "I tried to get another tour booked," she recalled, "but 'too late' . . . so this forced upon me the necessity of carrying a company of 50 people for four weeks—*idle!!!*" Later the Boston Opera House also postponed her appearance.[10]

When Loie and her muses arrived in Montreal for the first of their scheduled programs, there was some question as to whether they would be allowed to perform. The local archbishop objected on the grounds that her kind of dancing was both immoral and illegal. To show her what he had in mind—a belly dance or hootchy-kootchy—he moved the muscles under his vest. "Oh, father, you surely have traveled," she said. "But you never have seen one of my performances." She convinced him that these were very similar to religion. Not only did the show go on; it was "greeted by one of the largest houses, financially and otherwise, in the history of the Academy of Music" in Montreal.[11]

Before appearing at the Metropolitan in New York, Loie and her dancers made a one-night stand at the Academy of Music in Baltimore and another at the National Theater in Washington. In Baltimore they scored a "triumph" before a full house, and in Washington they "entertained a large and distinguished audience," though a critic there wrote: "To say that the audience was a unit in its appreciation of the dances would be a gross exaggeration." As for Loie's "Dance of the Hands," it was omitted at the National Theater after "there was a hitch in the lights and orchestra" and, "in desperation, her whispered calls for the curtain having gone unheeded, the dancer seized the green draperies and drew them about her with very apparent and excusable annoyance" as the curtain finally "descended amid ominous silence."[12]

Not till November 30 did the troupe make the first of its three appearances at the Metropolitan Opera House. Next day the *New York Times* recalled the spectacular effects of Loie's serpentine dances in former times. "Since then, however, Isadora Duncan and Maud Allan have revived the Greek dance, at least their own idea of the Greek dance," the *Times* went on to say, "and Miss Fuller's performance yesterday afternoon included examples of these latter-day conceptions as well as many of her own earlier ideas." The *Times* noted further: "A very large audience, which included many notable people, was in attendance, and the entertainment seemed to meet with approval."

One of the notable people in attendance was Isadora Duncan, who manifested something less than approval as she closely watched one of the soloists in particular—Gertrude von Axen. "Many said she suggested Duncan in her creative days," the *New York Telegraph* reported, "and Duncan looked as if she had something on her mind." In fact, she was thinking that Loie's new style drew too heavily on her own, and she was displeased to see the program getting such a good reception as it did.[13]

A greater hit than Gertrude von Axen was Rita Sacchetto. Sacchetto amazed the New York audience with her wild gyrations to the music of Chopin's "Tarantelle" as she played the part of a maiden who, bitten by a deadly tarantula, could save her life only by madly dancing. She charmed the Metropolitan Opera Company as well as the audience, and the company promptly hired her away from Loie, who had no recourse except to threaten a lawsuit. At the second Metropolitan appearance, on December 7, "popular interest in the occurrence was small" since the troupe had so badly "suffered a loss in the absence of the dancer Sacchetto."

During the week before the third Metropolitan performance, Loie's troupe played one-night stands in Boston and Springfield, Massachusetts, and Waterbury, Connecticut. In Springfield Loie sprained an ankle, and in Waterbury, while hospitalized, she had to be replaced by an understudy. Back in New York, she brought out her man muse, Chute, as a surprise to perform a duet with Thamara de Swirsky and thus, she hoped, to make up for the absence of Sacchetto. But Chute proved less impressive than Thamara, and she soon joined Sacchetto as a member of the Metropolitan Opera Company.[14]

After resting for a few weeks and celebrating Christmas, Loie and her dancers gave a series of eight Boston performances in January 1910. "Many, many Isadora Duncans, followed by many, many Loie Fullers—this is the impression left by last evening's performance at the Boston Opera House," the *Boston Transcript* reported a day after the opening. With regard to Loie's

"Dance of the Hands," the *Boston Traveler* commented: "Miss Fuller is especially well fitted for such a dance as she has beautiful hands which are marvelously long and slim and graceful despite the fact that she, herself, is so distinctly plump that her success in dancing is regarded by those who know her personally, as a wonderful demonstration of the power of mind over matter."[15]

Well attended though these and other performances were, they were too few to bring in enough money to meet expenses, and Loie soon was overtaken by old as well as new debts. In February courts in New York issued judgments against her for unpaid bills owed to a modiste, a production assistant, and a jeweler. When deputy sheriffs called at her New York hotel suite, she told them "her only asset at present was her ability to please the public" but she "expected to shortly take out on the road a company in vaudeville and make a lot of money."

> The deputies had departed and La Loie said, in that childlike way of hers: "The judgments against me were taken by default. I wasn't here when the papers were served; wasn't it stupid!"
>
> "Miss Fuller, is it true that all your solo muses are suing you for $1,000 each?"
>
> "I believe they say so, but how can they sue me if I don't refuse to pay them? The poor dears, I never said I wouldn't give them money."

It was Loie's turn to sue when three of her muses—Gertrude von Axen, Irene Sanden, and Orchidee—left her employ and went to work for William Morris, Inc., dancing at the Plaza Theatre in New York. The Morris agency advertised them as former members of the Loie Fuller troupe and called their act the *Ballet of Light*. Loie sought an injunction to prevent this, but failed to get it.[16]

Despite her troubles, Loie put on a cheerful face, telling reporters that Gabrielle Bloch, who had been with her on the American tour, was about to come back from Paris with more dancers.

"Will they take the place of the suing muses of New York?"

La Loïe and Her Muses

"I think so, and I am getting applications all the time. One Wellesley girl came to dance for me, and became so enthusiastic over herself that she is going to leave college and join my company." American girls would be "the leading dancers of the future," Loie predicted, because they had a "freedom of spirit" that was "lacking in those abroad."

American girls may have been eager to dance for her, but when Loie went out on the road again, in the late winter and spring of 1910, she had only seven or eight young women with her. And they were no longer playing at legitimate theaters, opera houses, or academies of music. Instead, they were reduced to appearing in vaudeville halls in Boston, New York, and other cities, where they had to compete for applause with such entertainers as aerialists, tumblers, and "knockabout comedians."

> The artist in the light fantastic was asked if she expected the average music hall patron—say, the delicatessen dealer of Seventh Avenue—to catch onto the point of these classical dances of hers, even with a glossary, concordance, and general explanation printed on the program. She was not in the least taken aback and replied that she did so expect.
>
> "The delicatessen man," said she, "is indeed more likely than the educated man to grasp the meaning of my dances. He *feels* them. It is a question of temperament more than of culture. My magnetism goes out over the footlights and seizes him so that he *must* understand—in spite of his delicatessen."

Whatever the reason, the vaudeville crowds seemed to appreciate natural dancing at least as much as the presumably more highly cultivated theatergoers had done. Loie and her remaining dancers, given top billing everywhere they went, took one place "by storm" and got four curtain calls at another.[17]

One question was asked, a question that had come up repeatedly since the Montreal archbishop first raised the moral issue: "Is it necessary, for art's sake, to make young girls appear without fleshings and in bare feet, with naught to shield their forms save a few folds of filmy gauze?" Loie herself believed "there is something about the thinnest covering that spoils the lines under the drapery and really makes the effect more commonplace and suggestive than the beautiful simplicity of the nude limbs." Still, the United States was supposedly puritanical, and the New York antivice crusader Anthony Comstock exerted considerable influence as a censor of literature and art. Comstock would have liked to ban the whole tribe of "barefoot dancers"—Loie Fuller, Isadora Duncan, Maud Allan, Ruth St. Denis— all of whom performed in the United States during the 1909–10 season. But in this case Comstockery did not prevail. Noting that most of the leading dancers of the new style were fellow Americans, a dance critic boasted: "The nation which has been the most pitiably enthralled by the ideals of a decadent Puritanism has become foremost in this cult of physical beauty."[18]

Not for four years did Loie revisit the United States. During those years, as she passed from age forty-eight to fifty-two, she continued to develop her dancing school in Paris and to give performances in France and elsewhere in Europe.

It took some time for her to regroup after the disheartening American tour. While doing so, in the winter and spring of 1910–11, she was called to London to supervise the lighting for one play and the choreography for another. By June 1911 she was again ready with her troupe.

The troupe had changed somewhat. Now numbering forty, it no longer included star soloists or other grown-ups except for the twenty-year-old American Orchidee, who had rejoined it after reconciling with Loie. The rest of the members ranged in age from five to fifteen, and nearly all of them, despite Loie's publicly declared preference for American dancers, were English. They went under such names as Peach, Plum Pudding, Kitten, Birdie, Little Thing, and Angel.

Talking to a Paris critic—"with that English accent which, in a woman's mouth, makes French a language of strange musical sounds"—Loie described her performers with grandmotherly affection, referring to them alternatively as her "pupils," her "babies," her "darling little girls," and her "dear little dancers." She could absolutely depend on them, she said. "They

La Loïe and Her Muses

do the right thing because it is right and because an inner voice tells them to do it. They dance in the same way, giving heed only to their own inspiration. Now, inspiration of this kind never makes a mistake!"

The girls were prepared to offer dances similar to those of the American tour, interpreting the music of Schubert, Mozart, Debussy, and Mendelssohn. For her own solos, the "indefatigable" Loie had some new creations that were "works of genius," according to a reporter who watched her rehearse. One of these creations, the "Ultraviolet Dance," would "flabbergast the scientific world." Others were the "Dance of Steel," in which "cold beams of light seemed to collide"; the "Pansy Dance," in which "the flowers opened up under the dancer's step"; the "Black Lily," "a tragic dance"; and the "Bluebird," "a dream, a winged poem."

Loie was "royally welcomed" back to Paris, "the scene of her first triumphs, and by the children of her first admirers," when she and her troupe got an opportunity to appear at a charity gala for the benefit of an orphanage. They presented four matinees at the Théâtre de la Gaieté-Lyrique (one of several government-subsidized theaters in the city) in June 1911. They seem to have been unable to secure any more engagements until the following December, when they appeared in six matinees at the Femina theater.[19]

For want of something better, Loie agreed to a European tour not as her own impresario but as an employee. One of her employers and financiers was the same Mrs. T. Alexander Clarke who had bankrolled her previously. Mrs. Clarke sent an agent, a Monsieur Lhomme, along with the dancers to handle their business affairs as they traveled about in Spain, Portugal, and southern France from January to April 1912. Loie nevertheless had to concern herself with business as well as art on the tour. While in Marseilles, she received telegrams tentatively offering engagements in Nice and Cannes. "But for terms one must go and fight for them," she complained to Gab, who stayed in Paris. "Mr. Lhomme tells me to go alone, but I need a man to treat with men when it comes to technical contracts, terms etc."

It turned into a miserable tour, as Loie confided to Gab in letter after tearful letter. From Porto, Portugal:

> I took a fearful cold in the wagon lit [sleeping car] in my nose
> & on arriving in Lisbon I could get no room any where that

had a fire in it. No fireplace no stoves no steam. Theatre no fire. *Cold cold colder* than Paris by five times at least.

I got more cold. Here worse still. Cold, cold—and every day Lisbon & here rain rain rain.

I have got an oil lamp in my room but it doesn't do anything but smell. I am having the fight of my life to keep off the bronchitis.

From Marseilles: "The whole bunch of us are living per day on less than the allowance I was to have." From Toulouse: "How unjust Mrs. Clarke is" (in thinking Loie was using illness as an excuse for missing a performance).

> *They are too ready* (and against their own interests in the tour) to believe bad things of me without hearing me, *and a guilty criminal* even has the right to answer before he is judged. I know it is because down in their hearts they do not like me & they are easier to believe bad than good. . . . I am beginning to feel the hurt of their frankly cruel accusations so deeply that I *do* not get over it & the injustice of it is getting just a little more than I can bear, but I will go on doing the best I can. But I tell you Gab I just *can't bear it*. I cry so much I can't see.

When the time came to return to Paris, Loie needed 839 francs for railroad tickets but had only 20 francs in her pocketbook. Spending some of that on a telegram to Mrs. Clarke, she said it would have been better all along to send money directly to her rather than sending it to Lhomme and then joining with him to dispute her accounts.

Loie won some plaudits for her pains. At a banquet in Marseilles she and her girls charmed the other guests as one girl represented Saint Francis preaching to the little birds, another evoked the movement of water and wind, and a third gave the impression of sorrowfully tearing the petals from a rose. "Miss Loie Fuller is again at the peak of her worldwide fame," a Marseilles paper declared after the subsequent theater appearance. But the tour made no money for her or for anyone else involved.[20]

La Loïe and Her Muses

The next season, 1912–13, Loie remained in Paris to perform at the Bouffes-Parisiens, a small theater noted for the risqué and the downright bawdy. She, with the "chaste evolutions" of her innocent girls, was said to be "charged with purifying the temple." Here, with the accompaniment of a symphony orchestra, the troupe offered a full program, which included the following numbers: "Little Trifles" (Mozart), "Great Black Bird," "Great Veil," "Cavalcade," "Nell Gwyn" (three country dances to the music of Sir Edward German), "Ballet of Light," "Wandering Souls," "Dance of the Hands," "Flecks of Light," "Furies," "Fire Dance," and "Butterflies." In the spring of 1913 the dancers appeared in the much more spacious and more reputable Théâtre des Champs-Elysées, recently refurbished, to interpret the *Nocturnes* of the impressionist composer Claude Debussy—pieces that seem made to order for Loie's technique, since they were intended to suggest various effects of light and shade.[21]

In December 1913 Loie and her girls were honored when they were chosen to perform, though only for two matinees, at the Odéon, one of the oldest and most prestigious theaters in Paris, famous for serious drama both classical and modern. Honored again, the troupe was invited to appear, in February 1914, at a gala sponsored by the king of Greece and intended to benefit victims of the recent Balkan Wars. According to Gab, a tremor ran through the spectators in the Athens stadium when Loie, with her magic, brought to life the ancient Greek statue Winged Victory.[22]

Back in Paris, Loie and her school were billed at the Théâtre du Châtelet, a roomy edifice for spectacular shows and ballets, from May 4 to 20, 1914, but the opening had to be postponed for a day because of the unexpectedly long time it took to install the necessary electrical equipment. The girls began the program with their familiar number *A Midsummer Night's Dream*. "Mendelssohn's glorious music is interpreted with a charm that moves the audience to constant applause," the *London Daily Mail*'s Paris edition reported. "The scene is a forest glade, and the stage fills with dancing merry gnomes and fairies, who appear as figures in a shepherd's dream." Then came Edvard Grieg's *Peer Gynt*, which was "once again a delight to watch." But far more spectacular was the interpretation of the modernistic Russian composer Igor Stravinsky's *Fireworks*. Two other pieces, *The Thousand*

and One Nights and *The Orchestration of Colors*, were composed by Armande de Polignac with Loie in mind. Mme Polignac surprised the audience at one performance when she took the place of Gabriel Pierné as orchestra conductor.[23]

※

Always more serious about Loie than Americans were, French critics gave as careful attention to her career with the dancing school—though not necessarily as much approval—as they had previously given to her serpentine and other dances. Now competing for the attention and approval of the critics, however, were not only her old rival Isadora Duncan but also the newly created Ballets Russes, which was rousing artistic and intellectual Parisians to a veritable balletomania. At the same time, motion pictures were beginning to draw so many customers as to threaten to monopolize the commercial entertainment of ordinary folk.

When the Russian dancers under the direction of Sergey Diaghilev debuted in Paris on May 19, 1909, they made a sensation comparable to what Loie had done when she first appeared there nearly seventeen years before. On this historic May 19 the crowd at the Théâtre du Châtelet, in a frenzy of enthusiasm, rushed forward at the conclusion of the performance and tore off the orchestra rail. From 1909 to 1914 the Ballets Russes maintained its popularity as the dancers made frequent reappearances in Paris, featuring the high-leaping Vaslav Nijinsky and the graceful Anna Pavlova and Tamara Karsavina.

This was a revolutionary kind of ballet, one that offered great vigor and storytelling power to replace the comparatively insipid routines of the traditional kind. Instead of the usual tutus, prescribed gestures, and formalized steps, the Ballets Russes displayed freedom, originality, and variety in costumes, sets, and movements.

The company's first choreographer, Michel Fokine, made known his principles of the ballet in a 1914 letter to the *Times* of London. Among these principles were the following: Dancers should express the feelings and ideas of the characters they portray. They should use their entire body to do so.

La Loïe and Her Muses

Dancing should be integrated with scenery, costuming, and music. The music—no longer merely a rhythmic waltz, polka, or whatnot—should convey the same thoughts and emotions as the dancing.

In developing his theory, Fokine had learned a good deal from watching Isadora Duncan when she appeared in Russia in 1905. Her dancing showed him new possibilities of movement, though Diaghilev no doubt exaggerated when he said, "Isadora's influence on Fokine was the very foundation of his creative activity."[24]

"Isadora Duncan has clearly had an influence on the recent ideas of Loïe Fuller, whose earlier inventions were more original," the critic Paul Souday declared. Most French critics, like most American ones, thought Loie conducted her school in imitation of Duncan's. "It seems to me that the little girls taught by Loïe Fuller are less concerned with precision than are the little girls instructed by her illustrious rival," Georges Pioch remarked. "On the other hand, Loïe's pupils have more of a light-footed gracefulness, and their gambols create a more fluid and varied fantasy."

"Isadora sculpts. Loie Fuller paints. It is useless to compare them." So wrote Louis Vauxcelles, who nevertheless went on to compare the two, judging Loïe's work less bookish, more spontaneous.[25]

"Isadora has talent, Loie has genius," averred Claude Roger-Marx, who as a boy had learned to dance the serpentine from Loie. He was the son of Roger Marx, lately editor of the *Gazette des beaux-arts,* who for years had been her voluntary and most effective publicist. After his father died, in 1913, Claude continued to look out for the reputation of the longtime family friend. She confided in him, and he expressed her point of view. He wrote on one occasion (November 28, 1912):

> We have been dazzled by Nijinsky in "The Blue God" and "The Afternoon of a Faun." We have seen Prince Igor's bowmen hurl their weapons toward the sky, the Firebird discover a supernatural people beneath some fantastic trees, Petrouchka die, and Zobeide stab herself at the Sultan's feet. Ought we to forget that this tremendous movement of renewal owes its élan to a modest, thoughtful, and pretty woman who has returned to us—Miss Loïe Fuller?

To Claude Roger-Marx and to others Loie explained her theory of the "dance of the future": "The dancer ought to be an instrument that projects rhythms expressing all human emotions," she told Roger-Marx. "The dance is visual music, it reaches out in silence, it is a symphony of gestures that convey thought." To another interviewer she said:

> I seek to create a harmony of sound, light, and music. Holding this ideal, I am particularly interested in modern music, so pictorial that it opens a vast field for imagination and innovation.
>
> Music is the joy of the ears. I want it to be also a feast for the eyes and, with that aim, to make it pictorial, to cause it to be *seen*. Oh! that dream, that obsession—to materialize the evanescent. Torch in hand, I tread unknown paths. How happy I would be if everybody whom beauty stirs and sincerity attracts could follow me!

Loie may have exaggerated her own uniqueness and significance, but she certainly deserved credit for a high degree of originality, and her ideas paralleled if they did not anticipate those of the famous Russian choreographer Fokine. Like him, she insisted that the dancer should use the entire body as an instrument of expression and that music and movement should reinforce one another. There were differences, of course, between her philosophy and his. He aimed to coordinate dancing, music, costuming, and scenery, while she concentrated on dancing, music, color, and light. She wanted to give pictorial effects by abstract means that stimulated the imagination; he relied on a more direct and concrete appeal to the senses.[26]

Both Loie and Duncan prepared the way for the Ballets Russes, according to Camille Mauclair, a symbolist poet, an art critic, and a friend, counselor, and biographer of Rodin. Mauclair wrote (December 24, 1911):

> We have recently attended other demonstrations of the lost art which they [Loie and Duncan] are attempting to revive. The Ballets Russes have shown us other marvels, two veritably supernatural beings, the dancers Tamara Karsavina

and Nijinsky. These two owe their fascination neither to the magic of lighting nor to music, and the imitation of ancient Greek dancing is not their thing. But the perfection of their bodies, their exquisite grace concealing their muscular strength, makes them weightless, airy creatures that fly about the stage and seem to create their own atmosphere of Oriental legend.

These Ballets Russes dancers, in Mauclair's opinion, were engaged in essentially the same enterprise as Loie and Duncan: all were trying to renew the dance by restoring an age-old tradition, one that "considered the human body as a symbol and human gestures as a form of language."[27]

Some critics, much less flattering to Loie, refused to accept her theory—and her practice—of the dance as a visible expression of the meaning of music. With reference to her girls, one wrote: "Their dances do not present any kind of meaning, nor do they fit the titles that are given them or the music by which they are accompanied." Several commentators agreed with this judgment. "We may question whether a particular piece of music can ever be transplanted to the material domain. Isn't it the very essence and charm of music that it allows us to create our own dream?" "Debussy's music carries me to great heights, and the dreams I owe to it suffer a bit when confronted with her [Loie's] artistic realizations."

> The evening show began with the charming music written by Mendelssohn for "A Midsummer Night's Dream" . . . for certain episodes of a specific drama. For this drama Mme Loïe Fuller substitutes a fantastic scenario: "In the forest a shepherd daydreams of fairies, gnomes, and elves." The development of the scenario does not amount to much more than an impression of nightgowns. . . .
>
> The same can be said with regard to "Peer Gynt" by Edvard Grieg. During the Death of Ase some young girls—always in long white tunics—come to lament around a dead infant, but Ase is the mother of Peer Gynt. Anitra's Dance is not, either in Ibsen's or in Grieg's thought, a quadrille of damsels

painted many colors. Besides, it makes no sense to have the same quadrille and the same motley serve for both Anitra's Dance and the Hall of the Mountain King.

Most critics gave Loie credit at least for creativity in lighting effects. According to one, her career could be summed up thus: "There once was a woman who caused the light to dance." And, this commentator added, she was still doing so, ceaselessly researching and inventing, always fresh and original, even as she approached the "autumn" of her life. But some observers were far less complimentary. One described some of her projected scenery as splotches of color that looked like enlarged slices of cancerous tissue. He went on to dismiss her lighting effects in general as old hat and a sign of mawkish taste. "The magic lantern was all the rage around 1889, the year of the illuminated fountains [at the 1889 Universal Exposition]; dare I say that it has lost a great deal of its interest since the invention of the cinematograph?"[28]

Since the invention of the movie projector, the slide projector had indeed been losing its charm as an instrument of commercial entertainment. The first commercial moving-picture shows took place in Paris on December 28, 1895, and in New York on April 23, 1896. Soon music halls and vaudeville houses were adding movies to their variety programs, and some of the buildings were being converted into movie theaters, while other cinemas were being newly constructed. By 1914 there were some 260 movie houses in Paris alone.

In the early days of filming, Loie herself had performed the serpentine once or twice before a movie camera. Later she and her pupils had occasionally appeared on the same program with such acts as "the Pathégraph exhibiting amusing and interesting up-to-date pictures" or the "bioscope" depicting "among other things an Exmoor Stag Hunt, Scenes in Ireland, and Beachy Head Lighthouse in a gale."

As yet, however, the moving pictures could not come close to doing what Loie aspired to do with her blend of dancing, music, color, and light. Movies were still soundless and colorless. The films of Loie dancing had to be tinted by hand, and, hardly more than a curiosity, they failed to give the viewer any conception of what it was really like to watch her perform in person.

La Loïe and Her Muses

Most of the movies were mere one-reelers, offering little drama that could compare with that of stage plays. Not till 1915 did the cinema art make its great leap forward with D. W. Griffith's production *The Birth of a Nation*. Within a few years Loie would turn her own special talents to the art of moviemaking.[29]

Since 1905 Loie had considered the family hotel at 3 Cité du Retiro as her permanent address. By 1912 she and Gab had begun to think of finding a place where they could live together, and while Loie was on the road Gab wrote her:

> Now I am in pourparlers for two flats. One is two enormous rooms bath room steam heated, rez-de-chaussée, in a house where flats are 16.000 Frs a year. I can sleep on a divan in the sitting-room and you have the bed-room—or I found this other funny flat in Avenue Trochot, Montmartre[—]you know like a garden, Brieux [an acquaintance] leaves [lives] in rez-de-chaussée and the first floor [h]as verandah funny little terrace etc.—you saw him before with me. It is electricity now in it and bath room but no steam heat. Which do you like best?

The steam heat would surely have appealed to Loie, but she and Gab rented neither of the two flats.

By 1913, however, Loie had moved into more imposing quarters than the Cité du Retiro. Her new dwelling, at 18 rue Boissière, "away up on the tip-top of a high eminence reached by a flight of stone steps," was part of a "curiously sequestered block of modern apartments with distractingly similar stone façades," as an American visitor described the place. "They are bright, airy, and comfortable, and from the windows one looks down over the gardened stretch of the Trocadero and beyond to the great Eiffel tower." It was a "situation unsurpassed in Paris."

While calling that airy apartment home, Loie rented a large room in

Passy for her atelier. Here she had very little furniture: a few chairs, a large divan, a piano, some boxes for costumes and accessories, consisting mainly of gauzy tunics and soft scarves. Here on a December day a French critic found her dressed in an ample fur coat as she conducted rehearsals for a show that she was about to present. "The fur coat is surprising," the Frenchman thought. "One is used to seeing Mme Loïe Fuller moving about unencumbered in the midst of flying veils and gauzes."

Loie did not remain long at 18 rue Boissière. By the summer of 1914 she was residing at one of the most deluxe hotels in the city, the Plaza-Athénée, on the avenue Montaigne. Gab lived some distance away, in an apartment at 41 Quai des Grands-Augustins.[30]

Loie was used to first-class accommodations, whether she could afford them or not, and she often could not. At one time she hoped to make money from a business venture, the Tanagra Electra U.S.A. Company, Limited, which was organized for the distribution of a newly invented electrical stage device. "I have brought people together who purchased the rights for America, for England, for Austria & Italy," she explained. "The American Company worked with English capital is in the hands of Senator J. A. Cantor of New York." Cantor was her friend of long standing who years earlier had been rumored to be her prospective husband.

Another American whom Loie interested in the project, Mrs. Maud Chance, became one of Loie's many personal benefactors. Maud and her sister Mazie vacationed together with Loie and Gab at a French seacoast resort in the summer of 1912. Afterward Mazie complained that Loie and Gab had sponged off her and Maud. Loie "was always in the way and ate their breakfasts, & they were tired out with her & wanted to get rid of her but couldn't." Deeply offended, Loie protested that she and Gab could not afford to contribute more than they did until she "was again earning income." She insisted that, anyhow, she had already repaid with her friendship and, in particular, with her help in trying to find a new husband for Maud, a widow.

Mazie also complained about Loie's handling of one of the company's stage devices, one that she and Loie jointly owned. "She accused me of placing the Tanagra machine where it could be seized for my debts," Loie wrote to Maud, "and yet she had been told again & again that Gab was doing

La Loïe and Her Muses

the business, and my name did not appear in anything but the receipt for the machine." It probably would have made little difference if the thing had been seized, since the Tanagra Electra U.S.A. Company apparently never got off the ground.[31]

When Loie's memoirs were republished as *Fifteen Years of a Dancer's Life* (1913) in London and Boston, she could expect some royalties, but her returns from the American edition were delayed. This was her own fault. The English edition had appeared without her foreknowledge, and she asked "by what right" the "London people" had published her book. The American publisher, Small, Maynard & Company, took her query to mean that the French publisher, Juven, had no right to authorize republication. Small, Maynard refused to pay royalties until Mrs. Clarke, still looking out for Loie, set her lawyers to work.[32]

Another of Loie's benefactors was John Winchester De Kay, an American in his thirties who, though well-off as a financier and newspaper publisher, liked to write about truth and beauty and showed his distaste for materialism by declaring: "A world that is ready to give up Apollo and the Muses for the telephone, telegraph and railroads, prizes information more than life." At one of the Flammarions' parties Loie introduced De Kay to Rodin, and in 1908 Rodin did a bust of him, which he called "Dante." A year or so later, De Kay received a bill of 10,000 francs for the sculpture. He objected that, according to Loie, Rodin had wanted to do the bust simply because he thought him a good model. Loie, De Kay said, had asked him repeatedly if he could spare a few hours for the sculptor. He also said he did not know her very well, though he had "assisted her on several occasions with large sums of money." He nevertheless paid Rodin the 10,000 francs, but despite continual appeals he did not succeed in getting a copy of the bust until after Rodin's death in 1917.[33]

Not long after modeling De Kay's bust, in the old atelier at 182 rue de l'Université, Rodin made a big change in his living and working arrangements. The French government had taken over the Hôtel Biron, an eighteenth-century mansion serving as a convent school, and was renting rooms in it to artists. Here, at 77 rue de Varenne, Rodin began to occupy several rooms in October 1908. After July 1912 he was the sole tenant of the building, which was to become the Musée Rodin in return for his gift of all his works to the state of France. In the meantime he spent most of his time here, while Rose Beuret remained at the villa in Meudon.

When he first moved into the Hôtel Biron, at the age of sixty-eight, Rodin had a new mistress, a bulimic but beautiful forty-four-year-old American, née Claude Coudert. Her husband, an impecunious French aristocrat, styled himself the Duke—and so she was known as the Duchess—of Choiseul-Beaupré. The Duchess proceeded to extend her control over Rodin and his work, which more and more consisted of profitable but unimaginative sculptures of well-to-do Americans such as John Winchester De Kay.

While with the Duchess in Dijon in 1908, Rodin remembered Loie with a Christmas card, much to her delight. Before long, however, Loie and other old friends of his found it necessary to deal with the Duchess as with a kind of gatekeeper. Loie once misremembered the title Choiseul-Beaupré and abjectly apologized:

> Dear Sweet Little Woman
>
> I ought to say dear sweet little flower, for that is what you are—a flower. You are like a delicate plant with a long name. One never forgets the plant, the flower or the perfume. They are learned in a single instant, never to be forgotten, but one always forgets a name, which is often hard to learn & more difficult still to remember. Whenever I have occasion to remember you, or think of you, your eyes are instantly before me, but the name—Oh! I have suffered—during my years in Paris—more through trying to learn peoples names and remember them (and then doing it all over again) than through any thing else, for I am constantly encountering somebody I have met or seen before, whose name I cannot recall, nor pronounce it when I do, and to write it down is tout en l'histoire [i.e., out of the question]. Duchess is very easy for me, but Duchess "so and so" isn't.

When Loie sent Rodin a Happy New Year note on January 1, 1912, her French quickly failed her, and she continued in English, confident that

"that dear friend of ours, who is so good, the little Duchess," would translate for her. As late as May 1912 Loie still felt it necessary to kowtow to the Duchess when wishing to introduce people to Rodin. She then wrote her:

> So far as asking the maitre to see strangers, I hope you believe in me enough to say that he has too much to do to see them. I want them to see his art and work, especially at Meudon, but I know some of his most beautiful things are at 77 [rue de Varenne] and I don't know if I might ask the maitre to let me show any body these without him.
>
> It is for the truth I admire you so much, so you can see I would understand & appreciate it with me—and if you don't want those people, just tell me so. Perhaps I might take them to Meudon one day when the maitre is not there and perhaps I might come to 77 with just the Count Primoli—and do tell me right out—anything.

A couple of months later Rodin broke with the Duchess, and Loie no longer had to flatter her in order to gain access to him. Soon she was again freely socializing with him and "Madame Rodin," as friends called his old mistress Rose Beuret—inviting them, on a typical occasion, to go with her in her car to call on the Flammarions and have dinner with them in the country.[34]

While recovering her place in the society of her idol Rodin, Loie was renewing her acquaintanceship with another of her idols, Princess Marie of Romania. In 1912, ten years after meeting the princess, Loie began to correspond with her, sending her photographs of her "children" and news of their projected tour, which was to include Madrid, where Marie's favorite cousin, Eugenia, was queen. "I have written to the Queen," Marie responded. "I have told her how we had known each other and what a liking we had kept for each other although we had never met since."

The next year, not yet recovered from the phlebitis that followed the birth of her sixth child, Marie made a brief stop, her first, in Paris. There, beset by well-wishers from the Romanian community, she could spare only a little time for Loie. Loie could not take her to see Rodin, because he was away,

Loie and her dance troupe pose in front of the Sphinx in early 1914. (Courtesy of the Musée d'Orsay, © R.M.N.)

but he had given Loie one of his bronzes to send to Marie. "I lovingly thank you," Marie wrote Loie after returning to Romania. "It was indeed a joy to meet again after all those years and to feel that there was no difference between our feeling for each other of then and now as if we had only parted the day before." Marie promised to arrange an appearance for Loie and her troupe in Bucharest. "I loved your little girls and wish only that I had had more time to talk with them and get them accustomed to me."

Loie and Marie continued to exchange letters. Marie told about her children, about a fairy story she was writing, about her relief work among Romanian soldiers afflicted with cholera during the Second Balkan War. She sent Rodin a photographic portrait of herself and addressed to Loie a letter for her to deliver personally to him, thanking him for the bronze he had given Loie to give her. In return, Rodin invited Marie to his atelier and thanked her for the portrait and for the letter that "the great woman of genius Loïe Fuller" had brought him.

In January 1914 Loie looked forward to a tour that would take her once more to Romania and the princess. "Ah, how I wish you were here," she wrote to Rodin from aboard a packet boat in the Mediterranean, "—the sea like glass—the sunshine warm—the air like summer—beautiful, beautiful." She and her girls stopped in Cairo and had their picture taken in front of the Sphinx, then gave their performances in Athens, and finally headed for Bucharest to appear at the Opéra Lyrique. En route, she received a telegram from Marie saying: "alas am in deep mourning [because of a death in the royal family] and would only be able to go to rehearsals all the same would love to see you idea about my fairy story being produced on the stage enchants me."[35]

10

*Little Loïe
and
Big Alma*

*A*s it did to millions of others, the Great War of 1914–18 deflected the career of Loie Fuller. It interrupted her schedule of dances in Europe and caused her to turn to the United States as the main venue of her performances. These became subservient to her larger objective, which was primarily to alleviate the suffering of war-torn France and Belgium and secondarily to acquaint Americans with French art, emphasizing that of Rodin. Her achievements in war relief and art promotion were made possible by her association with Alma Spreckels, the wife of one of California's wealthiest men.

Alma Emma Charlotte Corday le Normand de Bretteville was born on a farm near San Francisco in 1881, nineteen years after Loie. Alma's impecunious parents, natives of Denmark, traced the family ancestry to a noble refugee from the French Revolution—hence the namesake Charlotte Corday, who was guillotined after assassinating the Revolutionary extremist Jean Paul Marat. Alma grew up to be a beautiful, imposing young woman, an artist's model, six feet tall. For five years the mistress of Adolph B. Spreckels, she became his wife after he inherited a sugar-business fortune and the title of Sugar King. She bore him three children before he lost his potency, presumably because of syphilis.

Full of energy, Alma occupied herself with social affairs, but these did not satisfy her. She was interested in art. After the construction of the new Spreckels mansion, one of the most impressive in San Francisco, at 2080 Washington Street, she wanted to fit out her room with the finest of eighteenth-century furnishings. So, in the spring of 1914, though unacquainted with the French language, she set out alone on a shopping trip to Paris. There she found more than she was looking for. "She found Loie Fuller, the dancer, and Auguste Rodin, the sculptor, and through them," as her biographer has written, "she found a whole new direction to her life."[1]

Loie and Alma met at one of the city's most fashionable restaurants—Loie remembered it as Paillard's, Alma as Ciro's—where the dinner host was the Paris representative of New York art dealers whom Adolph Spreckels had alerted. Alma's cousin Pierre, the Marquis de Bretteville, called at the Hotel Plaza-Athénée for Loie, one of several invited guests who were known as fanciers of art. Several years afterward Loie recounted (in the

Alma Spreckels, whom Loie inspired to help found the Legion of Honor Museum in San Francisco and the Maryhill Museum in Goldendale, Washington. (Courtesy of the Dance Collection, the New York Public Library for the Performing Arts.)

third person) what was to her a most significant occasion, one that began with her accompanying the marquis:

> Entering a motor it was not long till they arrived at that splendid place where the cuisine is superb, Paillard's, & mounting a short flight of stairs, they came upon a woman & there they stood face to face, these two women who did not either of them care to meet the other, each of them having enough to do without spending time in making useless acquaintances. One of them was tall & of the Juno type, the other petite and looking for all the world like a little plump figure out of a Dresden china group, [and they] stood facing each other for quite a minute before either of them spoke & the little one putting out her hand said, "You are sensitive, too sensitive. You must not let people hurt you." The tall beautiful woman smiled and said, "It is true but how could you tell?" "Instinct," the other replied, "& we can't explain instinct, can we?" And the ice was broken!

Alma did, indeed, feel quite ill at ease in the presence of so many French-speaking celebrities, and at the table she was relieved to be sitting beside the fellow American who talked excitedly about a close friend, the famous sculptor Rodin.[2]

Loie wanted Alma to meet her famous friend, and together the two went to look for him, first at the Biron house and then at the Meudon villa, where they peeked through the windows at his statuary collection, but they could not find him at either place. When Alma went shopping for art, Loie accompanied her and gave her advice. Forget about antiques, she said, and concentrate on the works of living artists. Alma was grateful. "I used to be a student at the Mark Hopkins Art School," she later recalled, "[but] I knew nothing of art and imagined that all things antique were worth owning. Loie Fuller and I became great friends and she taught me that ugly things were also made in the old days and you had to learn to distinguish."

Alma was in England, preparing to sail for home, when Loie telephoned her to say she had finally found Rodin, and she persuaded her to come back and meet him. At Meudon, Loie introduced her as a moneyed woman who wished to collect and exhibit his works. With an uncertain memory, Alma afterward wrote, quoting Loie: "'Well,' she said, 'Master, Mrs. Spreckels has a museum in San Francisco, and I want you to let her have some of your works, and here is a photo of the museum.' And with that, she showed him a large photo of 2080 Washington St. I was on the spot, as I did not like to tell Rodin that Loie had a vivid imagination, and that it was our home."

In this instance it was Alma herself who had a vivid imagination, for her account is inconsistent with Loie's contemporary correspondence with Rodin. He had his suspicions about Loie's and Alma's project, for he could not help remembering his unhappy experience when, eleven years earlier, Loie undertook to exhibit his works in New York and left him with a worthless promissory note. She now protested to him (in French):

> I am flabbergasted by the impression you are under. I must make you understand. Mrs. Spreckles [sic] invited me to return with her and spend several days (or weeks) in San Francisco.
>
> I have plenty to do here, for we have a great tour—beginning in Vienna on September 20—and a dozen summer performances on shipboard in the Mediterranean.
>
> But when I understood that Mrs. Spreckels wanted to do something for San Francisco, it occurred to me that perhaps *you* could profit from it, and after having turned down her invitation I offered to accept *if I could be useful,*—and I promptly made her acquainted with your grand and beautiful works.
>
> Then she suggested that I arrange for next year (while I am there this summer) an art exhibition—in her beautiful house (you have seen the photograph)—an exhibition like the one I did in New York, only this time it is *she,* instead of myself, who will bear the expense. Under these circumstances I shall go to San Francisco, because with my help she *can* perhaps obtain for you and your work the justice that they deserve.
>
> After the project is arranged I have more to do. Your agent

Little Loïe and Big Alma

will take the necessary oversight, since I know nothing about the commercial aspect.

No personal consideration has entered my head.

When I interested Mrs. Spreckles in our master Rodin, I had something grand in mind. She told me (without having seen your work), "You can ask the master (if agreeable to both of you) whether we can buy from him his *première oeuvre* for the museum that you will help me found in San Francisco—and whether we can build the Tower of Labor instead of the museum."[3]

For the time being, however, Loie could neither expect nor afford to stay long in San Francisco. Not only did she have the Vienna engagement beginning September 20, but she also had a contract for a later appearance in Switzerland and was hoping to arrange a tour in Germany. Meanwhile, to pay her debts and keep her troupe together during the summer, she needed money, lots of it. Her new business manager and financial backer, Nathan Van Beil, had invested a good deal in the enterprise, but he was running short of funds and becoming rather desperate himself.

Van Beil, an American, had become acquainted with Loie and her dancing girls at least as early as July 14, 1909, when, as one of the Flammarions' guests, he watched the "muses" perform on the lawn at Juvisy. Then in his seventies, he looked the part of a successful businessman, rather stout, with hair parted in the middle and combed sideways, a gray mustache and a Van Dyke beard, and rimless pince-nez glasses. Much of the time he held an expensive cigar, the kind with a long-lasting ash. Agnes Van Beil, his second wife, quite pretty, was much younger than he and looked even younger than she was. The Van Beils became good and generous friends of Loie and Gab. "They are not poor, so they will take a good time along with them," Loie once wrote regarding a pleasure trip that she and Gab were about to take with them. Eventually the friendship was so close that Loie and Gab habitually referred to Van Beil as "Dad" or "Daddy" and to Mrs. Van Beil as "Auntie."

Another investor in Loie's enterprise was her old friend Jacob Cantor, who currently (1913–15) served as a Democratic congressman from New

York. Previously he had been a member of the state senate, and Loie, Gab, and the Van Beils continued to call him "senator." Early in 1914 Van Beil, facing what he and Loie considered a financial emergency, renewed an appeal to Cantor for a further investment of twenty thousand dollars. "There were two ways to succeed," Van Beil explained to him. "One was an immediate result in the music halls for big money weekly. The other was for bigger money in the operas, but this would take time. As either was a sure thing I chose the latter.... Now every opera in Europe is at last open to us." Loie added her assurance that they were offering a business opportunity, not asking for charity: "Dear Senator it was for what Dad saw could be made & not really *for me*, as I fear you think it was.... Oh! if I had known it would or could have been a care to you, I would have cut my hand off before I would have accepted it. Twenty years ago I would not be a block in your advancement & that cost me more sacrifice than it would have been now not to have had Dad's help. Success does not tempt me, if it gives you care." Here Loie implied that when, some twenty years earlier, there were rumors of an impending marriage between her and Cantor, he had in fact proposed to her and she declined, even though acceptance would have meant relief from the financial pressure she then faced. Despite her touching plea, Cantor did not respond with the necessary funds, and Van Beil had to borrow them at high interest.[4]

Counting on the contracts she already held, and anticipating more of them, Loie could look forward to the 1914–15 season as probably the best ever for her school of dancers. The future continued to look bright even after June 28, 1914, when a Serbian nationalist assassinated Archduke Francis Ferdinand, heir to the Austro-Hungarian throne, and Austria-Hungary began to threaten war against Serbia. Parisians carried on as usual with their summer gaiety, including the fête of the sun atop the Eiffel Tower. Here a group of astronomers and other scientists met every year to dine and watch the sunset. Prominent among them was Flammarion, who had involved his friend Loie in meetings of the Savants' Society and who now invited her to the Eiffel affair. The scientists "held their breaths in wonderment and surprise" as Loie, on that highest platform, daringly executed for them her own conception of an Egyptian sun dance.[5]

By the time Loie embarked for Montreal, on the Canadian liner *Lauren-*

tic, Austria-Hungary was at war with Serbia, and hostilities were beginning quickly to spread to other countries. At sea, on August 3, the *Laurentic* passengers received by "wireless telegraph" the distressing news that Germany had declared war on France. Loie, concerned for the safety of the Rodins and the Flammarions, immediately cabled and wrote to "Very Dear Master," begging him to arrange for all of them to proceed to Dieppe, where Mrs. Van Beil would receive them and conduct them across the Channel to England, whence they must sail promptly for America. After Loie landed she repeated the message by cable and by mail, assuring them that Mrs. Van Beil would pay their expenses, but received no reply.[6]

In San Francisco, after delivering some Rodin sketches and plaster molds that she had brought for Alma, Loie encouraged her to go ahead with the project for establishing a museum. Alma must begin accumulating more and more pieces, the money for which would have to come from her husband, who granted her a generous but not unlimited allowance. After a couple of weeks, Loie left to return to France and bring back additional Rodin statuary. She got as far as New York, where she used Cantor's law office as her headquarters, and where she received a cablegram from Gab saying she "must not sail on any pretext" for the time being. So she postponed her voyage.

Back in San Francisco, after the three-day train ride from New York, Loie continued to get letters and cables from Gab, who had been sending them in a constant stream. "And I love you Loie dearest with all my heart," Gab kept assuring her. "Love again *dear dear* Loie." But regarding money problems and relations with the Van Beils, Gab repeatedly insisted: "Do nothing without consulting me first by cable and having my reply." Gab was in London with the "children," as was Agnes Van Beil, while Nathan Van Beil traveled to Washington to confer with "Senator" (Congressman) Cantor. Naturally, the war was on everyone's mind. "In *the end* we win, but before I am sure the Germans be in Paris," Gab wrote. "They are north now, very much in France." In the first Battle of the Marne, September 6–9, 1914, the French and their British allies stopped the German advance but were far from winning the war. "If I had big money I would buy an auto and go to fetch wounded after the battle," Gab said, suggesting the kind of ambulance service that was soon to preoccupy her.

For the moment, another and less generous thought crossed Gab's mind. "Just seen Isadora lent her school to Red Cross," she reported. "Speaking of school, what we must do and where is lot of money is to make your school at once when you return. You have all the advantage on Isadora now but after *it be too late*. Every body want to send children to you not her. You must have a house like hers (rented)." Actually, the prospects for Loie's school were dim. The anticipated Austrian and German tour was, of course, completely out of the question now, and even the Swiss contract was canceled when cities in neutral Switzerland ordered the closing of all places of public amusement for an indefinite period.[7]

As for Duncan, Loie felt sympathetic rather than rivalrous upon reading a newspaper story headlined "The Fate of the House Built on Sin." It began: "Death, disaster, misery in many forms still overtake those who transgress against the elementary laws of God and man." The first example was that of Frank Lloyd Wright, who had run off with another man's wife, Mamah Cheney, who in turn was murdered at Taliesin, the house he had designed for her. The second example was that of Duncan, who without the sanctity of marriage had given birth to two children, both of whom were accidentally drowned in the Seine. "It is terrible to publish something like that," Loie wrote to a friend in Paris, sending her a clipping of the article. "I think Isadora Duncan has suffered enough . . . truly this is too much. Poor woman, poor great artist."

With regard to the war, Loie could not be neutral, though her native country proclaimed itself to be. According to what she read in the papers, the war could become unimaginably horrible with the development of strange new weapons—a "gun that discharges poisonous gases," "airships with lenses and mirrors" that concentrate the sun's rays on the enemy, and even an "atomic bomb" that "releases the energy of matter and causes everything it touches to explode." If the United States would stop all foreign trade, it could stop the war in a week and thus prevent these horrors, or so Loie momentarily believed. She composed a ten-page essay on that theme and sent it to Van Beil with a letter in which she greeted him as "Dearest Daddy" and signed herself "Your loving *daughter*." But the more the war escalated, the more she consecrated herself to the Anglo-French cause.[8]

To make up for the dancing engagements that the war had cost her in

Europe, Loie looked for opportunities in the United States, and she found one right in San Francisco. Here, in 1915, was to be held a great exposition to celebrate the opening of the Panama Canal. On September 15, 1914, Loie signed on behalf of herself and her absent manager, Van Beil, a contract with the Panama-Pacific International Exposition Company. During the following summer at the exposition, according to the contract, she was to put on four performances a month, provide twenty pupils and ten electricians, pay all travel and transportation expenses, and receive 50 percent of the gross receipts. She hoped also to get an engagement at the Metropolitan Opera House in New York, but failed to do so.[9]

Among the exhibits at the Panama-Pacific International Exposition would be those at the French pavilion. While the French government would provide some displays of national art, Alma could supplement these by lending objects she had acquired or expected to acquire. This kind of generosity would strengthen Loie's bargaining position vis-à-vis Rodin.

Before Loie left San Francisco again, Alma took her to a shack where Arthur Putnam lived in poverty with his wife. Putnam had sketched and sculpted animals until surgery for a brain tumor left him partially paralyzed. His work so impressed Loie that she offered to take a number of his plaster molds to France and have them cast by Rodin's founder. Alma agreed to pay for this. She was also going to pay, of course, for the Rodin pieces that Loie promised to obtain (and did obtain).

When about to sail from New York on the American liner *St. Louis,* October 10, 1914, Loie consigned to the ship's purser for safekeeping a box containing approximately seventy-seven hundred dollars in gold coins, readily convertible into francs. "To be delivered to your order at Liverpool," she advised Gab in a hasty note; "if anything happens to me, you must claim it."[10]

Once arrived in England, Loie confronted a set of self-imposed assignments that were to keep her extremely busy during the fall and winter of 1914–15. Not only did she have to acquire as many Rodin pieces as possible for the projected San Francisco museum and for the Panama-Pacific Exposition, but she also intended to undertake a grand-scale work for the relief of wartime suffering in Belgium and France. Meanwhile, she must see that her children were properly taken care of and that those due to perform in San Francisco were safely transported there, along with the necessary stage properties and lighting equipment.

The immediate task was to find Rodin. There had been an exhibition of his works in London, and according to Gab's information he was still somewhere in England, but she did not know where. Eventually finding him in London, Loie offered to buy, for Alma, the works on exhibit there. She was too late: he had already promised them to the Victoria and Albert Museum. Anyhow, Alma was unwilling to pay as much as Rodin was asking. "She wants too many things for the money she has available," Loie later explained to Rodin, while expressing the hope of obtaining another collection of Rodin pieces.

> I am expecting a telegram and if she so decides I will come at once with the money because I know, my dear Master, as you have told me, that there is no point in coming on her behalf without the money—you know that kind of Americans better than I do!
>
> If by chance she tries to communicate directly with you, thinking she can succeed better with you than with me, would you let me know? Perhaps she thinks I keep part of the money for myself, but, on the contrary, I don't know how I could come see you with so little as she is willing to give me. But the war may be long, and I must be sure that you have all the money possible before I leave . . . and if I insist and stand firm she will give you what you ask.

When Loie left London for Paris, she expected to see Rodin there and talk further with him about the purchase of his works.[11]

When Rodin left London for Paris, however, he did not tarry there but promptly went on to Rome. "My heart was broken when you left," she wrote him, ". . . without waiting a minute here in Paris!" She continued to occupy herself with packing up for her San Francisco show, and even after sending off forty-eight boxes she still had more of them to fill with personal and

Little Loïe and Big Alma

theatrical things. Then, with authorization from Alma, she decided to follow Rodin to Rome and do business with him there.

Accompanying her to Rome was Mrs. Van Beil, to whom she had recently sent the following:

> *An Ancient Prayer.* "Oh Lord I implore Thee to bless all mankind & bring us to Thyself and keep us to dwell with Thee."
>
> This prayer was sent to me & it is to be sent all around the World. It was said in ancient times that all those who wrote it would be safe from calamity & those who passed it by would meet with misfortune.
>
> Copy it & send it to 9 persons within 9 days. The 11th day you will meet with great joy. Please do not break the chain.

Did Mrs Van Beil break the chain? Regardless, she was destined to meet with serious misfortune within a few months. For the moment, though, she was cheerful enough. "We took a sleeper in Paris and did not have to change until we arrived 36 hours afterward—it rained when we got here, now it is dull but dry," she reported to her husband from Rome. "Loie turns herself upside down to make me happy—God bless her."[12]

The Rome mission was successful, culminating in three agreements on December 16 and 24, 1914, and January 1, 1915. According to these, Loie was to make a down payment on eight specified bronzes but could take possession of them only when she or Alma paid the balance on each and it was cast by the founder, Eugène Rudier. Loie bought six other pieces outright—*The Thinker* (large-scale), *The Bronze Age, Bust of Rochefort, Saint John, The Sirens,* and *The Prodigal Son*—all of which reached San Francisco in time for the exposition.[13]

Before leaving Rome, Loie asked Rodin to give her some twenty of his sketches and allow her to publish them in an album. Copies of this, she explained, would be sold at the exposition, and the proceeds would be used to benefit the wounded veterans of France. Rodin, not entirely trusting her, wanted to be absolutely certain that all the profit would be spent for that purpose. He agreed to her proposal, but only on the following condition: he could, if he wished, require that the gross receipts be sent directly to him,

Rose Beuret, Rodin, and Loie in a rooftop garden in Rome about December 1914. (Courtesy of the Musée Rodin.)

so that, after reimbursing her for the costs, he could forward the balance to the appropriate authorities.

Despite his misgivings, Rodin took pride in cooperating with Loie on this occasion, as he indicated to Armand Dayot, supervisor of the Beaux-Arts school and organizer of the French section at the San Francisco exposition. Dayot had sent Rodin a telegram begging him to return at once to Paris "for the glory of our country. Don't abandon it at this moment. France has need of all its powers and especially of Rodin." "Do you think I have been wasting my time in England and Rome?" Rodin protested. "From here I have been making arrangements for the San Francisco exposition, which is taking beautiful shape, thanks to you and Monsieur Guiffrey [curator of the Louvre], and thanks also to Loïe Fuller."[14]

After Rodin, Loie had started enlisting other French notabilities in her campaign to raise money for the war wounded, and back in Paris she concentrated on the effort. Her plan was to beg or buy books and photographs, persuade the authors or subjects to sign them, and then ship them to the United States to be sold or raffled off. Accumulating a bunch of volumes by a particular author, she would take them and him to a restaurant in her car, and he would do the signing after lunch. Among the famous writers who obliged were the astronomer Flammarion, the Egyptologist G. C. C. Maspero, the novelist Pierre Loti, and the poet and novelist Gabriele D'Annunzio, an Italian who was trying to get his country into the war on the side of the Allies.

Eager to add her old friend Anatole France to the list of contributors, Loie posted letter after letter to him but got no reply. "I am desolate because I can't find you," she lamented. When she learned he was out of town and unavailable for a book-signing luncheon, she sent him leaves of paper for his signature, to be pasted in his books. At last he responded, and she wrote him again:

> Very Dear Master
>
> Thanks and thanks again—a thousand times—for your dear and beautiful lines—and for the signatures I thank you yet again. And now I would like to request something very, very great of you, for France, and a great sacrifice on your part. Will you earn money for the wounded, the soldiers of France and Belgium? Will you agree to go to North America and give some lectures on the war—to defend France against the propaganda being made in America by the Germans? . . . A Belgian woman has made a lecture tour in the United States, and she has returned with 1,400,000 francs. And *you* could get much more.

But the seventy-year-old author, patriotic though he was, did not see his way clear to making the kind of sacrifice that Loie proposed.[15]

Writing (in English) to Madame Raymond Poincaré, wife of the president of the French republic, Loie explained that her charity work was intended to benefit not only wounded soldiers but also the needy families of painters, sculptors, writers, musicians, and actors. She asked that President and Madame Poincaré sign some of their photographs and books. One large picture was to be inscribed to Mrs. Adolph Spreckels.

> She is the wife of the great Sugar King & although she was born in San Francisco she is the grand niece of the old Marquis de Bretteville—& her heart is French to its very depths. She is the one who sent me here on a great mission. . . . I am so grateful to God that I can be doing even so little—for my heart [and] my soul are in the country which gave me real life, the life of spirit, friendship, & art—France—and while I am not much good myself I can help *immensely* the wife of the great financial King of the West to be.

Readily providing the requested signatures, Madame Poincaré invited Loie and her girls to visit the presidential mansion, the Palais de l'Elysée. Afterward Madame Poincaré suggested that her husband reward the children, but Loie demurred. "They are paid every week a salary to send home to help their people who are poor," she explained, "but they have not yet learned to expect or look for presents for doing their duty to themselves & to me." She would be much pleased, though, if the president would say a word of appreciation to the Van Beils, to whom she and her girls owed everything: "Our lives are made happy and our work made possible by an old gentleman philanthropist of 80 years of age and his wife who is over 60. They are giving us their whole lives and spending their fortune for us. If it were not for them, we could never think of our art. They are making a great Temple for me to give to my children when I am gone, where they shall be the professors in art, science & literature for which they are now being educated."

One more favor Loie asked of Madame Poincaré, who was quite ready to grant it also. "Mrs. Spreckels is going to send over cases of food and clothing which she hopes you will be willing to distribute." One of the conspicuous

Little Loïe and Big Alma

items, appropriately enough, would be sugar, of which Alma had already shipped a thousand kilos.[16]

In addition to the Poincaré pictures, Loie obtained an autographed painting of King Albert I of Belgium, another of General Joseph J. C. Joffre, commander in chief of the French army, and signed photographs of Joffre and also of General John D. P. French, commander of the British Expeditionary Forces in France. To General French she wrote regarding her charitable project: "This would not be complete without something from the two men who are leading civilization against the mighty goose step of oppression, Deutschland Ober [sic] Alles—thank you! I am only a woman & a nuisance, I expect, but I don't want Deutschland over me!"

Her old friend and admirer the artist Pierre Roche was glad to help her out. When sending her a drawing of his for her to reproduce, he expressed gratitude instead of expecting it: "It was nice of you, in the midst of all your occupations and extra occupations, to have thought of coming to see me." Besides pictures and books to sell—especially to French and Belgian communities in the United States—Loie was also accumulating lantern slides of French art and of alleged German atrocities to use in lectures she planned to give for the enlightenment of the American public.[17]

After four months in Europe, Loie summed up in reports to Alma what she had been doing for her and for the great cause. Loie was reproachful, feeling that Alma was unappreciative. "In spite of the fact that you are perhaps the only person in all the world who does not understand what I am doing means—I cannot help doing all the good I can, & as it is your money & not mine, I am able to put all the credit down to you," she wrote. "If you follow and carry out the plans I have laid & begun here, you will not only hold the place of the first woman in Cal, but in Paris as well, & I have no doubt you will receive for it the cross of the Legion of Honour."[18]

For some time, Gab had assumed responsibility for the children, but she had to give it up when she got her wish to serve as an ambulance driver for the army. Ambulances for her and for other volunteers were among the benefits that Loie intended to provide through her money-raising schemes. While Gab was on leave, she and Loie called on Rodin's secretary, Marcelle Martin, to cheer her brother, a wounded soldier convalescing under her care. Then Gab returned to the front, and Mrs. Van Beil departed for America with the children.

By the time Loie herself was ready to go, she was worn out, having worked day after day from eight in the morning till after midnight. She already had a bad cold when she left Paris, and she was compelled to take to her bed as soon as she arrived in London. There she stayed for a week or so and then, disregarding her doctor's orders, sailed on the liner *New York*. After six days at sea she was still in bed but was recovering from her bronchitis. She had to get well. "I have a great work to do in San Francisco," she reminded Rodin on one of the ship's postcards.[19]

When Loie arrived in San Francisco, in March 1915, the Panama-Pacific International Exposition was already attracting crowds. The exposition appealed to beauty with its brilliantly lighted Tower of Jewels and its Palace of Fine Arts mirrored in a reflecting pool, and to practicality with its Ford automobile assembly line and its demonstration of the U.S. Mint. Among the foreign exhibits, the French pavilion, a temporary replica of the Palais de la Légion d'Honneur in Paris, was about to open. Seeing it, Alma decided she must have a permanent replica of the same building to house her Rodin collection.

To hail this collection, which Loie was making possible, Alma staged in the Spreckels mansion what a local newspaper described as the "greatest celebration of art ever held in the West and, at the same time, one of San Francisco's most brilliant social functions." Loie gave the society folks a lecture on Rodin's works, illustrating it with some of the slides she had brought with her from France. "When our day shall belong to the past, when generations have come and generations have gone, the immortal works left by Rodin will remain, and his genius will stand like a giant in the storm—unshaken, unmoved," she declared. "Rodin, the magician who has brought out of human nature the best and crystallized it into bronze, is the apostle of simplicity, and has shown the world that only the true simplicity is truly great."[20]

Loie and her troupe were scheduled to begin performing at the exposition on June 1. Meanwhile the girls remained in Philadelphia, and Loie wondered how she was going to get them to San Francisco. She found it hard even to keep up with their salaries. One mother, writing from England, complained that her daughter was not receiving the shilling-a-week pocket money she had been promised. Van Beil, in New York with his wife, could not help; he was so ill that for a time he was not expected to live. "I know of course what an awful struggle you had to get the means for transportation," Cantor apologized to Loie from New York. "Unhappily, we were strapped here, and could not raise a dollar, otherwise you know I would not put you to all that annoyance, embarrassment and anxiety." Cantor did pay for the girls' board and room in Philadelphia, and he provided money for food and extras on the trip, so that the troupe could finally depart, under the supervision of Loie's English secretary, Beresford, a man. Alma, who no doubt had bought the railroad tickets, assumed responsibility for the girls' maintenance after their arrival in San Francisco, while they waited to begin their performances and earn their keep.

Van Beil never arrived. Embarking at New York with Mrs. Van Beil, to go by ship through the recently opened Panama Canal, he died en route. The news, though not entirely unexpected, came as a terrible shock to Loie, as it did to Gab when Loie cabled it to her. "Poor Dad, poor Dad!" Gab replied and proceeded to warn Loie against acknowledging any monetary indebtedness to Cantor or to Van Beil's estate. Gab elaborated:

> *You* never received money directly from Senator. It was always Daddy, so they cannot prove. Also as you know Daddy managed at his own idea, signing his own contract (Chatelet etc) touching *all the money* not even giving you 5 francs, so you have all proves for you. *It was his own speculation.* If they say, it is funny at his old age to make speculation like that, you only answer, why he made it himself as a speculation and also because he & Mrs V B were found [fond] of the children and of the work. That is the stand you must take.

Certainly Loie could not afford to assume any new debts, since she was already so far behind with old ones, among them a fairly large sum that she had owed for several years to her former benefactress, Mrs. T. Alexander Clarke. "Now that Daddy is dead, & it may take some time before Auntie can rely on any thing much," Loie confided to Alma, "I must not do things that would perhaps make it necessary for me to have to depend on others, especially you." She was, of course, already depending on Alma.[21]

At the time of Van Beil's death, Loie was busy preparing to put on a pageant a few days later to celebrate the opening of the new municipal auditorium across the bay in Oakland. The performers were local lasses, not her own "children." "I expect to find some stars among the several hundred girls, some who will go far in the art of dancing," she had announced when inviting all the young women of Oakland to sign up at a hotel ballroom. According to the *Oakland Enquirer,* she was going to "arrange the greatest ball in all the city's history." Whether it proved the greatest or not, the pageant (on April 30) elicited praise for her "contagious enthusiasm" and her "great artistic soul."

While Loie was in Oakland, Anna Pavlova, formerly of Diaghilev's Ballets Russes, appeared in the new auditorium, "but she danced only on little stage one end," as Loie gossiped to Gab. "She don't adjust herself to other places or fashions (till she sees us). She had Sat mat & eve $5000 receipts. But . . . all people were saying Oh Miss Fuller is coming we must go & see her" at the San Francisco exposition.

Loie was more enthusiastic about a quite different kind of entertainer among the first ones to appear at the auditorium. This was William F. Cody, with whose show she had played her first important role as an actress a third of a century before. As gallant a showman as ever, though racked by disease and debt, Cody was now reduced to a kind of circus appendage. He had not forgotten Loie, "a very particular long-time friend," and on his behalf the director of the Sells-Floto Circus & Buffalo Bill Co. arranged "nice reserved seats" for her and the twenty-five members of her troupe. "Did you see the girls rise and wave to Colonal Cody when he came round?" a fellow spectator asked her. "I know he liked that."[22]

Besides her activities in Oakland, Loie was preoccupied with rehearsing for the exposition and with helping Alma plan to raise money for their French and Belgian charity. "Am so pushed and busy," she informed Gab. "Alma is opening a house as studio for artists works to be sold & half goes to charity over there, same as the books. Sat next [May 29] she gives an illuminated fete in the garden & I make of children a *dance Opal* in honor of a great opal (5000 frs) a present she had to the charity to be raffled off. I got beautiful silks & coloring them my self. Same occasion I have 50 girls from Oakland to dance same as there." The opal dance, which Loie had choreographed for the occasion, was worthy of the huge black gem it celebrated, a gift from an Australian. Numerous as they were, the colorfully lighted dancers made an impressive scene as they gamboled on the grass in front of sheets that had been hung as a backdrop.[23]

The next Tuesday evening, June 1, Loie and her company began their exposition performances in Festival Hall, an auditorium she considered beautiful, decorated as it was with paintings she had chosen, among them one of herself. Colossal indeed was the program of "Colossal Scenic Productions," incorporating practically all the acts of the past few years and culminating in a grand finale in which the Oakland girls took part. The eighty-piece Exposition Symphony Orchestra provided the music. On the following day the *San Francisco Call* reported:

> La Loie Fuller's first appearance in America at Festival Hall last night was a triumph. Before a crowd of fully 3500, including the city's foremost art lovers, the world famous danseuse and her company of pretty girls interpreted musical masterpieces in the dance, presenting new terpsichorean creations.
>
> In color effects, revelry, spirit and art the dances charmed the large audience, winning great plaudits for the artists. Loie Fuller's appearance . . . was made the occasion of a great assemblage of society folk. The boxes were bright with the gowns of belles and matrons, and the sparkling of jewels added to the splendor of the spectacle.[24]

Crowds continued to attend and applaud the four performances a month in Festival Hall, but when Loie took the show to the Mason Opera House in Los Angeles, it got no such enthusiastic reception. This was Loie's own fault. Her manager, L. W. Buckley, had agreed with the opera house's manager, W. T. Wyatt, that she would appear with her company for six nights and two matinees, beginning on Monday, July 19. The terms were quite generous, her share of the gross receipts rising to 70 percent if the total should reach eight thousand dollars. A few days before the opening date, however, she telegraphed to Fred Cummins, her representative in Los Angeles: "I received copies of L.A. papers of last Sunday in which I see I am absolutely ignored. Does Mr Wyatt think I am an ordinary act or does he realize I am the only artist in my line in the world. Being slighted so, I feel terribly embarrassed and will not sign any contract nor will appear at present. If Mr Wyatt wishes to negotiate with me direct I will give his negotiations consideration for probably a later date."

In a flurry of telegrams Cummins begged Loie to reconsider, and Wyatt warned: "If Fuller does not arrive Monday somebody will pay heavy damage—sale for Monday very good." Loie changed her mind, but too late to appear on Monday, and Buckley asked Wyatt to postpone the opening until Tuesday. On Tuesday Loie and her troupe finally arrived, but not their baggage, so Wyatt had to return two nights' receipts to disappointed patrons. This "double disappointment," he told Cummins, "not only killed the business for the Wednesday night performance but undoubtedly has hurt it considerably for the balance of the week." By week's end the receipts totaled only $1,089.25, and Loie's share did not even cover her expenses.

A financial fiasco, the Los Angeles appearance was also a critical failure. The *Los Angeles Times* critic, who remembered seeing Loie perform as a "slender wisp of a girl," found her essentially unchanged. "She looked from 38 to 42 [she was fifty-three], plump, but not ungraceful. She did not really dance and now I know that she never did." Her art was only a "trick of light." Still, word had come from San Francisco that "her production in that city was one of the finest features of the fair year." She must have brought much less than her full company (she did not bring her Oakland girls) to Los Angeles. "She has treated us as people of established reputation often do treat us. She has brought us her second best, or at least only half of her best. Los Angeles never loses anything by slights of this kind." Inadvertently, Loie had prodded the inferiority feelings of Angelenos.[25]

"I am terribly sorry to hear that Loie's performances were not a success," Gab wrote to Alma. "Poor little Loie! I am afraid she has her head full with the work begun for the artists, the Charity work and this terrible War." Her head continued to be full of projects. After concluding her series of shows in Festival Hall, she produced an open-air pageant at the exposition on Fine Arts Preservation Day, October 16. The pageant, *Elaine,* retold the story of the "lily maid of Astolat" who pined and died for Sir Lancelot. Along with aerial stunts and other events, Loie's spectacle was intended to start a money-raising campaign for the preservation of the exposition's Fine Arts building. Later Loie put on several other shows in the Bay Area for the benefit of French and Belgian victims of the war.[26]

Also for the benefit of the French and the Belgians, Loie and Alma kept selling the autographed books, pictures, and such things that Loie had sent or brought from France and was continuing to acquire from there. But Alma thought of an even better fund-raising scheme, namely, to use many of these and other items as prizes in a gigantic raffle. Since she feared a lottery would be considered illegal, she called her project a "tombola." For prizes—besides the gifts from Loie and the great black opal from the Australian—she obtained a valuable racehorse from her husband, a Model T car from Mrs. Henry Ford, and a town lot, a piano, a Victrola, and a sewing machine from other donors. There was a prize for every ticket, each of which cost one dollar. On a single day Alma sold a thousand tickets, and by the time of the final drawing she and Loie had found buyers for eighteen thousand of them.[27]

In what time Gab could spare from her ambulance service in France and Belgium, she took charge of distributing to the intended charities, including her own ambulance corps, the funds that Loie and Alma raised through benefit performances, book and picture sales, and the tombola. "We go to the front in Belgium for civilians to deliver ourselves with ambulances and military . . . with the obus [shells] upon our head, and the shrapnells," Gab wrote regarding one of her trips to Ypres. "What I have seen I cant explain—civilians dying of hunger, orphelins [orphans] without food, beds etc."

Loie wanted Gab always to communicate with her in strict confidence. "Now, I have many times told you to cable me only Loiful or Loie Fuller San Francisco Western Union & *they know to give it* to Amer Ex where I go every day." But Gab once made the mistake of addressing a telegram to Loie in care of Adolph Spreckels's office—much to the consternation of both Loie and Alma. Adolph Spreckels disliked Loie and, proud of his German ancestry, disapproved of her and Alma's pro-French activity, despite his gift of the racehorse to their tombola. So the two women kept secrets from him. "You gave information to a German husband of what we are doing & *now therefore it cant be done at all*," Loie now protested to Gab. "What on earth made you send that cable to the care of that man?"[28]

Most of the time, Loie and Gab and Alma cooperated cheerfully in their joint enterprise. "But how wonderful is all what Alma is doing and you too," Gab wrote to Loie, "and I am glad to work as I do for you two." Gab informed Alma with regard to Loie: "She is so good, people take advantage of it, but I am sure she will follow your advice as I know how really fond of you she is." "She is good," Alma agreed in a letter to Gab, "but she is the Artist she does not understand Business." And Loie confided to Gab her attitude toward Alma: "She is made of the right stuff and I have tried to use all the nobleness in my character (& suffering of self & the suffering of others *has helped* me to be noble) . . . and Alma has responded. We have our stones to pass for we are but human but we do not let the stones ruin or hurt us nor spoil our ideas of the great work we have to do."

Gab was upset, however, when Loie announced to her a new phase of the great work that she and Alma had to do. "For your sake we are going to organize the greatest tour of Bienfaisance the world has ever seen," Loie wrote. What she had in mind was a series of lectures and performances in big cities throughout the United States. Gab objected that such a tour would not pay, that Alma would "not feel responsible any more" for Loie once she had left San Francisco, and that "the children must return at once to London" or there would be "trouble with the parents." "Now, Loie . . . if I don't receive at the latest the 17th [of November 1915] a cable from you stating that the children are sailing at the latest before the end of the month *I absolutely refuse to have anything more to do with you*."[29]

Not till January 1916 did Loie send the children to London, for Gab to meet them at the dock, she having forgotten her recent threat. Loie herself soon followed, but with the intention of returning very soon for her American tour. One reason for these Atlantic crossings, her sixth and seventh since the war's outbreak, was to bring back some more of Rodin's works.

With Loie's encouragement, Alma had continued to buy Rodin pieces from her marital allowance, and when that ran out she borrowed money to keep on buying them. Spreckels, on learning of it, asked her not to do so again, for fear it might harm his credit. As the Panama-Pacific Exposition approached its end, Alma would soon be able to take from the French pavilion the pieces she owned and had lent, but the French government could be expected to retain those she had not yet paid for. So Loie, writing to Rodin, begged him to allow Alma time to raise the money she owed on them. Loie thought of herself as laboring for the cause of both Alma and France. She explained to Armand Dayot, organizer of the French exhibit at the exposition: "I shall stay till all is done—but I must often bear hasty and cruel words. I go to sleep weeping, & then I remind myself, nothing is done in this world for our friends without sacrifice, so what I am doing to help make Mrs. S. be a great woman will bring good to France later on, for little by little we shall have Mrs. S. become a great art patron & when she is free to spend her fortune she will understand how & where to do it."

Loie, having already led Alma to found an art museum, was to succeed in making her a great art patron, one who knew how to spend her inheritance after her husband's death.[30]

11

More Missions to America

Undeterred by U-boat–infested waters, Loie Fuller voyaged to America and back twice more in 1917 and 1918, thus bringing to a total of one dozen her Atlantic crossings during the war years. She was carrying out additional self-imposed missions to the United States. Despite recurring illness, she pushed ahead with her usual determination and drive as well as her usual disregard for personal finances. The consequences were noteworthy: on the one hand, aid to war victims in Romania and further aid to those in France and Belgium; on the other hand, the founding of a second art museum, this one in the state of Washington, not to mention some dubious encouragement to a third, in Ohio.

It was her devotion to Queen Marie of Romania that brought Loie back to the United States in May 1917, twelve months after her departure from there. During those twelve months she had divided her time between France and England, finding some remunerative employment for her troupe in London and sharing the hazards of war in both countries. At night the earth shook when the terrifying zeppelins dropped their bombs. As an expert in illumination, Loie conceived of using light to shield Paris against the air attacks. She explained her scheme in a sixteen-page proposal, with several crude sketches, which she sent to a French army officer. Her idea was, first, to detect the approach of enemy dirigibles by a sound-magnifying device; second, to keep them visible as targets and meanwhile dazzle the crews by means of the city's street lights intensified by reflectors and supplemented by powerful searchlights. She proposed a similar plan for London. "In strategy, who knows," she wrote, "*Light* is something to be reckoned with in the future."[1]

One day, as Loie sat writing in her room at the luxurious Hotel Plaza-Athénée, a huge shell exploded somewhere "and the whole city trembled." Three times the previous night she had hurried to the basement with other hotel guests at the sound of dropping bombs, a sound that was all too familiar. The daytime shelling from afar, a new threat, was even more terrifying. Yet it was not nearly so terrible as what was happening to Marie, as Loie learned soon afterward when a British army officer brought her news from Romania.

The wartime fate of that country was, in general, well known. King Ferdinand favored Germany and Queen Marie the Allies, while Romanian nationalists eyed territories that Austria-Hungary held. After two years of neutrality, Romania declared war on Austria-Hungary, August 22, 1916, and less than four months after that, on December 6, the enemy occupied the capital, Bucharest. The government then took refuge in Jassy, near the Russian border.

On November 23, 1916, while still in Budapest, Marie wrote a several-page letter to Loie in response to Loie's repeated offers of assistance. "By what words can I begin, it is so long, so long since I have written to you, and such terrible events have fallen on me lately that I stand small before them—with wide open eyes full of tears." Not only was her country invaded; her youngest child, her "little life-bud," had died in an epidemic. Now she was busy nursing others, having converted the palace into a 120-bed hospital. She also kept going "everywhere, into all corners of the country," wherever she could be of encouragement or aid. "Oh! Loïe, we will want help from all sides," she acknowledged. "Good-bye for today—I put my heart in these pages as I can do but for few."[2]

This letter was several weeks old by the time Marie had given it to the British army officer in Jassy and he had made his way to Paris and delivered it to Loie. Previously Loie had been excited by the idea of going to Romania and, in consultation with Marie, making plans for the relief of the Romanian people. But she lost track of a wealthy American she expected to accompany her, and then she came down with another of her bronchitis attacks, this one so severe that it kept her in bed for nearly two months.

When Loie recovered she decided: "In order to get large supplies and money to really help, I must go to America." She told Marie (in a letter to be forwarded by the Romanian legation in Paris): "Again, I was to go to you, and instead of that, I am leaving for America, where I can serve you best. Shall I ever come to you? God knows." A warm and grateful note from Marie inspired Loie to reply: "Your dear, dear and again dear letter . . . has filled my heart with love. I never knew till now how dear you are to me."

The Romanian minister to France, A. W. Lahovary, enthusiastically approved of Loie's project. "It's quite possible that Americans are not as well acquainted with Romania as they are with Belgium," Lahovary advised her. "So it's necessary, above all, to make every American know what Romania is and who the Romanians are." This was an assignment that Loie gladly took upon herself.

More Missions to America

Before leaving Paris, Loie went to the American embassy to see about the possibility of a U.S. government loan for Romania. While at the embassy, she got the word that Congress had declared war the previous day, April 6, 1917. This was great news. No longer neutral, the United States could be expected to give financial support to its fellow belligerents, among which Romania seemed especially deserving from the viewpoint of Loie and her Romanian friends. President Woodrow Wilson had proclaimed the "self-determination of nations," the rights of small states, and (in one of his Fourteen Points) the redemption of Romania from the Germans. Loie kept on calling at the embassy and appealing to the counselor: "If we ask your good offices, if we seem unduly pressing and exigent, forgive us, but it is because people are starving—and there is not a moment to be lost!"[3]

Why not appeal to the president himself by way of his wife? Waking at four one morning with an inspiration to do so, Loie proceeded to write Mrs. Wilson a letter that, when typed, filled twelve pages. She quoted from one of Marie's letters, recounted her own friendship with the queen, and described her as a stronger character than the king. "(One would not believe this to look at them because the Queen looks like a Fairy Princess who ought to have a golden chariot and white horses waiting for her somewhere near by.)" The gist of Loie's message: "If only America could offer Roumania a credit through her Queen—the people would be saved, the country saved, for not one country in the world is so in the hands of powerful pro-Germans!"

After landing in New York, Loie went immediately to Washington, D.C., where Red Cross representatives were holding a national convention. There she hoped to "tell the story of Roumania" but was too late to speak, the program having already been arranged. She proceeded, nevertheless, to organize the American National Committee for Roumanian Relief, to use her powers of persuasion upon officials of the Red Cross and the federal government, and to travel about the country speaking for the cause and collecting money, clothing, and food. After only a few weeks of strenuous effort she telegraphed Marie a preliminary report in which she said that already local organizations of the Red Cross were sending sizable amounts and the national organization was giving $700,000. She added: "Have obtained government loan of many millions for Roumania." Here she was overoptimistic. In fact, the U.S. government did not grant Romania anything until after the war, when it provided $25 million in cash loans and nearly $13 million in supplies.[4]

Loie still hoped to go to Romania and present Marie a check for ten thousand dollars she had collected. Marie had been expecting a visit from her. She wrote her on October 17, 1917:

> Have you given up the idea of coming here yourself? I have always been awaiting you eagerly, longing to see you, to talk to you, to hear many things. . . . How happy I would be to have you here in spite of the none too inviting state of Jassy, but I feel it would do my heart good to talk to you. I wonder where you are and what you are doing. Did you really set out to come to me as your telegram promised? All that has remained unexplained. I don't know where to send you this letter, so I give it to the American missionary. Your name is so well known that I suppose you can be found anywhere.
>
> A strange world we are living in now! rather a terrible world with much horror mixed with much grandeur. I would like to talk it over with you. I always feel that our souls are very near.
>
> Good-bye Loïe dear—I hope these lines will reach you somewhere and bring you my love and trust and hope.

By the time these lines reached Loie, she no longer had a chance to go and talk things over with Marie, no matter how sincerely and desperately she might reciprocate Marie's feelings. The Bolsheviks had seized the Russian government, to start fighting a civil war instead of the Allies' war and leave the German armies unopposed on the eastern front. The Germans soon overran the northern part of Romania, and the Bulgarians the southern part. Her country occupied, Marie was hardly in a position to receive loans from the U.S. government or visits or even communications from her American friend. Loie would have to wait until the Bulgarians and Germans had surrendered before she could reconsider her Romanian trip.[5]

More Missions to America

{ 249 }

When, on her travels for Romanian relief, Loie first stopped in Cleveland, she received a heart-warming welcome from local lovers of art. They were fascinated by this foreign-appearing fellow American, who came dressed in the uniform of the Romanian Red Cross, and they expected great things of her. The Cleveland Museum of Art, only a year old, needed to build up its collections, and she presumably could facilitate the process, what with her influence among the artists of France. Before long, however, the Clevelanders, grateful but disillusioned, would begin to look on Loie as more a deadbeat than a donor.[6]

Chance had led Loie to Cleveland and its museum. A Cleveland woman, Emery May Holden, after graduation from a finishing school, went to Paris to be with her intended, who had a job in the American embassy there. She volunteered to give some of her time to the Appui Belge, an organization for Belgian relief in which Gabrielle Bloch was involved. Soon Holden, Gab, and Loie were getting together every once in a while for dinner, lunch, or tea. Inevitably, Loie introduced Holden and her hometown friend Lucy Upton to Rodin, and he not only sold Holden one of his bronzes but also gave her a plaster fragment and a seventeenth-century ivory statuette for her to present on his behalf to the Cleveland Museum of Art, which now attracted Loie's interest.[7]

Holden's aunt and foster mother, Roberta Holden Bole, daughter of the founder of the *Cleveland Plain Dealer,* was one of the museum's most generous friends. Loie, during her stays in Cleveland, enjoyed the hospitality of Mrs. Bole as her houseguest. Through Mrs. Bole she met the director of the museum, Frederick Allen Whiting.

Whiting arranged for Loie to present two slide-illustrated talks, "Rodin and Rivière" and "Beautiful Roumania." Afterward he was pleased to report that the "attendance exceeded the capacity of the lecture room." He was also pleased to accept, for the museum, a number of art objects as gifts from Loie, among them an original plaster of one of the Burghers of Calais and a bronze foot by Rodin, a marble figure of Chastity by Théodore Rivière, and a statuette of Loie herself by Pierre Roche. Whiting accepted several other pieces as joint loans from Loie and Rivière's widow. On behalf of the trustees, he extended his official thanks to Loie, adding that the museum was grateful for her "interest which prompted the gift from Mr. Rodin of

Loie posing as a thinker beside Rodin's The Thinker *in the Cleveland Museum of Art, 1918. (Courtesy of the Cleveland Museum of Art.)*

the XVIIth Century Ivory figure of Christ and the small plaster original of a leg"—the items that Rodin had presented through Emery May Holden. Whiting closed his letter "with appreciation of past favors, and hoping that we may have still further active cooperation with you."[8]

Loie, also hoping for further active cooperation, offered Whiting a deal he could not refuse. He understood it thus:

> Miss Loie Fuller owns a collection of 48 pieces by Rivière which she lent to the California Exposition, which were insured for $37,000 or more, also a collection of 33 medals by [Victor] Peter, and some drawings by Rodin. These she would like to lend to the Museum here with the possibility that ultimately they might come to us as a gift, but she has borrowed money on them to make further payments to Madame Rivière and to Mr. Peter, who were in need owing to the war, and it is necessary for us to make advances on her note—or, in other words, to secure a loan here for about $18,000 in order to remove them from California—this to be repaid to us a little later.

To enable Loie to get a loan, Whiting persuaded four prominent businessmen, including the president of the museum's board of trustees and two members of its advisory council, to cosign a one-year note on the Cleveland Trust Company. For the security she offered, nineteen Rodin drawings and two Eileen Gray lacquers, she could borrow only nine thousand dollars, just half as much as she wanted.[9]

Loie promptly took her check for nine thousand dollars to San Francisco, where the collection of Rivières and other pieces, which she had exhibited at the Panama-Pacific International Exposition, were stored as collateral in the vaults of her creditor, the Anglo & London Paris National Bank. While her Cleveland loan was not enough to pay off her San Francisco debt, it somehow enabled her to maintain ownership of the collection, which she had been in danger of losing. "I came here *only* to save the collection," she explained to Gab. "Mrs. Bole and the museum did that . . . & to think it is all due to two girls—Emery May and Lucy."[10]

Mrs. Bole did not exactly reciprocate Loie's warm feelings. She replied to a query from Whiting:

> Yes, I do want to pay all the bills against Miss Fuller up to the time she left Cleveland. I told her I would do so. She left behind here some $800.00 in debts which I agreed to pay on condition she did not come back to Cleveland any more before going to Roumania. I told her that Mr. Bole objected to my giving at the rate I had been for the six weeks she was in this part of the country. . . . She continued to order things after she had left and charged them to me, so after the amount had gone over a thousand dollars I wrote her and told her I could not support her any further. . . .
>
> "La Loie" has now written that she *must* stop in Cleveland on her way east. I don't know quite what to do about it. She has also written to ask for certain money that has been donated to the Roumanian and Belgian books. I have refused to send that as it was donated for immediate relief for those two countries and not for her running expenses.
>
> I believe her to be entirely honest but so extravagant that she is constantly in hot water as to funds and is obliged to ask assistance in every direction.
>
> I am afraid we shall all have to be very firm with her or there will be no end to our obligations.[11]

Whiting, like Mrs. Bole, had not been firm enough with Loie, and there now seemed no end to his obligations—or to hers. His obligations to the museum and to its financial pillars, the men who had cosigned her note, could not be met until hers were, and these were long delayed. For three years after the due date, she put off payment of the principal and lagged behind with the interest. Whiting, his relationship with the cosigners increasingly touchy, kept reminding her, more plaintively than angrily, of her debt. His impression of her character, meanwhile, became even a bit harsher than Mrs. Bole's: "it has seemed to me that this is the case of a person with an artistic temperament who allows her artistic temperament to run away with her and possibly of one who is inherently honest but who does not understand the value of an exact statement of fact."[12]

Eventually Alma Spreckels paid the debt to the California bank and took the collateral, so Loie did not keep that collection after all. Another wealthy friend finally reimbursed the Cleveland Trust Company and acquired the lacquers and the Rodin drawings.[13]

The friend who reimbursed the Cleveland Trust Company—and who founded a museum at Loie's suggestion—was Samuel Hill, generally known as Sam Hill. About five years older than Loie, born to a Quaker family in North Carolina, Sam Hill remained a Quaker but was hardly Quakerlike in his behavior. After an education at Haverford and Harvard, he rose to the position of legal adviser to James J. Hill (no kin), the builder of the Great Northern Railway. He married the boss's daughter, Mary, fathered two children by her, then separated from her but obtained no divorce, she being a devout Roman Catholic. In time he had three more children by a succession of three mistresses.

After leaving James J. Hill's employ, Sam Hill made a fortune in multifarious business ventures, and he spent money as compulsively as he garnered it. Restless, hyperactive, sometimes manic, he threw himself into a variety of projects, some of them praiseworthy, others harebrained. Like his father-in-law, the "Empire Builder," he devoted himself especially to the development of the Pacific Northwest. He led the good-roads movement in the state of Washington and the surrounding region. As symbols of his business success, he acquired a mansion in Seattle, an estate in Stockbridge, Massachusetts, and a ranch of seven thousand acres near the Columbia River, a ranch he named "Maryhill" after his wife, daughter, and mother-in-law. Here, in 1914, he began to build as his future home a chateau worthy of a French aristocrat—the edifice that, before he finished it, Loie talked him into making an art museum.[14]

Tall and handsome as a young man, Sam Hill was paunchy and jowly but still rather impressive, with abundant gray hair and a bushy mustache, by the time Loie met him, which she did with Alma Spreckels as intermediary in 1915. Loie and Sam later discovered common interests, in particular the Romanian cause—he was the wealthy American with whom she expected to visit Queen Marie in 1916. At one point he suggested, by cable, that the three of them meet in Petrograd for Christmas, he to arrive by way of Japan and Siberia. He authorized Loie to draw one thousand dollars from his Paris account for her travel expenses, and she did so, even though she never made the trip. Long before Christmas she ceased to hear from him. "I have had no word," she wrote to Marie, "—and I fear information has been given to the Germans and something has happened."[15]

Communication between Loie and Sam Hill having been restored, she let him know that she still counted on him in the Romanian cause and intended to get together with him during her 1917 stay in the United States. An opportunity arose in July, when she had business in San Francisco and time enough to go on from there to Portland. She was traveling with a young Romanian army officer, carrying a telegram from Marie, and naming Sam vice president of her national committee "for the Roumanian and Belgian work," as she telegraphed him while en route. "Have wonderful things to tell you."[16]

Sam met Loie in Portland. From there, it was about a hundred miles up the Columbia River to Maryhill. No highway had yet been built that far on either side of the river, but the Union Pacific Railroad ran along the south bank, and the Spokane, Portland, and Seattle along the north. The S. P. & S. train stopped at the Maryhill station, where Sam was trying to establish a town as part of a land-promotion scheme. From here it was only a few miles, most of it uphill, to Sam's chateau, which Loie had heard much about and now had a chance to see with her own eyes.

Its site as desolate as it was grand, the building stood on a bench of barren land high above the Columbia. Beyond the river, to the south, the undulating semidesert of Oregon stretched away to the horizon. At a distance downriver rose Mount Hood, its cone shape etched in almost Euclidean perfection on a clear day. On days when mist gathered about its base the peak appeared to float in midair. But Loie was more interested in the house than in the scenery. The walls of poured concrete were up, and the flat roof was on, but the interior was unfinished. The perfect spot for an art museum, Loie immediately concluded.

At the end of her first visit to the place, Sam (who had an office and a

More Missions to America

hotel in the town) handed Loie the following typewritten statement, dated July 24, 1917: "After the eloquent pleading of today, I have decided to dedicate my new chateau at Maryhill, Washington, to a museum for the public good, and for the betterment of French art in the far Northwest of America. Your hopes and ideals shall be fulfilled, my dear little artist woman." At the same time, Sam gave Loie a message for the artists of France, telling them: "In the autumn of 1918 you can arrange with our friend Loie Fuller to hold the first salon, when we will open the museum with our first exhibit." (In fact, twenty-three years were to pass before the museum officially opened.)[17]

From Maryhill, Loie accompanied Sam to Seattle, then took a train to Portland, to go the rest of the way to San Francisco by boat. While at the Portland station, she penciled a letter to Whiting, the Cleveland museum director, giving him an account of her transactions with Sam:

> I tried to write you on the train but my eyes & head were both so bad I had to give it up. A great pain has got into my head and it makes me dizzy when the train is going. I came to see Mr. Hill about 4 things. One was the collection [of Loie's art objects in the San Francisco bank]. He had no ready money, is land and property poor, but he has business in hand which will give him a large capital later on & then he will help....
>
> 2nd I wanted to see his great house just finished in Washington State at "Mary Hill." It is marvellous a regular King of Bavaria Palace. My object was to get it for a museum—and I succeeded. Mr. Hill ... will put it [in] my hands for direction. He has agreed that it shall be formally opened autumn of next year. I will get the artists to begin by making an exhibition—a salon, & the same exhibition can go first to you if you want it.
>
> 3rd I wanted his signature as Vice President of the Ntl[Romanian and Belgian relief] Committee and that is done.
>
> 4th I wanted to see him about my trip to Roumania & the expenses for it, in order to be sure, & he is paying them for me for two people.[18]

When Whiting asked him about her character, Sam replied that he had "never heard Miss Fuller's integrity questioned." Still, he began to have doubts about her museum project. Was Maryhill too remote? Would artists actually make their works available? "The highway the railway and river forming direct communication with Maryhill solves the future," Loie assured him by wire. "Am very earnest and nobody must be permitted to spoil the plan. France and the artists of France and indeed all modern art will take care of the problem and bless you from their hearts as I do now."

Sam continued to hesitate. True, Oregon was expected to build a Columbia River highway the next year, and Washington "at the earliest opportunity." But Sam still wanted reassurance about the interest of the French. "I have closed down the work here until I hear from you, as I do not wish to put in any steel partitions which will have to be taken down," he wrote to Loie from Maryhill in November 1917. He needed definite word by February 1918. "I hope by that time to open up the work again and finish the house for occupancy in case it is not desired to use it for the purpose indicated to you in my letter of July 24th, 1917." Loie replied from Paris: "Everybody here is simply crazy about your Museum and the most wonderful ideas are being evolved for it."[19]

In any event, Sam would have had to go slow with the museum building because of recurring cash-flow problems, though these did not prevent him from reconstructing Stonehenge as a war memorial in 1918 or erecting a Peace Arch on the Canadian border a little later. To make the museum a reality, Loie had to keep pushing.

※

In furthering the development of American museums, Loie had made use of her friendship with French artists, particularly Rodin. Her friendship with Rodin lasted to the day of his death. Before that, however, Loie lost her wonted ability to obtain his works directly from the sculptor, whether as purchases or as gifts.

During his last years, as in earlier times, Rodin was surrounded by adulatory women, each with her own agenda and each jealous of the others. Prominent among them were his secretary, Marcelle Martin, his biographer Judith Cladel, and his student Jeanne Bardey. After her husband's death, Jeanne Bardey succeeded in making herself and her daughter, Henriette, favorites of Rodin. Jeanne was forty-four, ten years younger than Loie, when the two met in May 1916. In a short time they were "like sisters." Jeanne and Henriette included Loie when they entertained Rodin at their apartment.

Rodin gave intimations of mortality when, in May and again in July 1916, he suffered strokes, the second of which caused him to fall down the stairs at Meudon. Jeanne, thinking it time for him to make his last testament, invited a lawyer to the villa to draw up a will. This named Jeanne and Rodin's longtime mistress Rose Beuret as his "joint residuary legatees." Loie, present for the occasion as a special friend of both Rose and Jeanne, watched while Rodin and Rose signed the document.

A few days later, again at Meudon, Loie asked Rodin for a large bronze of his *Balzac*. Others had previously made the same request, and he had always declined it, being unusually possessive of this particular sculpture. Still, accepting the two thousand francs that Loie offered him, he now gave her permission to have a casting made, with the understanding that she would also have to pay the founder. But she never got possession of the *Balzac*.[20]

The reason was that Rodin lost control of his own works. On September 13, 1916, he signed an agreement by which he presented to the French state all his collections of art and all his rights to their reproduction and sale. On the same day he signed another paper giving "absolute power to administer his artistic property" to Léonce Bénédite, the prospective curator of the Rodin Museum, which was to be established in the Biron mansion.

Bénédite, an aggressive bureaucrat, promptly took action against Loie. He not only canceled her *Balzac* order but also held up the delivery of eight other pieces. What was worse, he impugned her honesty in a letter to Alma Spreckels. He asked Alma how much she had paid for a marble *Siren* that Loie had bought from Rodin for her. "I should also like to know," Bénédite wrote, "if it is in response to an order given by you that Miss Loïe Fuller has asked for the following works," and he listed the eight in question. He made his main point offensively clear:

> Knowing the admiration you profess for the work of the Master and your desire to see it more fully represented in the collections of the San Francisco gallery, I have the honour to beg you henceforth to address yourself, if you have occasion to do

so, directly, without any intermediary agent, to the Administration of the Rodin Museum.

I may add that the prices of reproductions are fixed by the administration of the French State. Such being the case, it will be more advantageous for you to address yourself directly to it, as there will be no commission to pay to intermediary agents nor any possible raising of prices by them.

"The want of justice towards one & the lack of confidence in one are the hardest things to succeed against," Loie later wrote to Alma. "One can do a hundred percent more with trust, confidence & a free hand."[21]

Loie, keeping on good enough terms with Rodin's secretary, Marcelle Martin, continued to visit Rodin and Rose Beuret from time to time and to eat breakfast or lunch with them. On Christmas Day 1916 she was their dinner guest, along with two French servicemen. Several days later she paid them another visit, this one in the company of a French journalist, who afterward recalled:

> On January 2, 1917, a cold day, we rode in her eternal "taxi" from l'Etoile to Raspail Boulevard, where an atelier of dolls awaited us. She said: "Would you like to have your emotions stirred by Meudon?" The automobile stopped near Rodin's closed iron gate. He was ill and not seeing anybody, but all gates open before Loïe. In a modest little provincial dining room, a few steps from the royal riches he has bequeathed to France, Rodin sits ponderously and seems shut in behind his Moses beard. At times his mind fails him. Seated nearby, now reduced to only a shadow of her former self, Madame Rodin looks at him, and the poor woman remains silent. Loïe Fuller, after chatting awhile, disappears in the house of the great artist she is so fond of. She busies herself seeing to everything, arranging everything. Meanwhile, Rodin talks of the grandeur of Egyptian art. Suddenly his ideas escape him again, and he falls back into meaningless infantilisms, then recovers his train of thought.[22]

More Missions to America

Christmas dinner, 1916, with Rose Beuret, Rodin, Loie, and two unidentified soldiers. (Courtesy of the Cleveland Museum of Art.)

Though Loie and others referred to Rose Beuret as "Madame Rodin" and treated her as his wife, she and Rodin had never married. They finally did so on January 29, 1917. Loie, confined with bronchitis, could not attend the ceremony. Rose, too, became ill with bronchitis, then pneumonia, and sixteen days after the marriage she was dead. "As you know, my thoughts have been with you and Madame Rodin all the time," Loie promptly wrote to Rodin. "And now that I have received the terrible news, my sorrow is all the greater for my not being able to be with you at such a moment. I will come as soon as I can leave my bed. With all my friendship and sadness, my dear master. You know how I loved Madame Rodin."

Loie continued to visit Rodin and ask favors of him. Early one morning she flustered his secretary, nurse, and maidservant when she arrived unexpectedly to get him to sign some volumes that she was going to send to America. The secretary asked him if he had not already autographed the same kind of things for Loie. At the moment he could not remember exactly, and he told the secretary to invite her back for breakfast the following day.[23]

While Loie was in the United States, Rodin grew steadily worse, and soon after her return to France he died, on November 17, 1917. She was grief-stricken at the news. "We have lost something that was here of the Divine," she scrawled in a four-page private lamentation. "We have lost our great Creator." It was as if a tremendous part of her own life had ended, Rodin having figured so largely in it for so many years.

The great man was buried a week later. There was a wintry chill in the air so mourners gathered for the funeral in the garden of the Meudon villa. Among them were many women, but Bénédite, who was in charge, had selected only men as speakers, some of whom had scarcely known Rodin. Despite Bénédite, the feminist writer Séverine managed to have the last word, presenting the final eulogy. Jealousy among the female admirers of Rodin had not died with him. When making her diary entry for the day, the catty Judith Cladel could not help noting that Loie had been dressed "in a hideous get-up vaguely resembling a combination of nurse's uniform and the Salvation Army."[24]

Rodin's death meant an increase in the value of his works, including those that Loie owned and those she had acquired for Alma. In letters to Alma she discussed the subject. Rodin's molder Eugène Guioché, she once wrote, "made the Master's hand for me by the order of the Master, & I would not for the world have it go to a founder for there would be *no* way by which I could be sure he would not keep a cast of it, & it would no longer be unique."[25]

Loie and Gab continued to preoccupy themselves with charitable activities. A nurse with the Belgian Red Cross, Gab was attached to a hospital in "free"

More Missions to America

Belgium, the small area unoccupied by the Germans, where she had been providing relief since the start of the war. Queen Elizabeth of Belgium sponsored the Aide Civile et Militaire Belge, which supervised relief in that part of the country. After Loie visited the hospital and other institutions of the ACMB, the queen's lady-in-waiting, Countess Van den Steen, praised her as "a real witness of our work" and said "we have the fullest confidence in her." "Gifts of money or in kind will be most gratefully received and may be sent to Miss Loie Fuller, who will forward them to us." In response to Loie's persuasion, the first lady of France, Madame Poincaré, had agreed to serve as patroness of the organization's French branch.[26]

By 1918 Loie had acquired a new royal sponsor—Henriette, Duchess of Vendôme, Princess of Belgium—with whom she enjoyed a closer relationship than with the queen. When Henriette held a fund-raising rally at her Paris residence, Loie stood on the lawn and, according to one of those present, harangued the crowd "like an apostle." Henriette enthusiastically approved when Loie proposed to raise yet more money by lecturing in the United States. "Your suggestion regarding the work to which I am giving my best efforts touches me deeply," the duchess responded in one of her always affectionate letters. "Go to America, tell the American people all you wish to."[27]

In preparation for the trip, Loie acquired a new passport, which gave the following description of her: "*Age* 49 years, *Stature* 5 feet 2 inches, *Forehead* medium, *Eyes* blue, *Nose* turned up [retroussé], *Mouth* medium, *Chin* round, *Hair* dark brown, *Complexion* fair, *Face* round." (The passport form did not call for her weight. As for her age, it was in reality fifty-six.) She sent ahead four crates, containing among other things such personal items as "1 box Confiserie Carleton, 1 box chocolates, 6 bottles perfume—Gloire de Ninette, 1 lot of pink ribbon, 2 neck chains with pendant—3 pearls (imitation), 2 pairs ear studs pearls (imitation), 1 neck chain—pearls (imitation)." In New York, "Fuller was taken off the ship dangerously ill" with bronchitis, and she remained bedridden in a New York hotel for about two weeks.[28]

When Henriette learned of Loie's illness, she wrote her: "I am *so* sorry and anxious to know if you are quite well again—your own active energetic lively self!" Loie was indeed her lively self by the time she reached San Francisco, near the end of June, but her plans were already going awry. "We have

Sam Hill and Gab Bloch at the left, beside one of the ambulances for which Loie, along with Alma Spreckels, helped to raise money. (Courtesy of Maryhill Museum of Art.)

had serious difficulties since you left," Henriette informed her. "Our French and Belgian authorities find it impossible to give an official commission for French and Belgian war works to someone who is not French or Belgian." Instead of starting on a lecture tour, Loie stayed in San Francisco to resume her unofficial war work in cooperation with Alma Spreckels.[29]

Alma, too, had run into trouble with Belgian officialdom. On behalf of the queen, she was collecting lots of money to provide milk for orphans, when the Belgian minister to the United States, Baron de Cartier, stepped in to make her stop. Under her auspices, Rotary Clubs in six western states and the territory of Hawaii placed milk bottles in frequented spots for people to drop pennies into. "I requested both Mrs. Spreckels and the California Committee for Relief in Belgium and France to give up their milk

More Missions to America

bottle stands and leave this field of activity to the Gamma Phi Beta Sorority," the Baron acknowledged. College girls were to take over from Rotarians, and a rival committee was to get credit for the system that Alma had originated!

"I don't have to beg anybody to do charity for them," Alma protested to Countess Van den Steen, who had the ear of Queen Elizabeth. "I only did it because I loved Miss Fuller. I respected and admired Her Majesty, and of course I wanted to try to do something for poor Belgium and the little children, and of course I have French blood in my veins—it is the Call of the Blood."

Loie tried to smooth over the difficulties. She advised Gab by cable: "Request Elizabeth and Henriette Vendôme to take no steps against Alma following her telegram of complaint." Alma's charity was "too successful," Loie explained; this "caused jealousy and efforts here to discredit and stop her," but "all will be arranged." Alma, she said, had sent Queen Elizabeth more than $14,000 and Madame Poincaré almost $11,000. Gab would soon receive $5,000 for her ambulance service. "Miss Loie Fuller, who interested me to do this work, shares with Miss Bloch the charge of keeping up the ambulances," Alma informed the Countess Van den Steen.

Yielding in the battle of the bottles, Alma quit collecting money for the milk fund. "Alma could continue but refuses quarrel," Loie telegraphed to Gab. "Therefore tell Her Majesty and Madame Poincaré Alma retires to work for American Hospital and Museum. Alma's husband has promised one hundred thousand dollars for Museum." While looking to her museum, Alma did not completely retire from her Belgian and French relief activities. With Loie's aid, she continued to play a leading role in the American branch of Aide Civile et Militaire, the Commission for Aid Civil and Military.[30]

But Loie and Alma ran into resistance from the Commission for the Relief of Belgium, an international organization that Herbert Hoover headed. The California branch of the CRB looked on Loie and Alma as interlopers, though these two insistently pointed out that they confined their attention to *free* Belgium, which the CRB ignored while ministering to the much larger occupied territory. "In Fresno the Hoover Committee discredited Miss Fuller, taking away from her the goods she had collected there." Alma related. She and Loie believed that their rivals were pro-German. Foremost among them was Mrs. Vernon Kellogg, the wife of a professor who had studied in Germany and whom Hoover had appointed as his liaison with the German authorities in Belgium. "Because of this she is a friend of Mr Hoover's, & that explains it all," Loie told Gab. Alma added that "her father was Mr. Hoffman (a German)," and both Loie and Alma suspected (erroneously) that Hoover himself was of German descent and hence pro-German.[31]

After their rebuff by the Belgian authorities, Loie and Alma dealt with Aide Civile et Militaire through Gab, who remained an official representative of the organization. At Loie's suggestion, Gab asked Henriette to "accept that the Commission for Aid Civil and Military" should "work for a surgical ambulance for French and American soldiers," the money to be sent either to Henriette's lady-in-waiting or to Gab. Henriette agreed, and Alma guaranteed 300,000 francs for the mobile operating room, the "auto-chir." By the time the money was raised, the war was over and the unit was no longer needed, so the fund was divided among a soldiers' convalescent home, a cancer hospital, and the care of the poor. Gratefully, Henriette wrote to Loie: "My thoughts go so often to America towards you, my dear and valiant friend!"[32]

Henriette, an acquaintance of Hoover, had appealed to him twice to facilitate Loie's lecture tour. "Will you help Miss Fuller to arrange that her work shall be endorsed by the Government because I understand that no work is allowed without it." After four months in San Francisco, Loie had not had time to go to Washington and apply for the necessary endorsement. By now, she was tired of having to fight the Belgian minister for the privilege of assisting his people. "I am disgusted and feel like sending it all to the devil," she complained to Gab. "I work so hard out of my own pocket at my own expense for such thanks."

One thing more than made up for all the bickering and frustration—the armistice of November 11, 1918. Now that the war was ending in victory for the Allies, Loie could look forward to communicating with Queen Marie and even, perhaps, to visiting her.[33]

12

The Lily of Life

*L*oie Fuller sailed from New York for Liverpool on December 10, 1918, the same day that President Woodrow Wilson left for Paris to attend the peace conference and help redraw the map of Europe. With Queen Marie in mind, Loie worried about the postwar fate of Romania in particular. The Germans having systematically looted that country, poverty and hunger prevailed there. But peace did not, as Prime Minister Ion Bratianu sent troops into Transylvania, Bessarabia, Bukovina, and the Dobruja to annex those territories and double Romania's area and population.

On shipboard Loie ran into an American newsman of her acquaintance who was on his way to cover the peace conference. "I must win him over for the Queen!" she vowed in her diary, and she succeeded in doing so. Another reporter she met was more of a challenge, being a socialist and presumably hostile to royalty. To him she argued that Marie was at heart both a socialist and a democrat. The most important ally she made among her fellow passengers was Robert L. Owen, an influential U.S. senator from Oklahoma. "Another talk with Mr Owen, several talks with *Mrs* Owen," she recorded. "He will see the members of the Conference & plead Roumania's cause."

In London—where the Wilsons, en route to Paris, were guests of King George V and Queen Mary—Loie proudly watched from the Carlton Hotel as a royal procession went by, the king and the president side by side in one open four-horse carriage, the queen and Mrs. Wilson in another. Many in England and on the Continent expected Wilson, the great exponent of the self-determination of nations, to work miracles in the making of peace. "If President Wilson could do justice by all and for all to the satisfaction of everybody," Loie sagely thought to herself, "it would be more than our Saviour could do." Convinced that Germany should be punished for war guilt, she was indignant when a Polish woman she knew told her that England and Germany were equally to blame.

> But I said Germany *began* the war, declared the war first. Oh no she didn't she said. War had already been begun on Germany by Russia. Oh she said my work has brought me in contact with nearly all the great working men—like Mr. Hoover. I had a long talk with him over the German question & he thought as I did. He agreed with me, and he said the cruelties

LOIE FULLER

& atrocities had been grossly exaggerated for the sake of Propaganda, and (she continued) he was in a position to know because he was in Belgium for so long when it was in the hands of the Germans! My astonishment can be better imagined than described to hear one of my dearest & best friends expressing such views even privately to me.

Loie persisted in believing that for centuries "the Prussian spirit of militarism was rampant" in Germany, and the "people of Germany therefore must be born through generations to a new thought."

While in London, Loie "began to try & interest people in Roumania further" by seeking assistance for a stage production of a fairy story, *The Lily of Life*, which Queen Marie had written for her youngest daughter. In the story a young princess, in love with a handsome prince, her older sister's lover, goes in search of a lily that will cure him of his life-threatening malady. After a long and dangerous journey she brings back the magical flower and saves the prince's life, then dies of a broken heart when he marries the older sister. (This theme of self-sacrificing devotion appealed to Loie; it was the kind of devotion that she felt toward Marie.) Lady Cunard agreed to form a committee to promote the production, and a producer "was ready to read a scenario but of course there was none."

When Loie heard that one of Marie's sons, the fifteen-year-old Nicholas, was at the Ritz Hotel in London, she was thrilled with anticipation. "Oh, I must go & see him & get news of the Queen!" she thought. "I hurried over to the hotel to find the Prince, and I was received instead by the meanest, burliest, most brutal man I had ever met. It was Joe Boyle!" Colonel Joseph W. Boyle, a Canadian, had been a sailor and a prizefighter before striking it rich in the Klondike gold rush and serving as a soldier of fortune in the recent war. A favorite of Queen Marie, he was at the moment engaged in two missions in her behalf: arranging for Nicholas to enter Eton College and trying to facilitate the shipment of food supplies to Romania.

According to Loie's contemporary account, Boyle told her he knew Herbert Hoover, now in charge of American relief in Europe, "& Mr Hoover had plenty of food on the way which Roumania could have but even Mr Hoover could not give it to him *without it was paid for in American actual*

The Lily of Life

money." Loie put Boyle in touch with Senator Owen, "and the senator advised him how to get the money." The senator "then left for Paris & at once had interviews with all the men necessary, including Mr Hoover, & then & not until after Mr Owen had taken these steps, was the matter arranged."[1]

After arriving in Paris, early in January 1919, Loie hoped to see Hoover and get his approval for her separate Romanian relief enterprise. L. H. de Friese, an acquaintance of Hoover's, wrote a letter of introduction for her. "I have known her . . . for many years and if there is another woman whose heart is as big as the entire world I have not met her," Friese assured Hoover. "There seems to have arisen differences on the Pacific Coast between Mrs. Spreckels and certain banking friends of mine and Miss Fuller on the one side and friends and supporters of yourself on the other," he conceded. But Loie and her wealthy sympathizers "can undoubtedly go on doing certain good work for Roumania without in the slightest degree interfering with your own great and world wide efforts." Whatever the reason, it appears that Loie never took or sent this letter to Hoover and never secured an interview with him.

Loie was still interested in Belgian as well as Romanian relief. Henriette, Duchess of Vendôme, sister of Belgium's king, expected Loie to put together a memorial volume, a "book of gold," which would make a lot of money for the mutual cause. "With 25% of the proceeds destined for me from the sale of your book on my works and on the war," Henriette promised when Loie visited her at the Château Saint-Michel in Cannes, "I shall build a Palace of Industry and Arts, of which I here name you the Director for your life time." Loie soon feared her life time would be short. On March 4 she wrote from Marseilles:

> I have been desperately ill again & nearly died something terrible. I stiffled [stifled] all the time & little by little I lost the power to breath[e]. The lungs filled with water. I had a slight attack in London. . . . Then I can down to Cannes to see the Duchess of Vendome about my work for her & I fell ill again following as before a slight cold. I was there over 3 weeks instead of 3 days. Got out of bed to be brought here in a motor car to get a sleeper to Paris. . . . I was instantly put to bed, where for over two weeks I have been struggling, & where I

still am. I was so ill I forgot—every thing—but now I am better my affairs rush over me.

When Loie finally got back to Paris, she was put to bed again.[2]

It was an especially unfortunate time for Loie to be confined, now that Queen Marie was in Paris. The queen had come to press Romania's territorial claims upon the leaders of the peace conference. Securing an audience with President Wilson, she found him standoffish, and when he referred disapprovingly to the anti-Semitism that prevailed in her country, she reminded him of the anti-Negro and anti-Japanese prejudice in his. Still, the peacemakers eventually gave Romania what Marie asked for. Meanwhile she shone as the cynosure of the city's diplomatic and social scene, entertaining and being entertained by many of the most prominent.

In the midst of her social whirl, Marie did not neglect Loie. If the commoner could not go to the queen, the queen would go to the commoner, so she called on Loie at the Hôtel Plaza-Athénée. The two had much to talk about, this being their first reunion since 1912. As tokens of her esteem, Marie gave Loie two notes, one of them authorizing her to "create and wear a special uniform" with the queen's Romanian cross as her insignia, and the other giving her the "fullest authority" to produce and present Marie's stories on the stage and screen. Loie was thinking particularly of *The Lily of Life,* and not only for the stage. "It is a silent fairy play and I can cinematograph it."

Loie and Marie were also concerned, as usual, about the problem of getting food supplies to Romania, as was Sam Hill, who happened to be in Paris. "Mr. Hill came in and in my little bedroom she met great people who undertook to help Roumania," Loie wrote soon afterward. "She sent me back a letter from the train and said it was like a fairy tale and Mr. Hill had gone to Roumania with some great men."

Before Marie left the room in the Plaza-Athénée, Loie showed her a telegram from Aix-les-Bains, a resort in southeastern France, where the Young Men's Christian Association was providing entertainment for Yankee soldiers waiting to be sent home, and where Marie had recently stopped to greet them. "Queen's visit a triumph," ran the telegram. Underneath the message, Marie now wrote in her bold hand: "I will never forget my memorable visit to American soldier boys, mine in the same cause."

The Lily of Life

In Aix-les-Bains Marie had had an opportunity also to see some of Loie's dancing girls, who, before four thousand soldiers at a time, were giving six to eight performances a day at the YMCA casino. The girls were in the care of Mrs. Nathan Van Beil, about whom the program director had his doubts. "I am quite sure the poor old lady is no longer a responsible person," he cautioned Loie. When Loie proposed to withdraw her dancers on short notice, he protested: "Of course, we appreciate the fact that you have certain claims to the girls and that the work here has received a real service from you in the contribution of the girls' services to us, but, on the other hand, the Y.M.C.A. has helped you to be free from the responsibility of them and Mrs. Van Beil, both financially and morally, for over a year."[3]

The war to end war, to make the world safe for democracy, raised expectations high but soon left them dangling. Some of the early disillusionment found expression in the poem "Nineteen Hundred and Nineteen" by the great Irish symbolist William Butler Yeats. The poem is rather enigmatic, and Loie figures in it rather enigmatically. It begins:

> Many ingenious lovely things are gone
> That seemed sheer miracle to the multitude....

It proceeds to say, among a great many other things:

> When Loie Fuller's Chinese dancers enwound
> A shining web, a floating ribbon of cloth,
> It seemed that a dragon of air
> Had fallen among dancers, had whirled them round
> Or hurried them off on its own furious path;
> So the Platonic Year
> Whirls out new right and wrong,
> Whirls in the old instead;
> All men are dancers and their tread
> Goes to the barbarous clangour of a gong.

Thus, somehow, Loie had become one of the symbols of the age. But if the poet meant that her dancing was entirely a thing of the past, he was less than prescient. True, she no longer enwound a shining web herself, but her students continued to do so, and she kept devising new ways for them to disport with a floating ribbon of cloth.

Loie persisted despite recurring ill health. She signed a contract with the Coliseum Theatre in London for her company to perform there for four weeks in May at £350 or $1,750 a week. But, getting to work too soon after her March illness, she had to remain in Paris and take to her bed again. Twice she postponed the performance, then was told that another postponement would mean cancellation.

> So my friend Miss Bloch took the next train & got there for just *one day* to rehearse in—but they opened—*successfully*. . . . I was however to change the play the second week. I could not come [to London] and they made it the third week. Then I came (carried here) only to be unable to do anything, then they gave me another fortnight seeing themselves how ill I was. Then I was carried to the theatre and on a sofa lying down so weak I was unable to move myself I directed in [a] whisper to another to direct the work. It was a success, a great success, but I could not do it the following weeks so the management postponed till August and because of the success, he will keep the entire season open for us if we can fill it.

"If I were not determined," she explained a little later, "I would sometimes be discouraged when I am so ill."[4]

By summer Loie was well enough to work not only at choreography but also at her "silk business," she and her girls dyeing silk scarves for sale. During the fall and winter of 1919–20, however, she was desperately ill again—so ill that at one point "the doctors attending me did not think I would live." After eight more weeks in bed, she had to go back to London to renew her engagement at the Coliseum Theatre, though she could "scarcely walk yet." From London she wrote to Gab: "Sat. Went to theatre, too cold couldn't stay. Orchestra & girls had to rehearse without me." The show must go on, and it did.[5]

The Lily of Life

By April 1920, having borrowed Gab's flat, more spacious than her own hotel room, Loie was "very very hard at work" on her stage version of *The Lily of Life*. She was especially pleased with the way one of her scenes turned out. "It is the scene where the Little Princess passes through many lands and climates accomplished by throwing scenes upon a great curtain behind her by two great lanterns from behind the curtain. Side lights upon her, etc. The effects are extraordinary. She finally reaches the Lily of Life, brilliantly illuminated in a nest of serpents, which form themselves into a bridge and over which she passes to reach the Lily of Life."

In anticipation of staging and filming this and other stories of Marie's, Loie and Gab formed a partnership, which they called "Loïe Fuller Enterprises." Unfortunately for them, as things turned out, they took in as a third partner a recent U.S. Army major by the name of Paul C. Turner. According to the partnership agreement, Loie was to engage in theatrical and artistic undertakings of whatever kind, and Gab and Turner were to be the firm's representatives "vis-à-vis de toutes personnes," each of the two to be paid 25 percent of the net receipts.[6]

"I wonder if our play will really be able to come out—how anxious I shall be," Marie wrote. In her letters the queen confided her personal problems—her troubled mother, her disloyal son—and what a comfort Sam Hill had been on his recent visit. "I suffered every degree of humiliation & torture which would have been unendurable had not Mr. Hill been the angel that he is. We sat hand in hand." Loie was an even greater and more constant comfort. "My heart is moved by an immense gratitude mixed with wonder at all the astonishing work you do for me from your bed of suffering," Marie assured her. "You are one of the things that helped me to remain as I ought to be."

Loie longed to visit Romania, to commiserate with Marie and discuss the scenario for *The Lily of Life*, but had to keep putting off the trip because of her health. Finally, in the spring of 1920, she got to Bucharest for a stay at the royal palace, Cotroceni. "All well, happy," she telegraphed from there to Gab in Paris, adding: "Gab be careful don't go to bed & sleep with a lighted cigarette." When Loie left the palace, however, she was no longer quite sure that all was well. "We parted that morning as the loving friends that we are and you ask me what is the matter? Had you hurt my feelings?" Marie responded to Loie's subsequent query. "Why this question? Did somebody say something unkind to you, because it certainly was not I, that morning when you came to say good-bye to me, I in my bed."

Marie had accepted Loie's invitation to attend the play's premiere, for which Loie succeeded in obtaining that most exalted of venues, the Théâtre National de l'Opéra. While making arrangements for Marie's stay in Paris, Loie had to assure her that the duchess of Vendôme was mistaken in telling her that the show had been called off. It had merely been postponed, Loie telegraphed. "Representation Opera House June twenty-six. Enormous success predicted." Later the play was rescheduled for July 1, 1920.[7]

In its one presentation at the Opéra, *The Lily of Life* proved as successful as Loie had hoped. "Last evening Queen Marie of Rumania saw at the opera a fairy tale she had written . . . turned into magic reality by the art of Mme. Loie Fuller and her pupils," the *New York Times* reported under a July 2 dateline. "It was the most brilliant night there has been at the opera since before the war. All Social Paris, with large delegations from the American and English colonies, was there."

The program listed as director of the play not Loie but her partner Paul C. Turner, though he was not mentioned in the reviews. Part of the proceeds were to go to the relief of war orphans in Romania.[8]

❦

Alma Spreckels was in Paris in time for the play. She had discontinued her campaign for Belgian charity after Herbert Hoover discouraged it. According to an Associated Press report, "Mr. Hoover insisted that Europe must get to work, and not depend any longer on assistance from the United States."

Alma, proud of what she had accomplished, felt unappreciated. "The temporary total sent by me to date is $115,785.83 besides food, clothing, auto, etc.," she informed Loie in October 1919. "My friends all think that considering the wonderful work that I did for Belgium that I was treated very shabbily." When Queen Elizabeth of Belgium went to California, she pinned a royal medal on ten women but completely ignored Alma. Loie, after an audience with the queen, told Alma she would probably send her a medal. "She need not derange herself to do so," Alma replied. "My ancestors worked for Royalty for ages but, thank God, I live in the little old United States."

Queen Elizabeth's sister-in-law Henriette, Duchess of Vendôme, continued to cultivate Loie in the hope that she would put together that "golden book" to be sold for the benefit of needy Belgians. "I am worried about our book," Henriette wrote her (in English) when the project lagged. "I want so badly money for our works." When Loie tried to reassure her, Henriette responded with "tender love and thanks for all the trouble you are taking for my dear works." And Henriette sent her a medal she had got on a prayerful pilgrimage to Lourdes. "Ware [sic] this blessed medal," she advised; "elle vous portira bonheur [it will bring you good luck]." She offered to pay Loie's expenses for a money-raising tour of the United States; Loie planned to make the trip but kept postponing it because of her illnesses and her other obligations.[9]

Loie also would have liked to revisit the United States for another reason, namely, to participate more closely in planning the California Palace of the Legion of Honor, to which Alma turned her full attention after discontinuing her work for Belgian charity. From a distance, Loie followed the San Francisco developments as closely as she could, giving advice and ordering art objects. Alma, she learned, had chosen the "exact spot" for the museum, a two-block square donated by the city park commissioners and located on high ground overlooking the bay and the Golden Gate. "Loie it is wonderful that I have gotten Adolph to give $320,000 for this work in the face of unkind opposition of people very close to him."

Loie advised: "Regarding your little theatre in the Museum, I hope you will be able to construct that when I am there to indicate how to light it as I did with the Boston Opera when I went expressly to Boston from Paris when they were building the Boston Opera; they constructed it following my instructions with regard to lighting."

Alma wanted to know whether it would help the project if she went to Paris and conferred with French artists and government officials. Loie told her to come on but to deal only through her. Viewing herself as a kind of Rodin apostle, she put it this way: "Remember, the future of our museum, with all the Master wants for it, is in my hands, & it will not fail if no one interferes."[10]

Loie, in cooperation with Alma's cousin Pierre de Bretteville, spent considerable time in making preparations for Alma's visit. Bretteville secured rooms at the Plaza-Athénée for Alma, her brother, and a young San Francisco woman accompanying them. Loie and Bretteville conferred with artists and officials about arrangements for an elaborate reception. On the afternoon of May 26, 1920, soon after Alma's arrival in Paris, the Société Nationale des Beaux-Arts, representing the minister of fine arts, held the reception in the Grand Palais, honoring Alma for her services to French art and to the French cause during the war.[11]

Remaining in Paris for the summer, Alma succeeded, with Loie's assistance, in obtaining a number of art objects from the French government. She seemed to make a hit with some of Loie's artist friends, who no doubt saw in her a market for their wares. Pierre Roche told Loie how pleased he was with Madame Spreckels' appearance at the Société Nationale and how her good grace and charming amiability had captivated everyone. Quite different was the impression she made on one of Loie's American friends, a woman who wrote Loie at the end of the summer:

> The great plan inspired by your own heart & soul is of deepest interest to me, but somehow I cannot seem to apply even a part of this interest to Mrs. S. I can think of her only as the fortunate puppet she is, with you to pull the strings and make her dance to a purpose. If I can tell you the honest truth, I thought her one of the deadliest women it has ever been my misfortune to meet. She has indeed been lucky that through you her only asset, wealth, is devoted to a noble and far reaching purpose.[12]

Henriette gave a tea party for Alma and promised to help her with her museum by "collecting works of art which will represent a little of our French soul and spirit." But the duchess gradually lost hope of getting much in return from Loie. "Dear, after the Queen of Romania, do some-

The Lily of Life

{ 277 }

thing for us," she was reduced to pleading. Eventually her lady-in-waiting wrote: "Her Royal Highness thinks you have been more and more absorbed by the Queen of Romania." Still, the duchess graciously sent her best wishes for the success of Loie's film version of *The Lily of Life*.[13]

Loie devoted the fall and winter of 1920–21 mainly to her cinematography, in which she had the close cooperation of Gab Bloch (who now took the name of Gab Sorère). They began without experience, Loie having hardly even seen a movie, since the flickering hurt her eyes. They also lacked a script and so were compelled to improvise in converting the stage pantomime into a motion picture. Fortunately, Loie was acquainted with Léon Gaumont, one of France's largest film producers and distributors, who had shot a sequence of her serpentine dance many years earlier. From Gaumont she was able to obtain facilities, equipment, and expertise, though she soon had occasion to disagree with the experts and to teach them a few tricks of her own.

The cast consisted of Loie's pupils and two other people. Twenty-two-year-old René Chomette, appearing in his first movie, took the part of the prince, and an actress and singer known as Damia played the roles of both the queen and the witch. Chomette learned a good deal about moviemaking from Loie. A few years later, under the name René Clair, he made his debut as a screenwriter and film director with *Paris qui dort* (Paris asleep), which showed traces of her technique. Still later, he became one of the leading French directors, scoring successes with fantasy films in both Paris and Hollywood.

Loie and Gab spent several weeks with a cameraman shooting in and around Nice and Cannes. From her Cannes hotel Loie wrote one October day to a man she hoped would help promote the film:

> All day Monday & yesterday I was not well. I am not accustomed on account of being so fat to eat two big meals a day but I gave myself a *real* holiday because it was such a pleasure to be with you & I *do* love to eat but I can't always let my self

free like that. Any how, I was very happy—& then I took a day off . . . & twice I had the doctor here, my eyes were also very bad, and one of my little girls is ill, so I was worried too, but still I went on with my work. . . . (Then I am going off into the town to take my girls out shopping & to a lunch, & I shall only get back by evening, as I must go to the dentist in the afternoon) and I would like you to write out the form of a contract you would like.

As if Loie did not have troubles enough, the filming was taking much longer than she and Gab had anticipated. "The exterior parts have been made in the south of France & the interior parts are being made here," she wrote on December 2 after returning to Paris. "The film is about half done, but how quickly the other half can be made we do not know." Then she was "taken sick" again. "And there is so much work to be done."[14]

The interior scenes were shot in the Gaumont studio, where the film was then edited and processed. When Loie asked to see the negative, she was told "a positive of the whole thing would be made," and then she could cut out what she decided not to use. She objected: "I want to cut it out of the negative first and save that expense!" After examining the negative, she decided to keep segments of it instead of the positive where they gave the effect she desired on the screen. Some of the sequences, negative and positive, were in slow motion. To achieve this effect, Loie had directed her girls to move as slowly as possible and had urged the "operator" to crank the camera as fast as he could. She also used her ingenuity with the illumination in the studio. "We did not want the place all lighted up in the usual way. On the contrary we wanted the light concentrated, and we brought in our own lights," she recalled five years afterward. "Since then the negative, the slow-up machine and concentrated light have become *regulations* in the film industry."

As finally edited, the movie begins with the young prince choosing the older of the two sisters, Mora, as his bride. A fade-in, with a curtain opening from one side to the other, reveals silhouettes of the couple embracing. When the prince is stricken by his strange illness, the younger sister, Corona, learns the secret of the Lily of Life from an old book. Superimposed on one of its pages, the prince's face appears and disappears. Corona, secretly in love with him, goes in search of the miraculous flower. In an enchanted forest she comes upon dancing nymphs, whose movements are so slow as to seem dreamlike. She returns with the lily after fearsome adventures and an escape from giant hands that reach out for her. Once the prince is restored to health, he favors Mora with his first kiss. Corona, her heart broken, fades into the darkness as night falls. At dawn a lifeless form is discovered close by a cypress tree.[15]

The film was scheduled for its first showing at the Gaumont-Palace Théâtre in Paris on Saturday, February 26, 1921. Loie looked forward to the occasion with both high hope and serious doubt. She confided to Marie:

> While the world is crying out for better films, the public—through those who buy—are wanting the dime novel or serial stories of crime & adventure. So we are not sure we shall find the great market for a pure & beautiful simple film such as ours. Indeed I almost fear to show it to the sort of men who I see are the agent buyers of films.
>
> We must do however as all others do. We must rent a theatre & an orchestra & give a special representation to the Trade or in other words to those very men who, I feel sure, will judge our film from the standpoint of hair breadth escapes etc. like the films they do buy & which they declare the public wants. If it had been launched in Roumania under your direct patronage it would have been different, I feel sure of that. As it is I show it next week, with strings pulling at my heart, as they never did for any thing else I have done.

Paris cinema critics of the avant-garde gave the picture flattering reviews. "For the first time a moviemaker, la Loïe Fuller, using all the resources appropriate to the new art, has constructed a film with almost no literary compromises, one in which the rhythmic movement of the characters and the skillful play of light and shadow suffice to create the expression and impart the emotion," Jean Galtier-Boissière declared in *Le Crapouillot*. "The cinema being the art of 'moving *plastique*,' this film is without doubt the first attempt at the autonomy of the silent art."

Though a critical success, the picture proved a financial failure. It needed large sales if it were to make a profit, one half of which Loie promised Marie for her charities. She explained to Marie:

> It cost all together some 400,000 francs which is very little for a big successful film to cost, & any body else would have spent the double on it & then not succeeded probably—but (foolish me) *we didn't think it would cost us 100,000. Ah! we didn't know* that we would have to rent a whole factory & pay I don't know how many thousand francs a day for it, because of the way they charge for things, only afterwards one knows & the days crept into weeks & months—with electric current like gold to pay for *all the time.*

Loie exhibited the film in London, contracted with a company to distribute it in France, and named a man as her "exclusive representative" for the United States, Canada, and Cuba. But the picture drew few spectators in England or France and none on the other side of the Atlantic, where exhibitors held to "the belief that the only personages who attract audiences in America are people like Charlie Chaplin, Douglas Fairbanks, Mary Pickford, et al."[16]

Loie's and Gab's loss would have been even greater if they had not found an investor willing to risk some of his money on the enterprise. To help pay their bills, Gab had some resources of her own, and Loie was profiting from the appearances of her dancers, who continued to perform when not acting for the film. She no longer had to go along with them. "I have prepared a performance for my school of girls to give," she explained in September 1920, "which can be done without me." She was present and in charge, however, when the girls began a week's engagement at the Théâtre des Champs-Elysées just two days after the first showing of the film.

The performance was a potpourri of numbers old and new, including an interpretation of Mendelssohn's *Midsummer Night's Dream* music. Among the many distinguished people in the audience was the twenty-nine-year-old composer Darius Milhaud, whose *Saudades do Brasil* served as accompaniment for one of the dances. Reviewers called to mind the scarf-waving performer who had debuted in Paris almost thirty years before and whom wags had dubbed "Loïe Foulard" (pronounced "Foolar"), meaning "Loie Scarf." Now that she had passed the torch to her disciples, she achieved through them her well-known enchantment of both the eye and the ear, or so the critics said. They still took her art seriously. As one of them commented, "The Théâtre des Champs-Elysées has paraded before us the most diverse forms of the ballet: the Russians of various styles, the Swedish company, Isadora Duncan's troupe, Loïe Fuller's." He asked: "Will there someday come out of these juxtapositions a new synthesis of the dance?"

Loie obtained other engagements for her school, some in England and some in Spain. When possible, she secured contracts that guaranteed her a fixed sum rather than a percentage of the proceeds. An example is the agreement she made with the management of the Grand Casino Sardinero in Santander for a seven-day appearance, with top billing, beginning on August 30, 1921. She was to be paid ten thousand francs, 10 percent of which was to go to an agent. Her show was to last thirty-five to forty minutes and was to be changed completely at least once during the period of the contract. She would furnish and take charge of not only performers but also electricians, projectors, scenery, and curtains, and she would be responsible for all expenses of travel and transportation.[17]

While Loie earned what she could from such engagements, creditors and bill collectors hounded her, as they had done throughout most of her career. Her largest and most long-standing debt was the one she owed the Cleveland Trust Company. F. A. Whiting, director of the Cleveland Museum of Art, learning from her about her filmmaking and her school's performances, hoped more and more desperately that she would clear enough from these activities to repay the Cleveland bank. He kept trying to find out about her financial condition from mutual acquaintances in Paris, among them Emery May Holden (now Mrs. R. Henry Norweb), who had been responsible for Loie's introduction to the Cleveland Museum in the first place. "Ever since her famous trip to Cleveland I have ceased to have anything to do with her," Holden haughtily replied to one of Whiting's letters. Later she said she had heard the film was finished and the girls had been dancing, which probably had "brought in some money. However Miss Fuller is living at an expensive hotel as she always has done."

Finally, on March 23, 1921, Whiting sent Loie what amounted to an ultimatum, informing her that the bank would not renew her note again: "The bank has given the endorsers until May 1 to sell the security or collect from you, and has notified them that the bank will take action to collect from them on that day, so that, as I have written before, it will be necessary for me to go through the unpleasant experience of demanding the money from these good friends and paying the note on May 1, unless you come to the rescue." Loie dreaded the prospect of a sale of the security, consisting of Rodin drawings she treasured, but she simply did not have the money to pay off the note. She could not come to the rescue, but Sam Hill could, and did.[18]

Sam Hill held Loie in high esteem, as he indicated by the strange request he made of her during one of his stops in Paris. "If I should die on this side of the Atlantic and the body be accessible I should like to have the same burned and the ashes put in an urn (a simple one) and sent to Maryhill Washington," he wrote her. "You are authorized to attend to this or may direct others to do so." (Actually, Sam outlived Loie by three years, died on the other side of the Atlantic, and was duly cremated, his ashes being placed, as he intended, in a crypt near his Stonehenge replica.)

Sam also had a high regard for Loie's art, particularly her *Lily of Life* film, which he tried to help Loie promote while he was on another of his frequent European trips. "Mr Hill thinks it beautiful," Loie told Marie, "but he is an idealist." Pleading for an extension of Loie's loan, Sam telegraphed to the Cleveland bank: "Miss Fuller's remarkable film is attracting attention account its originality and cleanliness. I believe [it] will be highly remunerative." When the bank declined to extend the loan, Sam paid it off, took the art objects that had served as security, and divided them between a Minneapolis museum and Maryhill.[19]

If Loie late in life showed signs of anti-Semitism, these reflected her devotion to Marie, the sovereign of a notoriously anti-Semitic country. They also reflected her disillusionment with Paul C. Turner, her one-time partner, a Jew. But such expressions do not jibe with her long and close association with people who were wholly or partly of Jewish heritage. Among them was Jacob Aaron Cantor, the New York lawyer, state senator, and congressman on whom she depended for legal and financial support and with whom she was once rumored to be considering marriage (he died on July 2, 1921). Of greater import was Roger Marx (1859–1913), who did more than anyone else, as she gratefully acknowledged, to induce Paris to take her seriously as an artist—and whose family accepted her as practically a member. Still more significant was Mrs. Marx's cousin Gabrielle Bloch, Loie's lifelong intimate, who apparently was never fazed by Loie's freakish ideas or by her (more or less imaginary) love affair with Marie.

In 1921 Loie planned another trip to Bucharest—a long train ride, leaving on a Thursday and arriving on a Sunday, for a one-week visit. "*I do not need a suite of rooms, or even a room with bath,*" she assured Marie. "On the divan where you sit, a screen around it & I will be up & out of the way at 7 o'clock." Later in the year she saw Marie in the resorts of Saint-Lunaire and Paramé in France, where the queen repeatedly hosted an "open air theatre fête."

Meanwhile Loie and Marie exchanged letters more frequently than ever, Loie's written, as always, in a scarcely legible scrawl, Marie's in a beautiful, bold hand. Loie addressed hers "My Beloved One" or "My Beloved, Beloved," and signed them "Thy Loïe." Marie used the somewhat more restrained salutation "My Loie" and signature "Your Marie." But Marie's letters as well as Loie's were affectionate, soul-baring, and extensive, running to eight, ten, sixteen, and even twenty-one closely written pages. Loie did not hesitate to tell the queen how to live her life (just as she told Alma how to live hers), and the queen sometimes felt called upon to parry Loie's overtures. She once wrote:

> All those who really know me, come to care for me overmuch. . . . I am not possessable, never was possessed by anyone as I was always the ruling power, not they. . . .
>
> I must be disappointing sometimes, as you feel unusual possibilities in me, but you can only fix half my attention as in spite of the great work of love you are doing for me [the

Queen Marie of Romania in an embroidered native costume. She inscribed this photograph to Gab Bloch in 1926. (Courtesy of the Dance Collection, the New York Public Library for the Performing Arts.)

Lily film], in spite of my being the central thought of your existence, I have a separate life, am held by a thousand things we have never even had the time to tell each other.

You love the ideal that you have made out of me, but do you think that you really know me? that is what I sometimes wonder. I think you would still love the "real me" but it is perhaps different to the Marie who has for so long lived in your soul....

This is a long rambling letter as I have not written for many a day. There is no "business" in it at all Loïe dear it is just from my soul to yours.

Again, after receiving advice from Loie, Marie responded:

Yes, Loïe dear, I understand what you mean about the miserable unemployed, about those who suffer in absolute want whilst others live in luxury and comfort....

Oh! I know what you think of my home, as I have often thought of it myself—of my golden dresses, my treasures around me, my pearls—and you would like me to cast it all away in one grand gesture of resignation.

If I thought that through that I could make the world a happier place—Oh! then indeed I would find the courage to do so....

Your American spirit shies at a title, but am I not more truly democratic with my crown than most of your rich American millionaires?...

Loïe dear, don't imagine that I did not understand what you meant by saying you wished I could make *evident visible* gestures which the poor can see. I always did so as much as I could and shall continue doing so.

Loie undertook to guide Marie's reading, and Marie once acknowledged: "Seldom has anything interested me as much as the book you sent me 'concerning something people do not wish to believe.'" Probably this particular book was *The Protocols of the Learned Elders of Zion*, which Loie had given

Marie. The *Protocols*, a basic text of anti-Semitism, passed as the report of an 1877 conclave at which Jews and Freemasons plotted to set up and control a world state. A baseless forgery, the document was exposed as such by the *Times* of London in 1921.[20]

Hoping that Marie would soon visit the United States, Loie wanted her to prepare the way with a gesture toward the country's Romanian immigrants, many of whom could be expected to give the queen an unfriendly reception. So Loie drafted a message for Marie to send them in advance. "In America there are many of our people, mostly of the Jewish race," the message ran. "Can it be possible that they do not know that they are living in my heart, and that they are of our people—are of our country—and that I am Queen of All my people in fact and in spirit?" Marie, with her striking penmanship, made copy after copy of this communication, one for each of the forty-eight states. Loie then entrusted the letters to Turner, who agreed to distribute them through Jewish organizations, of which he gave her a list.

After the presentation of *The Lily of Life* at the Opéra, however, Loie and Turner had a falling-out. "He abused me in a language I had never heard, composed of terrible threats and epithets which made me think he was of unsound mind," Loie wrote a couple of years later, "but his position and race made me stand for it, for the Queen's sake, if he would . . . help her win over his race for Roumania." Loie's forbearance did not last long. With Gab as a supporting witness, she sued Turner in a local court (le tribunal civil de la Seine) to break the partnership agreement with him, which she accused him of having violated. She won the case, but she was not through with Turner.

While keeping the queen's letters that he was supposed to deliver, Turner demanded twenty-five thousand and then thirty-five thousand francs from Loie. This sum was due him, he averred, for "having organized and directed the play" at the Opéra and for having "advanced considerable money" in an effort to promote the film. When Loie refused to acknowledge such a debt, he threatened to "take necessary legal steps" and finally wrote dunning letters to Marie herself. The queen, as she confessed to Loie, "felt physically sick" when she read "those insolent lines" from that "horrid man."[21]

To deal with Turner, who now resided in New York, Loie and Marie could rely on one of the most powerful of American corporation lawyers, William

Nelson Cromwell. He rates at least a footnote in the diplomatic history of the United States as the lobbyist who persuaded Congress to pay $40 million to a French company for its canal rights, thus making possible the American construction of the Panama Canal. A friend of Marie's, he served as president of the American Society of Friends of Roumania, eventually being honored with the Grand Cross of the Crown.

Continuing to instruct Marie, Loie composed two letters for her to copy and address as her own to Cromwell. One of these, referring to the queen's "message to the Jewish people of the U.S.A." and the fact that Turner was still holding the documents, asked the attorney to "take possession" of them. The other directed him to deny that Marie had ever seen, known, or had anything to do with Turner. Before mailing the package, Loie wrote to Marie: "I will consult my friend Gab who has a strong and wise head and if she thinks we ought not to fight this...." Later: "She tells me it is perfectly correct & to send it to you at once." Writing to Cromwell, Loie gave him her version of the entire affair and concluded in regard to Turner: "With his suave, oily and open frank smiling manner, he is a dangerous adventurer (and more) and now he is trying to blackmail the Queen."

Loie drafted so many things for Marie to copy and sign that Marie could not be sure about a certain statement attributed to her in the American papers. "As we have done such a mighty lot of work together it may be our message," she thought. "But as I do not *conceive* all the things we do together I cannot either remember which is which or how much I do under your instructions which proves to you the blind confidence I place in you."

When Turner gave out that Marie planned to visit America for a movie role, Loie suspected that he meant to "undermine the popularity of the Queen" by this false report. Turner's "race perhaps has sinister motives towards harming the prestige of the Queen," she explained to Marie's lady-in-waiting, Simone Lahovary; "or perhaps he is trying to *prevent her going to America where she would (by her visit) win all the support of even her own Jews.*" Actually, Marie had already concluded, on grounds of her own, that it was not a good time for her to make the American trip. As for Turner, he was finally so discouraged about the prospect of collecting from Loie or Marie that he assigned his claim to another man for a small fraction of the amount. He neither delivered nor returned the missives that Marie had addressed to her fellow Romanians in America.

In the midst of the Turner controversy, Loie received a kind of recognition as a Paris intellectual. The president and council of the University of Paris invited her to a reception for the president of Columbia University, Nicholas Murray Butler. Women were rarely included in such affairs at the Sorbonne. On the invitation card that Loie was sent, the word *Miss* had to be written over the printed word *Monsieur*.[22]

13

*Light
and Shadow*

*M*iss Loie Fuller's sparkling choreography again appears before the fascinated eyes of the Paris public, thanks to the beautiful Théâtres des Champs-Elysées, where this evening the famous dancer begins an important series of 'fantastic ballets,'" a Paris newspaper announced on June 10, 1922. "Her art, difficult to define, is a nice blending of shadow and light." This new show, premiering at the Champs-Elysées and playing there for three weeks, proved such a hit as to get started on a successful three-season run in Paris and on the road. It brought Loie a degree of prosperity that she had not enjoyed for many years.

In these *ballets fantastiques* she depended on gigantic shadows for her most startling effects. As a spectator on opening night described one of the acts, "Les Sorcières gigantesques" (The giant witches),

> The dancers are silhouetted on a brilliantly lit screen. Their shadows duplicate their movements on a much enlarged scale. The farther a dancer moves from the screen, the larger her "double" becomes. She approaches the front of the stage, and a shadow so huge that its head touches the ceiling pursues her, strides over the footlights, and merges into the darkness of the hall. Finally, an enormous hand clutches at a terrified group of dancers and closes upon them as they press against the screen. Never since the Grand Guignol of my childhood have I found the theater so entertaining.
>
> Voilà bien la Fuller! Hitherto, a shadow on the stage has been nothing but an accidental and often annoying presence, a threat to the laboriously built-up theatrical illusion. She takes hold of the shadow, tames it, and makes it an essential element of the show.

Other viewers were equally enthusiastic. "The effect is truly new, extraordinary, overwhelming." "Illusion reigns, the illusion of the dream and the nightmare." "Loie Fuller's art has been remarkably broadened since her debut." "She has created a genre, and she knows how to renew it. Once again she has carried off a most brilliant success."[1]

During the rest of the summer and the fall, Loie's dancers made a series of brief stops on a tour that took them through southern France and into Spain—to Vichy, Lausanne, Aix-les-Bains, Bayonne, Toulouse, Lille, Nancy, Orléans, and San Sebastian. During the winter they played for three weeks at the Coliseum Theatre in London, where the "Sorcerer's Dance" was said to be "a remarkable example of the success of Miss Loie Fuller's latest experiments in the realms of light, colour, and chiaroscuro." From the Coliseum the troupe went to the Alhambra in London for a week and then, during the spring, to La Scala in Antwerp for two weeks.[2]

In June and again in September 1923 the dancers appeared at the Opéra, where they followed a tedious performance of *Samson and Delilah* and "brought new life to the hall with their interpretation of 'Les Chimères,'" as one critic said of opening night. Another commented: "Some of the scenes—the gigantic Chinese shadows of the dancers doing incredible galops—have already been presented, last year, on the stage of the Champs-Elysées. They have achieved the same success here; indeed, the vast dimensions of the Opéra stage have magnified the fantastic effect."[3]

Touring again, the dancers played at various places in France and Spain during August, September, and October. Then, during December and January, they were back in London for a four-week stay at the Coliseum Theatre. The king and queen were expected to attend, and the *Sketch* headlined its account: "Ogre's Hand and Foot as a Royal Entertainment." Afterward, in 1924 and 1925, the show was once more on the road.[4]

As in earlier years, all or nearly all the members of the troupe were English. They still went by such whimsical names as Peach, Bobtail, Fairy, Smidge, Smiles, Finesse, Buttercup, and Chocolate. Their pay varied, but Loie indicated a beginner's 1924–25 compensation when she wrote to Edward C. Kidman in London: "It is agreed that your little girl, Minnie Kidman, is engaged in my Company of Dancers at a salary equivalent to £4. 10 sh [per month] whilst in France and £6 when the Company is booked in Germany and Tcheco-Slovakia." Also salaried was the Englishman S. Beresford, who had direct charge of travel and lodging arrangements for the troupe.

Loie continued to look after her "children" with motherly affection and motherly concern. "The girls all came to see me & my compartment was full all the time," she confided to Gab regarding one of their train trips. "I

Light and Shadow

was warned that *Bobtail went to Albert's room*. I had a talk with them. I did not tell them that, but I told them to be careful. His wife is not in accord with him, & it would be terrible for her to make trouble for Bobtail!" On the same trip Loie was disgusted when some of the girls went to the restaurant car instead of buying lunch baskets, which cost much less. "It makes me mad to see the girls spend their money like that & then grind me for more money (Beresford too) on the pretense *they cant pay* their expenses."

During one of the performances, in a backstage interview Loie in a torrent of words was expressing her opinions on various topics. "But suddenly she stops talking and takes on a severe look," her interviewer reported.

> From the black curtains there appears, gracefully, timidly, a girl with a milky complexion and copper-colored hair, who is wrapped in white veils like a first communicant.
> "Since when have you been using face powder?" Miss Fuller demands in a brusque, uncompromising tone. The recent sapphire dragonfly stands convicted of having taken advantage of the entr'acte to dust her sixteen-year-old skin with a white haze—so feminine!

As far as her pupils were concerned, Loie seemed to consider extravagance more reprehensible than dalliance with a married man, and cosmetics just as bad.[5]

Usually the cast consisted only of Loie's pupils, but at the June 1922 Champs-Elysées performances a special star also took part. This was Anieka Yan, an American who was said to bring a "different note" to the show, displaying a fine sense of both humor and music with her dance, the "Melancholy Jumping Jack."[6]

In making contracts for performances, Loie set her sights high. She once requested that an agent in England "arrange a tour of 15 or 20 representations in the *best* theatres or concert halls (*not* music, variety theatre halls)." She preferred a fixed and specified payment to a share of the proceeds. "My children go to the Grand Opera engaged & paid by the Opera," she rejoiced on one occasion. "It is *not* at our risk & peril, as they term it here in a contract taken on your own responsibility." The London Coliseum engaged her school for four weeks at 350 pounds a week, she agreeing to "change the programme weekly" and giving the management "the option of prolonging this engagement from week to week for a further period not exceeding 10 (ten) weeks." As a rule, however, Loie had to settle for a portion of the gross receipts, ranging from 50 to 75 percent. Typically, the theater provided the stagehands, electricity, and orchestra, while she was responsible for the scenery, lighting, sheet music, publicity, and everything else.

When Loie had an engagement at the Théâtre des Champs-Elysées in 1923, she exasperated the manager, Jacques Hébertot, by her failure to live up to the terms of the contract. Hébertot, who had been quite friendly, finally wrote her: "I really can't waste my time corresponding with you every day. I have reached the point where I must tell you that I am simply breaking our contract, and that I accept full responsibility for my decision. We shall see whether the courts will award you an indemnity, but, in any event, I would rather pay damages than spend a month in the circumstances that I foresee, playing to empty seats, because you, despite all our agreements, don't want to provide publicity—I mean the publicity that is customary and sufficient with theaters." There is no evidence that Loie, litigious though she often was, sued Hébertot for damages.[7]

Hébertot was willing to get rid of Loie and her pupils even though she and they consistently got high marks from the critics. "Never," one of the latter declared, "has theatrical art attained such perfection, such reality within the unreal." Even after Isadora Duncan and her school were no longer performing, some observers persisted in comparing Loie with Duncan, unsure as to which of the two owed the more to the other. Certainly, Loie had had the greater influence on the evolution of the stage, reducing the scenery to the barest essentials for creating the desired atmosphere, and depending more and more on lighting effects rather than painted properties. "What I have achieved is only a small part of what I would like to achieve," she told an interviewer. "I consider my work as just a start toward the grand symphony of light that will transform the theater of the future."[8]

The theater of the present, as of 1925, was being transformed by a quite different American dancer, whom Hébertot had engaged for the Théâtre des Champs-Elysées: Josephine Baker, tall and gangly, nineteen years old, born in Saint Louis, the illegitimate daughter of a Jewish merchant and a

Light and Shadow

black woman. Debuting in *La Revue nègre* at the Champs-Elysées, Baker "made her entry entirely nude except for a pink flamingo feather between her limbs; she was being carried upside down on the shoulder of a black giant." She proceeded to do the Charleston in a spectacularly wild and primitive way. Her act brought screams from the audience night after night as she created almost as great a sensation as Loie, now sixty-three, had done at the Folies-Bergère a third of a century before.[9]

While busy with her dance troupe, Loie had time to spare for her old friends, not only Gab Bloch but also Alma Spreckels and Queen Marie. Apparently she made a rather physical approach to Marie when visiting her in Bucharest in March 1922. Before Loie left, Marie gave her a hastily penciled note:

> Loïe dear—
> Since two years the conflict of this friendship which means so much to me has been the secret agony of my soul. . . . Yesterday evening it was agony also, but it was better that we should talk. You understand my point of view better now, as I showed you quite the human side of it. But I am ready to try and make it a possible and not an impossible thing. I would love for you [and me] to be able to be friends, but it must come about in quite a natural way as our talk did last night—one cannot *arrange* such things. Don't grieve over much. I know that you were longing to take me in your arms last night, and I have forgotten how to be anybody's child. I've always had to be strong and lonely and a stay for others since I was 17 so I never can be all soft—never—it is one of my tragedies—the strong have their tragedies as the weak do. God bless you my Loïe—I thank you for the courage you had last night.
>
> M.

Afterward the correspondence lagged. "It is ages since I have written," Marie explained in a letter of April 27, "but as you know I have been through my great anxieties," and she went on at some length about her queenly obligations.[10]

By that time, Alma was again in Paris, to remain throughout the summer, except when away on trips, one of them to Romania. While in Paris, she entertained lavishly. At one of her parties—attending Loie's show at the Théâtre des Champs-Elysées and then dining at the Hôtel Plaza-Athénée—the guests of honor were Marshal and Madame Joffre and the Grand Duke and Duchess Cyril of Russia.

Loie and Alma, as always, made an odd pair, as a French journalist discovered when breakfasting with them. Loie, he reported, wore a purple veil and a white cloth coat that looked like a deck blanket carelessly thrown over her shoulders. Behind her large shell-rimmed glasses she smiled with an expression that made her seem both exacting and domineering. Alma, "la Reine du Sucre," young, majestic, handsome, was dressed in clothes from the rue de la Paix (which a contemporary guidebook described as perhaps "par excellence *the* street of the fashionable shop").

The conversation turned to the San Francisco replica of the Paris Palace of the Legion of Honor. "You know, everyone will come," Alma said proudly but graciously. "I bought Rodin's works in Paris and am going to put them together in one hall. I want French art to be appreciated over there." Loie interrupted, to say sweetly but firmly: "Above all, America must *understand*. We must not talk money when you talk love. We ought to cancel your war debt. Besides, I would like to know exactly how much money France gave our ancestors [during the Revolutionary War]. I would make the figures public. And Rochambeau!"

Alma, along with two other American women, accompanied Loie and her troupe on a tour of southern France, where they stopped at a beautiful seaside hotel. "I unpacked, & an hour later Alma arrived—tired, hungry & in a wretched mood," Loie informed Gab in one of a regular series of letters to her. "We all felt better after dinner. I told Alma the reduced price of the rooms, & said of course I would pay for my room, but she said no indeed you are my guest. But under the circumstances I feel as if I am really the guest of the hotel, because they took off so much! They did it because they had them free for those two days & the manager wanted to do it for me. However, it is never *I* who do any thing, it is always that something is being done for me. Well, let it go!"

From Menton, near the Italian border, the four women left by car for Milan to catch the *Simploner,* a deluxe train, and take it to Bucharest. A visit with Queen Marie had been Alma's main objective all along, and Loie had given her instructions regarding it before she left San Francisco. "You will be just splendid to bring $20,000," Loie had written. "You must give 7000 of it to the Queen, for the hall chairs I am getting for you." Alma must also remember Marie's daughter, who was about to become queen of Serbia. "You must send her $1000 say 10,000 francs for her poor." In Milan the four travelers had time to go see the cathedral. "Wonderful" was Loie's reaction to the veritable wedding-cake architecture.

"We had a fine trip. Only us four in the whole car," Loie wrote to Gab on arriving in Bucharest. "Fine meals lovely scenery & slept Oh such a lot." Awaiting the Americans were two automobiles, one for servants and baggage, to take them to lodgings for the night. The next day they went by train to the hill resort of Sinaia, where Marie awaited them at the summer palace. "This will be a wonderful historical trip for the others," Loie thought.[11]

After Loie returned to Paris she received a "loving and precious letter" from Marie, to which she immediately replied: "How my heart gladdened when I saw the familiar and beloved hand writing—you had a moment that you had taken to write to your Loie." Loie had more to tell Marie about their lawyer William Nelson Cromwell and their legal difficulties with Paul C. Turner. Indeed, she had more to tell than she could conveniently write, so she made a quick trip back to Romania to talk with Marie in Bucharest.

Before leaving on her latest Romanian journey, Loie had made a shocking discovery. "I discovered a hard lump in my left breast," she recorded several weeks afterward. "I was terribly disturbed of course and wondered if it was cancer and how long I had to live." Her doctor found it to be an egg-shaped tumor, one that he considered benign. "It was harmless because it was not attached close to the body and could be pushed and moved about and he said I need not fear it to be a cancer." He also said there was no reason she should not go ahead with her Romanian trip. Once she was back in Paris,

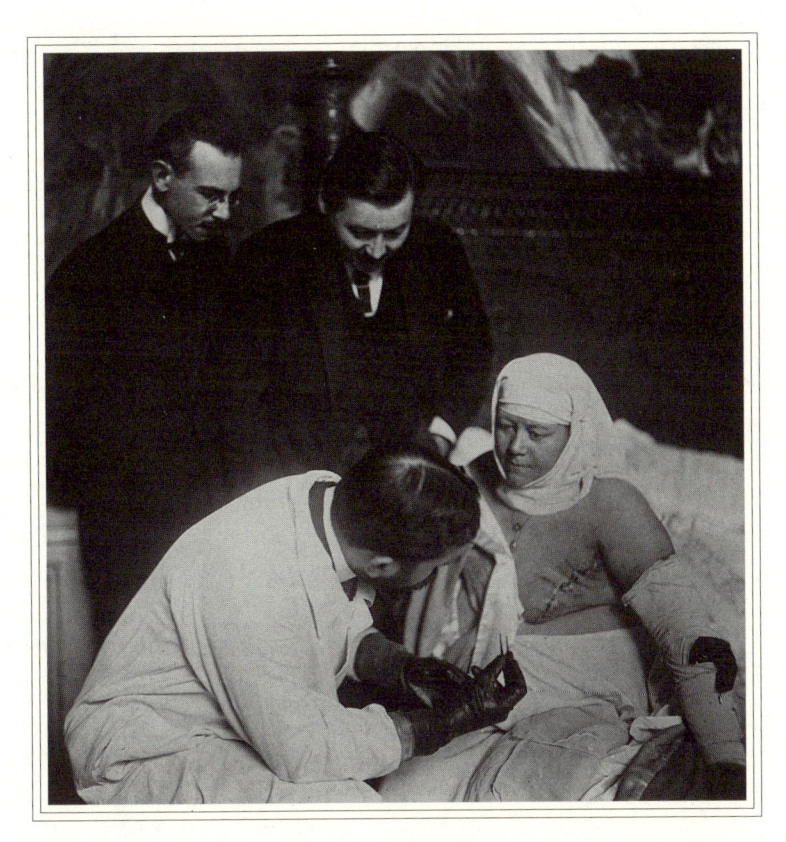

Loie after surgery for removal of a breast tumor in January 1923. (Photograph by Harry C. Ellis; courtesy of the Dance Collection, the New York Public Library for the Performing Arts.)

the tumor gave her more and more pain. "Now and then I had to hold up my breast most of the time to relieve it."

Gab, much concerned when surgeons proposed to operate, intervened to look for another way out. She, as well as Loie, had some acquaintance with the wife of Claude Regaud, a physician associated with Marie Curie in the Institute of Radium and probably the world's leading authority on radium therapy. Through Madame Regaud she promptly obtained for Loie an appointment with the doctor, who decided not to use such therapy in this case.

Light and Shadow

{ 299 }

So, on January 9, 1923, Loie underwent an operation in which not only the tumor in the breast but also the lymph nodes in the armpit were removed. To her immense relief, an examination of these revealed nothing malignant, but she was a long time recovering. After her eleven days in the hospital, during which she was overwhelmed with flowers from her countless friends, "some parts of the wound gave way" when she was driven home over rough cobblestone streets. She had to endure bandages and dressings for at least a month.[12]

Four months after the operation Loie had not yet quite recovered when she hosted an elaborate dinner party, with more than a dozen distinguished guests, to welcome Alma back to Paris. Alma's objective this time was to attend and help supervise an exhibit of French and American art, the proceeds of which were to go to the duchess of Vendôme's drive for the relief of war victims. The exhibit was sponsored by the California Palace of the Legion of Honor (which had not yet officially opened) and was held at the original Palace of the Legion of Honor in Paris. Scheduled to run from May 15 to July 15, it was postponed to June 6, 1923. Loie wanted her important friends to attend, especially Anatole France, to whom she appealed: "For some years I have worked for friendship between our two countries, and now that this exposition is here as an outcome and fulfillment, I would like so much for you to be at the inauguration on June 6, because you can add tremendously to the expressions of friendship at this gathering." But the novelist, apparently absent from Paris, did not get Loie's letter in time.[13]

To Loie, the San Francisco museum seemed largely a product of her own inspiration and effort, assisted by fate. She did not hesitate to let Alma know how she felt about the matter. "I am just re-reading one of your letters to Gab—wherein you say: *"I never got any thing I didn't pay for,"* she protested to Alma after Alma's return to the United States. She proceeded to argue at some length that the things she had got from Rodin for Alma were worth much more than Alma had paid for them. Thus unappreciated, Loie was reminded of old hurts.

> I never think of my experiences with you without tears springing to my eyes—I believe the pain will never leave me, [the pain] that comes when I live over again my visits to S. F.,

and yet I could not help doing it, because I saw what could be done.... And the love of the French for me (and America coming to the war rescue) all, all needed but *you*, and *God* made you French, it is all like a structure built from far away in the past—and just being completed now—a conscious thing coming from an unconscious one.... That is my work ... to convince others. Even as you were convinced from "Antiques only" to Modern Art, not modern art as the world knows it, but as the Master knew it and gave it in his message, which will take centuries to understand. The presence of the invisible in art—a thing undreamed of till he came as a messenger from the Infinite.

Loie persisted in giving advice about the San Francisco Palace and in obtaining items for it. But she was unable to be present when, six months after the death of Adolph Spreckels, the museum finally opened, in 1924. The opening took place on Armistice Day—appropriately enough, since the building was intended as a memorial to American soldiers who died in France.[14]

After nearly two decades of hotel living, Loie decided she could afford to rent a house again, now that she was prospering from the fairly full bookings of her dance troupe. She made what she considered a real "find" when, some time in 1923, she was shown the recently vacated mansion of the Grand Duke Alexander of Russia, located at 29 Boulevard de la Saussaye in Neuilly, a fashionable suburb at the west of Paris. She remained fond of the palatial residence after moving into it. "It has a garden, a very big garage, faces the sun all day long, has steam heat, and is beautifully furnished," as she later described it. There were five bedrooms on the third floor, three on the second, large living and dining rooms on the first, and a kitchen in the basement.

All this was more space than Loie really needed even with the sizable household staff she now employed, consisting of "a cook, a valet and two maids," not to mention a personal secretary. To help pay for the establishment, she briefly thought of turning it into a school for American boys.

Light and Shadow

She assured the man she had in mind as a prospective headmaster that the students could get free lessons from her close friends—astronomy from Camille Flammarion, radiology from Madame Curie, art history from Louvre director Jean Guiffrey, music from the composer Gabriel Pierné, French art from Inspecteur Général des Beaux-Arts Arsène Alexandre, painting from the widow of the painter Albert Besnard, and architecture from Henri Guillaume, who designed the San Francisco museum building for Alma.

The grand duke's house came with elegant wall decorations and with such furniture as "a writing table in old black oak, an English bookcase without glass and with the edges of the shelves trimmed in Spanish leather, divans covered with Persian carpets, and a screen of Coromandel lacquer." While delighting in these objects, Loie found opportunities to display some of her own artistic creations as well. "She continues to paint gorgeous effects on silk," an American reporter noted, "many of the finished pieces being already hung, tapestry fashion, on the walls of the living room."[15]

This technique of painting or dyeing cloth had occurred to Loie soon after she won fame for her serpentine dance on the Folies-Bergère stage in 1892. She wanted to produce similar effects of light and color when she was called upon for performances outdoors. "So Miss Fuller conceived the idea of colouring her voluminous draperies at random so that . . . the effect might be the same as that of shifting coloured lights at night but made more brilliant by sunshine and daylight." Thus, according to her own account, she hit upon a new kind of art, one that required no deliberate effort. By means of it, "a design could be created . . . to produce unconsciously a true and real expression of one's 'self.'"

Quite a few people of presumably good taste took this art form seriously, among them the decorative arts directors at the Louvre, who invited Loie to exhibit her work there. From February 22 to March 22, 1924, the prestigious museum presented a "Retrospective Exposition, 1892–1920," of her "Studies in Form, Line and Colour for Light Effects." The twenty-four pieces bore such titles as *Harmonious Spots, The Explosion, Sun Spots, Nocturnes (Night in the Sky), Chaos, Orgie* [sic] *in Colour, A Garden in the Jungle, The Garden of Dreams,* and *The Morning Sun.* The owners, who lent the pieces for the occasion, included not only Sam Hill, Alma Spreckels, and Queen

Marie but also the Baron Henri de Rothschild of the well-known Jewish banking family and Rudolph Valentino, one of the most popular of the American screen's leading men.[16]

This was not Loie's only contribution to the decorative arts. Reputedly, she still, in the 1920s as in earlier years, exerted a pervasive influence through her special kind of choreography. "She has stimulated modern decorative arts by 'inventing' color in motion, softness of tint, harmonious stain," one contemporary French critic declared. "All our lampshades, our cushions, our wallpapers, etc., derive from the clever work of Loïe Fuller."

The "genius of this woman" was confirmed once more, another Parisian averred, when she achieved a "miracle," a "triumph of light," at the 1925 International Decorative Arts Exposition in Paris. This exposition celebrated the arrival of a fresh style, known as Art Deco or *moderne*, which was looked upon as practically the antithesis of Art Nouveau, now considered old hat. Where Art Nouveau was sinuous and convoluted, Art Deco was inclined to be linear and sleek, suitable for mass production. But there was a reminder of Art Nouveau in the glorious spectacle that Loie put on for the exposition's opening gala. Here was also a reminder that, even in the heyday of Josephine Baker, Loie could still amaze Parisians with her showmanship.

This show Loie called *Sur la mer immense* (On the mighty sea), and she had her girls perform it to the piano accompaniment of Claude Debussy's *La Mer*. The scene was the monumental staircase of the Grand Palais, a building constructed for the 1900 exposition and now the site of the 1925 exposition. Stretched over the stairs was a tremendous expanse of silk cloth, hundreds of square feet of it. Underneath, invisible, the girls held up the cloth and manipulated it while projectors threw light of varying color and intensity upon it. The effect was fluid drapery, a silken sea that rose and fell, rolled and ran, seethed and foamed.

Several days later, on July 2, Loie put on a private performance for special guests. Seated on chairs in front of the huge staircase, they waited expectantly for the arrival of the guests of honor. At midnight the doors opened. Queen Marie entered, wearing a white dress, a diamond necklace, and a winning smile. She was accompanied by her husband, the king of Romania, and her daughter and son-in-law the queen and king of Greece.

A woman, her head covered by a modest, gray nun's veil, comes to greet the sovereigns. "Oh! Loïe," says Queen Marie, "what are we going to see?" Miss Loïe Fuller beckons. "Come on!" says Miss Fuller. "Come on!" She says it almost harshly. Then, almost humbly, she bows before this audience of kings, queens, poets, authors, and artists. She proceeds to work the miracle of bringing the sea up to our very fingertips and then subduing it with a gesture. This woman, this fairy, this creator has played with fire and flames and now gives us billowing waves and spectacular floods.

Beneath her little colorless veil Loïe Fuller looks alternately at the two sovereigns: the queen all in white, the sea all in blue. The smile of the queen meets the smile of the sea. It calms down and, quivering from edge to edge right up to the improvised throne, dies away.[17]

By the time of the Decorative Arts Exposition—twenty-five years after her triumph at the Universal Exposition and thirty-three after her sensational debut at the Folies-Bergère—it would seem that the art, career, and influence of Loie Fuller had reached their apogee. So the critic Legrand-Chabrier suggested in the magazine *L'Art vivant*. At the end of his long biographical and analytical essay, however, Legrand-Chabrier concluded that Loie's kind of "fantastic ballet" was still evolving and could possibly reach even greater heights.

In any event, Loie remained extremely popular. Further evidence of her popularity appeared when a Paris manufacturer asked to use her name on perfumes and cosmetics. A week after her special performance for Queen Marie, she signed a contract according to which she was to receive a percentage of the wholesale price of designated items. Later the firm obtained exclusive rights to the trademark "Les Parfums Loïe Fuller."[18]

From year to year, ever since the end of the World War, Loie had hoped to go back to the United States. Finally an opportunity came when she was invited to help the city of San Francisco celebrate its seventy-fifth anniversary, its Diamond Jubilee, in 1925. For this occasion she was to train local women to perform, as she had done in Oakland in 1915. One member of her own troupe would accompany her, to star as a solo dancer—the one who went by the name of Peach or, according to her present billing, Mademoiselle Pêche. Peach was no longer a young girl, having been with the troupe for nearly fifteen years.

For Gab's benefit, Loie kept a journal of the ocean crossing on the *Majestic*, the largest liner in the world. "Peach & I are very happy together," she wrote. She was annoyed when she realized she had forgotten to bring her white fox fur, and somewhat more concerned when she could not find her black fur, either, nor one of the several suitcases she thought her maid had packed. She did not keep on fretting, for there were interesting people to see and interesting things to do. For example: "We have met the 3 champion tennis players going over to play a tournament at Boston." When the August weather turned foggy and then warm, so warm she could not stop perspiring, she did not complain but insisted: "Well I like it hot & I dont like cold." Nor did she mind if she could not keep up with Peach. "Peach goes down stairs to swim but its too far down for me I cant stand it." When, after five nights, the *Majestic* docked at New York, Loie was in a complimentary mood: "Very fast & comfortable boat—lovely, elegant, superbe."

Heading west by train, Loie made a twenty-four-hour stopover in Chicago, where her younger brother, Delbert, worked as a humble stagehand in a local theater. Her older brother, Frank, lived in Florida. Other family—among them five cousins and two second cousins—resided in Hinsdale. Here she stopped again for twenty-four hours, during which she went to tea at a cousin's home, where several of the clan had gathered to greet their famous relative. They did not know quite what to make of her when she swept in with a dramatic flourish and proceeded to enact the grande dame. Actually, she was proud of the Fuller connection and was saddened to find that the family name had disappeared from her birthplace when Hinsdale recently annexed Fullersburg.[19]

In San Francisco she had a chance to express her family pride when a reporter called at her Saint Francis Hotel suite, which he thought looked like a flower show, it was so full of gladioli and other blooms, which Alma

Light and Shadow

and other friends had sent to welcome her. This reporter, like other new acquaintances in the city, was impressed by Loie's Americanism. "All American? Yes, indeed!" she said. "There were 800 Fullers at a family picnic. One cousin has 18 grandchildren. I never saw such a family. One of our forebears was a cousin of Tippecanoe Harrison."

Despite her Americanism, Loie seemed almost as exotic to this reporter as she did to her Hinsdale relatives. A "fat, vivacious, charming lady," she was wearing a "flowing purple gown" with a "purple coif," and at "something past 60" she was "still very much a prima donna." Though a "real American," according to another writer, "She looks now like a gipsy with kindly blue eyes and energetic, nervous hands—a Bedouin in a sandy colored veil and tortoise shell goggles."

Here in her native land, Loie voiced both positive and negative opinions about the country and its people. "Energy!" she exclaimed. "That's what America means to me." Nowhere in Europe, she declared, was there a vista to compare with what she could see from her high hotel window as she looked across San Francisco Bay to the Berkeley Hills. Yet she also said she found America a land of materialism where jazz was master of the dance and where "art in all its branches was manifested in an orgy of ugliness and distortion." (Could she have been thinking, in particular, of the jazzy art of Josephine Baker?)

"Loie Fuller's Fantastic Ballet," with "Mademoiselle Peche and Forty Dancers," accompanied by a symphony orchestra, was scheduled for seven evenings and one matinee, September 7–13, at the Columbia Theatre. There were to be nineteen numbers selected from Loie's accumulated repertoire, among them "The Gigantic Lily," "The Fantastic Shadows," "The Famous Fire Dance," and, as a finale, "On the Mighty Sea." Loie had only about a week in which to train her inexperienced performers and electricians for this elaborate program. During that week and the week of the performance she was so busy with training and directing that, until the last show was over, she had little time for visiting with Alma or enjoying the recently opened Palace of the Legion of Honor.

To get the job done, Loie "hurricaned about like an avenging warrior," according to one witness.

A direction not instantly obeyed, not heard, brought forth torrents of abusive language. Should, however, a caller draw her to her dressing-room, and the caller be "somebody," a transfusion of calm and sweetness would subdue her and a learned discussion of music, drapes, light, relativity flow in endless stream to be "Yes-ed" and "Oh-ed" and "Ah-ed" by the quite nonplussed listener. Curtain and performance the next minute when, seated on a hard stool, barely concealed behind the curtain, she never ceased her orders. Telling the dancers where to go, what to do, talking to them, ordering, commanding. Changing lights. "Look at that spot! You there! Look at that light! Look at that light! Look at that light! Damn you! Amber, amber, amber. Damn you, change that spot, XYZ." Occasionally rushing to change it herself.

And she got results. Some of the local sophisticates, viewing her as an aging eccentric and her art as "kindergarten stuff," had been inclined to snicker. "But when she produced her flowing sea of dancers beneath apparent miles of silks that undulated all with a fairy play of light, San Francisco forgot the individual for the effect, and a great vaudeville circuit booked her for New York's largest playhouse."

For the engagement at New York's Hippodrome, the Loie Fuller Dancers themselves were on hand, having just arrived from Paris. New Yorkers responded as favorably as San Franciscans, to judge by the *New York Times*, which gave the program a good review. The audience especially liked "Fantastic Shadows," in which "a huge hand appeared to brush away the screen figures," and "Golliwog's Cakewalk," in which they seemed to "disappear under a giant foot." But most memorable was "The Mighty Sea," which "filled the Hippodrome's wide proscenium with alternate waving gossamer and swimming forms to Debussy's music of 'La Mer,'" and which "recalled the famous Loie—O la! la Loie!—of her former American dancing days." Those days were long ago. "Miss Fuller's name is known to few of the younger generation."[20]

Light and Shadow

14

The Dying of the Light

*I*t was mostly a sad time, those last two years of Loie Fuller's life. She was frustrated as she struggled, against recurring and worsening illness, to get things done; disillusioned when her idol, Queen Marie, turned out to be only a human being after all, though still a loved and loving one; disappointed in the financial returns from her troupe's dancing—and in her hopes to recoup by means of new experiments in moviemaking; concerned for her future reputation, which she feared would be hurt by the publication of Isadora Duncan's book. Meanwhile, she was sustained by the persisting affection of those who had long been dearest to her, not only Queen Marie but also Sam Hill, Alma Spreckels, the "children," and, most intimately, Gabrielle Bloch.

Reminders of mortality had come with the deaths of Loie's famous friends Anatole France (October 12, 1924) and Camille Flammarion (June 3, 1925). To help the latter's widow start a career of her own, Loie in January 1926 wrote to an old acquaintance, Zoë Beckley, of the Famous Features Syndicate, in New York, to inquire about the possibility of arranging an American lecture tour for Mme Flammarion. Beckley recommended an impresario, then added: "We went to the Hippodrome when 'The Mighty Ocean' was showing, and saw Mademoiselle Peache [sic], who gave us the regrettable news that you were not well enough to come at that time to America." Loie was unable to keep up the strenuous pace she had set for herself at the San Francisco jubilee the previous month.

While trying to arrange an American tour for Mme Flammarion, Loie was doing the same for Marie Curie's daughter Eve. Loie had not seen Mme Curie for some time when she renewed their association by inviting her and Eve, then nineteen, to lunch so Eve could play the piano for her. "I love you very much," Loie wrote Mme Curie afterward, "& your little girl has walked & played herself right into my heart." Loie arranged for Eve to take lessons from another of her distinguished friends, Gabriel Pierné. When Eve was twenty she gave her first public recital, which led *Le Temps* to comment that she showed promise but was yet to fulfill it. A few months after that, early in 1926, Loie heard from another of her old acquaintances, Ona M. Talbot, of Fine Arts Enterprises, in Indianapolis, that Eve's name was "absolutely unknown in America from the box-office value," but because she was "Curie's daughter she might command a straight fee of five hundred ($500.00) dollars" a performance.

Talbot agreed to "arrange with a New York manager," and Sol Hurok of New York contracted with Gab, June 30, 1926, to handle a "piano recitals tour of America (U.S.A., Canada, Mexico and Cuba)" by Eve during the winter of 1926–27. Loie composed a press release for her. Mme Curie, the statement ran, was training her daughters Irene, twenty-eight, and Eve, twenty-one, for careers in science, but Eve had chosen a musical career instead. She wore her hair "shingled like a boy" and was "a first class chauffeur, a very practical 20th century girl, of the latest modernity." "She is pretty as a picture, with eyes that burn as she talks, first in one language, then in another."

But Eve got cold feet. Before long she wrote (in English):

> Dear, dear Miss Fuller,
> I thought again about all our business yesterday and this morning, and also today after I saw M. Hurok. I am awfully ashamed and anxious in writing these words to you, because I know and I felt every day how much you worked on that business, and how much time you and Gab loosed [lost] on that, and what love for me you showed in that whole thing. I know, as we signed a contract together, that you *can make me go* to U.S. in January. But I am *sure* now, and *today more than ever*, that honestly I *cannot go* and undertake that tour without working one year more.... I write that to you too late, and with a very great remorse, but with all my love and a very, very deep hope that *you* will, *you* only, understand that, and that you will consent to give all this business up.

Loie consented, though the decision was almost as embarrassing for her as it was for Eve. Not only did Loie and Gab possess a financial stake in the business, but they had sold a share in it to at least one other person. "Mrs. Riley, who had taken an interest in Miss Curie's concert tour for $2,000, wanted the money back when the tour was put off," Loie confided to Sam Hill. "But I had bought some things for myself at artists' prices— 50% discount—a fine fur coat and some beautiful golden dresses and coats to match, which I had never put on—and as she wanted something of the kind, she took them instead of the money."[1]

The Dying of the Light

Mme Curie donated some books for the museum that Sam and Loie were planning. Having appointed Loie as one of its five trustees, Sam frequently sought her advice—"Please write me at once the name you prefer for the Maryhill Museum"—and sent her checks to pay for items she was collecting or for their shipment to the state of Washington. She proposed setting up rooms devoted to various subjects, among them Romania, Greece, Napoleon, Marshal Joffre, and Madame Blavatsky. Helena Petrovna Blavatsky (1831–91), the founder of the Theosophical Society in New York, had won tens of thousands of followers with her offbeat doctrines of universal brotherhood and mystical religion, featuring reincarnation.

Loie finally decided to donate to Maryhill the hands of famous people—cast by one of Rodin's molders—which she had been collecting for some time and which she highly prized. Earlier she had said: "I am going to offer them to a great museum in America, my old and only home. I am *chez-moi* in Paris, it is true; I should be after living here so many years and after the great kindness French people have shown me, but I'm an American, and my heart is true to my country." Apparently no great museum in her country was much interested in the pieces; at any rate, a small, inchoate museum there was going to get them. They included the hands of Queen Marie and Sam Hill, of course, those of Eve Curie and of Loie herself, and those of Victor Hugo, Auguste Rodin, Sarah Bernhardt, Rudolph Valentino, Camille Flammarion, Marshal Joffre, and a dozen others. According to Loie, the casts were made in such a way as to reflect the character of each person. "Look at these hands of Marshal Joffre," she said. "This pair is of clenched fists as if he were saying that now famous phrase: 'They shall not pass.'"[2]

Alma credited Loie as cofounder of another museum, the one in San Francisco, writing to her: "We have done a big work together and that mighty building stands, no matter what." Having bought a chateau in Paris, Alma was preparing to visit France with her children in the summer of 1926. "The White Star is sending my Rolls Royce for me via the Panama Canal & then on board the Olympic & then getting me a driver, & two days after we are in Paris I will have my car. Isn't that lovely?"

In Paris that summer Alma met a man who Loie thought would make an ideal husband for her. The handsome and charming Alexander P. Moore had succeeded as a Pittsburgh newspaper editor and owner and had made a creditable record as U.S. ambassador to Spain. He was perhaps best known, however, as the fourth husband of the late Lillian Russell, whom he had married in 1912, when he was forty-three and she was fifty. An Iowa-born actress and singer, Russell was still remembered as the paragon of pulchritude for her time, the 1880s and 1890s. She and Loie, fellow performers on the New York stage, had been close acquaintances. Loie kept urging Alma to marry Moore, who seemed willing enough, but Alma could not quite be persuaded. "Anyway I don't want to mix up in his affairs," she finally told Loie. "He is a strange man."

Moore was in Paris that summer to publicize the Sesquicentennial Exposition in Philadelphia and to induce important people to visit it. In Versailles he attended a performance of Loie's dancers and was so impressed that, by cable, he immediately urged the sesquicentennial committee to engage them for the exposition. Loie herself needed no invitation from the committee to induce her to cross the Atlantic again. She was already planning to go, without her dancers, to accompany Queen Marie on a tour of the United States. This trip was the fulfillment of a dream that Loie had nourished for several years—a dream that now turned into a nightmare.[3]

"Where can I communicate with Loie," Marie telegraphed to Gab on August 13, 1926, "or will you let her know that our dear plan for this autumn progresses exactly as we wish. She can go ahead." Marie was yielding at last to the importunities of Loie, who had long argued that the queen could benefit her country by making herself known to Americans and thus winning their goodwill. The queen could now justify the trip, for she had a specific objective, Sam Hill having invited her to stop at Maryhill and dedicate his museum, even though the building was not yet in shape for use.

With the go-ahead from Marie, Loie began to cooperate with Sam in making the necessary arrangements. Before long she was able to let her know by telegram: "John H. Carroll representing Howard Elliot Chairman of the Northern Pacific Railway and Daniel Willow President of the Baltimore and Ohio Railway and Hale Hold President of the Chicago Burlington and Quincy Railway Company place at your disposal a special train for your

The Dying of the Light

entire visit to America." Then she embarked for New York, to serve as an advance agent and help lay out the itinerary.

When she landed she was met by Mrs. C. C. Calhoun with an offer that proved difficult to refuse. Mrs. Calhoun represented the Women's Universal Alliance for the Mothers' Memorial, a group that proposed to construct a monument to motherhood in Washington, D.C. To raise money for the project, she wanted Loie's dancers to give a benefit performance at the Metropolitan Opera House, where she had secured a date. With *The Lily of Life* on the program and Queen Marie as the guest of honor, an excellent gate could be expected, and Loie was promised 50 percent of it. Even so, she could not afford to bring her troupe and her equipment all the way from Europe for a one-night stand. She was given to believe that other engagements would follow, however, and an invitation from the Sesquicentennial Exposition in Philadelphia now did so, in response to the earlier recommendation from Moore. Thus persuaded, she sent for her girls—and soon had reason to regret it.

By this time, the projected royal visit was becoming an embarrassment to all concerned and especially to Marie. Newspapers in both Europe and America gossiped about the strange intimacy between the commoner and the queen. The former was taking charge of the latter, it seemed to many Romanian officials, and they grew increasingly unhappy about the matter. From Washington, the *New York Times* reported: "At the [Romanian] Legation today denials were made of reports that the Chargé d'Affaires had resigned because of the alleged activities of Loie Fuller, the dancer, in New York, although it was admitted that some irritation had been caused."

Loie decided that, to save the queen further embarrassment, she must discontinue and disavow any effort to manage the trip. From her rooms in the Plaza Hotel, where she was confined by another of her bronchitis attacks, she issued a statement in reply to rumors that she was seeking to "participate in making arrangements for welcoming Queen Marie." The statement ran: "I have nothing whatever to do with the visit and mission of her Majesty the Queen of Roumania except to manifest a lifelong devotion to one whom I consider the noblest woman in the world." In saying this, Loie was not telling the whole truth, and she resorted to downright prevarication when she assured a *Times* reporter that "her arrival here at the same time as Queen Marie's visit" was "a mere coincidence." She told him she had come to stage her ballet in Philadelphia and New York, and she "denied that she and her dancers would accompany Queen Marie on her Western tour." A part of this was true: the dancers were not going to accompany the queen on her trip.[4]

The *Leviathan*, with Marie and her entourage on board, docked at New York near dawn on Monday, October 18, 1926. At about ten o'clock that morning a messenger from the queen arrived at the Plaza Hotel to deliver to Loie "a large official envelope," in which she found various documents and manuscripts, among them the following:

> Monday.
> Loie dear—
> early this morning I put the last words to this, waking up before anyone came to me, seeing the sun rise and the first sight of land. God bless you Loie—here I am. I know you have had a hard time of it, but here I am and it is your work—one day they'll know it. When and how am I going to see you, make contact with you? Of all people it is you my Loie that I want—like a child its mother. I love you my Loie.
>
> Marie

It was some time before Marie had a chance to make contact with Loie. At noon a procession of soldiers, sailors, and marines set out from the Battery to escort the queen through showers of ticker tape to City Hall, where Mayor Jimmy Walker greeted her. That afternoon the royal party left for Washington, D.C., to pay a courtesy call on President and Mrs. Calvin Coolidge at the White House.

In Philadelphia, where Marie was an honored guest of the Sesquicentennial Exposition, she attended the Loie Fuller Dancers' interpretation of another of her stories, *The Queen's Handkerchief*. Then, after returning to New York, she made her scheduled appearance at the Metropolitan Opera House for their performance of *The Lily of Life* on the evening of October 24.

This proved a social and financial disaster. Ever since the program was

The Dying of the Light

announced, it had been under fire from hostile newspapers, especially the most vicious of them, the *New York World*. They complained of the high ticket prices, resented Loie's getting half of the take, and insinuated that the whole thing was a scam. A rumor circulated to the effect that the queen did not really intend to be present. Consequently, large numbers of ticket buyers demanded their money back, "taking up all of the time of the ticket sellers for three days when they should have been selling tickets instead," as Loie recalled. "So Her Majesty was welcomed by half a house instead of a large audience." The gross receipts amounted to only $17,000 instead of the $50,000 or $60,000 that the treasurer of the Women's Alliance had originally estimated. The treasurer declared that 50 percent for Loie was "equitable and just," since the organization could give her no guarantee, and she "had the expense of bringing her entire troupe from Europe and their upkeep and overhead in New York." Actually, Loie lost money on the deal. After this fiasco, other American engagements failed to materialize, and during her stay in the United States she continued to bear the expense of maintaining her troupe.[5]

More disappointments came after Loie joined the queen's party on her special train, the *Royal Rumanian*. The train had reached Spokane, Washington, when Loie finally overtook and boarded it, together with Gab, Alma, and May Birkhead, a *New York Herald* reporter who was referred to as Loie's press agent. Greeting the four women was jovial Sam Hill, who had just arrived and was assigned to the same car. Though Loie's "friends endeavored to keep correspondents aboard the train from reporting her presence," they could not stop a *New York Times* man from wiring his paper the next morning: "Miss Fuller and the Queen are understood to have had a long conference last night." Loie, also telegraphing to New York City, informed William Nelson Cromwell, the attorney for both herself and Marie: "She received threatening telegram . . . it is this delicate position I found her in when I arrived yesterday."

After an overnight run from Spokane, the train pulled into the Maryhill station on November 3, 1926. Loie "watched the long caravan of automobiles whisk the queen and her party and hundreds of curious visitors up the hills and along the lonely road to the museum commanding the Columbia." Still keeping in the background, Loie stayed on the train and thus missed the climax of the trip, the dedication of the building she had not seen since the summer of 1917, when she inspired Sam to convert it into a museum. It now looked more like a ruin than a building under construction, though it was bravely decorated for the occasion in the Romanian colors: red, yellow, and blue. In an extemporaneous speech Queen Marie dignified the occasion and defied her critics, first explaining why she had come to this strange and desolate place:

> Samuel Hill once gave me his hand and said if there was anything on earth I needed I had only to ask. Some may even scoff, for they do not understand. But I have understood. So when Samuel Hill asked me to come overseas to this house built in the wilderness, I came with love and understanding....
>
> Some have wondered at the friendship of a Queen for a woman whom some would call lowly. That woman is Loie Fuller. Her name has often been slighted. That woman stood by me when my back was to the wall. That woman gave me life in my hour of need. She went all over America getting aid for my people. This has almost been forgotten by the rest of you, but I could no longer be silent.
>
> In this democracy there should be no gap between the high and the lowly. As woman to woman, I wish that there would be no doubt in any heart that that woman gave me hope.

Loie "knew nothing of what had happened until the Queen's party returned to the train, and even then it was not the Queen who told her," the *Times* man reported. "Loie Fuller, a tired, sick little woman in black, seeming very old, wept behind her horn-rimmed spectacles when they told her. 'I never dreamed she would do anything like that,' she sobbed. 'I never dreamed it.'"[6]

The dénouement was much less gratifying for Loie and for her traveling companions Sam and Alma. Getting under way again, the train crossed the river into Oregon, where the state's governor welcomed the queen and her party. A string of about thirty brand-new Lincoln touring cars, provided by the Ford Motor Company, took them down the Columbia River Highway (one of the fruits of Sam's good-roads agitation) to Portland. Sam was riding in the lead car with the governor, the queen, and her longtime friend and aide Major Stanley Washburn. When Washburn had the governor leave the queen's car to make room for a detective, Sam objected. He and Washburn got into a violent argument, which led eventually to Sam's ejection from the royal train.

At Portland, Alma abruptly left the party and took off for home without saying good-bye to anyone, though she sent Loie a telegram as soon as possible. She had come down with tonsillitis, she explained, which developed into something like strep throat and left her "very sick." She did not mention that she also suffered from something else—her disappointment at not being invited to the official Portland dinner. Her greatest disappointment, however, was her inability to bring the queen to San Francisco and have her grace the Palace of the Legion of Honor with her presence.

Colonel John H. Carroll, in charge of the *Royal Rumanian,* sided with Major Washburn in his continuing dispute with Sam. In Seattle, after Carroll and Sam ate lunch with Marie in her car, Carroll announced that Sam would not continue with the royal party. Loie was flabbergasted. The next morning, after the train had headed east, she went to Marie and persuaded her to call Carroll and Washburn to a meeting. The queen was "bewildered and upset, trying to find the bottom of things," Loie afterward related to Sam. "She told them she had not been the one to ask you to leave the train and gave orders that you should be called back, and they said they would." But they did not.[7]

The queen was no longer in command of her own expedition, if indeed she ever had been. Her lady-in-waiting, Simone Lahovary, now took over as the royal spokesperson, giving the reporters on board her own version of events. Mme Lahovary, once a resident of Paris, had a long and close friendship with Loie but concluded that, in the present circumstances, she must choose between Loie and Marie. As the train approached Great Falls, Montana, it was "made known by a Rumanian official in the Queen's suite" that Loie would not remain until the end of the tour but would leave it perhaps as soon as the next day, when the train was due in Denver. "The Queen felt, this official said, that much of the discord of recent days had centred around

Miss Fuller's presence on the train, and she wished her to go, even though she regarded her as her friend. Queen Marie was said to be very loath to take this action, but had come to feel in Miss Fuller's case, as in the case of Samuel Hill, who left the train at Seattle, that the confusion centring around her presence was endangering her prestige in America, and her official position as the Queen of Rumania forbade her yielding too completely to personal sentiment." So reported the *New York Times* correspondent, and other newspapers gave similar accounts.

Mme Lahovary's story was not only fallacious but also gratuitous, since Loie had never intended to continue to the end of the tour. Soon after boarding the train, she had said in a telegram to Cromwell: "will be myself New York Tuesday," that is, November 9. She needed to be there to negotiate a contract for what promised to be a very profitable series of American appearances by her dancers the next year. Before the train reached Denver, Marie sent Loie the following hasty and blotty note:

> Loie dear
> I am sorry you will not remain and that you need to get back to N.Y. Do not be disturbed by the reports in the papers. I never thought of dismissing you my dear friend how could it be? You know how I love and trust you.
> Marie

At Denver, on November 10, Loie, Gab, and May Birkhead boarded a special car that Colonel Carroll had provided gratis and that was attached to a regular eastbound Burlington train. Loie was carrying a "written message regarding legal matters" from the queen to Cromwell. Marie and the rest of her entourage were meanwhile taken up Lookout Mountain, where they visited the grave of the old showman with whom Loie had trod the boards so long ago—William F. Cody, Buffalo Bill.[8]

After a week in New York, Loie and Gab sailed for France on the White Star liner *Majestic*, both of them in first-class accommodations, of course. The dancers, nineteen of them, were in second class on the same ship. When Loie arrived at her Neuilly home on the night of November 26, she was "worn out from her American experiences and ocean trip," and she was

The Dying of the Light

still angry at the American newspapers for their falsehoods about her and Queen Marie, as she told a correspondent for one of the papers. She felt some consolation, however, in having had a part in the queen's "triumphal reception" and in having signed what she confidently but mistakenly believed was a lucrative contract that would bring her dancers back to the United States "for the whole of 1927."

To correct the falsehoods, Loie began to put together a collection of Marie's letters, which she had carefully saved for years. This correspondence, together with Loie's commentary, she hoped to publish as a book with the title *The World Asks* (as if the world cared!). Marie endorsed the project and gave it her cooperation, writing an introduction, providing additional letters, and asking only that Loie show her what she was going to include. It would be a book "telling a simple tale of love and confidence," Marie assured Loie. "It is horrible to think that our great love and belief in each other should stand besmirched before the world."[9]

As queen of a country with an uncertain future, one facing a dynastic crisis and the threat of communism, Marie had troubles of her own, which she kept confiding to Loie. Her husband, King Ferdinand, was dying of cancer. Her son Prince Carol had abdicated as heir apparent and was living in Paris with his mistress, Magda Lupescu, much to Marie's embitterment. As a neighbor of his, Loie saw the prince from time to time and came to sympathize with him to some extent. She repeatedly tried to bring about a reconciliation between him and his mother, who was neither offended by her advice nor inclined to follow it.

Taking time to write long letters, Marie continually reassured Loie of her own steadfastness, despite what had happened on the *Royal Rumanian*. In defense of her lady-in-waiting, Mme Lahovary, she said: "She, because of the scandal raised, believed that your name attached to mine was harming me—so her friendship to you went to the wall . . . my faith in you never wavered." Again: "One day, when your long struggle will be over, you will enter a light more marvelous than all the wonderful lights that you, light's great master, lit for us poor mortals, here, on this suffering earth. It may not be in this world that you will enjoy recognition, faithful Loïe, but should you go to the Better Land before your Queen, your memory will always be kept sacred at least in one heart!"

"This time last year with what excitement we were preparing for that great event," Marie wrote later, on July 3, 1927, with reference to their plans for the American trip. "Reality is never quite like the dream!"

Loie, too, had learned about dreams and reality. Despite Marie's assurances, she could not help puzzling over the treatment she and Sam had received on the train. "Remember I have not had one minute alone with her since it all happened," she reminded Sam. "It is only by correspondence that we have been able to get at anything, but I will see her soon and everything will be threshed out between us." In fact, she never saw Marie again, and things were never quite threshed out. She later told Sam that she was "struggling against that terrible result of the U S visit, where she [Marie] had not the strength of character or moral courage to do anything," that is, anything to prevent Sam's dismissal. "Love her? Yes, one's heart cannot change—but the idol is broken & a human being fills its place. One must learn that idols do not exist. They are a chimera living in one's soul & heart, & humans *cannot live up to them,* so the fault is not hers, it is mine! & realization has burned so much I stand inert, confused, holding a bleeding heart in my hand looking at it wonderingly, & with an aching all over me.... My enthusiasm is gone—*but gone for all things.*" Loie still had work to do, however, and she was determined to keep "struggling to carry on."[10]

It seemed fabulous, the agreement they signed before leaving New York, and that is just what it proved to be—a fable.

According to its terms, Loie and Gab, the parties of the first part, were to provide two companies of dancers to tour the United States for forty-eight weeks, beginning on January 3, 1927. The girls would perform in moving-picture theaters for twenty to thirty minutes not more than three times a day. For each of the two companies, the parties of the second part were to pay $2,000 per week (less 10 percent for "booking charges") plus 25 percent of receipts over $10,000 at any performance. These parties were also to be responsible for all transportation and travel expenses, and they were to give a $4,000 advance on or before December 18, 1926.

Loie calculated that, in the course of the year, this contract would bring

The Dying of the Light

in approximately $200,000, enough to pay her debts and make her and Gab at least temporarily affluent. But no advance money had come when December 18 came, nor had Loie heard from the New York impresarios when January 3 arrived. While the weeks passed, she avoided making European engagements that would conflict with the American proposition. "So I just couldn't give up the idea that they were going to keep the contract—and in waiting for them, I got into debt deeper and deeper," she confessed to Sam. The parties of the second part never executed the contract.

By the time Loie began to look for new engagements, it was too late for her to salvage much from the 1926–27 season. She was making a hopeless effort to collect damages from the proprietor of a Berlin variety theater who had canceled a contract for the month of November. During the spring she managed to line up a few performances here and there, but not till July, when the girls were scheduled for a summer tour of twenty nights, would they begin to pay for their keep. Even so, they were leaving their mark on Paris entertainment. Loie complained to Alma: "Two of the theatres here are copying our big 'sea' without any conscience whatever. One is the Moulin Rouge and the other is the Palace—in their big revues. Peach went the other night to the Palace and came home furious—so mad she could hardly speak! 'But,' I said, 'Dear—the whole world has been doing that with Madame for thirty-five years. It is a little late to get mad about it now!'" Still capable of the kind of originality she had shown in "The Mighty Sea," Loie was getting ready to put on "an exhibition of light in relief, where the colors thrown on the screen look as if they were cut. I can not begin to describe them—they have to be seen."[11]

Loie was also demonstrating her ingenuity again as a moviemaker in collaboration with Gab. Since filming *The Lily of Life,* the two had made another picture, *Visions de rêve* (Dream visions), with similar techniques and with the girls as performers. This showed, among other remarkable events, elves with butterfly wings doing a round dance, a fairy wedding party with angelic heralds descending a ladder of flowers, and the great white bird and the great black bird swooping down from a dizzying height. It was made possible by Madame Ernesta Stern, who allowed the use of her property and contributed 15,500 francs with the understanding that she was to receive one third of all profits and that every copy of the film would indicate that it was shot in the garden of her Nice estate. Nearly three years had gone by since that movie was made (in 1924), and there were no profits to divide with Mme Stern, but Loie and Gab nevertheless had high hopes for their latest cinematic venture.

This was a much more ambitious project. Loie and Gab now formed a company, issued ten shares of stock, and sold them for 25,000 francs apiece to wealthy investors, who included some of Gab's relatives. A few of the subscribers were slow to pay up, but Loie remained extremely optimistic as the filming proceeded. The costs were low because it would not be necessary to rent a studio or buy much equipment, since she already had access to most of what she needed. She and Gab would have to hire an "operator," or cameraman, but not a producer or director, and the girls could do their acting during their periods of unemployment. "So we can sell *cheap* & still make a 500% profit," Loie boasted to Sam. "So far it [the film] is very fantastic & lovely, & we expect that to get us out of all our difficulties." Supposedly, this success would more than make up for what had been lost as a result of the Metropolitan Opera fiasco and the nonfulfillment of the subsequent American contract.

The scenario was something that Gab adapted from "Coppelius and the Sandman" by E. T. A. Hoffmann (1776–1822), the great German author of grotesque and gruesome tales. In this story an evil spirit takes possession of a maker of eyeglasses and causes him to do strange, satanic things. In Gab's version the man finally frees himself and the world from the evil spirit. "Oh! yes! we must have a happy ending," Loie said, "—who wants to go to the movies to go home weeping, revengeful, filled with hatred or remorse?"

To tell the tale on the silent screen, Loie and Gab made further experiments in trick photography.

> For instance: The manner of showing how people can be seen walking in mid-air—on nothing at all—or flying through the air, free of all material except the sky. How streams of light can be produced in little round spots, which, when rushed across the screen, blend into a curious irregular stream of light, which can be produced in no other way. How empty spectacles can seem to be producing eyes—eyes which jump

out of the glasses or fall down away from them, melting like tears.

Reflections from mirrors counter reflected. Shadows of people and things which take on the form of fantastic monsters.... Everything is light, shadow, shade and color. People are the trees—or trees are made out of people. People walk on the water, not in it—on it! The soul leaves the body—and looks like a spirit. Several people together make one monster, and suddenly they separate into people again. Objects dance in the air.

So Loie wrote as an "interview" she intended for publicity.

The filming, in the garden and the garage of the Neuilly chateau where Loie lived, took longer than she had anticipated, continuing through the spring and summer of 1927. At the end of September, when there was beginning to be a chill in the air, she was still working along with the others despite the onset of another bad cold in the head and chest. "While I am not able to go where they take the pictures, they consult with me and I can give advice," she told Alma, dictating a letter from her bed. "But our furnace is broken and there is heat only in my room and in the dining-room for the others—so I am not able to go downstairs into the drawing room where they examine the pictures and do the cutting and putting together."

Soon after that, Loie had to leave the chateau because the owner, the Grand Duke Alexander of Russia, wanted either to sell or to occupy it. "Gab is working hard on the film and also getting her little house arranged which she has taken here in Neuilly," Loie wrote to Eve Curie. "Gab says that I can go into her house when it is ready, but I do not know when that will be." So Loie moved back into the Hôtel Plaza-Athénée, where her illness took a turn for the worse. The film remained incomplete.[12]

There was other unfinished business—planning for the Maryhill Museum, writing an autobiography, making sure of posthumous fame. There was even the task of seeing to the fulfillment of another person's life. "You know,

Alma," Loie said, "your whole life points to a woman of great destiny, and it was my destiny to be the instrument by which it was to be done—and it is not finished." Alma Spreckels, occasionally declining a request for a loan or an offer of something for sale, did not always respond in the way that Loie wished her to. Yet Alma acknowledged Loie's permanent importance to her. "I want you to know Loie that I love you with all my heart and soul," she wrote. "Nobody but you and I understand this friendship. I am yours Loie forever."

Ill though she was and busy with other things, Loie persisted in gathering items for Maryhill. For some time she had been accumulating sheet music covers picturing famous people, and now she found an additional and quite abundant source. M. Witmark & Sons, a firm founded by a Jewish immigrant from Prussia, was the largest publisher of sheet music in the United States. One of the sons, Julius, who as a boy soprano had toured with Loie's "concert company" many years before, possessed a large collection that he was willing to donate to the museum, together with such additional examples as he could find. "Will you not try and get music covers of dancing too?" Loie urged him. "Write to me often and keep me posted. With renewed expressions of love and friendship."

Maryhill needed her presence and her promotional talents, Loie believed. She wanted to go there and talk to businessmen, especially those connected with hotels, banks, railroads, streetcar and bus lines, tour companies, and the sale of artworks. "I want to talk to them about what to do to make tourists come to Maryhill, and what to do to make them want to stay there when they do come." Sometimes she thought she ought to "migrate to Maryhill and remain there and work from there until the Museum is opened."

But she had in mind another idea that must first be started on the way to realization. "For a long time, you know, we have thought about a building here in Paris," she reminded Sam. "We want it to be a Loie Fuller American Museum—headquarters for the Maryhill Museum." According to the plans that she worked out in some detail, this building would presumably be not only self-supporting but also profit making. On land to be provided free by the French government, it would be built in a hollow square around a "garden court," with museum space on the ground floor and twenty apartments on five upper floors. Sam, however, was not convinced that the apartments could be rented for as much as Loie estimated, and neither he nor any of his moneyed friends could be persuaded to finance the project.[13]

While planning that monument to herself, Loie also tried other means of perpetuating her name. She kept working on an autobiography, a book she intended to be much more comprehensive than her published memoirs, *Fifteen Years of a Dancer's Life,* or her manuscript about Queen Marie and herself, *The World Asks.* With the autobiography she made little more progress than to jot down some miscellaneous scraps of reminiscence.

These included bits of shameless self-flattery. "Her meteoric career," Loie wrote in the third person, "placed her in a firm position by the force of her character—unselfish, generous, unthoughtful of herself, always thinking of and living for others, she has already made history—and one day her story will become a legend like Prometheus, because she invented an eternal flame, where silk and light so reproduce fire . . . like the real fire of Prometheus."

Yet she could also be disarmingly modest. "I was born in America but I was made in France," she declared. "To France I owe all, every thing the world has given me." Along with hundreds of thousands of others, French and American, she rejoiced in the wave of Franco-American fellowship that surged when Charles A. Lindbergh landed at Paris on May 21, 1927, after the first solo flight across the Atlantic. Lindbergh, she thought, had given a "fine example" of the best kind of diplomacy, the people-to-people kind, with no "ceremony" or "protocol."

Loie had never advocated the attainment of female suffrage or other women's rights through political organization and agitation. Yet she believed in a kind of feminism, a kind that had nothing to do with politics. As she once wrote to Gab,

> Equality's the thing.
> Therefore make thyself worthy
> To be any man's equal!

In other words, women should make themselves equal by virtue of personal achievement. That is what Loie herself was doing, as Jules Clarétie indicated in his 1907 *Le Temps* article, in which he said women were "more and more taking men's places" as lawyers, writers, physicians, and whatnot, and Loie was creating a "feminist theater."

Loie expressed her view of the achieving woman in an essay she once wrote, "The Boston Blue-Stocking." This term refers, she said, to "the woman who has crammed her head as full of learning and knowledge as any man ever has his."

> Whether she teaches school, lectures publicly, writes for high-minded exclusive journals, for a sensational newspaper, publishes books or opens a lawyer's office, becomes a surgeon, dentist or regular M.D. you can make up your mind she knows what she's doing! . . .
>
> Certainly she can hold her own anywhere and anyhow. It may not be the old-fashioned quality we call womanliness, but it competes with every thing and itself—and gets there. That is the thing nowadays, especially with the self-made American—get there. If you don't, you're not made, that's all, neither self nor any other kind of made.

Loie got there.

In reminiscing, she confessed to some rather embarrassing moments. There was, for instance, the time when she got into an automobile with Queen Marie, and the door was slammed on her finger. She groaned, and Marie suggested that she try the Coué technique, which Loie had just been praising. Dr. Emile Coué, in the 1920s a well-known proponent of cure through autosuggestion, advised patients to keep saying: "Day by day, in every way, I am getting better and better." So Loie started repeating and Marie and the others in the car joined her: "Ce pass-pass-pass-pass-pass-pass till there was no end of it, & the pain did pass but I am still wondering whether it was really Coué, or the pride to keep up to what one says that made the pain go."

Recalling Rodin, Loie revealed feelings of a kind that she had never expressed in her letters or in her published memoirs. "I went with the great sculptor Rodin once to see a church & I stood there at least 3 hours while he contemplated every blessed thing in the place—at least 3 hours standing there like a fool," she now wrote. "I didn't see any fun in it at all. And when we got out the master whispered softly *we hadn't enough time!* (Gee!)." She did not claim to have influenced Rodin's art, though she could justly have made such a claim. As Hélène Pinet has pointed out, her "explosions of vivid color are rediscovered" in his watercolors.

For a person who seemed to associate on equal terms with so many of the highly learned, she made a quite unexpected admission:

> I was not crazy about people who are all the time saying clever things, or making highly intellectual remarks. I had much rather they would say of themselves I am very clever—very intellectual—but I won't bother you, unless you desire it—because that would give one a chance to escape if they wanted to. It's always so uncomfortable to have someone telling you things you don't understand & don't want to, & it's rather disagreeable to be told things as if you didn't know any thing yourself, and then besides how can one be really & truly interested just because it is something that interests some body else. Education is wonderful but nobody wants it rubbed in like, & it's terrible to be expected to ask the right question in the right place at the right time when you don't even know what they are talking about & you don't want to know. Some times I think I'd rather get religion than education.

Concerned as she was for her reputation, she might have been a little less self-revealing than she often was in her autobiographical jottings.[14]

Loie suddenly saw a threat to her reputation when she heard what Isadora Duncan was saying in her autobiography. Duncan began her chapter 10 by quoting an acquaintance who once remarked of Loie: "She is not only a great artist but she is such a pure woman. Her name has never been connected with any scandal." Scandalously heterosexual herself—and obviously a bit jealous—Duncan proceeded to intimate that Loie was just as scandalously homosexual. It was in these memoirs that she told how, in 1901, she had found Loie in Berlin "surrounded by her entourage. A dozen or more beautiful girls were grouped about her, alternately stroking her hands and kissing her." And Gab was a "scarab" among "brightly coloured butterflies," one whose "enthusiasm for Loie Fuller possessed her entire emotional force."

Homosexuality was still "the love that dare not speak its name." People remembered all too well the trial, conviction, and disgrace of Oscar Wilde. More recently there had been the case of Maud Allan, one of the dancers whom, along with Isadora Duncan, Loie claimed to have launched. In 1918, while Allan was performing in London, a scandal sheet ran an article, "The Cult of the Clitoris," giving the unmistakable impression that she was a lesbian. She sued for libel but lost the case after it "degenerated into a debate about Wilde and homosexuality in general."

Loie now contemplated a lawsuit of her own. "Two different American newspaper representatives and two other different people friends of Isadora all came to me separately to inform me that she gave them each to read a scurrilous and false chapter on me in the manuscript of her book which she is sending her publishers in America," Loie cabled to Cromwell, her lawyer in New York. Again: "All I would ask now is for you to notify Boni Liveright publishers that I hear false disreputable things will appear about me in Isadora book and that we would hold them responsible if published." But Cromwell could not prevent Boni & Liveright from publishing *My Life* by Isadora Duncan (1927) with the chapter that Loie had objected to as "scurrilous and false."

By the time the book came out Duncan was dead. She had been trying out a sports car when her long scarf caught in a wheel and strangled her. That was in Nice, where a year earlier, at the age of forty-eight, she had resumed her dancing career after a lapse of some years. Loie attended one of her new recitals and obtained her signature on the program. But she did not attend the funeral, which was held in Paris, or the cremation and the placing of the ashes in the columbarium at Père-Lachaise. Even if she had been inclined to go, she was too ill to leave her bed. She did not have long to live, herself.[15]

For some months Loie had been finding it a struggle to get anything done, even when she was not bedridden. She confided to a male friend in the spring of 1927, not long after her sixty-fifth birthday:

The Dying of the Light

Oh! I am so tired—so tired! All inside me is so tired—just tired out. Have you ever been so tired you could not even undress to go to bed? Well, I am just that way all—the—time, except when some activity spurs me on. Then when the moment is over of mental activity, it all comes back again—and the tired feeling hurts me so that tears come in spite of me. Isn't it dreadful?

I wonder if it is always like that with people when they get old. Is that terrible fatigue—age? I don't know, but when I see old people walking slowly along I understand. They are too tired to move! . . .

There is so much to do—so much that has got to be done, and I put off—put off—because I am *too tired!* . . .

As I am writing this there is a sensation of vibration throughout my system, but not evident. My eyes close with almost each word I write, my head is heavy and little "hurts" come in my head, first here and there. My face is uncomfortable from, I suppose, the nerves. I am sleepy—I wonder if it is because I slept only very late last night. But I always [go to] sleep late—from twelve to two is my *"wakest"* time. I was born at two a.m.

During the last three months of the year (and of her life) Loie was confined to her room at the Plaza-Athénée. It was a room with a view, high enough that she could look out at the Seine and, beyond the river, at the roofs, domes, and steeples of the Left Bank. She could also watch the sky, which never ceased to fascinate her with its changes of light and shade. "There are still so many things that can be done with light—light—light!" she remarked to a visitor, a newsman for the *Paris soir,* who reported: "She was crazy about light."

Loie had frequent visitors, as many as five or six of them crowding into the room, as they did one day when her three favorite students—Peach, Finesse, and Fairy—were rehearsing there. In the small chamber Peach somehow found space in which to dance, and she was sensitively interpreting a "poem of the sea" while Loie lay stretched out on the bed, a silent spectator, having practically lost her voice because of her bronchitis. Suddenly she sat up. She had some comments to make, and she was not going to let her hoarseness stop her. "The words burst forth, striking and picturesque," as one of the people in the room remembered.[16]

Loie seemed to be improving when, near the end of December, her bronchitis turned into pneumonia. Gab and other close friends began to keep a day-and-night vigil at the bedside. One night Loie complained of difficulty in breathing, and Gab called the doctor, who brought in a pulmotor, which gave temporary relief. On New Year's Eve a telegram arrived from Queen Marie. Loie dryly remarked that Marie was extravagant in wishing her "bonne année" ("happy new year") when "bonne journée" ("have a nice day") would have been enough.

On New Year's Day another telegram came from Marie, who must have heard from Gab that Loie was dying. This one said: "Good-by, Loie, La Belle Loie, my best beloved." Soon after it was read to her, Loie went into a coma. She died several hours later—at two o'clock in the morning. Gab now had the sad duty of closing the eyelids of the one she had loved so faithfully and so long.[17]

"According to the expressed wish of the deceased," a Marseilles paper stated, "there will be no religious ceremony." No doubt that was indeed Loie's wish, since she was in no conventional sense a religious person (despite Anatole France's statement that she was "profoundly religious"). A funeral was nevertheless scheduled for the morning of January 4, 1928, at the American Cathedral of the Holy Trinity (Episcopal).

In the church's large auditorium, the attendance that bitterly cold morning seemed rather slim. Yet an impressive number of notable people were present, among them artists, actors, writers, and representatives of the American, French, and Romanian governments. Others at the funeral included Loie's cousin Kate Fuller, a longtime resident of Paris; Raymond Duncan, Isadora's brother; and Eve Curie. Loie's "children" were absent, off on a tour in Egypt.

Conspicuous among the mourners, Gab wore a black cape that contrasted sharply with her hair, now completely white and thrown back over the cape. Close friends addressed their condolences to her. "I thought Loïe was getting better, and can scarcely believe this sudden blow, so awful for

The Dying of the Light

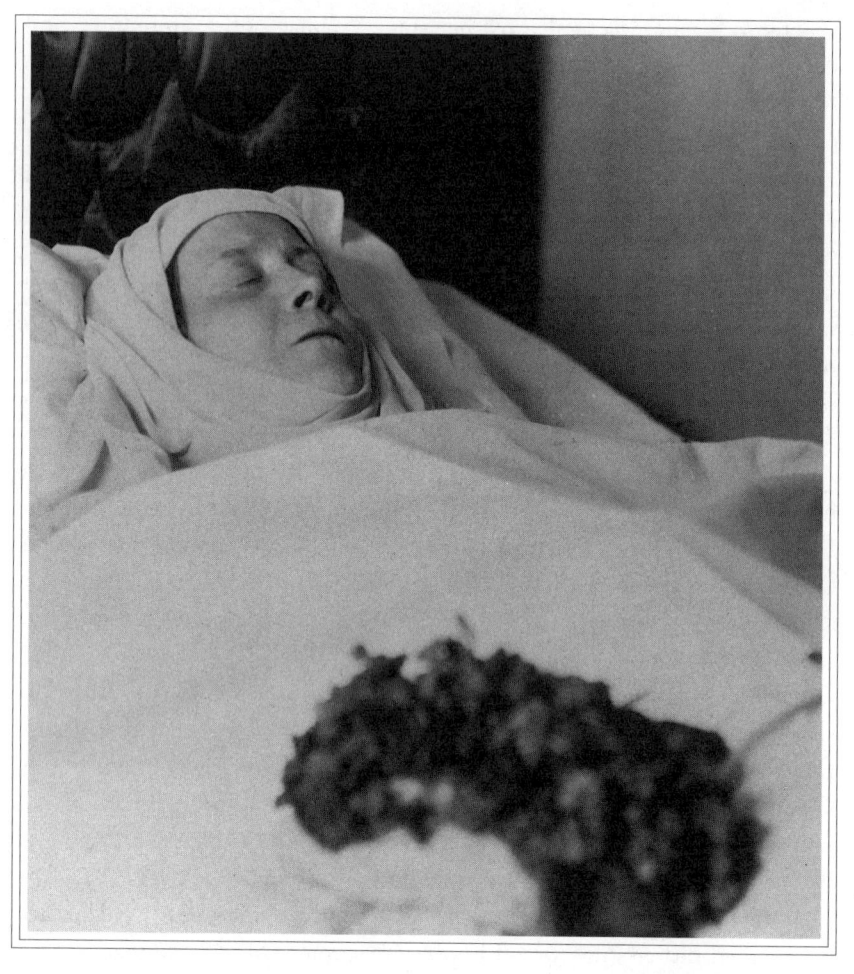

Loie on her deathbed in her room at the Plaza-Athénée hotel, Paris, January 2 or 3, 1928. This picture was taken by Harry C. Ellis, who photographed her so often and for so long that he might almost be considered her official photographer. (Courtesy of Maryhill Museum of Art.)

all those who loved Loïe," Eve Curie had written as soon as she learned the sad news from the newspapers. "I embrace you very tenderly and very firmly, dear Gab, and think of you and of our Loïe."

After the service, which was short and simple, a small group of those who had been closest to Loie followed the hearse to snow-covered Père-Lachaise cemetery. Adorning the coffin were two magnificent bouquets beribboned in the Romanian red, yellow, and blue. One was from Queen Marie, the other from Prince Carol.

In accordance with Loie's instructions, her body was cremated. From the tall chimney of the crematorium rose whirling spirals of smoke that made one observer think of Loie's whirling draperies of long ago. It was the "last manifestation of the sublime dancer." Her ashes, in a ceramic urn, were placed in a columbarium receptacle not far from Isadora Duncan's.[18]

The Dying of the Light

EPILOGUE

It was too much, of course, for Loie Fuller to think, or to hope, that someday her story would become "a legend like Prometheus"—Prometheus the fire bringer, the life giver, of Greek mythology. Even if her expectations had been far less grandiose, she would surely have been disappointed in her reputation as it existed during the first several decades after her death. True, when she died she was the subject of a great many newspaper obituaries, most of them extremely complimentary, and in the ensuing years she was honored by various re-creations and memorials. In comparison with Isadora Duncan, however, she received little attention in books and magazines and was generally rated as less important in the history of the dance. If not a forgotten woman, she was a poorly remembered one.

As Loie's legatee, Gabrielle Bloch got practically no money but did receive a number of art objects. Through her lawyer she promptly requested the return of the things that Loie had left on loan at the Cleveland Museum of Art. "I have gone over all the items which were lent here by Loie Fuller and certainly none of them are of the slightest interest for us," a presumed expert informed the Cleveland director. "They are terrible!" Which goes to show that, with art experts as with the rest of us, beauty is in the eye of the beholder.

Gab also inherited the Loie Fuller Dancers and, through them, helped to keep alive the memory of her dear friend. Under Gab's direction the troupe continued to perform for about ten years, until the approach of World War II. The girls remained a familiar sight as they traveled about in their white robes, white slippers, and red cloaks. They were "petites Loïes Fullers," reminders of their late exemplar.

"The famous creator of the serpentine, she who first had the idea that electricity could contribute to the dance, some time ago closed her eyes to that light of which she had demanded so much," *La Vie parisienne* noted in 1933. "But some devoted hands have preserved her legacy, and her pupils survive as priestesses of rhythm, light, and color." The following year Gab (using the name Sorère instead of Bloch) made and exhibited films of the girls performing "Les Ballets de Loïe Fuller." One critic praised her for maintaining artistic as well as cinematic integrity, and another commented that filmed dances were usually pedantic and boring, but these could be enthusiastically recommended.[1]

Queen Marie remembered Loie with mixed emotions. Several months after Loie's death she complained to Alma Spreckels that she had given Loie 200,000 francs for three Rodin sculptures and had never received them. "I know that our faithful Loie, who always wanted to help me with my poor, knowing the colossal demands put upon me, would be desperate if she thought that because of her death I had lost all that money," Marie wrote. "Now, where she is, she no doubt sees 'through a glass darkly' but alas she can send me no message." Marie also said that Loie had acquired, for Alma's benefit, furniture and other goods from the Romanian royal palace at a fraction of their value. "Loie comes and sweeps my house of memorable treasures but my poor get nothing."

Before Marie died, in 1938, she published two volumes of memoirs (1934, 1935), the first covering the years to the beginning and the second to the end of World War I. In the first volume she did not so much as mention Loie, though she had met her in 1902 and had renewed the friendship in 1912. In the second, consisting mainly of diary excerpts, she included no more than a brief mention in the entry for April 27, 1917: "I have news from Loie Fuller, who is going off to America, whence she hopes to send me many provisions for my hospitals. I hope she will not be blown up! She is a wonderful friend and such an enthusiast."[2]

Both Loie and Marie were commemorated in the Maryhill Museum, the completion of which was delayed by Sam Hill's death in 1931 and then by several years of litigation over his will. Alma was largely responsible for making possible the museum's opening, which took place on what would have been Sam's eighty-third birthday, May 13, 1940. She was also largely responsible for its subsequent development until her own death, at the age of eighty-seven, in 1968.

Though never publicly acknowledging Loie's help with the Palace of the Legion of Honor, Alma determined to do Loie justice by dedicating to her a Hall of the Dance at Maryhill. For this Loie Fuller gallery she proceeded to

Epilogue

collect sculptures, drawings, posters, and photographs. "It was Loie Fuller who really inspired Sam Hill to make the museum at Maryhill," she reminded its first curator. "It was Loie Fuller who introduced Sam Hill to the Queen of Romania, and she also helped him get a great many things for your museum."

Regarding her Maryhill activities, Alma also wrote: "What I am doing is in memory of Sam Hill, Queen Marie, and Loie Fuller, a great happiness that I am able to do it, and a great privilege." The museum is a monument to all three—and to Alma as well.[3]

A different Loie commemoration was the work of Ruth St. Denis (Ruth Dennis). Once called the "First Lady of American Dance," St. Denis with her husband, Ted Shawn, operated the influential dancing school and company Denishawn in Los Angeles from 1915 to 1931. One of their students, equally influential in turn, was Martha Graham. Continuing to perform, with great popular success, St. Denis acknowledged her own and other modern dancers' debt to Loie Fuller: "She brought appurtenances—lights and veils—to dance and where would I be, pray, without my lights? where would Isadora have been without her simple lighting effects? where would the theatre dancers of today find themselves without Loie's magnificent contributions?" To express her appreciation, St. Denis performed *The Ballet of Light* in the Hollywood Bowl on August 3, 1954. The program described her dances as "Reminiscences of Loie Fuller, to whom the Hollywood Bowl performance was a tribute."[4]

To observe the fiftieth anniversary of her death, the Palace of the Legion of Honor in San Francisco put on an art exhibition and a performing arts festival, "In Celebration of Loie Fuller," which was scheduled to run from December 10, 1977, to February 26, 1978. This was the work of Margaret Haile Harris, a former Legion of Honor guest curator. She had planned a much more comprehensive exhibition than the legion proved able to finance, and afterward she looked for a museum that could accommodate the entire show.

The result was "Loïe Fuller: Magician of Light," a tremendous loan exhibition, lasting from March 12 to April 22, 1979, at the Virginia Museum of Fine Arts in Richmond. Objects were provided by thirty-two lenders, among

Epilogue

them Maryhill and the Cleveland Museum of Art. Included were more than 140 sculptures, paintings, posters, drawings, and photographs, all of them reflecting Loie in one way or another. There was even the showing of an old film in which she could be seen as a performer in action.[5]

In displaying Loie Fuller memorabilia, the Virginia Museum was also displaying Art Nouveau. By this time, books on Art Nouveau were appearing more and more frequently, and almost every one of them contained at least a single Loie Fuller illustration or some reference to her as the personification of the movement. These books helped to keep her memory alive among students and fanciers of art.[6]

From September 30 to November 30, 1987, Loie was featured in an exhibition of photographs at the Musée Rodin in Paris. She or her pupils appeared in 54 of the prints, Isadora Duncan and her girls in 11, the French dancer Adorée Villany in 10, and Ruth St. Denis in 2. The shots had been taken between the late 1890s and 1914, many of them for Rodin's possible use in making sketches or sculptures. By that time, shutter speeds of one-hundredth and even one-thousandth of a second were possible, but only Loie and her pupils were shown in action photos; the rest of the dancers merely posed for the camera.[7]

In September 1988 Loie was spectacularly brought to life at the International Dance Biennale in Lyons, France. There, a German dancer from Munich, Brygida Ochaim, presented a twelve-minute piece of original choreography that invoked the spirit of Loie's performances without attempting to reproduce them exactly. Ochaim and her associate, the American lighting designer and video artist Judith Barry, did not pretend to have discovered Loie's secrets of light and color. They did not need them. They had the advantage of technology unknown to Loie, such as computer-controlled projectors and, to create the effect of smoke and flame in the fire dance, laser beams. To round out the program, a film clip revealed one of Loie's pupils tripping across a lawn with silk billowing behind her, and another clip showed a segment of Loie and Gab's 1921 movie, *The Lily of Life*.[8]

It remained for the Villa Stuck Museum in Munich to present, under the direction of Jo-Anne Birnie Danzker, the greatest of all Loie Fuller exhibitions. On display there, from October 19, 1995, to January 14, 1996, were more than half again as many items as had been shown at the Virginia Museum in

Epilogue

1979. A century after her sudden rise to fame, Loie was being more tellingly remembered in France and Germany than in the country of her birth.

❧

They were often compared, to the disadvantage of the one or the other, while they were alive, and the same kind of disparaging comparison continued after they were dead. In January 1928 a Loie obituary in a New York newspaper began: "In the last two months [actually, Isadora Duncan died three and a half months before Loie] two of the most noted women in the world of dance have passed away. Loie Fuller has followed Isadora Duncan. There is scarcely any just comparison between the two, because Miss Duncan was in reality an artist, while Loie Fuller during her long stay in Paris gained no greater credit than attaches to a clever mechanician." Some of the obituaries in Paris newspapers played a similar theme. "Her art had nothing to do with choreography," declared one. "La Loïe Fuller was first and foremost an ingenious electrician." Another Paris paper gave a more positive emphasis: "Did she dance? No. And yet that is the way fire dances." A Berlin periodical also put the matter nicely: "The effect of the dance creation that made Loïe Fuller famous consists less in the art of the dance than in the charm of color and light."

Loie herself more than once had said essentially the same thing. She said it again in an autobiographical note not long before her death: "'Light' and 'Color,' thrown on great masses of silk, was my real representation and not dancing at all." She produced her effects, she explained, by "rhythmical movement" that was "called dance for want of a more appropriate title."[9]

Whatever it was, would her kind of performance have a lasting effect? "In her day she was perhaps the most widely imitated woman in the theatre, but it has been some years since her type of work has been popular," the *New York Times* opined. "Perhaps the most significant thing she did artistically was to direct attention in some degree to the possibilities of lights and draperies in combination."

But at least a few French critics thought, at the time of her death, that Loie would have a significant and permanent influence—a greater one than Duncan would have. Prophetically, Georges Martin wrote regarding Loie:

Epilogue

So brilliant was she that she dazzled an entire epoch. There is not one *modern style* [i.e., Art Nouveau] work from around 1900 that, in its waving curves, does not maintain a trace or a reflection of Loïe Fuller's dances, like an impregnation of that poetry so very Anglo-Saxon, phantasmagoric, childish, and charming, which was her distinctive hallmark.

The *modern style* is perhaps unfashionable now. But it will receive its due someday, for it has prepared the way for the style of the present, as is shown by Loïe Fuller's example. Her choreography has not become outdated. Adapted, transformed, made more serious and, in a sense, more masculine, it lives on in that of Isadora Duncan, who was one of her students and who, in turn, inspires contemporary artists.

Still more laudatory, Michel Georges-Michel credited Loie with having revolutionized choreography. "She freed the dance from the thin shackles of the tutu, of Italianism, and of academic gestures." She led and Duncan followed, far less successfully, according to this critic.

Loie seemed preferable to Duncan even in the opinion of one of the critics who considered her a mere lighting expert. Her effects, André Rouveyre contended, were comparable to those of modern illuminated signs, such as the "multicolored electric cascades" that nightly advertised Citroën cars on the Eiffel Tower. Still, Rouveyre thought that, among professional dancers of the prewar years, Loie was "certainly one of the most likeable, at least for her personal charm," whereas Duncan "had little to offer—and that little with presumptuous self-conceit—except enormous dislocations and grimaces, which aimed for the sublime and fell ridiculously short of it."[10]

Appraisals of Loie Fuller and Isadora Duncan, so various in 1928, continued to range widely in subsequent years. Experts have disagreed.

On the one hand, the great English ballerina Dame Margot Fonteyn has belittled Loie in a rather catty way. "Loie Fuller was as different from Isadora Duncan as theatre is from nature. Loie had theatrical sense in the highest degree. Her performances, however, were more gimmick than dance and did not endure. And as for Loie Fuller herself, she got very fat."

On the other hand, the great Russian dancer and choreographer Michel

Epilogue

Fokine, who helped to launch Diaghilev's Ballets Russes, has expressed a very high opinion of Loie, ranking her as one of the leading contributors to modern dance. "I consider the greatest manifestations of recent times to be the separate and so dissimilar achievements of Isadora Duncan, Loie Fuller and Ruth St. Denis," Fokine declares. "Duncan has reminded us of the beauty of simple movements. Loie Fuller introduced the effect of lights and shadows, of the combination of the dance with floating veils. Ruth St. Denis has acquainted us with the dances of the East."[11]

When in 1916 the Ballets Russes first appeared in the United States, American critics were unaware of the troupe's background, the American dance historian Elizabeth Kendall has pointed out. "It was the Europeans and especially the Russians who analyzed and built upon the dance inventions of Loie Fuller and Isadora Duncan," Kendall notes. She adds: "It is clear that Ruth St. Denis and Isadora Duncan both stemmed from Loie Fuller, though each took off in a separate direction."

"The earliest modern dancers were not trained ballet dancers and had to devise a system of movement that was suitable for their individual expressive needs," another authority, Don McDonagh, has written. An "exploration of form" became necessary. "The exploration started with Loie Fuller, Isadora Duncan, and Ruth St. Denis and accelerated in the 1930's with the specialized technical contributions of Martha Graham and Doris Humphrey and the historic generation of modern dance."[12]

Thus in the 1970s and 1980s Loie ranked along with Isadora Duncan as one of the significant pioneers of the modern dance, in the judgment of American experts on the subject. In 1990 a Mexican writer, Alberto Dallal, rated Loie even higher. Dallal traces the origins of modern dance mainly to American "show business." "Viewed in this aspect," he argues, "the figure of Isadora Duncan tends to lose its luster, and the personalities of Loie Fuller, Maud Allan, and Ruth St. Denis emerge with greater vividness and brilliance." Loie in particular stands out, according to Dallal. Her art "contains elements that are repeated throughout the history of extravaganzas in the United States."[13]

Nevertheless, Isadora Duncan has received much more attention than Loie, both in dance histories and in biographical literature. A 1991 computer printout of Library of Congress holdings shows Duncan ahead 48 to 4—

Epilogue

forty-eight titles concerning Duncan, only four for Loie. These four consist of the "gypsograph" of Pierre Roche and Roger Marx (1904), Loie's own *Fifteen Years of a Dancer's Life* (1913), Margaret Haile Harris's Virginia Museum Exhibition catalog (1979), and the Brandstetter and Ochaim book (1989).

At the end of the twentieth century Isadora Duncan was much better known than Loie. Most educated Americans could identify the one; few had ever heard of the other, and those few were either residents of Hinsdale or Monmouth, Illinois, or people interested in Art Nouveau or the history of the dance.

Isadora Duncan may have been better known because she was more truly a great dancer, or because she was more beautiful, or because she had a more conspicuously sexy and scandalous life, or because she was simply fated to become the more famous of the two. Or it may be that Loie suffered from the handicap of versatility. Instead of being concentrated in one area, her talents and accomplishments were distributed over several fields. She was not only a pioneer of modern dance but was also an actress, an impresario, a playwright, a contributor to stage lighting and cinema techniques, a cofounder of two art museums, and the very personification of Art Nouveau. She was more than a dancer; she was more than Isadora Duncan.

Loie deserves to be much better remembered than she has been. Even if not quite a legend like Prometheus, she is at least entitled to a promethean reputation, the word *promethean* being defined as "creative, boldly original."

APPENDIX

A List of Artists and Their Representations of Loie Fuller

Though Loie Fuller the performer died in 1928 and audiences' recollections of her spectacular movement and colored lights dimmed over time, magnificent images of Loie and the effects she created have been captured and preserved by at least seventy artists. Her impact on the Art Nouveau world was so profound that more art representing her was produced than for any other woman up to the present.

Museum goers at the Virginia Museum of Fine Arts, the Museum Villa Stuck in Munich, and the Musée d'Orsay have been thrilled in recent years to see the dancer's performances recreated by entire shows devoted solely to Loie Fuller and her art. Other famous art institutions such as the Maryhill Museum in the state of Washington, the Metropolitan Museum of Art, the Boston Museum of Fine Arts, the Musée Rodin, the Cleveland Museum of Art, and the Museum of Modern Art in New York have each presented notable Loie pieces as part of their permanent and special exhibitions.

Internationally, private collectors continue to compete with the museums and with each other for the dancer's posters, bronzes, pâte de verre sculptures, and other items—both because they recall Loie's onstage magic and also because she serves as the symbol for the Art Nouveau spirit. The auction houses Sotheby's in 1996 and Bonham's in 1995 have offered Loie lots. Bonham's consignment was not artistic representations but letters and notebooks composed by Loie herself. This written material, not discovered until the late 1940s backstage in a York, England, theater, is interesting when read in relation to other Loie letters unfortunately scattered in depositories from Paris to London, New York, Cleveland, and Washington state. A few letters are in private collections, as are other scarce ephemera such as postcards and periodicals with Loie articles and pictures.

An additional medium of visual arts, photography, should also be noted. Images of the personal and professional Loie have fortunately been preserved through the work of several noteworthy photographers. The Musée

Rodin and the Musée d'Orsay archives have the best collections of original Loie pictures, taken by Eugène Druet, Isaiah W. Taber, R. Moreau, Samuel Joshua Beckett, B. J. Falk, and Rider. They also have pieces of the thirty-year, or more, chronicle of Loie's life documented by Harry C. Ellis, who might be considered her "personal photographer." Ellis's photographs were intimate records of her private life, such as the photos of Loie and her mother; Loie after breast surgery; and, finally, a tranquil Loie on her deathbed.

When one considers all of the "fine" and "decorative" art representing Loie Fuller; the special effects and dancer-themed art influenced by her; the letters and other ephemera; and the original photographs, it becomes clear that a list of everything would be neverending. Instead, the following compilation concentrates on "known" pieces of Loie Fuller art in a wide variety of mediums, much of which has been displayed in the special shows at the Virginia Museum of Fine Arts and at the Museum Villa Stuck. Scholars who are interested in learning more about the pieces at these exhibitions can study catalogs at the respective institutions and at the New York Public Library for the Performing Arts.

AUBURTIN, Jean-François [Francis] (1866–?), French
    Poster: *La Loïe Fuller et son école de danse,* color lithograph, ca. 1914; 167 × 128.5 cm.

BAC[Bach], Fernand Sigismond (1859–1952), German, worked in France
    Poster: *La Loïe Fuller/aux Folies-Bergère,* color lithograph, 1892; 148.5 × 107.5 cm.; also in 77.5 × 61 cm.

BERNSTAMM, Leopold (dates unknown), nationality unknown
    Sculpture: *Loïe Fuller,* bust, date unknown; piece is now lost; size unknown.

BOOKPRINTER, Anna Marie [Valentien, Anna] (1862–1947), American
    Ceramic dish: *Loïe Fuller,* made at Rookwood Pottery, Cincinnati, 1903; 10.2 × 15.2 × 8.9 cm.

BRADLEY, Will (1868–1962), American
    Book illustration: "The Serpentine Dance," black and white, in *The Chap-Book,* December 1, 1894; 19 × 11.4 cm.

Appendix

CARABIN, François Rupert (1862–1932), French
  Bronze: *Loïe Fuller*, 1896–97; 20.5 × 20 × 15 cm.
  Bronze: *Loïe Fuller*, 1896–97; height 22.5 cm.
  Bronze: *Loïe Fuller*, 1896–97; height 22 cm.
  Bronze: *Loïe Fuller*, 1896–97; height 19.5 cm.
  Bronze: *Loïe Fuller*, 1896–97; height 18.5 cm.
  Bronze: *Loïe Fuller*, 1896–97; height 18.8 cm.
  Bronze: *Loïe Fuller*, 1896–97; height 21 cm.
  Bronze: *Loïe Fuller*, 1897–98 (M. Harris), 1901–2 (Museum Villa Stuck); 17 cm.
  Ceramic luster: *Loïe Fuller*, 1897–98; height 52.5 cm.
  Ceramic luster: *Loïe Fuller*, 1897–98; height 46 cm.

CHALON, Louis (1866–?), French
  Bronze: *Loïe Fuller*, ca. 1894 (M. Harris), ca. 1903 (Museum Villa Stuck); 22.2 × 16.5 × 16.5 cm.
  Bronze: *Loïe Fuller*, ca. 1903; 22.2 × 20.3 × 10.6 cm.

CHÉRET, Jules (1836–1932), French
  Pastel on paper: *Loïe Fuller*, undated; 118.7 × 80.3 cm.
  Poster: *Folies-Bergère/La Loïe Fuller*, color lithograph printed in four combinations of colors, 1893; 124.2 × 85.5 cm.
  Poster: *Folies-Bergère/La Loïe Fuller*, color lithograph reproduced in *Les Maîtres de l'affiche*, 1897; 38.9 × 29.2 cm.
  Poster: *Folies-Bergère/Loïe Fuller*, color lithograph, 1897; 123 × 87 cm.
  Poster: *Folies-Bergère, La Danse du feu*, color lithograph, 1897; 122.5 × 83.5 cm.

CHOUBRAC, Alfred-Victor (1853–1902), French
  Poster: *Folies-Bergère/tous/les soirs/à 10h. 1/2/L'originale/Loïe Mystérieuse*, color lithograph, 1893; 150 × 99.5 cm.

COLIN, Paul (1892–1985), French
  Gouache on paper: *Maquette for Loïe Fuller poster*, 1925; 150 × 112 cm.
  Poster: *Champs Elysées/Music Hall/Les Féeries fantistiques/de la Loïe Fuller*, color lithograph, 1925; size unknown.

CROZIT (dates unknown), nationality unknown
  Watercolor on paper and cellophane: *Fire Dance: Study of Loïe Fuller*, no date; 29.9 × 22.7 cm.

DAUM FRÈRES, French, founded 1878 in Nancy
  Sculpture: *Loïe Fuller*, pâte de verre, 1900; size unknown.

Appendix

DÉCORCHEMENT, François-Emile (1880–1971), French
   Sculpture: *Loïe Fuller*, pâté de verre, sculpted by R. Raymond, ca. 1912; height 17.1 cm.

FEURE, Georges de [Georges Joseph van Sluijters] (1868–1928), Dutch, worked in France
   Poster: *Tous les soirs à 10 heures à la/Comédie Parisienne/La Loïe Fuller/dans sa/création/nouvelle/Salomé*, color lithograph, 1895; 130 × 94 cm.

GARNIER, Jean (dates unknown), French, active 1890–1910
   Bronze: *Danse serpentine*, 1893; 41.3 × 22.2 cm.

GAUTIER, F. (dates unknown), French
   Poster: *La Loïe Fuller/From the Album/Souvenir to/La Loïe Fuller/on her 550th Night/From the Students "Des Beaux-Arts"/Paris, March 24th 1895*, color lithograph, 1895; 54 × 41 cm.

GÉRÔME, Jean-Léon (1824–1904), French
   Sculpture: *Loïe Fuller, ou La Danse*, white marble, 1903; 87 × 47 cm.

GRÜN, Jules-Alexandre (1868–1934), French
   Poster: *Loïe Fuller*, color lithograph, 1901; 160 × 109.8 cm.

HASKELL, Ernest (1876–1925), American
   Pen sketch: *Loïe Fuller*, 1901; size unknown.

HEINE, Thomas Theodore (1867–1948), German
   Woodblock illustration: *"The Serpentine Dance"* in *Die Insel* 5 (1900); size unknown.

HOETGER, Bernhard (1874–1949), German, worked in France 1900–1911
   Bronze: *Loïe Fuller*, ca. 1901 (Museum Villa Stuck), ca. 1910 (M. Harris); 26 × 35.6 × 29.2 cm.
   Bronze: *Tempête*, ca. 1901; height 31 cm.

HOUSSIN, Edouard Charles-Marie (1847–1917), French
   Sculpture: *Loïe Fuller*, white marble, ca. 1893; 22.2 × 29.2 × 19 cm.
   Bronze portrait mask: *Loïe Fuller*, 1897; height 30.5 cm.

LARCHE, François-Raoul (1860–1912), French
   Gilt bronze table lamp: *Loïe Fuller*, 1901; height 33 cm.
   Gilt brass table lamp: *Loïe Fuller*, before 1909; height 33 cm.
   Gilt bronze table lamp: *Loïe Fuller*, ca. 1901; height 45.4 cm.
   Gilt bronze table lamp: *Loïe Fuller (Fond Memories, 1883–1908)*; height 45 cm.

Appendix

LARSSON, Gotfride (dates unknown), nationality unknown
  Bronze: *Loïe Fuller,* ca. 1894; 39.4 × 15.2 cm.
LELONG, René (dates unknown), French
  Oil [?] on canvas: *La Loïe Fuller, Queen of Light,* 1910; size unknown.
LEMMEN, Georges (1865–1916), Belgian
  Conté crayon on paper: *Loïe Fuller,* ca. 1900; 46 × 69.5 cm.
LEROLLE, Henry (1848–?), French
  Oil [?] on canvas: *Loïe Fuller,* ca. 1893; piece is now lost; size unknown.
LEVASSEUR, Henri Louis (1853–?), French
  Bronze: *Loïe Fuller,* ca. 1894; 38.1 × 19 cm.
LEYMARIE, Auguste-Louis (dates unknown), French, active ca. 1910–25
  Poster: *Les/Danseuses/de Loïe Fuller,* 1922; 79 × 119.5 cm.
LOPES-SILVA, L. (1862–?), French
  Poster: *Nouveau/Théâtre/Bouton/d'Or,* color lithograph, 1893; 150.5 × 97 cm.
LOUCHET, Charles (dates unknown), French
  Gilt Bronze: *Loïe Fuller,* undated; 22.5 × 17.1 cm.
LÖWENTHAL, Arthur Imanuel (1879–?), Austrian
  Bronze: *Untitled,* 1903; 38.1 × 20.3 × 10.2 cm.
LUCAS, E. Charles [Charles-Louis] (dates unknown), nationality unknown
  Poster: *Folies-Bergère/La Loïe Fuller,* color lithograph, ca. 1893; 99.7 × 152.4 cm.
MARS-VALLET, Marius (dates unknown), French
  Bronze table lamp: *Loïe Fuller,* ca. 1900; 114.3 × 86.4 cm.
MASSIER, Clément (1845–1917), French, and
LÉVY-DHURMER, Lucien (1865-1953), French
  Charger: *Untitled,* stoneware with luster glaze, ca. 1895; diameter 49.5 cm.
MAURIN, Charles (1856–1914), French
  Pastel on paper: *Loïe Fuller,* ca. 1898; 61.5 × 45 cm.
  Pastel on paper: *Loïe Fuller,* ca. 1898; 61.4 × 45.5 cm.
  Pastel on paper: *Loïe Fuller,* ca. 1898; 59.7 × 45.7 cm.
  Pastel on paper: *Loïe Fuller,* ca. 1898; 59.7 × 45.7 cm.
  Pastel on paper: *Loïe Fuller,* ca. 1898; 58.4 × 45.7 cm.
  Pastel on paper: *Loïe Fuller,* ca. 1898; 59.7 × 43.2 cm.

Mazza, Aldo (1880–?), Italian
   Pastel on paper [?]: *Loïe Fuller,* 1914; size unknown.

Meunier, Georges (1869–1939), French
   Poster: *Loïe Fuller at the Music Hall,* color lithograph, 1898; 120 × 86 cm.
   Poster: *Folies-Bergère/Loïe Fuller,* color lithograph, 1898; 124 × 88 cm.

Micael-Lévy, C. (dates unknown), French, active 1885–1915
   Bronze: *Loïe Fuller,* ca. 1894; 29.2 × 17.8 × 7.6 cm.

Moser, Koloman (1868–1918), Austrian
   Watercolor: *Loïe Fuller, Butterfly Dance,* ca. 1900; size unknown.

Noury, Gaston (1866–?), French [?]
   Gouache: *Untitled,* lead pencil on paper, date unknown; 22 × 15 cm.

Orazi, Manuel (1860–1934), Italian, worked in France
   Poster: *Loïe Fuller,* color lithograph, 1900; 200 × 65 cm.
   Poster: *Théâtre de/Loïe Fuller/Exposition Universelle/rue de Paris,* color lithograph, printed in three editions in three different color schemes, 1900; 201 × 60.5 cm.

Paget-Fredericks, Joseph (1905–63), American
   Watercolor: *Loïe Fuller: Oiseau de la nuit,* ca. 1925; 32.8 × 45.8 cm.
   Watercolor: *Loïe Fuller: Winged Victory,* ca. 1925; 35.8 × 48.7 cm.

PAL [Paléologu, Jean de] (1860–1942), Romanian, worked in France 1893–1900
   Poster: *La Loïe Fuller/Folies Bergère,* color lithograph, ca. 1893; 123 × 83 cm.
   Poster: *Folies-Bergère/Tous les soirs/La Loïe Fuller,* color lithograph, ca. 1896; 130 × 89.5 cm.
   Poster: *Folies-Bergère/Tous les soirs/La Loïe Fuller,* color lithograph, ca. 1897; 78 × 58 cm.
   Poster: *Folies-Bergère/Tous les soirs/La Loïe Fuller,* color lithograph, 1897; 92 × 63 cm.
   Poster: *Folies-Bergère/Tous les soirs/La Loïe Fuller,* color lithograph, 1897; 132 × 95 cm.
   Poster: *Folies-Bergère/Tous les soirs/La Loïe Fuller,* color lithograph, 1897; 132 × 95 cm.
   Poster: *Folies-Bergère/La Loïe Fuller,* color lithograph, ca. 1897; 124 × 83 cm.

Poster: *Folies-Bergère/Tous les soirs/La Loïe Fuller*, color lithograph, ca. 1897; 124 × 84 cm.
Poster: *Folies-Bergère/Tous les soirs/La Loïe Fuller*, color lithograph, date unknown; 85.5 × 57 cm.
Poster: *Apollo Théâtre/La Loïe Fuller*, color lithograph, date unknown; 140 × 105 cm.

PFEFFER, Clara (dates unknown), American
Gilt bronze: *Untitled*, ca. 1903; 39.4 × 20.3 × 8.9 cm.

POSS, Jan (dates unknown), nationality unknown
Line drawing: *Loïe Fuller*, 1981; size unknown.

REISSNER STELLMACHER AND KESSLER (dates unknown), nationality unknown
Bronze luster: *Loïe Fuller*, ca. 1900; size unknown.

RENAUD, Francis (dates unknown), French [?]
Bronze: *Loïe Fuller*, black patina, 1901; height 26.7 cm.

RIVIÈRE, Théodore Louis-Auguste (1857–1912), French
Sculpture: *Loïe Fuller*, white marble, ca. 1898; 23.5 × 24.1 × 16.5 cm.
Sculpture: *Loïe Fuller: Lily Dance*, white marble, ca. 1898; 40.6 × 43.2 × 22.9 cm.
Biscuit porcelain: *Loïe Fuller Dancing*, Sèvres, date unknown; 24 × 19 cm.
Sculpture: *Loïe Fuller*, white marble, ca. 1898–99; size unknown.

ROCHE, Pierre [Massignon, Fernand] (1855–1922), French
Oil on canvas: *Loïe Fuller*, ca. 1893; 55.9 × 45.7 cm.
Oil on canvas: *Loïe Fuller*, ca. 1894; 41 × 32.5 cm.
Bronze: *Loïe Fuller*, ca. 1894; 53.4 × 17.8 × 17.8 cm.
Bronze weathervane: *Loïe Fuller*, ca. 1896; height 68 cm.
Bronze: *Loïe Fuller: Fire Dance*, ca. 1897; height 54.5 cm.
Bronze finial: *Loïe Fuller*, 1900; 10.5 × 7.7 cm.
Bronze medal: *Loïe Fuller*, 1900; diameter 7.2 cm.
Bronze medal: *Loïe Fuller*, two pieces, 1900; 19 cm. obverse, 18 cm. reverse
Sculpture: *Loïe Fuller*, used over entrance to her Exposition Universelle pavilion, 1900; size unknown.
Silver medal: *Loïe Fuller*, 1900; diameter 7.2 cm.
Bronze medal: *Loïe Fuller as Comedy*, cast from 1901 plaster model, date unknown; diameter 48.9 cm.

Appendix

Bronze medal: *Loïe Fuller as Drama,* cast from 1901 plaster model, date unknown: diameter 48.9 cm.
Clay bas relief: *Loïe Fuller Dancing,* date unknown; 18 × 19.5 cm.
Plaster cast for coin: *Loïe Fuller,* date unknown; diameter 1.93 cm.

ROCHE, Pierre, and
DAMMOUSE, Albert-Louis (1848–1926), French
Plaque: *Loïe Fuller,* pâte de verre in gilt bronze frame cast by Dammouse, presentation to Alma Spreckels, ca. 1903; 11.4 × 6.8 cm.

ROCHE, Pierre, and
MARX, Roger (1859–1913), French
Portfolio: *La Loïe Fuller,* 27 unbound pages, paper wrapper, and 14 pages illustrated with gypsographs, text by Roger Marx, edition of 130 copies, 1904; 26 × 20 cm.
Gypsograph: *Loïe Fuller Dancing,* red, 1904; 9 × 5 cm.
Gypsograph: *Loïe Fuller Dancing,* blue, 1904; 9.5 × 9 cm.
Gypsograph: *Loïe Fuller Dancing,* white, 1904; 10 × 7 cm.

RODIN, Auguste (1840–1917), French
Bronze: *Head of Loïe Fuller,* set on black marble base, date unknown but Rodin sold Dec. 16, 1916; piece is now lost; height 18 cm.

ROYAL BAYREUTH HELIOSINE (dates unknown), German
Ceramic dish: *Untitled,* ca. 1900; diameter 13 cm.

STEVENS, A. E. (dates unknown), nationality unknown
Poster: *Loïe Fuller,* color lithograph, date unknown; 218 × 102 cm.

STOLTENBERG-LERCHE, Hans (1867–1920), German/Norwegian
Gilt bronze vase: *Loïe Fuller,* ca. 1897; 14.6 × 14 cm.

STUDENTS, L'Ecole des Beaux-Arts, Paris, French
Twenty-three watercolors: *550th Performance of Loïe Fuller at the Folies-Bergère,* 1895; various sizes.

TERESZIUK [Tereszizck], Paul (dates unknown), Austrian, active 1895–1925
Bronze: *Loïe Fuller,* ca. 1897, 36.8 × 15.2 cm.
Porcelain lamp: *Loïe Fuller,* produced by A. Forster & Co., Vienna, date unknown; height 66 cm.

TÉTERGER, Henri (1862–?), French
Bracelet: *Untitled,* of linked dancers, ca. 1900; size unknown.

TOULOUSE-LAUTREC, Henri de (1864–1901), French
Lithographs: *Miss Loïe Fuller,* edition of 50 prints, printed in black, in-

Appendix

dividually tinted with watercolors and sprinkled with gold, silver, or bronze powder, 1893; approximate sizes 40 × 28 cm.
Oil [?] on canvas: *Au Music-Hall: La Loïe Fuller,* 1892; size unknown.
Oil [?] on canvas: *La Loïe Fuller aux Folies-Bergère,* 1893; size unknown.
Oil [?] on canvas: *La Loïe Fuller sur la piste,* 1893; size unknown.

TRETTER, Anna (1956–), German
India ink/cigarette ash on paper: *Hommage au Loïe Fuller,* 24-item series, 1991; 132 × 248 cm.

WALTER, Almaric-V. (1859–1942), French
Sculpture: *Loïe Fuller,* pâté de verre, sculpted by Jean Descomps, 1920–30; 19.3 × 28.9 cm.

WANDT, Ernest (1872–?), Belgian
Gilt bronze: *Loïe Fuller,* ca. 1897; 33 × 16.5 cm.

ANONYMOUS
Poster: *La Loïe,* color lithograph, printed by George H. Walker & Co., Boston and New York, ca. 1893; 107.5 × 71.5 cm.

ANONYMOUS
Poster: *La Loïe Fuller/aux Folies-Bergère,* color lithograph, printed by Dupuy & Fils, Paris, ca. 1893; 78 × 61 cm.

ANONYMOUS
Poster: *La Loïe Fuller,* color lithograph after a B. J. Falk photo, ca. 1896; 72.4 × 49.5 cm.

ANONYMOUS
Poster: *La Loïe Fuller,* color lithograph, 1897; 213 × 98.5 cm.

ANONYMOUS
Gold Brooch: *Untitled,* with precious stones, ca. 1901; 5.5 × 2.5 cm.

Abbreviations used in the notes:

AMR	Archives of the Musée Rodin, Paris
ARSENAL	Bibliothèque de l'Arsenal, Paris
BIB. NAT.	Bibliothèque Nationale, Paris
CMA	Archives of the Cleveland Museum of Art, Cleveland, Ohio
GB	Gabrielle Bloch
LF	Loie Fuller
LOCKE	Robinson Locke scrapbook of Loie Fuller clippings, NYPL
MARYHILL	Archives of the Maryhill Museum of Art, Goldendale, Washington
NYPL	Loie Fuller Collection, New York Public Library for the Performing Arts, Lincoln Center, New York City
OPÉRA	Bibliothèque de l'Opéra, Paris
ORSAY	Archives of the Musée d'Orsay, Paris
SFPALM	San Francisco Performing Arts Library and Museum, San Francisco

NOTES

CHAPTER 1. FROM "LOUIE" TO "LOIE"

1. Margaret Haile Harris, *Loïe Fuller: Magician of Light* (Richmond: Virginia Museum of Fine Arts, 1979), 16, says Loie was "born Mary Louise Fuller" and later changed her first name to Marie. The federal census taker in 1870, when Loie was eight years old, put down the name as "Maria," which he would have derived from "Marie" more likely than from "Mary."

2. Loie recalled this family history in autobiographical fragments that she wrote in 1927 and that are preserved in the Loie Fuller Collection (1914–28), NYPL. According to the "Family Record" in the Fuller family Bible, "Reuben was born Sept 8th 1827," and "Reuben Fuller was married to Delilah R. Eaton Aug 24th 1850." Xerographic copy courtesy of Pat Woodstrup.

3. LF, *Fifteen Years of a Dancer's Life, with Some Account of Her Distinguished Friends* (London: Herbert Jenkins, 1913), 16–17. "Loie Fuller was born in the hotel where Lincoln stayed. It was owned by her grandfather and managed by her father" (Mrs. T. E. Clarke to Maurice Needham, ca. 1925, copy in the Chicago Historical Society). The date of birth is probably January 22, 1862, but is difficult if not impossible to verify, since Du Page County, Illinois, birth records for the period are nonexistent.

4. George E. Ruchty Jr., *The Fullers of Fullersburg, 1834–1923* (Hinsdale, Ill.: Hinsdale Historical Society, 1978), unpaginated; Loie to Frank Fuller, April 18, 1927, NYPL.

5. Reuben Fuller was listed in the Chicago City Directory for 1864–66, indicating that he had moved to Chicago as early as 1864.

6. LF, *Fifteen Years*, 20–23. Loie once told an interviewer: "I made my début at the age of two and a half years at a Sunday-school recitation party." *The Sketch*, London, April 12, 1893, 642–43.

7. Autobiographical fragment, 1927, NYPL; manuscript census for 1870.

8. On the Chicago fire, see Mabel McIlvaine, ed., *Reminiscences of Chicago during the Great Fire* (Chicago: Donnelly, 1915). These reminiscences were republished in David Lowe, ed., *The Great Chicago Fire* (New York: Dover, 1979), with a new introduction and seventy contemporary illustrations. The Fullers' house at 164 West Lake Street was located on land later taken by the Kennedy Expressway. The street has been renumbered.

9. LF, chapter topics for memoirs, ca. 1907, NYPL; *Monmouth Daily Review*, December 4, 1874, February 26, 1875. These and other quotations of Monmouth newspapers are taken from transcripts in the Hinsdale Historical Society.

10. *Monmouth Weekly Review*, March 5, 1875, and an undated clipping citing

"H. R. Moffet's history of Warren County" in the Hinsdale Historical Society. On the Illinois temperance agitation, see Ernest L. Bogart and Charles M. Thompson, *The Industrial State, 1870–1893,* vol. 4, *The Centennial History of Illinois* (Chicago: McClurg, 1922), 42–49. On *Ten Nights in a Bar Room,* see Harvey Wish, *Society and Thought in Early America* (New York: Longmans Green, 1950), 428.

11. *Monmouth Atlas,* December 31, 1875; LF, chapter topics for memoirs, ca. 1907, NYPL.

12. LF, chapter topics for memoirs, ca. 1907, NYPL. The 1878–79 edition of the *Lakeside Annual Directory for the City of Chicago* lists Reuben Fuller at 12 Rumsey Street but gives no occupation for him. The 1879 edition lists "Mrs. Delilah R. Fuller, notions, 63 Blue Island Ave., house 12 Rumsey," and "Frank R. Fuller, clerk," with the same addresses, but does not mention Reuben Fuller at all.

13. LF, chapter titles for memoirs, ca. 1907, NYPL; *New York Sun,* January 20, 1892, 5; Sally R. Sommer, "The Stage Apprenticeship of Loïe Fuller," *Dance Scope* 12 (fall–winter 1977–78): 24. The Chicago Historical Society has a practically complete file of Hooley's Theatre playbills and a fairly large number of Academy of Music playbills for the late 1870s and early 1880s. In none of these programs does the name Louie, Loie, Louise, or Mary or Marie Louise Fuller appear. The only Fuller to be found is Mollie Fuller, a fairly well known actress of the time, whose name appears in the Hooley's Theatre program for July 27, 1884.

14. Henry B. Sell and Victor Weybright, *Buffalo Bill and the Wild West* (New York: Oxford University Press, 1955), 130; Don Russell, *The Life and Legends of Buffalo Bill* (Norman: University of Oklahoma Press, 1960), 285–87; George C. D. Odell, *Annals of the New York Stage,* 15 vols. (New York: Columbia University Press, 1927–49), 12: 167; LF, chapter titles for memoirs, ca. 1907, NYPL; LF to Julius Witmark, June 15, 1927, Maryhill.

15. *Boston Herald,* April 21, 1896, March 24, 1909, January 2, 1910; *Toledo Blade,* April 25, 1896, clippings in Locke; Eugene Tompkins and Quincy Kilby, *The History of the Boston Theatre, 1854–1901* (Boston: Houghton Mifflin, 1908), 322.

16. *New York Times,* July 1, 1886, p. 4, c. 7; Bijou Opera House program for July 24, 1886, NYPL; Odell, *New York Stage* 13:39.

17. *New York Times,* September 14, 1886, p. 4, c. 6–7, September 24, 1886, p. 4, c. 7; *New York Daily Mirror,* September 15, 1886, 2; Odell, *New York Stage* 13:255; LF, *Fifteen Years,* 148–49.

18. Bijou Opera House programs for December 13, 1886, and March 31, 1887, LF Coll., NYPL; Odell, *New York Stage* 13:255; Nat C. Goodwin, *Nat Goodwin's Book* (Boston: Richard G. Badger, 1914), 140–43.

19. *New York Times,* July 29, 1887, p. 2, c. 2, July 30, 1887, p. 5, c. 3; September 13, 1887, p. 4, c. 7; *New York Sun,* September 18, 1887, 9; Standard Theatre program for October 15, 1887, NYPL; Odell, *New York Stage* 13:444–45, 560.

20. *New York Times*, December 1, 1887, p. 5, c. 2; Odell, *New York Stage* 13:453–54; *Chicago Tribune*, April 12, 1896, clipping, Locke.

21. LF to Eunice L. Rogers, May 31, 1887, and September 4, 1888. These, the earliest of Loie's letters known to be extant, are in private possession.

22. Odell, *New York Stage* 13:209–10, 212, 239, 250, 260, 309, 437; Tompkins and Kilby, *Boston Theatre*, 354, 352.

CHAPTER 2. THE SERPENT AND THE SERPENTINE

1. The *New York Dramatic Mirror*, September 21, 1889, clipping, Locke, mentioned a report that Loie had married "W. B. Hayes, nephew of Ex-President Hayes." But Roger D. Bridges, director of the Rutherford B. Hayes Presidential Center, Fremont, Ohio, states: "we checked genealogies, correspondence, etc., for information about a nephew who had a wife . . . named Loie. I confess that we struck out. Insofar as we can determine, Hayes had only one nephew (Rutherford Hayes Platt)" (Bridges to the authors, June 9, 1992).

2. In *Fifteen Years*, 101–3, Loie dates the Jamaica visit as occurring in 1890 and says she was accompanied by her mother, both of which statements are inconsistent with contemporary evidence.

3. This account of Loie's relationship with Hayes is derived from the *New York Sun*, January 20, 1892, 5, which reported the subject at great length, interviewing Hayes, Loie, and their respective lawyers, and quoting or describing correspondence, photographs, and other documents.

4. *New York Dramatic Mirror*, June 22, 1889, clipping, Locke; Odell, *New York Stage* 14:63.

5. *New York Dramatic Mirror*, September 21, October 12, 1889, clippings, Locke; publicity release, Globe Theatre, October 15, 1889, NYPL; *Tattler*, London, October 19, 1889, 122; *Echo*, London, December 6, 1889, 1; *Stage*, London, December 6, 1889, 9.

6. *Echo*, October 23, 1889, 4; *Stage*, October 25, 1889, 9; *Era*, London, October 26, 1889, 14; *Pelican* (previously the *Tattler*), November 2, 1889, 157.

7. *New York Sun*, January 20, 1892, 5; copy of death certificate by courtesy of Pat Woodstrup.

8. *New York Tribune*, January 20, 1892, 5; *Stage*, February 14, 1890, 9, and April 25, 1890, 12. Loie's reminiscence is quoted in Harriet Tarbox Darling, "And the First Was Loie: The Real Story of How an American Artist Created Her Contribution to the Dance," *Dance*, March 1926, 15.

9. *Stage*, October 24, 1890, 11; November 21, 1890, 11; March 5, 1891, 13; May 7, 1891, 12; J. P. Wearing, ed., *The London Stage, 1890–1899: A Calendar of Plays and Players* (Metuchen, N.J.: Scarecrow Press, 1976), 1:69, 79, 100, 115, 117, 118.

10. *Munsey's Magazine*, June 1892, clipping, Locke; John Parker, *The Green Book*,

Notes to Pages 21–31

or *Who's Who on the Stage* (London: T. Sealey Clark, 1909), 196–97; Wearing, *London Stage* 1:69. *Munsey's* says Loie "for eighteen months was with the Gaiety Company," but she does not appear to have been continuously with the company for anywhere near that length of time. Wearing says she appeared in *His Last Chance* at the Gaiety from October 13, 1890, to July 4, 1891, and Gabriele Brandstetter and Brygida Maria Ochaim, *Loïe Fuller: Tanz, Licht-Spiel, Art Nouveau* (Freiburg im Breisgau: Rombach, 1989), follow Wearing in making the same statement. Such contemporary evidence as there is, however, suggests that Loie appeared in the play (a curtain raiser for *Carmen-up-to-Data*) for only a comparatively few performances.

11. *New York Mail and Express,* undated [1891], clipping, Locke.

12. LF, *Fifteen Years,* 25–35. Loie says (p. 32), "the New York managers refused to touch" *Quack, M.D.,* but Odell, *New York Stage* 15:81, notes that the play opened at the Columbus Theatre in New York on October 20, 1891.

13. LF, *Fifteen Years,* 37–38; *New York Spirit of the Times,* January 12, 1892, and *New York World,* probably February 16, 1892, quoted in the *Toledo Blade,* March 19, 1892, clippings, Locke; *New York Times,* February 14, 1892, p. 13, c. 1, and February 16, 1892, p. 5, c. 2; *New York Post,* February 16, 1892, 7; *New York Sun,* February 16, 1892, 8.

14. *New York Sun,* January 20, 1892, 5; *New York Tribune,* January 20, 1892, 2; *New York Times,* January 20, 1892, p. 8, c. 6.

15. *New York Tribune,* January 29, 1892, 2, and January 30, 1892, 4; *New York Sun,* January 30, 1892, 5; *New York Times,* January 30, 1892, p. 7, c. 1.

16. New York City and County Court, Second District, docket, January 18–February 12, 1892, in New York City and County Archives; *New York Tribune,* February 17, 1892, 12; *New York Spirit of the Times,* February 20, 1892, clipping in Locke.

17. *New York Times,* 1893; January 17, p. 10, c. 1; January 18, p. 10, c. 2; January 19, p. 8, c. 3; January 20, p. 10, c. 4; January 29, p. 3, c. 3; February 10, p. 9, c. 1; February 24, p. 5, c. 5.

18. LF, *Fifteen Years,* 37–42; *New York Sun,* February 25, 1892, 8; *New York Spirit of the Times,* February 27, 1892, clipping, Locke; program, Madison Square Theatre, April 11, 1892, NYPL; Odell, *New York Stage* 15:40.

19. *New York Times,* March 15, 1892, p. 8, c. 2; Loie Fuller against New York Concert Company, Limited, Court of Common Pleas, March 1–June 17, 1892, ms. record in New York City and County Archives.

20. *New York Times,* June 17, 1892, p. 9, c. 4.

21. *Federal Reporter* 50:920–26, clipping, NYPL; *New York Times,* June 19, 1892, p. 20, c. 3.

22. Charles H. Hoyt and Charles W. Thomas, release (legal form), June 28, 1892,

NYPL; *New York Times*, June 28, 1892, p. 8, c. 5; Odell, *New York Stage* 15:13–14, 32, 37, 126; LF, *Fifteen Years*, 43–44.

CHAPTER 3. EXTRAORDINARY SUCCESS, EXTRAORDINARY FAILURE

1. LF, *Fifteen Years*, 47; *New York Spirit of the Times*, November 12, 1892, clipping, Locke. The newspaper report of Loie's shipboard performance was undoubtedly based on a letter from Loie herself.

2. *Berliner Illustrierte Zeitung*, 1892, quoted (in German) by Brandstetter and Ochaim, *Loïe Fuller*, 103. Brandstetter and Ochaim do not give the exact date of this issue of the paper, but the date was after Loie's debut in Paris.

3. LF, *Fifteen Years*, 47–50; *Le Figaro*, October 30, 1892.

4. The quotations are from Charles Rearick, *Pleasures of the Belle Epoque: Entertainment and Festivity in Turn-of-the-Century France* (New Haven, Conn.: Yale University Press, 1985), 83–84. See also Charles Castle, *The Folies-Bergère* (New York: Franklin Watts, 1985), 15–28.

5. This account is based on LF, *Fifteen Years*, 51–61; Raymond Bouyer, "L'Art aux Folies-Bergère: La Loïe Fuller," *L'Artiste*, October–November–December 1898, 365; and *Le Figaro*, October 29, November 1, 5, 1892. Loie's own story seems fanciful in many of its details.

6. *Le Figaro*, November 8, 9, December 9, 1892; January 26, 27, March 4, April 7, 1893.

7. *L'Echo de Paris*, November 8, 13, 1892; *Le Figaro*, November 12, 15, 17, 1892; February 11, March 4, April 18, 1893.

8. See the program for the matinee on January 29, 1893, a copy of which is in the Loie Fuller collection, Opéra.

9. *Le Figaro*, November 17, December 9, 1892; January 25, 1893; *L'Echo de Paris*, November 26, 1892.

10. *Le Figaro*, November 17, 1892; *L'Echo de Paris*, November 15, 24, 26, December 4, 1892.

11. *Le Figaro*, November 19, 21, 30, 1892; February 2, 16, 1893; *Le Siècle*, November 20, December 1, 1892; *L'Echo de Paris*, November 23, December 1, 1892.

12. *L'Echo de Paris*, December 4, 1892; *Le Figaro*, January 24, February 9, 1893; *New York Spirit of the Times*, February 25, 1893, clipping in Locke.

13. *New York Dramatic News*, April 15, 1893, 10; *Fifteen Years*, 82–83; LF, autobiographical fragment, ca. 1907, NYPL.

14. *Le Figaro*, February 9, 11, 1893; Stéphane Mallarmé, "Considerations sur l'art du ballet et la Loïe Fuller," *National Observer*, March 13, 1893, quoted in Harris, *Loïe Fuller*, 28; *Cri*, Paris, January 8, 1928, clipping, Dossier Rondel, Arsenal. On Mallarmé and Loie, see Frank Kermode, "Loïe Fuller and the Dance before Diaghilev," *Partisan Review* 28 (January–February 1961): 48–49.

15. *Chicago Tribune*, January 8, 1928, quoting Huysmans, clipping, AMR; *Le Figaro*, February 16, 1893; "Loïe Fuller Gavotte," sheet music in Opéra.

16. "A Chat with Miss Loïe Fuller," *Sketch*, London, April 12, 1893, 642–43; *New York Dramatic News*, April 15, 1893, 10.

17. LF, *Fifteen Years*, 146–47; LF, autobiographical fragment, ca. 1907, NYPL; Roger Marx, "Chorégraphie: Loïe Fuller," *Le Revue encyclopédique*, February 1, 1893, cols. 106–10, clipping, Opéra.

18. "A Chat." Another writer was led to believe that Loie "est née à Chicago (Etats-Unis) vers 1871." H. C. in *Le Revue encyclopédique*, ca. January 1893, col. 109, clipping, Opéra.

19. Ibid.; *Le Figaro*, January 18, February 1, 8, 1893.

20. "The Electrical Serpentine Dancer: A Chat with Miss Marie Leyton," *Sketch*, London, February 8, 1893, quoted in Brandstetter and Ochaim, *Loïe Fuller*, 15–16.

21. "A Chat"; Mrs. M. Griffith, "Loie Fuller: The Inventor of the Serpentine Dance," *Strand Magazine* 12 (London, 1894): 542; LF, *Fifteen Years*, 25–32; *Munsey's Magazine*, June 1892, and *New York Spirit of the Times*, August 19, 1893, clippings, Locke; *New York Herald*, August 27, 1893, clipping, SFPALM.

22. Darling, "And the First Was Loie," 58.

23. H. C. in *Le Revue encyclopédique*, ca. January 1893, col. 109; *L'Illustration*, January 14, 1893, 26; U.S. Patent Office Report, specification for Patent No. 518,347, clipping, NYPL; "A Chat."

24. *Le Figaro*, January 8, 1893; Rastignac, "Courrier de Paris," *L'Illustration*, January 14, 1893, 26.

25. *Le Figaro*, April 20, 1893; *Nos Parisienes*, ca. April 1893, clipping, Maryhill; *New York Dramatic News*, April 15, 1893, 10; H. C. in *Le Revue encyclopédique*, ca. January 1893; col. 109.

26. LF, *Fifteen Years*, 73–82.

27. "A Chat"; *Le Figaro*, May 10, 1893; *New York Times*, August 11, 1896, p. 4, c. 6.

28. *New York Times*, January 2, 1893, p. 2, c. 4; *New York Spirit of the Times*, February 25, 1893, clipping, Locke; *New York Dramatic News*, April 15, 1893, 10.

29. *New York Times*, January 29, 1893, p. 3, c. 3; February 10, 1893, p. 9 , c. 1; February 24, 1893, p. 5, c. 5; *New York Evening Journal*, September 6, 1900, clipping, Locke.

30. *New York Times*, August 11, 1893, p. 4, c. 6.

31. Garden Theatre program for week ending August 19, 1893, NYPL.

32. *New York Times*, 1893; August 17, p. 4, c. 5; August 18, p. 4, c. 7; August 20, p. 16, c. 1; August 25, p. 5, c. 5; *New York Theatre Magazine*, May 1900, clipping, Locke; Odell, *New York Stage* 15:570; Garden Theatre program for week ending August 26, 1893, NYPL.

33. Theater advertisements in the *New York Times*, 1893; August 26, p. 7, c. 7; September 1, p. 7, c. 6–7; September 3, p. 7, c. 6–7; September 11, p. 7, c. 7; Septem-

ber 25, p. 7, c. 7; Odell, *New York Stage* 15:318, 583, 595–96, 598–99, 624, 634, 781, 783; *New York Herald*, August 27, 1893, clipping, SFPALM.

CHAPTER 4. WHY CAN'T I BE SALOME?

1. *Le Figaro*, October 19, 21, 1893; *L'Echo de Paris*, October 20, 1893.
2. *Le Figaro*, November 29, December 24, 1893; Folies-Bergère playbill for November 30, 1893, in private possession; *L'Echo de Paris*, December 4, 1893, quoted in P. Hulsman and M. G. Dortu, *Lautrec by Lautrec* (New York: Galahad Books, 1964), 115.
3. *Le Figaro*, December 9, 1893; January 2, February 10, 21, 26, 1894; Castle, *Folies-Bergère*, 33–35, 47–50.
4. Griffith, "Loie Fuller," 540–41, 544.
5. LF, *Fifteen Years*, 82–83; Griffith, "Loie Fuller," 544–45.
6. *Le Figaro*, March 24, 1894.
7. *New York Spirit of the Times*, June 30, 1894, clipping, Locke; LF, autobiographical fragment, ca. 1907, NYPL; *New York Times*, February 23, 1896, p. 8, c. 1.
8. "The Career of a Dancer: La Loïe Fuller on Herself," *Black and White*, London, January 25, 1896, p. 118, clipping, Theatre Museum, London; Findlay Muirhead and Marcel Monmarche, eds., *Paris and Its Environs* (London: Macmillan, 1921), 73.
9. *New York Times*, February 25, 1893, p. 3, c. 6; September 5, 1894, p. 9, c. 2; June 9, 1895, p. 17, c. 7; *Boston Courier*, November 5, 1893, clipping, Locke.
10. S. L. B., "Li and Loïe Fuller," *Sketch*, London, December 30, 1896 (based on an 1895 interview), clipping, Theatre Museum, London; LF, *Fifteen Years*, 62–64.
11. Griffith, "Loie Fuller," 540; F. Raoul-Aubry, "Au Jour le jour: La Danse serpentine," *Le Figaro*, March 11, 1895, p. 1; *New York Herald*, August 27, 1893, clipping, SFPALM. LF's quote is from Exodus 15.20.
12. *New York Times*, January 24, 1896, p. 2, c. 6.
13. H. Montgomery Hyde, ed., *Oscar Wilde: Plays, Prose and Poems* (London: Orbis, 1982), 260–61, 305–25.
14. Roger Marx, "Loïe Fuller," *Les Arts et la Vie* 3 (May 1905): 271–73.
15. *L'Echo de Paris*, February 21, March 1, 3, 4, 1895; *New York Times*, March 17, 1895, p. 4, c. 7.
16. Roger Marx, "Salomé," *La Revue dramatique*, April 1, 1895, 127; Marx, "Loïe Fuller," 271–73; *Le Figaro*, March 5, 1895; *L'Echo de Paris*, March 6, 9, 1895; *New York Times*, March 24, 1895, p. 32, c. 2; Jean Lorrain, *Poussières de Paris* (Paris: Ollendorf, 1899), 143–44, as quoted in Harris, *Loïe Fuller*, 20.
17. A. B., "Loïe Fuller," *Le Monde illustré*, November 6, 1897, 364.
18. Mlle Montalbert, "A travers la dance," *Le Théâtre*, 17–18, undated clipping, Theatre Museum, London.
19. Gerstle Mack, *Toulouse-Lautrec* (New York: Paragon House, 1989), 160.
20. *L'Echo de Paris*, March 27, 1895; LF, *Fifteen Years*, 184–85; a copy of the

March 24, 1895, program cover in private possession; Friedlander to LF, March 24, 1895, NYPL. In her memoirs Loie mistakenly refers to the theater as the Athénée and to the occasion as her "six hundredth appearance in Paris."

21. *Le Figaro*, March 22, 25, April 8, 14, 21, 22, June 21, 30, 1895; *New York Spirit of the Times*, July 27, 1895, clipping, Locke.

22. Palace Theatre program, December 30, 1895, Maryhill; "Career of a Dancer," 118; S. L. B., "Li and Loïe Fuller."

23. LF, *Fifteen Years*, 111–18; *Muirhead's Paris*, 349.

24. LF, *Fifteen Years*, 101–10; LF to Eugène Poulle, September 29, 1894, and six undated letters of LF to Dumas, Dumas Papers, Bib. Nat.; *New York Times*, February 23, 1896, p. 8, c. 1.

25. Cornelia Otis Skinner, *Madame Sarah* (London: Michael Joseph, 1967), 3–4, 130–51; *New York Times*, February 23, 1896, p. 8, c. 1; *Boston Herald*, ca. April 21, 1896, undated clipping, Locke. LF, *Fifteen Years*, 84–95, gives a fanciful account of her first sight of Sarah Bernhardt on the stage and of her first meeting with the world-famous star. Loie was not a little girl but was at least eighteen and probably in her twenties when she first saw Bernhardt perform. She did not meet and perform for Bernhardt while at the Folies-Bergère (1892–94) but while in Manchester in the summer of 1895.

26. LF to Dumas, ca. July 6, 1895, Dumas Papers, Bib. Nat.; André Maurois, *The Titans: A Three-Generation Biography of the Dumas* (New York: Harper, 1957), 460; LF, "Alexandre Dumas at Marly," *Black and White* 10 (December 7, 1895): 726; LF, *Fifteen Years*, 105.

CHAPTER 5. THE MISTRESS OF FIRE

1. Gösta M. Bergman, *Lighting in the Theatre* (Stockholm: Almquist & Wiksell; Totowa, N.J.: Rowman & Littlefield, 1977), 256–63, 273, 275, 277–80, 288, 290, 315; David E. Nye, *Electrifying America: Social Meanings of a New Technology, 1880–1940* (Cambridge, Mass.: MIT Press, 1990), 30, 43; "Stage Illumination," *New York Times*, October 24, 1881, p. 5, c. 5, quoting the London *Telegraph*, October 10, 1881.

2. *L'Echo de Paris*, February 21, March 4, 1895. On Loie's patents of stage mechanisms, see Harris, *Loïe Fuller*, 19–20, and a newspaper clipping dated December 23, 1899, but unidentified, in Locke.

3. Aspects of Loie's lighting and staging techniques are described by her and by others in the following clippings in Locke: unidentified New York paper, February 2, 1896; unidentified Boston paper, ca. April 1896; *Toledo Blade*, April 11, 1896, quoting the *New York Sun*; *Boston Herald*, ca. April 21, 1896. See also the *New York Times*, March 1, 1896, p. 10, c. 5, and the following clippings in SFPALM: *San Francisco Chronicle*, March 21, November 24, 1896.

4. *New York Times*, January 24, 1896, p. 2, c. 6; *New York Herald*, August 23, 1896, clipping, SFPALM.

5. *New York Times,* February 23, 1896, p. 8, c. 1; February 25, 1896, p. 5, c. 6; *New York Sun,* February 23, 1896, unidentified New York paper, February 25, 1896, and *New York Spirit of the Times,* February 28, 1896, clippings, Locke; Koster & Bial's Music Hall program for March 9, 1896, NYPL.

6. *Footlights: A Journal for the Theatre-goer,* Philadelphia, March 21, 1896, 4, and an unidentified paper, April 5, 1896, quoting *Footlights,* clippings, Locke; Brooklyn Academy of Music program for March 23, 1896, NYPL.

7. *New York Times,* May 4, 1896, p. 8, c. 2; *Boston Herald,* May 5, 1896, clipping, Locke.

8. *Boston Herald,* April 21, 1896, and unidentified Boston paper, April 21, 1896, clippings, NYPL; Boston Theatre program for April 20–26, 1896, NYPL; Tompkins and Kilby, *Boston Theatre,* 442.

9. *New York Times,* May 4, 1896, p. 8, c. 2.

10. LF, autobiographical note, ca. 1907, NYPL.

11. Standard Theatre program for the week commencing September 7, 1896, NYPL; *New York Times,* October 8, 1896, p. 19, c. 3.

12. *San Francisco Chronicle,* November 8, 13, 24, 1896, clippings, SFPALM; California Theatre programs for November 23, 24, 25, and November 28, SFPALM.

13. Alberto Dallal, *La Mujer en la danza* (Mexico City: Panorama, 1990), 37–44; *New York Evening World,* January 3, 1928, clipping, NYPL; *Monmouth Daily Review,* February 5, 1897, transcript, CMA.

14. *New York Times,* February 25, 1896, p. 5, c. 6; "Loie Fuller and the Poetry of Color," *The Critic* 28 (March 28, 1896), 217; unidentified Boston paper, ca. April 21, 1896, clipping, NYPL; Hugh Morton, "Loïe Fuller and Her Strange Art," *Metropolitan Magazine,* ca. 1896, 277–83, clipping, Theatre Collection, NYPL.

15. *Boston Herald,* April 22, May 5, 1896, and *Chicago Press,* undated, clippings, Locke; *San Francisco Chronicle,* November 13, 1896, clipping, SFPALM.

16. *El Universal,* January 12, 15, 1897, quoted and paraphrased (in Spanish) in Dallal, *La Mujer en la danza,* 39–44.

17. *Le Monde illustré,* November 6, 1897, 364; *L'Echo de Paris,* September 24, 1898.

18. Folies-Bergère program for December 14, 1897, Opéra; *Le Figaro,* August 30, 1898; *Cri du peuple,* October 16, 1898, clipping, AMR.

19. Bouyer, "L'Art aux Folies-Bergère," 357–65. The translation of Rodenbach's poem is by Philippe Rein, as quoted in Frank Kermode, "Loïe Fuller and the Dance before Diaghilev," *Partisan Review* 28 (January–February 1961): 48.

20. *Le Figaro,* September 15, 1898; *L'Echo de Paris,* September 26, 1898; *Monmouth Daily Review,* October 13, 1898, transcript, CMA; Lyric Theatre program for February 2, 1899, Maryhill; The Editor, "La Loie Fuller and Her Artistic Advertisements," *Poster,* February 1899, 69–74, clipping, Theatre Museum, London.

21. Harris, *Loïe Fuller,* 19; Jean Lorrain, *Poussières de Paris,* 195–96.

22. For the description of Jean Lorrain, see Nigel Gosling, *The Adventurous World of Paris, 1900–1914* (New York: Morrow, 1978), 40.

23. *Monmouth Daily Review*, May 10, 1899, transcript, CMA; LF, autobiographical fragment, ca. 1907, NYPL; Arthur Lynch, reminiscence, unidentified English newspaper, ca. January 1928, Theatre Museum, London.

24. *New York Evening Journal*, undated clipping, Locke; *Monmouth Daily Review*, March 19, 1900, transcript, CMA.

CHAPTER 6. A THEATER OF HER OWN

1. Nathaniel Harris, *Art Nouveau* (New York: Exeter Books, 1987), 44.

2. LF, *Fifteen Years*, 146–47; LF, autobiographical fragment, ca. 1907, NYPL.

3. LF, *Fifteen Years*, 250–66; LF, autobiographical fragment, ca. 1907, and autographed photo, undated, NYPL; Emilia Cimino to Rodin, September 12, 1903, AMR, for the kinship between Mrs. Marx and Gabrielle Bloch.

4. Frederic V. Grunfeld, *Rodin: A Biography* (New York: Holt, 1987), 235–43, 442–43, 514–15.

5. Rodin to Roger Marx, November 26, 1897, Alan Beausire et al., eds., *Correspondance de Rodin* (Paris: Editions du Musée Rodin, 1985–92), 1:173; Ruth Butler, *Rodin: The Shape of Genius* (New Haven, Conn.: Yale University Press, 1993), 346.

6. LF to Rodin, September 14, 1898; undated, ca. 1898; October 12, 1899; April 4, 1900, AMR; LF to Rodin, May 1900, quoted in Hélène Pinet, *Ornement de la durée: Loïe Fuller, Isadora Duncan, Ruth St. Denis, Adorée Villany* (Paris: Musée Rodin, 1987), 8.

7. LF to Rodin, undated, ca. 1898; Emilia Cimino to Rodin, October 26, November 17, 1898; August 22, 1899; undated, ca. June 1900, AMR. On Cimino, see Butler, *Rodin*, 345–46.

8. Cimino to Rodin, March 22, April 22, 1900, AMR; Pinet, *Ornement de la durée*, 24–34; Jérôme Doucet, "Miss Loïe Fuller," *La Revue illustrée*, November 1, 1903, Dance Clipping File, NYPL.

9. N. Harris, *Art Nouveau*, 44.

10. "A Chat"; Bouyer, "L'Art aux Folies-Bergère," 364.

11. M. Harris, *Loïe Fuller*, 8.

12. Lincoln F. Johnson, Jr., "The Light and Shape of Loie Fuller," *Baltimore Museum of Art News* 20 (October 1956): 13.

13. Gilles Dusein, "Loïe Fuller: Chorégraphie de l'Art Nouveau," *La Recherche en danse* (1982), quoted in Pinet, *Ornement de la durée*, 6; Lara-Vinca Masini, *Art Nouveau* (Secaucus, N.J.: Chartwell, 1984), 42–44; Robert Schmutzler, *Art Nouveau* (New York: Abrams, n.d.), 9–10; Peter Selz and Mildred Constantine, eds., *Art Nouveau: Art and Design at the Turn of the Century* (New York: Museum of Modern Art, 1959), 16.

14. Yvonne Brunhammer et al., *Art Nouveau Belgium France* (Houston: Institute for the Arts, Rice University, 1976), 410.

15. Vivienne Becker, *Art Nouveau Jewelry* (New York: Dutton, 1985), 20.

16. M. Harris, *Loïe Fuller,* 30.

17. Ibid.

18. "La Loie Fuller and Her Artistic Advertisements," *Poster,* February 1899, clipping, Theatre Museum, London; M. Harris, *Loïe Fuller,* 37, 49–50, 73, 79. In this well-illustrated catalog of the 1979 Loie Fuller exhibition at the Virginia Museum of Fine Arts, Harris gives an excellent account of Loie in art.

19. *Toulouse-Lautrec: Prints and Posters from the Bibliothèque Nationale* (Paris: Bibliothèque Nationale, 1991), 47–51.

20. M. Harris, *Loïe Fuller,* 30.

21. Barbara Shapiro, *Pleasures of Paris: Daumier to Picasso* (Boston: Museum of Fine Arts and David R. Godine, 1991), 134.

22. M. Harris, *Loïe Fuller,* 30–31.

23. Brunhammer, *Art Nouveau,* 488; M. Harris, *Loïe Fuller,* 74, 77, 80; *Revue blanche,* May 15, 1899, clipping, AMR.

24. M. Harris, *Loïe Fuller,* 31.

25. Frederick Brandt, *Late 19th and Early 20th Century Decorative Arts* (Richmond: Virginia Museum of Fine Arts, 1985), 46.

26. Philippe Garner, *Art Nouveau Collectables* (Secaucus, N.J.: Chartwell, 1989), 117.

27. Philippe Garner, *Emile Gallé* (New York: Rizzoli, 1990), 121–22; Claude Anet, "Loïe Fuller in French Sculpture," *Architectural Record* 13 (March 1903): 278, clipping, Maryhill; Schmutzler, *Art Nouveau,* 229, for the quotation regarding Tiffany; Franco Borsi and Ezio Godoli, *Paris Art Nouveau: Architecture et décoration* (Paris: Marc Vokar, 1989), 171.

28. Philippe Julian, *The Triumph of Art Nouveau: Paris Exhibition, 1900* (New York: Larousse, 1974), 88–90, 174–75.

29. Borsi and Godoli, *Paris Art Nouveau,* 169–70; LF interview in an unidentified New York newspaper, ca. 1901, clipping, Locke.

30. Arsène Alexandre, "Le Théâtre de la Loïe Fuller," *Le Théâtre,* August 11, 1900, 23–25, clipping, Theatre Museum, London.

31. Unidentified Monmouth, Ill., newspaper, November 20, 1975, clipping, Hinsdale Historical Society.

32. Brunhammer, *Art Nouveau Belgium France,* 486.

33. Martin Battersby, *Art Nouveau* (Middlesex: Hamlyn, 1969), 39.

34. For contemporary descriptions of the theater, see Jules Rais, "Le Musée Loïe Fuller," *Le Siècle,* June 24, 1900, and Camille Mauclair, "Sada Yacco et Loïe Fuller," *La Revue blanche,* October 15, 1900, 277, clippings, AMR; F. Jourdain, "L'Architec-

ture à l'Exposition Universelle," *Revue des arts décoratifs* 20 (1900), quoted in Borsi and Godoli, *Paris Art Nouveau*, 37. On Orazi, see Brunhammer, *Art Nouveau*, 486; M. Harris, *Loïe Fuller*, 74; and Garner, *Art Nouveau Collectables*, 75–76, and on Bernhardt, 116.

35. Debora L. Silverman, *Art Nouveau in Fin-de-Siècle France* (Berkeley and Los Angeles: University of California Press, 1989), 298–300; Rearick, *Pleasures of the Belle Epoque*, 131–32.

36. Anet, "Loïe Fuller in French Sculpture," 270, 278.

37. Brunhammer, *Art Nouveau*, 77, for an illustration and a description of this gypsograph, a copy of which may be seen in the Virginia Museum, the Library of Congress, the New York Public Library, Lincoln Center, or the Newberry Library, Chicago. Roger Marx, "Loïe Fuller," clipping, NYPL, is a reprint of the essay. The (translated) quotation is from pages 355–56 of this reprint.

38. Julian, *Triumph of Art Nouveau*, 174–75; R. S., "The Exposition Theatres," *New York Times*, September 16, 1900, p. 18, c. 3, which is the source of all the quotations here.

39. LF interview, unidentified and undated New York paper, ca. 1901, clipping, Locke; Jean Lorrain, journal entry for July 6, 1900, clipping, Opéra.

40. Invitation card, LF to Rodin, June 25, 1900, AMR; unidentified New York paper, June 26, 1900, and LF interview in unidentified New York paper, ca. 1901, clippings, Locke; Lorrain, journal entry for July 6, 1900, clipping, Opéra; *New York Times*, September 16, 1900, p. 18, c. 3; *L'Evènement*, October 16, 1900, clipping, AMR.

41. Pinet, *Ornement de la durée*, 8–9, quoting a Rodin interview and Maillard to Rodin, September 18, 1900.

42. LF interview, ca. 1901, clipping, Locke; Mauclair, "Sada Yacco et Loïe Fuller."

43. LF interview, ca. 1901, clipping, Locke; Alexandre, "Le Théâtre de la Loïe Fuller."

44. *L'Echo de Paris*, July 10, 21, 25, 1900; program for "Fête donnée au Palais de l'Elysée," August 19, 1900, Opéra.

45. *New York Times*, September 16, 1900, p. 18, c. 3.

CHAPTER 7. SADA, ISADORA, MARIE, THE CURIES, RODIN

1. *New York Sun*, January 6, 1901; unidentified New York paper, January 1901; *New York Morning Telegraph*, February 23, 1901, clippings, Locke.

2. *Stage*, London, June 20, 1901, 12; July 18, 1901, 12; *London Illustrated News*, June 22, 1901, 884; *Era*, London, June 22, 1901, 388–89, Newspaper Library, London; Shaftsbury Theatre program for July 15, 1901, NYPL.

3. G. Montignac, "La Loie Fuller et Sada Yacco," *Le Monde illustré*, November 2, 1901, Dance Clipping File, NYPL.

4. LF, *Fifteen Years*, 207–8, 222, 231.

5. Isadora Duncan, *My Life* (New York: Liveright, 1927), 48–49, 68–69, 90–91.
6. LF, *Fifteen Years*, 223.
7. Duncan, *My Life*, 94–98.
8. LF, *Fifteen Years*, 151–52, 224–30.
9. Marie, Queen of Roumania, *The Story of My Life* (New York: Scribner's, 1934), 290, 346.
10. LF, *Fifteen Years*, 152–64; LF, "The World Asks," ms. memoir, ca. 1927, NYPL.
11. LF to "Cheres Amies," undated but probably April 1901, ms. in private possession. In this letter, in her not entirely correct French, Loie wrote: "J ai passer le matin hier avec les '*Curie*' / tres interressante le *Radium*."
12. Eve Curie, *Madame Curie*, trans. Vincent Sheean (Garden City, N.Y.: Doubleday, Doran, 1937), 232–33; LF to Rodin, telegram [April 1902], AMR.
13. Emilia Cimino to Rodin, October 1, 1901, and two undated letters, ca. October 1901, AMR; Beausire, *Correspondance de Rodin* 4:205, 211, 231, for identification of Carrière, Druet, and Mirbeau.
14. Alice D. Weston to Rodin, October 8, 9, 1901, AMR.
15. Butler, *Rodin*, 362–65.
16. LF, *Fifteen Years*, 122–26.
17. LF, reminiscence, ca. 1927, NYPL.
18. LF to Rodin [January 1903], AMR; unidentified Brooklyn newspaper, February 3, 1903, clipping, Locke.
19. H. Hamburg to Rodin, March 3, 17, 20, April 3, 1903; Emilia Cimino to Rodin, May 5, 1903, AMR. On Nellie Bly, see Brooke Kroeger, *Nellie Bly: Daredevil, Reporter, Feminist* (New York: Times Books, 1994).
20. Cimino to Rodin, April 28, May 5, 1903, and an undated 1903 letter, AMR.
21. Printed invitation card of the National Arts Club, May 6–16, 1903, AMR; *The American* (city unidentified, but not New York), May 8, 1903; *New York Times*, May 9, 1903; *New York Tribune*, May 10, 1903; *New York Mail and Express*, May 16, 1903, clippings, AMR. Grunfeld, *Rodin*, 445, misdates this exhibition as occurring in September 1903 and erroneously refers to it as "Rodin's first one-man show in America."
22. Cimino to Rodin, May 6, 10, 17, 1903, and "Memoranda for Members" of the National Arts Club for May 1903, AMR. These memoranda announce that Miss Emilia Cimino-Folliero will talk on Rodin's art. Later she signed herself E. C. Folliero. Possibly this name change indicates that she had been married. On Rodin's amour propre, see Butler, *Rodin*, 378.
23. Edwin Elwell, Curator of the Metropolitan Museum of Art, to Rodin, June 2, 1903, AMR; LF to Rodin, telegram, June 7, 1903; Rodin to LF, telegram, ca. June 8, 1903, Bausire, *Correspondance de Rodin* 2:87–88.
24. Tag for exhibit, June 26, 1903; note regarding "Oeuvres soi-disant vendues," June 1903; LF to Rodin, July 1, 1903, AMR. On the *Tower of Labor*, see Pinet, *Ornement de la durée*, 12, and Butler, *Rodin*, 334–37.

25. Geo. W. Adrian, Landlord, against Loie Fuller, Tenant, May 12, 1903, NYPL; unidentified New York newspapers, May 20, 1903, and July 1903, clippings, Locke.

26. Rodin to John W. Simpson, September 1, 1903, and Simpson to Rodin (French translation), October 28, 1903, Bausire, *Correspondance de Rodin* 2:87–93; and Simpson to Rodin (in the original English), October 28, 1903, AMR; Cimino to Rodin, September 12, 1903, and three undated 1903 letters from her to him, AMR.

27. LF to Rodin, July 16, August 15, 24, 30, September 2, 1903, and an undated letter from her to him, ca. September 1903, AMR.

28. *Tatler,* London, October 7, 1903, 31, clipping, Maryhill; Crédit Algérien to Rodin, October 16, 20, 1903; R. R. Moore to Rodin, October 21, 1903; René Cheroy to Rodin, memorandum, November 6, 1903, AMR.

29. Doucet, "Miss Loïe Fuller." What follows is all derived from Doucet's article except for a few supplementary sources as noted below.

30. Loie's vision problem is elaborated upon in two articles, undated but ca. 1902, the one from the *New York Morning Telegraph,* the other from an unidentified paper, clippings, Locke.

31. LF, *Fifteen Years,* 138–42; *Daily America* (city not specified), August 1902, clipping, Locke.

32. Loie had recently expressed her idea of playing with light as with sound in another interview: André Charlot, "Une Loïe Fuller qu'on ne connait pas," *Le Monde illustré,* September 19, 1903, 281, clipping, Opéra. "The luminous art being still in the embryonic stage, these ideas and theories can appear strange at first," but on reflection they appear reasonable enough, Charlot thought.

33. Loie was quoted as saying, around 1905: "I am not a dancer. No, I don't dance. I express, I express!" J. A. L. in *Avenue,* January 3, 1928, clipping, Arsenal.

CHAPTER 8. WANDERERS IN GLORY

1. Unidentified New York paper, July 15, 1905, clipping, Locke.

2. Note signed by LF and dated Montevideo, June 29, 1904, ms. in private possession; *New York Herald,* September 1905, clipping, Locke; E. C. to LF and GB, November 11, 1905, NYPL; Maurice-Verne in *Paris soir,* January 9, 1928, clipping, Arsenal.

3. LF to GB, October 28, 1905, three postcards, and October 29, 1905, postcard, NYPL.

4. LF, *Fifteen Years,* 208–10; Grunfeld, *Rodin,* 520–21.

5. LF to Rodin, August 4, 1906, AMR; Pinet, *Ornement de la durée,* 9:10.

6. LF, *Fifteen Years,* 171–75, 185–87; Grunfeld, *Rodin,* 520.

7. Raguet to Rodin, August 27, 1906, and LF to Rodin, undated, AMR; Pinet, *Ornement de la durée,* 10.

8. LF, *Fifteen Years,* 210–16; Suketaro Sawada, *Little Hanako* (Nagoya, Japan: Chunichi, 1984), 32–33.

Notes to Pages 160–174

9. Six letters of LF to Rodin, one dated May 17, 1907, another August 31, 1907, the others undated but all in 1907, AMR. In the museum archives is a printed note describing Rodin's head of Loie and a written note saying: "Vente Paris . . . 16 Dec. 1966."

10. *L'Echo de Paris,* September 15, 1907; LF to "Chere Amie," ca. November 1907, Orsay.

11. *Sketch,* London, March 6, 1907, clipping, Theatre Museum, London.

12. *L'Echo de Paris,* January 7, 1905; Nozière, "Une Fée," unidentified periodical, January 1907, clipping, Arsenal.

13. *Stage,* August 29, 1907, 16; *Era,* August 31, 1907, 15; *Sketch,* September 4, 1907, 240–41, all of London; also *Sketch,* August 28, 1907, clipping, Theatre Museum, London.

14. Felix Cherniavsky, *The Salome Dancer: The Life and Times of Maud Allan* (Toronto: McClelland & Stewart, 1991), 148–49 and passim. Cherniavsky assumes that Maud toured with Loie in 1907, but the year must have been 1906.

15. *New York World,* February 17, 1907, clipping, Locke; *Le Figaro,* May 7, October 2, 8, November 19, 1907; *L'Echo de Paris,* September 25, 1907.

16. Jules Clarétie, "La Vie à Paris," *Le Temps,* November 8, 1907, clipping, Opéra. Parts of this article, translated, is included in LF, *Fifteen Years,* and the quotation as given here is from pp. 286–87 of that book, with some alteration.

17. *Indianapolis Star,* November 24, 1907, clipping, Locke.

18. *New York Morning Telegraph,* November 17, 1907, clipping, Locke.

19. *Le Figaro,* November 10, 1907; *Evening Standard et St-James Gazette,* quoted in Théâtre des Arts program, dance file, NYPL; *Pittsburgh Gazette Times,* November 24, 1907, clipping, Locke; A. V., "Une Tête à cent expressions," *Femina,* no. 164 (November 15, 1907): 507.

20. *Le Temps,* November 8, 1907; LF, *Fifteen Years,* 282.

21. GB to W. J. Beresford, ca. 1904–5, NYPL; LF to Rodin, January 17, 18, 1907, and two undated letters, ca. 1907, AMR; LF to "Chere Amie," ca. 1907, Orsay.

22. W. J. Beresford to GB, ca. 1905, NYPL; Edmund Russell (LF's secretary) to Rodin, ca. 1907, AMR.

23. LF to Rodin, three letters, ca. 1907, AMR.

24. Eve Curie, *Madame Curie,* 243–46; LF to Rodin, July 12, 1907, AMR. LF's copy of Mme Curie's book is in the Maryhill Museum.

25. LF to Rodin, ca. 1907 and July 3, 1907, AMR.

26. LF to Rodin, ca. December 1906 or January 1907, AMR; LF to Anatole France, ca. 1907–8, Anatole France mss., Bib. Nat.

27. LF, *Fifteen Years,* 98–100, 273–81.

28. Félix Juven to LF, January 12, 1908 (misdated 1907); Elie Metchnikoff to LF, February 5, 1908; LF, autobiographical fragment, March 1908, NYPL.

29. LF to Mme Clarétie, 1908, and autobiographical fragment, 1908, NYPL;

Gladys Thomas to Rodin, two letters, 1908, AMR; LF to "Chere Amie," 1908, Orsay; *New York Times,* March 26, 1908, p. 1, c. 6; *New York Morning Telegraph,* March 27, 1908, clipping, Locke.

30. Mrs. S. H. Danovitch to Edward T. James, March 28, 1960, copy, Chicago Historical Society; *Chicago Record-Herald,* November 28, 1908; *New York Telegraph,* December 10, 1908; *Indianapolis Star,* December 27, 1908, and other newspaper clippings, Locke; LF, *Fifteen Years,* 15, 36, 62–72, and manuscript of chapter 1, NYPL.

31. LF to Mme Clarétie, 1908, NYPL; LF, *Fifteen Years,* vii–x, 127, 278–88.

CHAPTER 9. LA LOÏE AND HER MUSES

1. LF to Mrs. Jules Clarétie, ca. July 1908, NYPL; LF to "Chere Amie," ca. July 1908, Orsay; *Chicago Tribune,* September 20, 1908; *New York Telegraph,* October 4, 1908, clippings, Locke.

2. LF to W. G. Robertson, August 4, 1908, Walford Graham Robertson MSS, Huntington Library; Nina Auerbach, *Ellen Terry: Player in Her Time* (New York: Norton, 1987), 142, 352–59; Victor Seroff, *The Real Isadora* (New York: Dial Press, 1971), 96–101.

3. *New York Telegraph,* September 7, 1908; *Variety,* September 12, 1908, clippings, Locke.

4. *Musical America,* September 5, 1908; *Chicago Interocean,* July 14, 1909, clippings, Locke; *Sketch,* London, November 3, 1908, clipping, Theatre Museum, London; *New York Times,* February 14, 1909, pt. 3, p. 2, c. 7; LF to Rodin [February 1909], AMR.

5. *New York Sun,* April 1, 1909; *Boston Herald,* April 5, 1909; *Musical Leader,* May 20, 1909; *New York World,* May 20, 1909, clippings, Locke.

6. *New York Times,* June 19, 1909, p. 1, c. 6; LF to Rodin, June 29, 1909, AMR.

7. LF to "Cheres Amies," ca. 1908, Orsay; LF to Rodin, August 16, 1909, AMR; *New York Telegraph,* August 21, 1909; unidentified paper, ca. August 1909; unidentified Boston paper, September 26, 1909; Sterling Heilig, Paris dispatch, October 15, 1909, in unidentified paper; *Des Moines Register,* March 20, 1910, clippings, Locke.

8. *Dramatic News,* ca. October 5, 1909; *Washington Post,* October 12, 1909; *New York Telegraph,* November 28, 1909, clippings, Locke; Metropolitan Opera House program for November 30 and December 7, 1909, NYPL.

9. *Musical America,* ca. August 11, 1909; *Musical Courier,* August 21, October 11, 1909, clippings, Locke.

10. *New York Telegraph,* September 2, 1909, clipping, Locke; LF to Otto Kahn (draft), October 2, 1914, NYPL.

11. *Musical America,* September 18, 1909; *New York Telegraph,* October 31, 1909, clippings, Locke.

12. *New York Telegraph,* October 5, 1909; *Washington Post,* October 12, 1909; *Musical America,* October 30, 1909, clippings, Locke.

13. *New York Times*, December 1, 1909, p. 7, c. 3; *New York Telegraph*, December 1, 1909, clipping, Locke; Fredrika Blair, *Isadora: Portrait of the Artist as a Woman* (New York: McGraw-Hill, 1986), 204.

14. *New York Times*, December 5, 1909, pt. 3, p. 12, c. 4; December 13, 1909, p. 9, c. 1; December 15, 1909, p. 6, c. 2; *New York Telegraph*, December 13, 15, 1909, clippings, Locke.

15. *Boston Herald*, January 4, 1910; *Boston Transcript*, January 4, 1910; *Boston Traveler*, January 7, 1910, clippings, Locke.

16. *New York Tribune*, February 10, 1910; *New York Telegraph*, February 18, March 10, 11, 1910, clippings, Locke; *New York Times*, February 10, 1910, p. 7, c. 3; February 17, 1910, p. 9, c. 4.

17. *Boston Herald*, January 18, 1910; *Variety*, January 22, 1910; *New York Telegraph*, February 18, 1910; *Des Moines Register*, March 20, 1910; March 22, 1910; *Brooklyn Eagle*, April 5, 1910; *Cincinnati Commercial*, May 16, 1910; *Vanity Fair*, 1910, clippings, Locke. Loie discussed her career and her dance theories in two articles during this period: "Dances That Inspire," *Chicago Record*, February 27, 1910, 5–6, and "Eighteen Years of Dancing," *Green Book Album*, March 1910, 656–63.

18. LF interview, Paris, August 24, 1909, unidentified paper; *Philadelphia Evening Times*, February 21, 1910; *New York Mirror*, March 5, 1910; John Corbin in *Hampton*, July 1911, clippings, Locke.

19. Wearing, *London Stage* 1:90, 123; *New York Telegraph*, July 20, 1911, clipping, Locke; unidentified clippings, June 19, 22, November–, December 7, 1911, Arsenal.

20. Seven letters from LF to GB, undated but January–April 1912, and LF to GB, telegram, April 26, 1912, NYPL; unidentified Marseilles paper, April 13, 1912, clipping, Arsenal.

21. Program, Le Théâtre des Bouffes-Parisiens, 1912–13 season, and unidentified clippings, May 5, 7, 9, Arsenal.

22. Unidentified Paris periodicals, December 9, 14, 28, 1913, clippings, Arsenal; *Musical America*, December 13, 1913, clipping, Locke; Covielle, "Danse, musique, lumière chez la Loïe Fuller," *L'Eclair*, May 5, 1914, clipping, Opéra.

23. Unidentified Paris periodicals, April 29, May 5, 11, 1914, clippings, Arsenal; program, Théâtre Municipal du Châtelet, May 4–20 [1914], clipping, Opéra; *Daily Mail*, May 24, 1914, clipping, NYPL.

24. Richard Kraus, *History of the Dance in Art and Education* (Englewood Cliffs, N.J.: Prentice-Hall, 1969), 171–72; Francis Gadan and Robert Maillard, eds., *Dictionary of Modern Ballet* (New York: Tudor, 1959), 40–44, 147–51, 239–41.

25. Georges Pioch, November 10, 1912; Paul Souday, November 11, 1912; Louis Vauxcelles, May 10, 1914, unidentified clippings, Arsenal.

26. Claude Roger-Marx, "Les Danses de Loïe Fuller et d'Isadora Duncan," *Comoedia illustré*, February 1912, 320–21, clipping, NYPL; Roger-Marx, "Le Génie inconnu de la Loïe Fuller," and "A propos des 'Danses de l'avenir de Miss Loïe Fuller,"

unidentified clippings, November 20, 28, 1912, Arsenal; Roger-Marx, "Loïe Fuller et son école," *Comoedia illustré* 9 (May 20, 1914): 739–41; Covielle, "Danse, musique, lumière."

27. Camille Mauclair, "Danseuses," *Le Progrès,* Lyon, December 24, 1911, clipping, AMR.

28. J. Ch., November 10, 1912; G. Linor, ca. November 10, 1912; Georges Pioch, May 7, 1913, and May 9, 1914; Louis Schneider, May 11, 1914; and an unsigned article, May 25, 1914, unidentified clippings, Arsenal.

29. Rearick, *Pleasures of the Belle Epoque,* 189–95; M. Harris, *Loïe Fuller,* 32. For vaudeville programs featuring both Loie's dances and movie shorts, see London Hippodrome program, October 5, 1908, clipping, Maryhill; and an unidentified London magazine, November 3, 1908, clipping, NYPL.

30. GB to LF, February 3, 1912, NYPL; Laura Hubbard, "A High Priestess of Terpsichore," *Vogue,* September 1, 1913, clipping, Locke; Dominique Sylvaire, unidentified periodical, December 12, 1913, clipping, Arsenal; LF to Rodin, telegram, July 23, 1914, AMR.

31. Alicia Little to LF, January 23, 1912; LF to GB, ca. April 1912; LF to Mr. Rich, July 9, 1912; LF to Maud Chance, July 12, 1912; LF to Peggy, July 15, 1912, NYPL.

32. LF to GB, ca. 1913, NYPL.

33. GB to Rodin, ca. 1908; LF to Rodin, June 11, 1909; Charles Girvin (De Kay's secretary) to "Monsieur," August 3, 1909; De Kay to S. G. Archibald, August 20, 1917; De Kay's lawyer, receipt, October 1917, AMR; Grunfeld, *Rodin,* 530.

34. LF to the Duchess Choiseul-Beaupré, ca. 1912 and May 1912; LF to Rodin, January 1909; January 1, 1912; ca. 1913; ca. 1914; March 3, 1914, AMR; Grunfeld, *Rodin,* 484–85, 551; Butler, *Rodin,* 414–15, 459–64.

35. Marie to LF, April 2, 1912; May 16, 1913; February 8, 1914, NYPL; LF to Rodin, November 27, 1913; "debut 1914"; July 23, 1914, AMR; Marie to Rodin, February 7, 1914, *Correspondance de Rodin* 4:67–68; Marie, *Story of My Life,* 543–47, 550–59.

CHAPTER 10. LITTLE LOÏE AND BIG ALMA

1. Bernice Scharlach, *Big Alma: San Francisco's Alma Spreckels* (San Francisco: Scottwall Associates, 1990), 1–49 passim. For the quotation, see p. 48.

2. LF reminiscence, ca. 1920, NYPL; Alma Spreckels reminiscence, Maryhill; Scharlach, *Big Alma,* 55–60.

3. LF to Rodin, ca. July 1914, AMR.

4. LF to Peggy, July 15, 1912; Van Beil and LF to Cantor, ca. 1914; Adolphe Henn to LF, October 2, 1914; Agnes Van Beil to Kellogg, May 9, 1915, NYPL. Reproduced in M. Harris, *Loïe Fuller,* 29, is a photograph of the Van Beils and other guests at the Flammarions' on July 14, 1909.

5. Flammarion to LF, April 1, 1914, NYPL; *Washington Post,* July 18, 1914, clipping, Locke.

6. LF to Rodin, August 3, 11, September–, 1914; Mrs. Van Beil to Rodin, August 12, 1914, AMR.

7. GB to LF, August 17, 18, 19, 20, 24, 28, 1914, and Adolphe Henn to LF, October 12, 1914, NYPL.

8. LF to "Rayon de Soleil," October 5, 1914, and to Van Beil, October 6, 1914; two full-page clippings from an unidentified newspaper, "Copyright, 1914, by the Star Company"; poem and essay by LF, NYPL.

9. Contract (in French) between LF and the Exposition Company, September 15, 1914, and LF to Otto Kahn, October 2, 1914, NYPL.

10. Scharlach, *Big Alma,* 61–62; LF to Alma Spreckels, September 1, 1914, and to GB, October 10, 1914, NYPL. Loie, in New York, had asked Alma to send her gold certificates rather than a check, as the certificates could be exchanged for gold.

11. GB to LF, September 8, 9, 1914, and LF to Rodin, ca. October 1914, NYPL; GB to Rodin, October 8, 1914, AMR.

12. LF to Rodin, ca. November 1914, AMR; LF to Mrs. Van Beil, ca. 1914, and Mrs. Van Beil to Van Beil, December 12, 1914, NYPL.

13. Copies of the agreements are in AMR and are printed in *Correspondance de Rodin* 4:106–8, 110, 112–13.

14. Rodin to LF, January 1, 1915, and to Dayot, January 20, 27, 1915, *Correspondance de Rodin* 4:114–16, 118–19.

15. LF to France, six undated letters, ca. January–February 1915, Anatole France MSS., Bib. Nat.

16. LF to Mme Poincaré, six undated letters, ca. February 1915, Papiers Poincaré, Bib. Nat.

17. LF to General French, ca. February 1915, and Pierre Roche to LF, February 8, 1915, NYPL; LF to Mme Poincaré, ca. February 1915, Papiers Poincaré, Bib. Nat.

18. LF to Alma Spreckels, two undated letters, ca. February 1915, NYPL.

19. Marcelle Martin to Rodin, January 29, 1915; LF to Rodin, telegram, February 15, 1915, and an undated letter and a postcard, both ca. February 1915, AMR.

20. *Variety,* March 1915, clipping, Locke; Scharlach, *Big Alma,* 63, 66, 71–72, 77.

21. Mrs. Briggs to LF, February 8, 1915; LF to Mrs. Briggs, ca. April 1915; Cantor to LF, April 10, 1915; GB to LF, April 20, 1915; LF to Alma Spreckels, ca. May 1915, NYPL.

22. *Oakland Enquirer,* April 14, 1915, clipping, SFPALM; John M. Burke to Fred Hutchinson, May 6, 1915; Harry Lafler to LF, May 13, 1915; Margaret Blake-Alverson to LF, May 16, 1915; LF to GB, ca. May 1915, NYPL.

23. LF to GB, ca. May 1915, NYPL; Scharlach, *Big Alma,* 79, 82.

24. *San Francisco Call,* June 2, 1915, clipping, Locke. Copies of the program are in SFPALM and NYPL.

25. Contract between Buckley and Wyatt, July 3, 1915; LF to Cummins, ca. July 14, 1915; Cummins to LF, July 14, 1915; Buckley to Wyatt, ca. July 18, 1915; Wyatt to

Buckley, July 18, 1915; Wyatt to Cummins, July 22, 1915; Mason Opera House account with LF, July 25, 1915, NYPL; Henry Christeen Warnack in *Los Angeles Times,* July 22, 1915, clipping, Locke.

26. GB to Alma Spreckels, ca. August 1915; LF to GB, November 22, December 9, 18, 1915, NYPL; *San Francisco Examiner,* October 3, 1915, clipping, and Columbia Theatre program, October 21, 1915, both in SFPALM.

27. LF to GB, four undated letters, 1915, NYPL; Scharlach, *Big Alma,* 83.

28. GB to LF, April 20, 1915, and LF to GB, November 1915, NYPL.

29. GB to Alma Spreckels, ca. July 1915, and to LF, October 27, 1915, and an undated letter, 1915; LF to GB, two undated letters, 1915; Alma Spreckels to GB, January 7, 1916, NYPL.

30. LF to Rodin, ca. November 1915, AMR; LF to Dayot, ca. November–December 1915, NYPL; Scharlach, *Big Alma,* 77–78.

CHAPTER 11. MORE MISSIONS TO AMERICA

1. Receipts for salary payments by LF, June 29, July 19, 1916; LF to GB, cables, December 6, 11, 14, 1916; undated fragment on defense of London, NYPL; LF to Captain Joseph Reinach, four letters, ca. November 1916, Joseph Reinach Correspondence, Bib. Nat.

2. Marie to LF, November 23, 1916; LF, autobiographical fragment, ca. 1920s, NYPL.

3. LF to Mme Poincaré, ca. November 1916, Papiers Poincaré, Bib. Nat.; Marie to LF, February 14, 1917, Maryhill; LF to Marie, March 22, 24, ca. April 6, 1917; Lahovary to LF, March 23, 1917; LF to Bliss, April 9, 1917, NYPL.

4. LF to Mrs. Woodrow Wilson, April 16, 1917, to Marie, June 14, 1917, and to GB, October 15, 1917; Walter Egan to LF, May 28, 1917, NYPL.

5. Assistant Secretary of State to LF, June 18, 1917; Jean to LF, November 10, 1917; LF to GB, ca. November 1917; LF to Samuel Hill, October 4, 1918, NYPL; Marie to LF, October 17, 1917, Maryhill.

6. The story is told from the museum's viewpoint in Henry W. Hawley, "Loïe Fuller and the Cleveland Museum of Art," *News & Calendar: The Cleveland Museum of Art* 20 (March–April 1980): 2–4.

7. Emery May (Holden) Norweb, Diary 1916–18, R. Henry Norweb Family Papers, Western Reserve Historical Society, Cleveland.

8. Whiting to LF, June 15, 1917; receipt for loans, June 18, 1917; lecture program, June 22, 1917; *Bulletin of the Cleveland Museum of Art,* June–July 1917, p. 93, August 1917, pp. 108–9, all in CMA.

9. Whiting to J. Nilsen Laurvik, June 4, 1917; to W. Frank Purdy, June 15, 1917; and to LF, June 21, 1917, CMA; Hawley, "Loïe Fuller and the Cleveland Museum of Art," 3.

10. LF to GB, October 3, 1917, NYPL.

Notes to Pages 242–252

11. Roberta Bole to Whiting, September 14, 1917, CMA.

12. Whiting to Laurvik, November 5, 1917, CMA. The CMA contain many letters of Whiting to LF and to others concerning the debt, 1918–21.

13. Whiting to W. B. Sanders, December 11, 1918; to J. Friedlander, December 20, 1918; and to LF, April 20, 1921; R. C. Foerster to Whiting, February 24, 1919; LF to Whiting, April 7, 1921; and E. S. Curtiss to Whiting, May 20, 1921, CMA.

14. John E. Tuhy, *Sam Hill: The Prince of Castle Nowhere* (Goldendale, Wash.: Maryhill Museum of Art, 1992), passim.

15. LF to Marie, ca. December 1916, enclosing copies of several telegrams exchanged between LF and Sam Hill in November 1916, NYPL; Scharlach, *Big Alma*, 63.

16. LF to Hill, telegrams, July 13, 17, 19, 1917, Maryhill.

17. Hill to LF, telegram, July 22, 1917, and two letters, July 24, 1917; Hill to the Artists of France, July 24, 1917, Maryhill.

18. LF to Whiting, ca. July 27, 1917, CMA.

19. LF to Hill, August 31, 1917, and Hill to LF, November 18, 1917, Maryhill; Hill to Whiting, October 27, 1917, CMA; LF to Hill, ca. early 1918, NYPL.

20. Jeanne Bardey to LF, June 24, 1916, AMR; Rodin to LF, July 24, 1916, *Correspondance de Rodin* 4:153; Butler, *Rodin*, 503–5; Grunfeld, *Rodin*, 599.

21. Bénédite to Alma Spreckels, ca. September 1916, AMR; LF to Alma Spreckels, ca. 1917, NYPL; Butler, *Rodin*, 509–10; Grunfeld, *Rodin*, 631.

22. Marcelle Martin to Conservateur, November 18, 1916, AMR; photograph of LF and others at dinner, December 25, 1916, CMA; Etienne Bricon in *Le Gaulois*, January 7, 1928, clipping, Arsenal.

23. LF to Rodin, ca. February 14, 1917; M. Tirel to Conservateur, May 2, 1917, AMR; Butler, *Rodin*, 508.

24. LF to Fumière, November 17, 1917, AMR; LF, meditation on Rodin's death, ca. November 17, 1917, Maryhill; Grunfeld, *Rodin*, 634; Butler, *Rodin*, 513.

25. LF to Alma Spreckels, ca. 1917, NYPL.

26. Ordre de marche for GB, May 8, 1916; Countess Van den Steen, letter of reference, April 22, 1917, NYPL; unidentified San Francisco newspapers, July 22, September 8, 1917, clippings, SFPALM.

27. Henriette to LF, April 26, 28, May 8, 22, 1918, NYPL; Etienne Bricon in *Le Gaulois*, January 7, 1928, clipping, Arsenal.

28. LF passport, February 6, 1918, NYPL; Constance Gould to Whiting, June 10, 1918; LF to Whiting, June 21, 1918; Whiting to LF, July 17, 1918, CMA.

29. Henriette to LF, June 8, July 24, 1918, NYPL.

30. Alma Spreckels to Van den Steen, June 27, July 4, 1918; LF to GB, July 4, 24, 26, 1918; Baron de Cartier to Eugene N. Fritz Jr., August 16, 1918, NYPL.

31. Alma Spreckels to GB, September 29, 1918; LF to GB, two letters, ca. October–November 1918, NYPL.

Notes to Pages 253–265

32. LF to GB, August 25, October 19, 1918; Henriette to LF, November 27, 1918, NYPL.

33. Henriette to Hoover, April 26, 1918, NYPL; Henriette to Hoover, April 28, 1918, Maryhill; LF to Sam Hill, October 4, 1918, and to GB, October 21, 14, 1918, NYPL.

CHAPTER 12. THE LILY OF LIFE

1. LF, journal of voyage, December 1918; account of Wilson in London, December 26, 1918; autobiographical fragments ca. December 1918–January 1919, NYPL; Hannah Pakula, *The Last Romantic: A Biography of Queen Marie of Roumania* (New York: Simon & Schuster, 1984), 240–41, 263–64.

2. L. H. De Friese to Hoover, January 8, 1919; Henriette to LF, February 3, 14, 1919, NYPL; LF to F. A. Whiting, March 4, 1919, CMA.

3. Marie to LF, March 11, 1919, Maryhill; Marie to LF, March 11, 1919; Gerry Reynolds to LF, ca. March 1919, March 17, 23, 1919; LF to Reynolds, March 21, 1919, NYPL; LF to F. A. Whiting, June 5, 1919, CMA; Pakula, *Last Romantic*, 271–87.

4. LF to McGuire and to Swain & Hoyt, May 9, 1919, NYPL; LF to Whiting, May 19, June 5, 1919, CMA. For the Yeats poem, see William Butler Yeats, *Collected Works* (New York: Macmillan, 1989), 1:240–41.

5. LF to Whiting, June 5, October 15, 1919, January 12, 1920, CMA; LF to Reed, ca. December 20, 1919, and to GB, December 29, 1919, NYPL.

6. LF to Whiting, April 10, 1920, CMA; Loïe Fuller Enterprises letterhead and partnership agreement, July 1920; LF to Crocker, September 1920, NYPL.

7. Marie to LF, June 6, November 13, December 15, 1919, and April 1, 1920, Maryhill; LF to GB, May 8, 1920, and to Marie, ca. May 1920, NYPL.

8. LF to Marie, May 29, 1920, NYPL; program, *Le Lys de la vie,* July 1, 1920, Opéra; *New York Times,* July 3, 1920, p. 8, c. 4.

9. Alma Spreckels to LF, ca. June 1919, October 20, 28, 1919; Henriette to LF, June 15, July 12, 1919, ca. 1919–20, NYPL.

10. Alma Spreckels to LF, ca. 1919–20, February 16, 1920; LF to Alma Spreckels, February 6, ca. March 1920, NYPL.

11. Bretteville to LF, April 5, 6, 16, May 7, 1920, NYPL; *New York Herald*, Paris ed., May 27, 1920, clipping in CMA; Scharlach, *Big Alma,* 111.

12. Pierre Roche to LF, May 26, July 6, 1920; Mary W. French to LF, September 17, 1920, NYPL.

13. L. Morel de Teincey to LF, June 3, 1920, March 7, April 23, 1921; Henriette to LF, December 11, 1920, ca. 1921, NYPL; Henriette to LF, June 20, 1921, Maryhill; Scharlach, *Big Alma,* 112.

14. LF to Mercanton, ca. October 1920, NYPL; LF to F. A. Whiting, December 2, 1920, CMA.

15. This account of Loie's 1920–21 cinematography is based on LF, ms. "inter-

Notes to Pages 265–280

view," April 1927, NYPL; M. Harris, *Loïe Fuller,* 32; and Brandstetter and Ochaim, *Loïe Fuller,* 67–71. My description of the movie follows closely Brandstetter and Ochaim, 71, who reproduce some still photos from it. These authors err, however, in saying that Gab "lebte seit 20 Jahren mit Loïe zusammen," and Harris misdates the moviemaking as of 1919.

16. LF to Marie, three letters (drafts), ca. February 1921; to Sir Oswald Stoll, ca. March 1921; and to Mr. Kirkup, June 28, November 1, 1921, NYPL. In Opéra is an undated program for *Le Lys de la vie* quoting several reviews of the film, including the one by Galtier-Boissière.

17. LF to F. A. Whiting, September 3, 1920, CMA; Raymond Charpentier and "Armory" in *Comoedia,* March 3, 1921, clipping in Theatre Museum, London; LF, contract, March 6, 1921; Margaret Chute to LF, April 4, 1921, NYPL.

18. Leon Wright to LF, January 13, 1920; John Ross to LF, January 19, 1921, NYPL; Whiting to Mrs. Norweb, ca. February 1921, and to LF, March 23, 1921; Mrs. Norweb to Whiting, May 6, 1919, and March 3, 1921, CMA.

19. Hill to LF, May 15, 1920, and to F. H. Goff, March 15, 1921, CMA; LF to Marie, ca. February 1921, NYPL.

20. LF to Marie, ca. February 1921, and to James K. Hackett, August 22, 1921, NYPL; Marie to LF, March 23, May 30, December 24, 1921, Maryhill. Pakula, *Last Romantic,* 394, states that Loie sent Marie a copy of the *Protocols* but does not give a source for the statement.

21. Marie to "Gentlemen," April 5, 1920, and to LF, February 14, 1922; *LF v. Turner,* June 5, 1921; LF to Lahovary, May 9, 1922, and to W. N. Cromwell, July 14, 1922; Turner to Marie, August 23, 1921, and ca. April 1922, NYPL.

22. Sorbonne to LF, July 13, 1921; LF to Marie, ca. December 1921, to Cromwell, February 3, 1922, and to Lahovary, May 9, 1922; Turner affidavit, August 9, 1922, NYPL; Marie to LF, January 1, 16, 1922, Maryhill.

CHAPTER 13. LIGHT AND SHADOW

1. Marcel Rieu, June 10, 1922; Paul Souday, June 11, 1922; Raoul Brunel, June 12, 1922; André Levinson, June 13, 1922; G. de Pawlowski, June 19, 1922; and G. Le Fèvre, June 20, 1922, unidentified clippings; Arsenal; Théâtre des Champs-Elysées program, June 10–30, 1922, NYPL.

2. Contracts for performances, 1922–23, NYPL; *Sketch,* London, February 14, 1923, clipping, Theatre Museum, London.

3. Académie de Musique et de Danse, Opéra, programs June, September 1923, Maryhill; Paris newspaper, June 12, 1923; Raoul Brunel, June 12, 1923, unidentified clippings, Arsenal.

4. *Sketch,* London, December 12, 1923, p. 541, clipping, Theatre Museum, London; contracts for performances, 1923, 1924, 1925, NYPL.

5. LF to GB, August 1, 1922, and to Edward C. Kidman, December 21, 1924,

NYPL; André Rivollet, "La Dernière incarnation de Miss Loïe Fuller," *Le Gaulois*, October 16, 1922, clipping, Arsenal.

6. Théâtre des Champs-Elysées program, June 1922, Arsenal; *La Danse*, August 1922, clipping, NYPL.

7. LF to Sam Hill, ca. October 1922, Maryhill; agreement, LF and Sir Oswald Stoll, December 8, 1922; Hébertot to LF, October 27, 1923; LF to Valerie Woodlane, ca. 1924, NYPL.

8. Marcel Rieu, ca. June 10, 1922; *Avenir*, June 12, 1922; Louis Schneider, June 12, 1923; André Rigaud, June 12, 1923, unidentified clippings, Arsenal.

9. Castle, *Folies-Bergère*, 170–72; Janet Flanner, *Paris Was Yesterday: 1925–1939* (New York: Viking Press, 1972), xx–xxi; Elizabeth Kendall, *Where She Danced* (New York: Knopf, 1979), 198–99.

10. LF to Alma Spreckels, ca. February 1922, NYPL; Marie to LF, ca. February 1922 and April 27, 1922, Maryhill.

11. LF to Alma Spreckels, ca. February 1922, and to GB, three letters, ca. July–August 1922, NYPL; *Le Gaulois*, October 16, 1922, clipping, Arsenal; Scharlach, *Big Alma*, 118–23.

12. LF to Marie, September 25, October 4, 1922, and to Cromwell, ca. October 1922; LF memorandum, ca. February 1923, NYPL; LF to Sam Hill, ca. October 1922, Maryhill; GB to Mme Regaud, ca. December 1922 and December 23, 1922; LF to Mme Regaud, December 25, 1922, Curie MSS., Bib. Nat.

13. LF to Anatole France, May 3, 1923, and later in May, 1923, Anatole France MSS., and LF to Mme Regaud, June 1, 25, 1923, Curie MSS., Bib. Nat.; Scharlach, *Big Alma*, 123–24, which misdates the opening of the exhibit as April 1923.

14. LF to Alma Spreckels, June 20, 1924, and ca. 1924, NYPL; Scharlach, *Big Alma*, 132, 137.

15. *New York Herald*, January 5, 1924, clipping; LF to Mr. Stevens, January 21, 1925, NYPL.

16. LF, press release draft, 1924, NYPL; Louvre announcement of LF exhibit, February 22–March 22, 1924, Maryhill.

17. Unidentified periodical, June 12, 1923; René Bizet, "Les Conquêtes de Loïe Fuller," *L'Intransigeant*, July 2, 1925, Pierre-Plessis in *Le Gaulois*, July 4, 1925, Arsenal; program draft, fragment, "La Mer," ca. July 1925, NYPL; Malcolm Haslam, *In the Nouveau Style* (Boston: Little Brown, 1990), 132–33; Brandstetter, *Loïe Fuller*, 76.

18. Legrand-Chabrier, "La Loïe Fuller d'une exposition à l'autre," *L'Art vivant*, November 1, 1925, 26–29, clipping, AMR; LF and Charles Davis, contract, July 9, 1925, NYPL.

19. LF to GB, August 1925; *New York Evening World*, January 3, 1928, clipping, NYPL; Mrs. T. E. Clarke to Maurice Needham, September 1925, copy, Chicago Historical Society; *Hinsdale Doings*, January 7, 1928; *DuPage Magazine*, December 1987,

clippings, Hinsdale Historical Society; Timothy H. Bakken, *Hinsdale* (Hinsdale, 1976), 266.

20. *San Francisco Call and Post,* August 29, 1925, clipping, and Columbia Theatre program for September 7–13, 1925, SFPALM; Uthai Vincent Wilcox, "The Wrath of God," *Dance,* ca. October 1925, clipping, Theatre Museum, London; *New York Times,* October 27, 1925, p. 20, c. 4, and November 1, 1925, pt. 8, p. 2, c. 5.

CHAPTER 14. THE DYING OF THE LIGHT

1. LF to Mme Curie, September 9, December 31, 1924, and January 2, 1925, Curie MSS., Bib. Nat.; Eve Curie to LF, January 15, 1925, and June 30, 1926; *Le Temps,* November 24, 1925, clipping; Beckley to LF, February 11, 1926; Talbot to LF, February 22, 1926; press release, draft, April 16, 1926; agreement, Hurok and GB, June 30, 1926, NYPL; LF to Sam Hill, April 8, 1927, Maryhill.

2. Sam Hill to LF, June 13, July 15, October 13, 1923; LF to Sam Hill, June 17, 1926; LF, affidavit, June 18, 1926, Maryhill; *New York Herald,* January 5, 1924, clipping; LF to Hill, June 17, 1926, NYPL.

3. Alma Spreckels to LF, May 6, 17, 1926, and June 6, 20, 1927, NYPL; Tuhy, *Sam Hill,* 240; Scharlach, *Big Alma,* 152–55.

4. Marie to GB, August 13, 1926; LF to Marie, ca. 1926; LF and Calhoun, contract, October 6, 1926; LF to W. N. Cromwell, March 15, 1927, NYPL; *New York Times,* October 16, 1926, p. 10, c. 4; October 17, 1926, p. 25, c. 2; October 25, 1926, p. 5, c. 1.

5. Marie to LF, October 18, 1926; LF to Alma Spreckels, June 18, 1927; LF, "The World Asks," NYPL; *New York Times,* November 7, 1926, p. 24, c. 2; Tuhy, *Sam Hill,* 237–40. Clare de Morinni, "Loie Fuller, The Fairy of Light," *Dance Index* 1 (March 1942): 50, taking her cue from the hostile reports, erroneously concludes that Marie and Loie "were involved in one of the more genteel rackets of the decade" and that the Metropolitan Opera House performance "was a simple device for obtaining easy money." Scharlach, *Big Alma,* 156, and Pakula, *Last Romantic,* 350–51, follow Morinni in giving the same unjustified impression.

6. LF to Cromwell, November 4, 1926, and two unidentified newspaper clippings, ca. November 4, 1926, NYPL; *New York Times,* November 4, 1926, p. 1, c. 2; Tuhy, *Sam Hill,* 242.

7. Alma Spreckels to LF, November 10, 1926, and LF to Hill, February 15, 1927, NYPL; *New York Times,* November 7, 1926, p. 1, c. 7, and November 8, 1926, p. 5, c. 2; Tuhy, *Sam Hill,* 245–48; Scharlach, *Big Alma,* 156, 162.

8. LF to Cromwell, November 4, 10, 1926, and to Alma Spreckels, November 10, 1926, NYPL; Marie to LF, November 9, 1926, Maryhill; *New York Times,* November 9, 1926, p. 12, c. 2; November 11, 1926, p. 2, c. 1; November 19, 1926, p. 3, c. 3.

9. Marie to LF, November –, December 28, 1926, and LF to Alma Spreckels, Feb-

ruary 14, 1927, NYPL; Marie to LF, March 15, 1927, Maryhill; *New York Times,* November 20, 1926, p. 2, c. 2; November 27, 1926, p. 2, c. 5.

10. Marie to LF, December 28, 1926; LF to Hill, February 5, 1927; LF to Marie, April 7, 1927, NYPL; Marie to LF, March 15 and July 3, 1927; LF to Hill, June 18, 23, 1927, Maryhill.

11. Agreement, LF and GB with David R. Hochreich and Frank M. Andrews, November 20 [postdated 26], 1926; complaint, *LF v. M. Marx,* December 1, 1926; LF to Alma Spreckels, February 14, April 25, 1927, and to Cromwell, March 15, 1927, NYPL; LF to Hill, April 8, July 3, 1927, Maryhill.

12. LF to Stern, March 27, 1924; to Cromwell, February 5, 1927; to Alma Spreckels, April 26, September 30, 1927; and to Eve Curie, August 16, 1927; LF, "An Interview with E. Guiochi," April 1927, NYPL; LF to Hill, April 8, July 3, 1927, Maryhill; *Ecouter,* January 7, 1928, clipping, Arsenal.

13. LF to Hill, February 15, 1927, and to Alma Spreckels, August 16, September 5, 1927; Alma Spreckels to LF, June 6, 1927, NYPL; LF to Julius Witmark, June 15, 1927, and to Hill, March 2, 8, June 6, July 2, 1927; Hill to LF, April 4, 1927, Maryhill.

14. LF to Alma Spreckels, June 6, 1927; manuscript autobiography (1927), pp. 23, 35, 39, and unpaged fragments, NYPL; Pinet, *Ornement de la durée,* 19–20.

15. Studio Isadora Duncan program, September 10, 1926; LF to Cromwell, May 25, June 1, 1927, NYPL; Duncan, *My Life,* 94–99; Flanner, *Paris Was Yesterday,* 28, 34; Hyde, ed., *Oscar Wilde,* 262–63.

16. LF to Nelson Morris, April 5, 1927, NYPL; Etienne Bricot in *Le Gaulois,* January 7, 1928, and Maurice-Verne in *Paris soir,* January 9, 1928, clippings, Arsenal.

17. René Lara in *Le Gaulois,* Jean Masson in *Journal,* Pierre Lazareff in *Midi,* all January 3, 1928, clippings, Arsenal; *New York Tribune,* January 3, 1928, clipping, NYPL; *Chicago Herald and Examiner,* January 15, 1928, clipping, SFPALM.

18. Eve Curie to GB, January 2, 1928, Maryhill; *Marcellais,* January 3, *Paris soir,* January 5, 9, *Irene,* January 5, *Volonté,* January 5, and *Excelsior,* January 6, 1928, clippings, Arsenal; *New York Times,* January 5, 1928, p. 29, c. 4.

EPILOGUE

1. Louis Paston to Whiting, February 24, 1928, CMA; *La Vie parisienne,* July 15, 1933, and *Quotidien,* June 29, 1934, clippings, Opéra; *Le Jour,* August 1, 1934, clipping, Arsenal; Sisley Huddleston, *Paris Salons, Cafés, Studios: Being Social, Artistic and Literary Memories* (Philadelphia: Lippincott, 1928), 257.

2. Scharlach, *Big Alma,* 174–75; Marie, *Story of My Life,* 2:172.

3. Scharlach, *Big Alma,* 249–51, 256; "Almighty Alma: Colorful Personality Plays Major Role in Maryhill Founding," *Maryhill Quarterly* 10 (fall 1993): 1–2.

4. Walter Terry, "The Legacy of Isadora Duncan and Ruth St. Denis," *Dance Perspectives,* no. 5 (1959): 30, quoted in Kraus, *History of the Dance,* 146; Hollywood Bowl program, August 3, 1954, Maryhill.

5. "In Celebration of Loie Fuller" program, 1977, and *Northwest Magazine,* January 22, 1978, clipping, Maryhill; M. Harris, *Loïe Fuller,* passim; *Richmond Times-Dispatch,* March 11, 1979, and *Richmond News-Leader,* March 12, 1979, clippings, Virginia Museum of Fine Arts.

6. See, for example, Borsi and Godoli, *Paris Art Nouveau,* 169–72; Brunhammer et al., *Art Nouveau,* 112, 164, 486; Garner, *Art Nouveau Collectables,* 68, 75–76, 114, 116, 117, 118; Haslam, *In the Nouveau Style,* 55; Julian, *Triumph of Art Nouveau,* 88–90, 174–75; Masini, *Art Nouveau,* 42–44, 45, 46; Robert Schmutzler, *Art Nouveau,* 9–10, 45, 229; Selz and Constantine, eds., *Art Nouveau,* 16; and Silverman, *Art Nouveau in Fin-de-Siècle France,* 298–300.

7. Pinet, *Ornement de la durée,* 24–67.

8. Anna Kisselgoff in the *New York Times,* September 21, 1988, clipping, NYPL.

9. Unidentified New York paper, clipping, and LF, autobiographical fragment, 1927, NYPL; *Berliner,* January 3, 1928, and *Le Gaulois,* January 7, 1928, clippings, Arsenal; Lucien Descaves, "Après les obsèques," *L'Intransigeant,* January 8, 1928, p. 1.

10. *New York Times,* January 15, 1928, pt. 8, p. 5, c. 1; Georges Martin in *Volonté,* January 3, 1928, and Michel Georges-Michel in *Paris soir,* January 5, 1928, clippings, Arsenal; André Rouveyre in *Mercure de France* 202 (February 15, 1928): 173–75.

11. Margot Fonteyn, *The Magic of Dance* (New York: Knopf, 1979), 92; Michel Fokine, *Memoirs of a Ballet Master,* trans. by Vitale Fokine (Boston: Little, Brown, 1961), 158, quoted in Blair, *Isadora,* 450.

12. Kendall, *Where She Danced,* 58, 85; Don McDonagh, *The Rise and Fall and Rise of Modern Dance* (New York: Outerbridge & Dienstfrey, 1970), 101–2.

13. Alberto Dallal, *La Mujer en la danza,* 38–39, 44–45.

BIBLIOGRAPHY

ARCHIVAL SOURCES

NEW YORK PUBLIC LIBRARY FOR THE PERFORMING ARTS, Lincoln Center, New York. By far the largest treasury of Loie Fuller documents. "Papers, 1892–1913," comprising 704 items, including most of the original manuscript of the LF memoirs. The "Loie Fuller Collection," approximately 1,800 items: correspondence with Gabrielle Bloch, Queen Marie, Alma Spreckels, and others, together with additional records. Also miscellaneous materials and the Robinson Locke scrapbook of press clippings concerning LF. (Robinson Locke, a newspaperman, drama critic, and collector of theater memorabilia, was a son of David Ross Locke, the publisher of the *Toledo Blade* and a humorist whose pen name was Petroleum Vesuvius Nasby.)

ARCHIVES OF THE MUSÉE RODIN, Paris. Letters from LF to Rodin and others, letters of Emilia Cimino referring to LF, and other documents.

ARCHIVES OF THE MARYHILL MUSEUM OF ART, Goldendale, Washington. LF correspondence with Queen Marie, Sam Hill, and Alma Spreckels; also ephemera.

ARCHIVES OF THE CLEVELAND MUSEUM OF ART, Cleveland, Ohio. Correspondence of LF and the museum's director and friends, mainly concerning LF's debt; also printed material.

BIBLIOTHÈQUE NATIONALE, Paris. Forty-odd letters of LF in the papers of Pierre and Marie Curie, Anatole France, Raymond Poincaré, and Joseph Reinach. Also files of *Le Figaro, L'Echo de Paris,* and other French periodicals.

ARCHIVES OF THE MUSÉE D'ORSAY, Paris. Approximately a dozen LF letters.

HUNTINGTON LIBRARY, San Marino, California. One LF letter.

PRIVATE COLLECTION of Richard and Marcia Current, South Natick, Massachusetts. Four LF letters.

BIBLIOTHÈQUE DE L'ARSENAL, Paris. Dossier Rondel and other clippings from French periodicals, including especially LF obituaries and reports of her performances.

BIBLIOTHÈQUE DE L'OPÉRA, Paris. Clippings regarding LF performances in Paris.

THEATRE MUSEUM, London. Clippings from English and French periodicals regarding LF performances.

NEWSPAPER LIBRARY, London. *The Stage* and other English theater periodicals containing reports of LF performances.

SAN FRANCISCO PERFORMING ARTS LIBRARY AND MUSEUM, San Francisco. Clippings concerning LF from San Francisco and Oakland newspapers.

HINSDALE HISTORICAL SOCIETY, Hinsdale, Illinois. Transcripts of articles concerning LF in Monmouth, Illinois, newspapers; also a variety of published material.

NEWBERRY LIBRARY, Chicago. Local histories and city directories.
CHICAGO HISTORICAL SOCIETY, Chicago. Local histories and collections of Chicago theater programs.
WESTERN RESERVE HISTORICAL SOCIETY, Cleveland, Ohio. Emery May (Holden) Norweb Diary, 1916–18, containing references to LF.
ARCHIVES OF THE CITY AND COUNTY OF NEW YORK, New York City. Records of law cases in which LF was involved.
WELLESLEY COLLEGE LIBRARY, Wellesley, Massachusetts. File of the *New York Times* in addition to other relevant periodicals and books.

In the notes of the present book, clippings from the repositories listed above are cited extensively but often incompletely, since many of the periodicals are inadequately identified. Only a few of the clippings are mentioned in the following list of books and articles, a highly selective list, confined to items that have had some relevance for this work.

BOOKS AND ARTICLES

Alexandre, Arsène. "Le Théâtre de la Loïe Fuller." *Le Théâtre* 4 (Paris, August 11, 1900): 23–25 [clipping, Theatre Museum, London].
Anet, Claude. "Loïe Fuller in French Sculpture." *Architectural Record* 13 (Chicago, March 1903): 270–78 [clipping, Maryhill Museum].
Auerbach, Nina. *Ellen Terry: Player in Her Time*. New York: Norton, 1987.
Battersby, Martin. *Art Nouveau*. Middlesex: Hamlyn, 1969.
Becker, Vivienne. *Art Nouveau Jewelry*. New York: Dutton, 1985.
Bergman, Gösta M. *Lighting in the Theatre*. Stockholm: Almquist & Wiksell; Totowa, N.J.: Rowman & Littlefield, 1977.
Bizet, René. "Les Conquêtes de Loïe Fuller." *L'Intransigeant*, July 2, 1925 [clipping, Bibliothèque de l'Arsenal].
Blair, Fredrika. *Isadora: Portrait of the Artist as a Woman*. New York: McGraw-Hill, 1986.
Bob, Tammie. "Loïe Fuller: Du Page's Dancing Daughter." *Du Page Magazine*, December 1987, 56–58 [clipping, Hinsdale Historical Society].
Borsi, Franco, and Ezio Godoli. *Paris Art Nouveau: Architecture et décoration*. Paris: Marc Vokar, 1989.
Bouyer, Raymond. "L'Art aux Folies-Bergère: La Loïe Fuller." *L'Artiste*, October–November–December 1898, 357–65 [clipping, Musée Rodin].
Brandstetter, Gabriele, and Brygida Maria Ochaim. *Loïe Fuller: Tanz, Licht-Spiel, Art Nouveau*. Freiburg im Breisgau: Rombach, 1989.
Brandt, Frederick. *Late 19th and Early 20th Century Decorative Arts: The Sydney and Frances Lewis Collection in the Virginia Museum of Fine Arts*. Richmond: Virginia Museum of Fine Arts, 1985.

Brody, Elaine. *Paris: The Musical Kaleidoscope, 1870–1925.* New York: Braziller, 1987.
Brunhammer, Yvonne, et al. *Art Nouveau Belgium France: Catalogue of an Exhibition Organized by the Institute for the Arts, Rice University, and the Art Institute of Chicago.* Houston: Institute for the Arts, Rice University, 1976.
Butler, Ruth. *Rodin: The Shape of Genius.* New Haven, Conn.: Yale University Press, 1993.
"The Career of a Dancer: La Loïe Fuller on Herself." *Black and White,* London, January 25, 1896, 118 [clipping, Theatre Museum, London].
Castle, Charles. *The Folies-Bergère.* New York: Franklin Watts, 1985.
Charlot, André. "Une Loïe Fuller qu'on ne connait pas." *Le Monde illustré,* Paris, September 19, 1903 [clipping, Bibliothèque de l'Opéra].
"A Chat with Miss Loïe Fuller," *Sketch,* London, April 12, 1893, 642–43.
Cherniavsky, Felix. *The Salome Dancer: The Life and Times of Maud Allan.* Toronto: McClelland & Stewart, 1991.
Clarétie, Jules. "La Vie à Paris." *Le Temps,* November 8, 1907 [clipping, Bibliothèque de l'Opéra].
Cocteau, Jean. *Souvenir Portraits: Paris in the Belle Epoque.* New York: Paragon House, 1990 (originally published in French, 1935).
Covielle. "Danse, musique, lumière chez la Loïe Fuller." *L'Eclair,* May 5, 1914 [clipping, Bibliothèque de l'Opéra].
Curie, Eve. *Madame Curie.* Translated by Vincent Sheean. Garden City, N.Y.: Doubleday, Doran, 1937.
Dallal, Alberto. *La mujer en la danza.* Mexico City: Panorama, 1990.
Darling, Harriet Tarbox. "And the First Was Loie: The Real Story of How an American Artist Created Her Contribution to the Dance." *Dance,* March 1926, 14–15, 58.
Derval, Paul. *Folies-Bergère.* Translated by Lucienne Hill. New York: Dutton, 1955.
Doucet, Jérôme. "Miss Loïe Fuller." *La Revue illustrée,* November 1, 1903 [clipping, New York Public Library for the Performing Arts].
Duncan, Isadora. *My Life.* New York: Liveright, 1927.
Flanner, Janet. *Paris Was Yesterday: 1925–1939.* Edited by Irving Drutman. New York: Viking Press, 1972.
The Editor. "La Loie Fuller and Her Artistic Advertisements." *The Poster,* February 1899, 69–74 [clipping, Theatre Museum, London].
Fonteyn, Margot. *The Magic of Dance.* New York: Knopf, 1979.
Fuller, Loie. "Alexandre Dumas at Marly." *Black and White* 10 (London, December 7, 1895): 726.
———. "Dances That Inspire." *Chicago Record,* February 27, 1910, Sunday magazine, 5–6 [clipping, Hinsdale Historical Society].
———. "Eighteen Years of Dancing." *The Green Book Album,* March 1910, 656–63 [clipping, Robinson Locke Scrapbook].

———. *Fifteen Years of a Dancer's Life, with Some Account of Her Distinguished Friends.* London: Herbert Jenkins, 1913.

Gadan, Francis, and Robert Maillard, eds. *Dictionary of Modern Ballet.* New York: Tudor, 1959.

Garner, Philippe. *Art Nouveau Collectables.* Secaucus, N.J.: Chartwell, 1989.

———. *Emile Gallé.* New York: Rizzoli, 1990.

Goodwin, Nat C. *Nat Goodwin's Book.* Boston: Richard G. Badger, 1914.

Gosling, Nigel. *The Adventurous World of Paris, 1900–1914.* New York: Morrow, 1978.

Griffith, Mrs. M. "Loïe Fuller: The Inventor of the Serpentine Dance." *Strand Magazine* 7 (London, May 1894), 540–45.

Grunfeld, Frederic V. *Rodin: A Biography.* New York: Holt, 1987.

Harris, Margaret Haile. *Loïe Fuller: Magician of Light.* Richmond: Virginia Museum of Fine Arts, 1979.

———. "Loïe Fuller: The Myth, the Woman, and the Artist." *Arts in Virginia* 20 (fall 1979): 16–29.

Harris, Nathaniel. *Art Nouveau.* New York: Exeter Books, 1987.

Haslam, Malcolm. *In the Nouveau Style.* Boston: Little, Brown, 1990.

Hawley, Henry H. "Loïe Fuller and the Cleveland Museum of Art." *News & Calendar: The Cleveland Museum of Art* 20 (March–April 1980): 2–4.

Henderson, Mary C. *Theater in America.* New York: Abrams, 1986.

Hubbard, Laura. "A High Priestess of Terpsichore." *Vogue,* September 1, 1913 [clipping, Robinson Locke Scrapbook].

Huddleston, Sisley. *Paris Salons, Cafés, Studios: Being Social, Artistic and Literary Memories.* Philadelphia: Lippincott, 1928.

Johnson, Lincoln F., Jr. "The Light and Shape of Loie Fuller." *Baltimore Museum of Art News* 20 (October 1956): 13.

Julian, Philippe. *The Triumph of Art Nouveau: Paris Exhibition, 1900.* New York: Larousse, 1974.

Kendall, Elizabeth. *Where She Danced.* New York: Knopf, 1979.

Kermode, Frank. "Loïe Fuller and the Dance before Diaghilev." *Partisan Review* 28 (January–February 1961): 48–75.

Kraus, Richard. *History of the Dance in Art and Education.* Englewood Cliffs, N.J.: Prentice-Hall, 1969.

Legrand-Chabrier. "La Loïe Fuller d'une exposition à l'autre." *L'Art Vivant,* November 1, 1925, 26–29 [clipping, Musée Rodin].

Lista, Giovanni. *La Scène futuriste.* Paris: Centre de la Recherche Scientifique, 1989.

———. *Loïe Fuller: Danseuse de la Belle Epoque.* Paris: Stock, 1994. [See Bibliographical Note below.]

Lorrain, Jean. *Poussières de Paris.* Paris: Ollendorf, 1899.

Lyonnet, Henry. "Fuller (Miss Loïe)," *Larousse mensuel*, July 1928, 757–58 [clipping, Musée Rodin].

McDonagh, Don. *The Rise and Fall and Rise of Modern Dance*. New York: Outerbridge & Dienstfrey, 1970.

McIlvaine, Mabel, ed. *Reminiscences of Chicago during the Great Fire*. Chicago: Donnelly, 1915.

Marie, Queen of Roumania. *The Story of My Life*. New York: Scribner's, 1934.

———. *Ordeal: The Story of My Life*. New York: Scribner's, 1935.

Marx, Roger. "Chorégraphie: Loïe Fuller," *La Revue encyclopédique*, February 1, 1893, cols. 106–10 [clipping, Bibliothèque de l'Opéra].

———. *La Loïe Fuller*. Paris: Maire, 1904. ("Gypsograph" by Pierre Roche, with preface by Anatole France.)

———. "Loïe Fuller." Preface by Anatole France. *Les Arts et la vie* 3 (Paris, May 1905): 265–73; (June 1905): 352–57 [clipping, New York Public Library for the Performing Arts]. (Same text as in the "gypsograph" above.)

———. "Une Rénovatrice de la danse." Preface by Anatole France. *Le Musée: Revue d'art mensuelle* 4 (Paris, March 1907): 91–114. (Same text as above.)

Masini, Lara-Vinca. *Art Nouveau*. Secaucus, N.J.: Chartwell, 1984.

Mauclair, Camille. "Sada Yacco et Loïe Fuller." *La Revue blanche*, Paris, October 15, 1900, 277–83 [clipping, Theatre Museum, London].

Maurois, André. *The Titans: A Three-Generation Biography of the Dumas*. New York: Harper, 1957.

Morinni, Clare de. "Loie Fuller, The Fairy of Light." *Dance Index* 1 (March 1942): 39–51.

Morton, Hugh. "Loïe Fuller and Her Strange Art." *Metropolitan Magazine*, New York, ca. 1896, 277–83 [clipping, New York Public Library for the Performing Arts].

Nye, David E. *Electrifying America: Social Meanings of a New Technology, 1880–1940*. Cambridge: MIT Press, 1990.

Odell, George C. D. *Annals of the New York Stage*. 15 vols. New York: Columbia University Press, 1927–49.

Pakula, Hannah. *The Last Romantic: A Biography of Queen Marie of Roumania*. New York: Simon & Schuster, 1984.

Parker, John. *The Green Room Book, or Who's Who on the Stage*. 4th ed. London: T. Sealey Clark, 1909.

Pinet, Hélène. *Ornement de la durée: Loïe Fuller, Isadora Duncan, Ruth St. Denis, Adorée Villany*. Paris: Musée Rodin, 1987.

Quinn, Susan. *Marie Curie: A Life*. New York: Simon & Schuster, 1995.

Rearick, Charles. *Pleasures of the Belle Epoque: Entertainment and Festivity in Turn-of-the-Century France*. New Haven, Conn.: Yale University Press, 1985.

Rivollet, André. "La Dernière incarnation de Miss Loïe Fuller." *Le Gaulois,* October 16, 1922 [clipping, Bibliothèque de l'Arsenal].
Rodin, Auguste. *Correspondance de Rodin.* Edited by Alain Beausine et al. 4 vols. Paris: Musée Rodin, 1992.
Roger-Marx, Claude. "Les Danses de Loïe Fuller et d'Isadora Duncan." *Comoedia illustré,* February 1912, 320–21 [clipping, New York Public Library for the Performing Arts].
———. "Loïe Fuller et son école," *Comoedia illustré* 9 (May 20, 1914): 739–41.
Rouveyre, André. "Loïe Fuller." *Mercure de France* 202 (February 15, 1928): 173–75.
Ruchty, George E., Jr. *The Fullers of Fullersburg, 1834–1923.* Hinsdale: Hinsdale Historical Society, 1978.
Russell, Don. *The Life and Legends of Buffalo Bill.* Norman: University of Oklahoma Press, 1960.
Sawada, Suketaro. *Little Hanako.* Nagoya, Japan: Chunichi, 1984.
Scharlach, Bernice. *Big Alma: San Francisco's Alma Spreckels.* San Francisco: Scottwall Associates, 1990.
Schmutzler, Robert. *Art Nouveau.* New York: Abrams, n.d. (originally published in Germany, 1962).
Sell, Henry Blackman, and Victor Weybright. *Buffalo Bill and the Wild West.* New York: Oxford University Press, 1955.
Selz, Peter, and Mildred Constantine, eds. *Art Nouveau: Art and Design at the Turn of the Century.* New York: Museum of Modern Art, 1959.
Seroff, Victor. *The Real Isadora.* New York: Dial Press, 1971.
Shapiro, Barbara. *Pleasures of Paris: Daumier to Picasso.* Boston: Museum of Fine Arts and David R. Godine, 1991.
Silverman, Debora L. *Art Nouveau in Fin-de-Siècle France.* Berkeley and Los Angeles: University of California Press, 1989.
Sommer, Sally R. "Loïe Fuller." *Drama Review* 19 (March 1975): 53–67.
———. "Loïe Fuller's Art of Music and Light." *Dance Chronicle* 4 (1981): 389–401.
———. "The Stage Apprenticeship of Loïe Fuller." *Dance Scope* 12 (fall–winter 1977–78): 23–34.
Tindal, Marcus. "Queen of All Dancers." *Pearson's Magazine,* 1901, 595–98 [clipping, Maryhill Museum].
Tompkins, Eugene, and Quincy Kilby. *The History of the Boston Theatre, 1854–1901.* Boston: Houghton Mifflin, 1908.
Toulouse-Lautrec: Prints and Posters from the Bibliothèque Nationale. Paris: Bibliothèque Nationale, 1991.
Tuhy, John E. *Sam Hill: The Prince of Castle Nowhere.* Goldendale, Wash.: Maryhill Museum of Art, 1992.
Wearing, J. P., ed. *The London Stage, 1890–1899: A Calendar of Plays and Players.* 2 vols. Metuchen, N.J.: Scarecrow Press, 1976.

Wilde, Oscar. *Oscar Wilde: Plays, Prose and Poems*. Edited by H. Montgomery Hyde. London: Orbis, 1982.

BIBLIOGRAPHICAL NOTE

The strength of Giovanni Lista's *Loïe Fuller* consists in its exposition and analysis of her performances, particularly those in Europe. The weakness of the book is to be found mainly in its treatment of her personal life, especially her earlier (and later) years in the United States. Of the following examples of factual errors, some are repetitions of those previously published, while others are new additions to the list. The author does not cite his sources, so it is usually impossible to know the basis, if any, for his statements.

The name Delilah is consistently misspelled as "Dalilah," and Reuben as "Ruben" or "Ruby."

Page 40. Lista says that Loie became a professional actress in Chicago in the 1860s. "Enfant prodige, la petite Loïe . . . déclamait Shakespeare," etc. Except for Loie's much later reminiscences, there is no evidence for this.

Page 44. "La famille s'installa donc à Monmouth . . . dans une ferme disposant d'un terrain assez vaste que Ruby fit aménager en ménage pour les chevaux destinés aux rodéos." In reality, when the Fullers moved to Monmouth they did not settle on a farm big enough for Reuben to raise horses for rodeos or on any other farm. The family lived in town in a hotel that he owned and operated.

Page 46. "A Monmouth. . . . Bien des années plus tard, elle raconta que lorsque la neige était tombée . . . ses deux frères se ralayaient pour l'emmener à l'école sur leurs épaules." Now, Loie was thirteen and her younger brother seven when they arrived in Monmouth. It is not likely that a seven- or eight-year-old boy, taking turns with an older brother, carried a thirteen- or fourteen-year-old sister over the snow to school on his shoulders.

Page 48. "Ruby . . . vendit la ferme . . . pour s'installer à nouveau à Chicago . . . il ouvrit cette fois-ci le Fuller's Museum, une taverne-saloon qui proposait boissons et spectacles. Le soir Loïe y dansait." In fact, Reuben operated the Fuller House in Chicago *before* moving to Monmouth, not afterward, and it was an ordinary boardinghouse, not some kind of "taverne-saloon" or nightclub, with Loie dancing for the customers.

Page 48. "Une année plus tard, le 24 mars 1874, Loïe débute officiellement sa carrière en participant à un recital dramatique de l'Academy of Music de Chicago." The chronology here is awry: the Fullers did not leave Chicago for Monmouth until 1875; they could hardly have been back in Chicago for a year by 1874. In any case, there is no good reason to believe that Loie began her professional career at the age of twelve—and Lista has already said (see page 40 above) that she began it even earlier!

Page 50. When Loie toured with Buffalo Bill (in 1883, Lista erroneously dates it):

"Son père . . . vient d'acheter une orangerie en Florida. . . . Isolé en Floride, il continue à soutenir financièrement les efforts de sa fille." Actually, Reuben was in no position to support Loie financially during the 1880s; she most likely was helping to suport *him*.

Page 54. Lista refers to "une note manuscrite où elle indiquait: 'La seule grande tragédie de ma vie qui aboutit à l'assassinat de mon père.'" He adds: "Le mystère est ici impénétrable." But the mystery is not impenetrable at all. The great tragedy of Loie's life, which culminated in the murder of her father, as she saw it, is explained in the present work.

Pages 59–61. Here is a very confused and inaccurate account of the "marriage" of Loie and William B. Hayes. According to Lista, Reuben died and could no longer finance his daughter; that is why she turned to Hayes for financial support. A "pasteur" with a Bible officiated at the marriage, and it took place *before* Loie and William Morris went to the West Indies. All this is wrong.

Page 72. "La dernière semaine du mois de décembre 1890. . . . Loïe entre ainsi dans la Gaiety Theater [sic] Company où, pendant dix-huit mois, elle remplaça des danseuses comme Letty Lind et Florence Saint-John avant de jouer sous son véritable nom dans les opérettes." This is not borne out by contemporary records, which show that Loie did not join the Gaiety Theatre Company during the last week of December 1890 and remain for eighteen months substituting for such dancers as Letty Lind and Florence Saint-John before she played anywhere in London under her own name.

Page 74. "Cette difficile période londonienne . . . prend fin en juillet 1891. Loïe est alors en mesure de rentrer à New York." Here the author contradicts himself: Loie could not very well have remained with the Gaiety Company for eighteen months if she joined it in late December 1890 and left London about six months later—in July 1891.

Pages 80–81. "Loïe propose en vain ses nouvelles danses dans différents théâtres . . . elle s'addresse enfin à William B. Hayes en le suppliant de l'aider encore une fois. . . . Il refuse. . . . Loïe ne comprend pas. . . . Sa fureur est telle qu'elle pense aussitôt à la pire des vengeances. Elle dénonce William B. Hayes pour bigamie." This is a fanciful and wholly erroneous account of Loie's case against Hayes. She charged him with bigamy not because he refused to give her financial aid when she was trying to persuade theaters to take her and her serpentine dance. She was already performing her dance in *Uncle Celestin* when the trial began. From Lista's account the reader would get no inkling of the true origin and outcome of the trial.

Pages 169–71. Here Lista discusses what he imagines is a lesbian love affair between Loie and a mysterious "Great Lady" about February or March 1893. Speculating as to the identity of the lady, he thinks she may have been the Countess Wolska. As his source, he refers to a chapter of Loie's manuscript memoirs that he says the publisher censored. An examination of the manuscript reveals a portion headed "My experience with a great lady." It begins: "I remember once, before I was known as La Loïe, a very great lady took me up, & patronized me." She proceeds to tell how she at first thought it would be great to have such a patron but soon found the woman so dictatorial as to be intolerable. This happened "before I was known as La Loïe"— that is, before her Paris breakthrough of November 1892, and not in February or March 1893. There is no hint of homosexuality in the anecdote, and it was not censored by the publisher. It was simply omitted because, like a number of other autobiographical anecdotes that Loie prepared for her book, it did not add up to much.

Pages 196–99. Here are descriptions of Loie's dances in the United States in 1893, but no mention of her role as an impresario with a failed play.

Pages 304–5. "En mai 1898 . . . Loïe décida de laisser le Grand-Hôtel . . . pour s'installer avec Gab dans un hôtel particulier au 24, rue Cortambert . . . une grande fête . . . Gab figurait parmi l'assistance." There is no reason to believe that in May 1898 Gabrielle Bloch moved in with Loie or attended the housewarming. In the original manuscript of her memoirs, as written in 1907, Loie said: "For eight years Gab & I have lived together, that is we have been as closely associated as two 'sisterly' sisters." She did not say that, ever since 1899, they had "lived together" in the sense of occupying the same house. The evidence indicates that Loie and Gab had separate residences throughout the pair's thirty-year relationship.

Page 314. "Et Rodin . . . n'arrivera pas à réaliser la sculpture de la danseuse américaine." But there is evidence that Rodin did, in fact, eventually make a bronze head of Loie.

Page 316. "Les expériences ou l'éducation de Loïe ont été profondément marquées, on le sait, par les idées et les théories du spiritualisme américain," Lista states. "C'est en effet sur cette base idéologique, c'est-à-dire à partir de la détermination du physique par le spirituel que Loïe Fuller a établi sa propre poétique de l'art et de la danse." There is no real foundation for these statements that Loie's education was deeply influenced by American spiritualism and that her conception of art and the dance was based on a belief in the determination of the physical by the spiritual. This is one of a number of fanciful interpretations by Lista.

Page 507. Lista says that, after the outbreak of World War I, Loie went to San Francisco to perform with her troupe at the Panama-Pacific Exposition and thus met Alma Spreckels: "La danseuse entre ainsi en contact avec . . . Alma." In fact, Loie had met Alma in Paris and first went to San Francisco to see her.

Page 591. "La rupture fut alors consommée, aussi violente, rapide, et brutale que leur relation avait été longue et profonde." This is an exaggeration. Between Loie and Queen Marie there was in 1926 no breakup so quick, violent, or complete as Lista here asserts.

Bibliography

INDEX

Page numbers appearing in italic type refer to pages which contain photographs.

Academy of Music (Baltimore), 201
Academy of Music (Philadelphia), 102
Africans, Fuller on, 173–74
Aide Civile et Militaire Belge, 262, 264
Aladdin, or The Wonderful Lamp (play), 20–21, 95
Albert I (king of Belgium), 236
d'Alençon, Emilienne, 58, 72, 74, 111, 134
Alexander (grand duke of Russia), 324
Alexandre, Arsène, 5, 134–35, 302
Allan, Maud: as dancer, 178, 201, 205, 341; as Fuller's student, 194; homosexuality of, 329
American National Committee for Roumanian Relief, 248
Ames, William, 10
anti-Semitism, 160, 283–84, 287, 288
arc lamp, for stage lighting, 94–95
Architectural Record, 138
Aronson, Rudolph, 33, 41–42
Art Deco, 303
Art Nouveau; contrasted with Art Deco, 303; decline of, 139–40; Fuller as personification of, 4, 120, *127*, 127–29, 131–34, 338, 340; Fuller's influence on, 343
Athenaeum Hall (London), 29
Auburtin, Jean-François, 344
audience, make-up of, 52–53, 100, 101, 180, 204
automobile, Fuller's experience with, 168–69, *169*
Avenue Theatre (London), 30
Axen, Gertrude von, 199, 202, 203

Bac, Fernand Sigismond, 130, 344
Baker, Josephine, 5, 295–96
The Ballet of Light (Fuller), 194, 199, 203, 337
Ballets Russes, 209–10, 211–12, 341
Bardey, Henriette, 257
Bardey, Jeanne, 257
Barrison Sisters, 72–74, 111
Barry, Judith, 338
Barrymore, Maurice, 103
Bates, Henry W., 24
Battersby, Martin, 137
Beaumont, Clara, 27
Beckett, Samuel Joshua, 344

Beckley, Zoë, 310
La Belle au bois dormant (play), 185
Bénédite, Léonce, 258, 261
Beresford, S., 238, 293
Bernhardt, Sarah; as actor, 79–80, 142; Fuller's relationship with, 85, 90, 91, 132, *133*, 185, 312; and Paris Universal Exposition, 134
Bernstamm, Leopold, 344
Berton, Pierre, 80
Beuret, Rose, 233, 260; Fuller's relationship with, 259–61; as Rodin's mistress, 122, 123, 154, 217, 218, 258
Bial, Albert, 100, 101
Big Pony (play), 20
Bijou Opera House (New York), 17–20
Bing, Samuel, 120
Birkhead, May, 316, 319
The Birth of a Nation (film), 214
Black, Susan, 10
Black and White (magazine), 85, 91
The Black Crook (play), 20
Blavatsky, Helena Petrovna, 312
Bloch, Gabrielle, 263; business partnership with Fuller, 160, 238, 274, 311, 321–23; charity work by, 236–37, 242–43, 261–62, 264, 265; cinematography by, 278; Isadora Duncan on, 149, 329; and Fuller's death, 331–33, 335; and Loie Fuller Dancers, 203, 273, 335; and Queen Marie's American tour, 316, 319; relationship with Fuller, 120–22, 124, 156, 168, 169–71, 189, 206, 207, 228, 230, 241, 284, 288, 296, 299, 310; residences of, 214, 215; and Van Beils, 226–27
Bly, Nellie, 157
Bole, Roberta Holden, 250, 253
Bookprinter, Anna Marie, 344
Boston Herald, 108
Boston Museum of Fine Arts, 343
Boston Opera House, 200–201
Boston Symphony Orchestra, 103
Boston Theatre, 17, 102–3
Boston Transcript, 202
Boston Traveler, 203
Bouffes-Parisiens, Théâtre des (Paris), 208
Bouyer, Raymond, 112
Boyle, Col. Joseph W., 269–70
Bradley, Will, 344

{ 391 }

Brandes, Carl Edvard, 67
Brandon, Olga, 68–69
Brandstetter, Gabriele, 342, 374–75n15
Bratianu, Ion, 268
Bretteville, Pierre de, 277
Brewer, Perceval, 13
Briand, Aristide, 180
Bridges, Roger D., 355n1
Broadway Theatre (New York), 69
The Bronze Age (Rodin), 232
Buckley, L. W., 240–41
Bust of Rochefort (Rodin), 232
Bust of Rodin (Claudel), 159
Butler, Nicholas Murray, 289

Calhoun, Mrs. C. C., 314
California Palace of the Legion of Honor (San Francisco), 276, 297, 300–301, 337
California Theatre (San Francisco), 104
Camille (novel, Dumas), 86
Camille (play), 81
Canada, Fuller performance in, 201
Cantor, Jacob Aaron, 77–78, 215, 226, 238, 284
Caprice (play), 24, 26, 27–29, 28, 32
Carabin, François Rupert, 131, 345
Carmen-up-to-Data (comic opera), 30
Carol II (king of Romania), 320, 333
Carrière, Eugène, 154
Carroll, Col. John H., 313, 318, 319
Carte, Richard D'Oyly, 60
Cartier, Baron de, 263–64
Casino Theatre (New York), 33–35, 41–42, 67
Chalon, Louis, 345
Chance, Maud, 215
Charlot, André, 366n32
Charly, Léon, 54
Chase, Pauline, 178
Cheney, Mamah, 229
Chéret, Jules, 129, 345
Chicago fire, 10, 75
Chicago Press, 110
Chicago Record-Herald, 189
Chicago Tribune, 194
The Chimes of Normandy (play), 26
China, Fuller's unrealized tour in, 103–5
Choubrac, Alfred-Victor, 345
Chute, Paul Jones, 199, 200, 202
Cimino, Emilia, 124–25, 154, 157, 158, 160
Cladel, Judith, 257, 261
Clair, René Chomette, 278
Clarétie, Jules: and Fuller's autobiography, 191; on Fuller's feminism, 326–27; Fuller's relationship with, 141, 142, 176, 195; and Hanako, 185–86; and *The Tragedy of Salome*, 178, 179–80, 182
Clarétie, Mme Jules, 186, 189, 191
Clarke, Mrs. T. Alexander, 197, 200, 206–7, 216, 239
Claudel, Camille, 122, 125, 159
Clemenceau, Georges, 180
Cleveland, Grover, 69
Cleveland Museum of Art, 250, 335, 343
coal gas, for stage lighting, 94
Cochran, Elizabeth Jane, 157
Cody, William F. ("Buffalo Bill"), 14–15, 239, 319
Colin, Paul, 345
Coliseum Theatre (London), 273, 293, 294–95
Collins, Marie, 70
Columbia Theatre (New York), 70
Columbia Theatre (San Francisco), 306
Columbus Theatre (New York), 32
Comédie-Française, 141
Comédie-Parisienne (Paris), 81, 83–84, 96
Commission for the Relief of Belgium, 264
Comstock, Anthony, 205
Constant, Benjamin, 116
Coolidge, Calvin, 315
Coolidge, Mrs. Calvin, 315
cosmetics, named after Fuller, 304
costumes, Fuller's use of, 61–62, 98–99
Coudert, Claude (duchess of Choiseul-Beaupré), 217
Coué, Emile, 327
Critic, 106
Cromwell, William Nelson, 287–88, 298, 316
Crozit, 345
Cummins, Fred, 241
Curie, Eve, 4, 154, 310–11, 312, 331–33
Curie, Irene, 311
Curie, Marie: and Eve, 310–11; Fuller's relationship with, 4, 153–55, 184, 302; and Maryhill Museum, 312
Curie, Pierre, 4, 153–55, 184

Dallal, Alberto, 341
La Dame aux camélias (Mucha), 132, 133
Damia (actress), 278
Dammouse, Albert-Louis, 350
D'Annunzio, Gabriele, 234
"Dante" (Rodin), 216
Danzker, Jo-Anne Birnie, 338
Daughters of the American Revolution, 6
Dawn Frères, 345
Davis, M. C., 10
Dayot, Armand, 233, 244
de Friese, L. H., 270

Index

De Kay, John Winchester, 216
Debussy, Claude, 208
Décorchement, François-Emile, 346
Delibes, Léo, 100
Depew, Chauncey M., 31
d'Humière, Robert, 179
Diaghilev, Sergey, 209, 210
Doucet, Jérôme, 163–65
Dressler, Marie, 103
Druet, Eugène, 125, *126*, 154, 344
Drury Lane Theatre (London), 30
Dubosq, M. J., 95
Duffy, Kate, 10
Dumas, Alexandre (*fils*), 4, 85, 86–90, *89*, 91
Dumas, Alexandre (*père*), 86
Duncan, Isadora: compared with Fuller, 177, 196, 201, 295, 335, 339–42; competition with Fuller of, 194, 229; Comstock's opposition to, 205; on Fuller, 202, 328–29; Fuller's influence on, 4, 149–51, 164; influence on dance of, 210, 211; photos of in exhibition, 338; and Rodin, 148–49
Duncan, Raymond, 331
Duse, Eleanora, 103

L'Echo de Paris, 53, 82, 96, 111, 130
Ecole des Beaux-Arts (Paris), 84, 350
Edison, Thomas A., 95
Elaine (Fuller), 242
electricity, 138. *See also* lighting, stage
Elizabeth (queen of Belgium), 262, 264, 275
Elliot, Howard, 313
Ellis, Harry C., 332, 344
Empire Theatre (Edinburgh), 84

Fairy (dance student of Fuller), 330
Falk, B. J., 344
fashion, Fuller's influence on, 54–55, 67
Felix A. Vincent Comedy Company, 14
Femina, 182
Femina theater (Paris), 206
feminism, Fuller and, 144, 182, 326–27
Ferdinand I (king of Romania), 151, 246, 303, 320
Feure, Georges de, 345
Feyton, Amy, 58
Fifteen Years of a Dancer's Life, with Some Account of Her Distinguished Friends (Fuller), 186–87, 189–92, 216, 342
Le Figaro (Paris): on Fuller, 50, 53, 72, 76, 83; hosts peace commissioners, 113; on Caroline Otero, 74; on Mabelle Stuart, 48
Finesse (dance student of Fuller), 330
Finland, Fuller's performances in, 172
Fireworks (Stravinsky), 208

Flammarion, Camille, 87: death of, 310; relationship with Fuller, 85–86, 197, 227, 234, 302, 312; and Rodin, 90
Flammarion, Mme Camille, 86, 87, 310
Fokine, Michel, 209–10, 211, 340–41
Folies-Bergère (Paris), 47–48, 50–54, 63, 72–74, 76, 111–12
Folies-Bergère/La Loïe Fuller (Chéret), 129
Fonteyn, Margot, 340
Ford Motor Company, 318
France, Anatole: death of, 310; and Fuller's art promotion, 234, 300; relationship with Fuller, 4, 116, 185, 191
Francis Ferdinand (archduke of Austria), 227
French, Gen. John D. P., 236
Friedlander, J. Henry, 84
Fuller, Delbert (brother): childhood of, 10, 14; as electrician for Fuller, 97, 101, 105; as stagehand, 305
Fuller, Delilah Eaton (mother), 87, *188*: death of, 187–89; and Fuller's childhood, 6–7, 10, 14; and William Hayes, 26, 66; poor health of, 63–64, 76, 105, 116, 146; relationship with Fuller, 109, 115; on tour with Fuller, 21–22, 29, 101
Fuller, Frank (brother), 6, 14, 96, 101, 305
Fuller, Ida Pinckney, 58, 70
Fuller, Jacob (grandfather), 6, 7
Fuller, Kate (cousin), 331
Fuller, Loïe, 9, *18*, *28*, *34*, *37*, *49*, *56*, *73*, *82*, *87*, *89*, *107*, *113*, *121*, *123*, *126*, *127*, *133*, *161*, *169*, *173*, *181*, *233*, *251*, *260*, *299*, *332*
artistic philosophy and technique: Art Nouveau, 120, 127, 127–29, 131–34, 139, 338, 340, 343; chemicals, 153, 155–56; compared with Duncan, 177, 196, 201, 295, 335, 339–42; competitors of, 41–43, 58, 70, 194, 209, 213–14, 229, 339–42; costumes, 61–62, 98–99; descriptions of, 55–57, 130, 190; development of, 105–6; incorporation of drama, 78, 80–81; influence on dance of, 65, 339–42; lighting, 20–21, 46, 95–96, 97, 99, 164, 185, 194–95, 213, 276, 279, 330; music, 100; "natural dancing," 194, 195–96, 198; philosophy of dance, 78–79, 211, 339; stage sets, 96, 111, 114–15, 147, 175
attributes and personal life. *See also* Fuller, Loïe, relationships; age of, 57–58, 75, 165, 191, 262; Americanness of, 101, 110, 141, 143, 306, 312; artistic representations of, 54, 112, 120, 124–25, 125–26, 128–32, *136*, *137*, 168, 250, 272, 343–51; character of, 5, 135, 164–65, 253–54, 256, 326; childhood of, 6–14, *9*; com-

Index

{ 393 }

Fuller, Loie (*continued*),
mand of French language, 55, 124, 159–60, 172, *183*; creativity of, 62; death and funeral of, 331–33; ephemera of, 343; feminism, 144, 182, 326–27; homosexuality of, 328–29; illegal marriage to William Hayes of, 24–26, 29, 36–40, 66; illnesses of, 7, 15, 54, 102–3, 163, 184, 185, 186–87, 189, 195, 207, 237, 247, 262, 270–71, 273, 278–79, 298–300, 310, 324, 329–31; injuries of, 112, 116–17, 202; intelligence of, 110–11, 200, 328; name of, 6, 7, 14, 51; photography of, 338, 343–44; physical appearance of, 4–5, 6, 75, 83, 109, 112, 163–64, 203, 262, 297, 306; posthumous commemorations of, 335–39; posthumous reputation of, 339–42; residences of, 10, 11, 13–14, 54, 76, 77, 115–16, 168, 214–15, 301–2, 330; robbery of, 116–17; rumored engagement to Senator Cantor of, 77–78; social entertaining by, 115–16, 184; temperance lecture by, 12

career: art promotion by, 131, 156–60, 225–26, 228, 230–36, 242, 243–44, 254, 255–61, 276–77, 283, 312, 325–26; autobiography, 186–92, 216, 326; beginnings of, 30–31, 32–36, 40–44, 46; charity work by, 11, 22, 53, 105, 206, 208; childhood performances by, 8, 12, 13; cinematography, 278–81, 322–24; dance school, 199, 205; decorative arts, 302–3; diplomacy by, 76–77, 113–14; education and training of, 5, 13, 15, 78–79; and finances, 22, 24, 37, 63–70, 148, 160, 197, 200, 203, 206, 207, 215, 226–27, 230, 235, 238–39, 251, 252–53, 254–55, 281, 282–83, 316, 332; as impresario, 26–27, 64–65, 67–70, 140–44, 147–48, 172, 179, 282; interviews with, 108–10, 163–65; invitation to University of Paris reception, 289; litigation against, 104, 203; litigation brought by, 27, 36–39, 40, 42–43, 134, 203, 287–88; and Loie Fuller Dancers, 194–206, 197, 219, 220, 235, 237–41, 292–95, 304–7, 335; at Panama Pacific International Exposition, 237–42; patents and copyrights by, 43, 61–62, 96; performances by, 14–22, 24–32, 47–55, 64–70, 72–76, 84–85, 100–105, 111–12; as playwright, 175, 177; publicity for, 50, 51–52, 52, 74, 110, 137, 141, 178; reviews of, 17, 18–19, 21, 26, 27–29, 30, 33–36, 50, 52, 67, 69, 81–83, 84, 105–8, 112, 114–15, 135, 142, 143, 147, 176–77, 178, 180–82, 201–3, 208, 209–13, 240, 241, 275, 280–81, 282, 292–93, 295, 304, 307; silk painting, 273, 302; theater built by, 125, 134–38; triumph of, 182; war relief, 230–36, 242, 247–49, 261–65, 270

relationships, 4, 120; with Sarah Bernhardt, 85, 90, 91, 132, 185, 312; with Gabrielle Bloch, 120–21, *121*, 124, 160, 169–71, 189, 206, 207, 228, 230, 238, 241, 274, 284, 288, 296, 299, 310, 311, 321–23; with Emilia Cimino, 157–59; with Jules Clarétie, 141, 142, 176, 191, 195; with the Curie family, 153–55, 184, 302, 310–11; with Alexandre Dumas *fils*, 86–91, *89*; with Isadora Duncan, 149–51, 164; with Camille Flammarion, 85–86, *87*, 227, 234, 302, 312; with Anatole France, 116, 185, 191, 234, 300; with Delilah Fuller, 21–22, 29, 101, 108–9, 115, *188*; with Hanako (Hisako Hohta), 171–75; with Samuel Hill, 283, 302, 310, 311–12, 321; with Marie, queen of Romania, 148, 151–53, 218–20, 247–49, 271, 274–75, 284–89, 296–97, 298, 302–4, 310, 312, 313–21, 327, 331, 333, 336; with Roger Marx, 85, 120, 122, 125, 189, 284; with Auguste Rodin, 116, 120, 122–25, 134, 141, 154–63, 171–75, *173*, 184–85, 189, 198, 216–20, 228, 233, 259–61, 260, 312, 327–28; with Alma Spreckels, 222–25, 235, 242–44, 296, 297–98, 300–301, 310, 312–13, 324, 325; with Van Beils, 226–27, 232, 235, 239; with Sada Yacco, 175

works: *The Ballet of Light,* 194, 199, 203, 337; "Black Lily" (dance), 206; "Bluebird" (dance), 206; "The Boston Blue-Stocking" (essay), 327; "The Butterfly"/"Le Papillon" (dance), 50, 51, *107*; "Dance of Steel," 180, 206; "Dance of the Flowers," 73; "Dance of the Hands," 199, 201, 203; "La danse du Lys," *113*; *Elaine* (pageant), 242; "Fantastic Ballet," 292, 306; "Fantastic Shadows" (dance), 307; *Fifteen Years of a Dancer's Life, with Some Account of Her Distinguished Friends* (autobiography), 186–87, 189–92, 216, 342; *Fifteen Years of My Life* (autobiography), 186–87, 189–92; "Fire Dance"/"La Danse de Feu," 83, 98, 99, 106, 147; "Firmament"/"La Danse du firmament" (dance), 98, 99, 106; "Golliwog's Cakewalk" (dance), 307; *Larks* (play), 15; *The Lily of Life* (film), 278–81, 283, 338; "Lily"/"Le Lis du Nile" (dance), 98, 99; *The Little Japanese*

Index

{ 394 }

Girl (play), 177–78; "The Mighty Sea" (dance), 307, 322; "Mirror dance," 114; "Night"/"La Danse du nuit" (dance), 98–99; "Opal dance," 240; "Pansy Dance," 206; *Quinze ans de ma vie* (autobiography), 186–87, 189–92, 216, 342; *Salomé* (pantomime), 80–85, 82, 96; "Serpentine Dance," 33–35, 34, 41, 43, 48–50, 49, 58–63, 106; "Sorcerer's Dance," 293; *Sur la mer immense* (pageant), 303; *The Tragedy of Salome* (play), 178, 179–82, 181; "Ultraviolet Dance," 206; "Violet"/"La Violette" (dance), 50, 51; *Visions de rêve* (film), 322–23; "White"/"La Danse blanche" (dance), 50, 98, 99, 101, 103; *The World Asks* (book), 320; "xxxx" (dance), 51
Fuller, Mollie, 354n13
Fuller, Reuben (father), 9: death of, 38; and Fuller's childhood, 6–8, 10–11, 13, 14; and William Hayes, 25, 27, 29; on tour with Fuller, 21–22

Gaiety Theatre (London), 29, 30, 59
Gailhard, Pedro, 47
Gallé, Emile, 132
Galtier-Boissière, Jean, 280
Garden Theatre (New York), 67, 69
Garnier, Jean, 346
Gaumont, Léon, 278
Gaumont-Palace Théâtre (Paris), 280
Gautier, F., 346
The Geisha and the Knight (play), 141
George V (king of Great Britain), 268
Georges-Michel, Michel, 340
Germany, Fuller's performance in, 46–47, 168–69
Gérôme, Jean-Léon, 346
Globe Theatre (London), 27, 29
Goodwin, Nat C., 17–20, 103
Graham, Martha, 337, 341
Grand Guignol theater (Paris), 140
Grand Opera House (Brooklyn), 15
Grau, Robert, 67, 69
Great Britain, performances by Fuller in, 27–32, 64–65, 114
Grieg, Edvard, 208
Griffith, D. W., 214
Grün, Jules-Alexandre, 346
Guiffrey, Jean, 302
Guillaume, Henri, 302
Guimard, Hector, 120
Guioché, Eugène, 261
gypsography, 131, 139, 342

Haggard, H. Rider, 21
Hamburg, A., 54
Hamburg, H., 156
Hanako (Hisako Hohta), 171–75, 185, 191
Harris, Margaret Haile, 337, 342, 353n1, 374–75n15
Haskell, Ernest, 346
Hayes, Amelia E., 36, 38, 40, 66
Hayes, Col. William B. (husband), 24–26, 36–40, 65–66, 191
Head of Balzac (Rodin), 159, 258
Head of Saint John the Baptist on a Platter (Rodin), 159, 232
health fads and alternative medicine, 163, 198, 327
Hébertot, Jacques, 295
Heine, Thomas Theodore, 346
Henriette (duchess of Vendôme, princess of Belgium), 262, 264–65, 270, 276, 277, 300
Hill, J. M., 16
Hill, James J., 254
Hill, Mary, 254
Hill, Samuel, 263: Fuller's relationship with, 283, 302, 310, 311–12, 321; and Marie, queen of Romania, 271, 274, 313, 316–17, 319; and Maryhill Museum, 254–57, 325–26, 336, 337
Hippodrome (New York), 307
Hippodrome (Paris), 175–76
Hoetger, Bernhard, 346
Hoffmann, E. T. A., 323
Hold, Hale, 313
Holden, Emery May, 250–52
Hooley's Opera House (Chicago), 16
Hoover, Herbert, 264–65, 269–70
Houssin, Edouard, 76, 131, 346
Hoyt, Charles H., 41
Hoyt & Thomas, 41, 42, 44
Hugo, Victor, 312
Humbug (play), 17
Humphrey, Doris, 341
Hurok, Sol, 311
Huysmans, J. K., 54

Les Idées vivantes (Mauclair), 130
Ingersoll, Robert G., 103
International Dance Biennale (Lyons), 338
International Decorative Arts Exposition (Paris), 303

Japan, Fuller's plans to visit, 146
Japanese performers, 141–44, 146–48, 171–75
Jefferson, Joseph, 103
Joffre, Gen. Joseph J. C., 236
Joffre, Marshal, 312

Index

{ 395 }

Judson, W. T., 10
Juven, Félix, 186

Kahn, Otto, 196–97
Karageorgevich, Bojidar (prince of Serbia), 186–87, 189
Karsavina, Tamara, 209, 211
Kawakami, 141, 146, 147–48
Keating, Anna, 40
Keen, Jule, 15
Kellard, John, 104
Kellogg, Mrs. Vernon, 265
Kendall, Elizabeth, 341
Kesa (play), 147
Kidman, Edward C., 293
Kidman, Minnie, 293
Koster & Bial's Music Hall (New York), 97, 100–101, 146

Lahovary, A. W., 247
Lahovary, Simone, 288, 318–19, 320
Lalique, René, 129, 132
Larche, François-Raoul, 131–32, 346
Larks (Fuller), 15
Larsson, Gotfride, 347
Legrand-Chabrier, 304
Lelong, René, 347
Lemmen, Georges, 347
Léonard, Agathon, 128
Lerolle, Henry, 133, 347
Levasseur, Henri, 347
Levey, Florence, 67
Lévy-Dhurmer, Lucien, 347
Leymarie, Auguste-Louie, 347
Leyton, Marie, 58–59
Li Hung-chang, 103, 104
Lichfield, Richard, 10
lighting: cinematic, 279; for Palace of Legion of Honor, 276; stage, and Fuller, 20–21, 46, 95–96, 97, 99, 146, 164, 185, 194–95, 213, 330, 337; stage, development of, 94–95
The Lily of Life (Fuller), 278–81, 283, 338
The Lily of Life (Marie, queen of Romania), 269, 274–75, 314, 315
limelight, for stage lighting, 94
Lincoln, Abraham, 7
Lind, Letty, 30–31
Lindbergh, Charles A., 326
Little Jack Sheppard (play), 17–19, *18*, 20
The Little Japanese Girl (Fuller), 177–78
Loïe Fuller (Brandstetter and Ochaim), 342
"Loïe Fuller: Magician of Light" (exhibition), 337
Loie Fuller American Museum, Fuller's plans for, 325–26

Loie Fuller Dancers, *197*, *219*: and Gabrielle Bloch, 228, 335; and Marie, queen of Romania, 220; performances by, 194–206, 237–41, 304–7; silk painting by, 273; and Van Biels, 235, 272
"Loïe Fuller Gavotte" (Hamburg), 54
Loie Fuller Theater/Le Théâtre de la Loïe Fuller (Paris), 134–35, *136*, *137*, *138*, 141–43
London Daily Mail, 208
London Times, 287
Lopes-Silva, L., 347
Lorrain, Jean ("Raitif de la Bretonne"), 72, 83, 111, 114–15, 142
Los Angeles Times, 241
Loti, Pierre, 234
Louchet, Charles, 347
Löwenthal, Arthur, 347
Lucas, E. Charles, 347
Lupescu, Magda, 320
Lyric Theatre (London), 114

M. Witmark & Sons, 325
Macdonough Theatre (Oakland), 104
MacKaye, Steele, 22
Madden, Minnie, 27
Mademoiselle Eve (play), 81
Madison Square Theatre (New York), 41–42, 44
Maillard, Léon, 142
Mallarmé, Stéphane, 54
Marchand, Edouard: and Fuller, 48–50, 51, 53, 63–64, 75; as manager of Folies-Bergère, 47, 72, 96, 111–12
Marie Alexandra Victoria (queen of Romania), 285; American tour by, 313–21; Fuller's relationship with, 148, 151–53, 218–20, 247–49, 271, 274–75, 284–89, 296–97, 298, 302–4, 310, 312, 327, 331, 333, 336; and Alma Spreckels, 298; and World War I, 246–49, 268
Mars-Vallet, Marius, 347
Martin, Georges, 339–40
Martin, Marcelle, 236, 257, 259
Marx, Roger: Fuller's relationship with, 85, 120, 122, 125, 189, 284; and Loie Fuller Theater, 134; writing on Fuller by, 55, 81–82, 139, 342, 350
Marx, Mme Roger, 160
Mary (queen consort of Great Britain), 268
Maryhill Museum: commemoration of Fuller at, 336–37, 343; Fuller's role in development of, 254, 255–57, 283, 312, 325–26; Queen Marie of Romania's dedication of, 313, 317
Mason Opera House (Los Angeles), 240

Index

Maspero, G. C. C., 234
Massenet, Jules, 198
Massier, Clément, 347
Mauclair, Camille, 130, 143, 211–12
Maurin, Charles, 347
Mazzo, Aldo, 348
McDonagh, Don, 341
Meltzer, C. H., 80
Mendelssohn, Felix, 195, 208, 212
La Mer (Debussy), 303
Merode, Cléo de, 134
Metchnikoff, Elie, 189
Metropolitan Museum of Art (New York), 343
Metropolitan Opera House (New York), 196–97, 200–201, 202
Meunier, Georges, 130, 348
Mexico, Fuller's tour in, 104–5, 110
Micael-Lévy, C., 348
A Midsummer Night's Dream (Mendelssohn), 195, 208, 212
Milhaud, Darius, 282
Miller, John, 10
Mills, Jenny, 58
Mirbeau, Octave, 154
mirrors, Fuller's use of, 96, 111, 114
modern style. *See* Art Nouveau
Modjeska, Helena, 85, 103
Le Monde illustré, 111
Monmouth Daily Review, 13
Monmouth Weekly Reivew, 12
Moore, Alexander P., 312–13
morality in art, 36, 86, 165, 204–5, 208
Moreau, R., 344
Morgan, John Pierpont, 159
Morinni, Clare de, 377n5
Morris, William, 24–25, 26, 27
Morris-Fuller Company, 25
Morse, Woolson, 20
Morton, Hugh, 108
Moser, Koloman, 348
motion pictures: Gabrielle Bloch's experience with, 335–36; as competition for Fuller, 209, 213–14; Fuller's experience with, 278–81, 322–24
Moulin Rouge (Paris), 322
Mucha, Alphonse, 132, 133
Municipal Casino (Nice), 100
Munsey's Magazine, 59
Musée d'Orsay (Paris), 343, 344
Musée Rodin (Paris), 338, 343–44
Muses. *See* Loie Fuller Dancers
Museum of Modern Art (New York), 343
Museum Villa Stuck (Munich), 338, 343, 344
Musical Courier, 200
My Life (Duncan), 329

National Arts Club (New York), 156–58
National Theater (Washington), 201
National Theatre (Mexico City), 104, 110
"natural dancing," 194, 195–96, 198
Nevada, Emma Wixom ("Western Nightingale"), 149
New York Daily Mirror, 18–19
New York Dramatic Mirror, 27
New York Dramatic News, 65
New York Herald, 189, 316
New York Post, 35
New York Spirit of the Times, 33, 60, 65, 84
New York Sun, 35, 355n3
New York Times: on Fuller's art promotion, 158; on Fuller's artistic influence, 65, 339; on Fuller's personal life, 77, 314, 316, 319; on William Hayes, 66; review of Fuller performances by, 17, 19, 21, 35, 67, 69, 105–6, 201–2, 275, 307
New York World, 35, 316
Niblo's Garden Theater (New York), 21
Nicholas (son of Marie, queen of Romania), 269
Nicholas II (czar of Russia), 172
Nicol, Will ("Nicola the Great"), 137
Nijinsky, Vaslav, 209, 210, 212
Nocturnes (Debussy), 208
Nos Parisiens, 63
Noury, Gaston, 348

Oakland Enquirer, 239
Ochaim, Brygida Maria, 338, 342, 374–75n15
Odéon, Théâtre de l' (Paris), 208
Olympic Theatre (Chicago), 14
Opera Comique (London), 30
Opera House (Harlem), 70
Orazi, Manuel, 137, 348
The Orchestration of Colors (Polignac), 209
Orchidee (dancer), 199, 203, 205
Otero, Caroline, 74, 111, 134
Our Irish Visitors (play), 17
Owen, Robert L., 268, 270

Paderewski, Ignace, 103
Paget-Fredericks, Joseph, 348
Pal (Paléologu, Jean de), 130, 348
Palace Theatre (Paris), 322
Palace Theatre of Varieties (London), 84, 162, 195
Palais de la Danse (Paris), 140
Palais de l'Elysée (Paris), 144
Panama-Pacific International Exposition, 237–38, 239–40
Panama-Pacific International Exposition Company, 230

"Les Parfums Loïe Fuller," 305
Paris Opéra, 47, 95, 275
Paris qui dort, 278
Paris soir, 330
Paris Universal Exposition (1900), 120, 125, 129, 132–38, 140–44
patents and copyrights, 43, 61–62, 96
Pavlova, Anna, 209, 239
Peach (Mademoiselle Pêche), 305, 310, 322, 330
Peer Gynt (Grieg), 208, 212–13
Peter, Victor, 252
Pfeffer, Clara, 349
Pierné, Gabriel, 80, 85, 209, 302, 310
Pierre (marquis de Bretteville), 222
Pinet, Hélène, 328
Pioch, Georges, 210
Plaza Theatre (New York), 203
Poincaré, Madame Raymond, 235, 262
Polignac, Armande de, 209
Poss, Jan, 349
The Poster, 114, 129
Pougy, Liane de, 134
Poulle, Eugène, 86–89
The Prairie Waif (play), 14–15
Primoli (prince of France), 90
The Prodigal Son (Rodin), 232
The Protocols of the Learned Elders of Zion, 286–87
Putnam, Arthur, 230

Quack, M.D. (play), 32
The Queen's Handkerchief (Marie, queen of Romania), 315
Quinze ans de ma vie (Fuller). *See Fifteen Years of a Dancer's Life*

radium, 153, 155, 200, 299
Raguet, Eugène, 174
Reed, Roland, 17
Regaud, Madame Claude, 299
Reissner Stellmacher and Kessler, 349
Renaud, Francis, 349
Renwood, Minnie, 41, 43
Researches on Radioactive Substances (Curie), 184
Revue blanche (Paris), 131
La Revue encyclopédique, 55
La Revue illustrée (Paris), 163
"Ride of the Valkyries" (Wagner), 100
Rider (photographer), 344
Riley, Mrs., 311
Rivière, Théodore, 131, 250, 252, 349
Roche, Pierre: art contributions by, 236; representations of Fuller by, 131, 136, 137, 139, 250, 349–50; on Alma Spreckels, 277; writing on Fuller by, 342
Rochefort, Victor Henri, 116
Rochegrosse, Georges, 80
Rodenbach, Georges, 112
Rodin, Auguste, 173, 233, 260, 350; and Fuller's art promotion, 131, 156–63, 231–34, 257–61; on Fuller's performance, 195; Fuller's recollections of, 191, 327–28; and Hanako, 174–75; inspiration of dance by, 199; introduction of to Fuller's friends, 154–55, 197, 250; at Paris Universal Exposition, 132; relationship with Fuller of, 4, 116, 120, 122–25, 134, 141, 154–63, 171–75, 184–85, 189, 198, 216–20, 228, 259–61, 312, 327–28; and Alma Spreckels, 222, 224–25, 237, 243–44; and Sada Yacco, 142
Roger-Marx, Claude, 120, 210–11
Rogers, Eunice L. (cousin), 22
Rothschild, Baron Henri de, 303
La Roulotte theater (Paris), 140
Rouveyre, André, 340
Royal Bayreuth Heliosine, 350
Rudier, Eugène, 232
Russell, Henry, 195, 198
Russell, Lillian, 22, 313
Russia, Fuller's cancelled tour in, 63–64

Sacchetto, Rita, 199, 202
Sada Yacco. *See* Yacco, Sada
Saikoku (play), 147
Saint Nicholas Garden (New York), 160
Salome (artistic subject), 79, 178
Salomé (Fuller), 80–85, 82, 85, 96
San Francisco Call, 240
San Francisco Chronicle, 104, 109
Sanden, Irene, 199, 203
Saudades do Brasil (Milhaud), 282
Sauvage, Henri, 134
Savoy Theatre (London), 171, 178
Schmitt, Florent, 179
Schultz, Lottie, 13
Sells-Floto Circus & Buffalo Bill Co., 239
"Serpentine Dance" (Fuller), 34, 49. *See also* Fuller, Loie, works; artistic representations of, 157; critics on, 106; development of, 33–35, 58–63; Fuller's ownership of, 41, 43, 48–50
Séverin, Fernand, 112
Séverine (writer), 261
Sewell, Robert, 10
Shaftsbury Theatre (London), 30
Shaw, Alice, 67
Shawn, Ted, 337
She (play), 21, 95, 147

Index

The Shogun: A Tale of Old Japan (play), 146
silk painting, 273, 302
Silvestre, Armand, 79, 80, 81, 85
Simpson, Jean, 161
Simpson, John W., 161
Simpson, Kate, 161
The Sirens (Rodin), 232
Sketch, 57, 64, 293
skirt dance, 30, 32
Société Nationale des Beaux-Arts, 277
Sorère, Gabrielle. *See* Bloch, Gabrielle
Souday, Paul, 210
Sousa, John Philip, 103
South America, Fuller's performances in, 168
Spanish-American War, Fuller on, 113–14
Spreckels, Adolph B., 222, 242, 244
Spreckels, Alma Emma Charlotte Corday le Normand de Bretteville, 223; art collection by, 237–38, 261, 302; charity work by, 239–40, 263–64, 265, 275–77, 300; financial assistance to Fuller by, 230, 254, 270; and Marie, queen of Romania, 316, 318; and Maryhill Museum, 336–37; relationship with Fuller of, 222–25, 235, 242–44, 296, 297–98, 300–301, 305–6, 310, 312–13, 324, 325
St. Denis, Ruth, 205, 337, 338, 341
St. John, Florence, 31
Stage (London periodical), 27
stage crew, 96–98, 112
stage mechanisms, 96, 114–15, 147, 175
Standard Theatre (New York), 20–21, 69, 103
Standing, Guy, 69, 78
Stein, Marten, 47, 48
Stern, Ernesta, 322–23
Stevens, A. E., 350
Stevens, Edward A., 100, 103
Stoltenberg-Lerche, Hans, 350
Strand Magazine, 74–75, 76
Stravinsky, Igor, 208
Stuart, Mabelle, 48
suffrage, female, 326
Sur la mer immense (Fuller), 303
Swirsky, Thamara de, 199, 202
symbolist movement, 4, 54

Taber, Isaiah W., 344
Tableaux Vivants theater (Paris), 140
Talbot, Ona M., 310–11
Tanagra Electra U.S.A. Company, 215–16
temperance, 12
The Tempest (Rodin), 159
Le Temps (Paris), 184, 310
Ten Nights in a Bar Room (play), 12

Teresziuk, Paul, 350
Terry, Ellen, 194
Terry's Theatre (London), 30
Téterger, Henri, 350
theater, growth of in U.S., 14
Théâtre de la Gaieté-Lyrique (Paris), 206
Théâtre des Arts (Paris), 179
Théâtre des Champs-Elysées (Paris), 208, 281–82, 292, 295–96
Théâtre du Châtelet (Paris), 208, 209
Théâtre Marigny (Paris), 195
Théâtre National de l'Opéra (Paris), 47, 95, 275
The Thinker (Rodin), 159, 232, 251
Thomas, Gladys, 189
The Thousand and One Nights (Polignac), 208–9
Tiffany, Louis Comfort, 132
Toulouse-Lautrec, Henri de, 83, 130, 350–51
Tourgée, Albion W., 103
Tower of Labor (Rodin), 159
The Tragedy of Salome (Fuller), 178, 179–82, 181
Tretter, Anna, 351
Troubetzkoy, Paul (prince of Russia), 198
Turned Up (play), 19–20
Turner, Paul C., 274, 275, 284, 287–89, 298
Twenty Days, or Buffalo Bill's Pledge (play), 15
Two or One? (play), 30

Uncle Celestin (musical comedy), 33, 34
El Universal, 104, 110
Upton, Lucy, 250, 252
Urquhart, Isabelle, 69, 78

Valentino, Rudolph, 303, 312
Van Beil, Agnes: and Loie Fuller Dancers, 228, 272; relationship with Fuller of, 226, 232, 235, 239
Van Beil, Nathan, 226–27, 228, 235, 238
Van den Steen, Countess, 262, 264
Vaughan, Kate, 30
Vauxcelles, Louis, 210
Victoria (princess of Germany), 77
La Vie parisienne, 335
Villa Stuck Museum (Munich), 338, 343, 344
Villany, Adorée, 338
Virginia Museum of Fine Arts (Richmond), 337–38, 343, 344
Visions de rêve (Fuller), 322–23
The Visit (Brandes), 67, 68–69

Wagner, Richard, 100
Walker, Jimmy, 315
Walter, Almaric-V., 351

Index

Wandt, Ernest, 351
Washburn, Maj. Stanley, 318
Washington, Gen. George, 69
Weston, Alice, 154
Wheeler, A. C., 20
Whiting, Frederick Allen, 250–53, 256, 282–83
Wilde, Oscar, 79, 329
William Morris, Inc., 203
Willow, Daniel, 313
Wilson, Mrs. Woodrow, 248, 268
Wilson, Woodrow, 248, 268, 271
Witmark, Julius, 15, 325
Wolska, Countess, 85–85
Women's Universal Alliance for the Mothers' Memorial, 314

The World Asks (Fuller), 320
World War I: effect on Fuller's career of, 222, 227–29, 246; Fuller's opinions on, 268–69; and Marie, queen of Romania, 246–47; and relief efforts by Fuller, 230–36, 242, 247–49, 261–65, 270
Wright, Frank Lloyd, 229
Wyatt, W. T., 240–41

Yacco, Sada, 141–44, 146–47, 148, 175, 191
Yan, Anieka, 294
Yeats, William Butler, 272–73
Yoshikawa, Kaoru, 174–75

Zephyr (play), 30, 31, 32
Zingoro (play), 147